# West's Law School Advisory Board

---

**JESSE H. CHOPER**
Professor of Law and Dean Emeritus,
University of California, Berkeley

**JOSHUA DRESSLER**
Professor of Law, Michael E. Moritz College of Law,
The Ohio State University

**YALE KAMISAR**
Professor of Law, University of San Diego
Professor of Law, University of Michigan

**MARY KAY KANE**
Professor of Law, Chancellor and Dean Emeritus,
University of California,
Hastings College of the Law

**LARRY D. KRAMER**
Dean and Professor of Law, Stanford Law School

**JONATHAN R. MACEY**
Professor of Law, Yale Law School

**ARTHUR R. MILLER**
University Professor, New York University
Formerly Bruce Bromley Professor of Law, Harvard University

**GRANT S. NELSON**
Professor of Law, Pepperdine University
Professor of Law Emeritus, University of California, Los Angeles

**A. BENJAMIN SPENCER**
Professor of Law,
Washington & Lee University School of Law

**JAMES J. WHITE**
Professor of Law, University of Michigan

# CONSTITUTIONAL LAW
## Fifteenth Edition

By

**Philip J. Prygoski**
Professor of Law
Thomas M. Cooley Law School

**WEST.**
A Thomson Reuters business

Thomson Reuters created this publication to provide you with accurate and authoritative information concerning the subject matter covered. However, this publication was not necessarily prepared by persons licensed to practice law in a particular jurisdiction. Thomson Reuters does not render legal or other professional advice, and this publication is not a substitute for the advice of an attorney. If you require legal or other expert advice, you should seek the services of a competent attorney or other professional.

© West, a Thomson business, 2008
© 2010 Thomson Reuters
© 2011 Thomson Reuters

    610 Opperman Drive
    St. Paul, MN 55123
    1–800–313–9378

Printed in the United States of America

**ISBN:** 978–0–314–27149–5

# TABLE OF CONTENTS

| Chapter | | | Page |
|---|---|---|---|
| I. | Introduction | | 1 |
| II. | Analytical and Exam Approach | | 3 |
| | A. | Analysis of Constitutional Questions. [§ 1] | 3 |
| | | 1. Read the Constitution | 3 |
| | | 2. Read the Assigned Cases in the Casebook | 3 |
| | | 3. Consider the "Real–Life" Implications of the Case | 3 |
| | B. | Base All Your Arguments in the Constitution. [§ 2] | 4 |
| | | 1. The Constitution Is the Supreme Law of the Land | 4 |
| | | 2. The Supreme Court Is the Ultimate Arbiter of the Constitution | 4 |
| III. | Overview of Constitutional Law: A Summary of the Major Areas of Constitutional Law | | 5 |
| | A. | Types of Constitutional Questions. [§ 3] | 5 |
| | B. | Judicial Review. [§ 4] | 5 |
| | C. | Separation of Powers. [§ 5] | 6 |
| | D. | Federalism. [§ 6] | 6 |
| | E. | Individual Rights. [§ 7] | 7 |
| | | 1. Which Government Is Acting? | 7 |
| | | 2. Identify the Interest That Has Been Abridged | 7 |
| | | 3. Place the Abridged Interest in the Constitution | 7 |
| | | 4. Ascribe Constitutional Weight to the Interest Abridged | 7 |
| | | 5. Set the Appropriate Level of Scrutiny for a Court to Use | 7 |
| | | 6. Balance | 8 |
| IV. | Judicial Review and Limitations on Judicial Review: The Constitutional Basis for the Exercise of Federal Judicial Power | | 9 |
| | A. | Article III of the Constitution Establishes Federal Courts. [§ 8] | 9 |
| | | 1. Original Jurisdiction of the Supreme Court. [§ 9] | 9 |
| | | 2. Appellate Jurisdiction of the Supreme Court. [§ 10] | 9 |
| | | 3. Ways to Appeal to the Supreme Court. [§ 11] | 10 |
| | B. | Does a Federal Court Have Jurisdiction? Will It Exercise It? [§ 14] | 10 |
| | | 1. Determine Jurisdiction Exists. [§ 15] | 10 |
| | | 2. Even if Jurisdiction Exists, Should a Federal Court Refuse to Hear a Case? [§ 19] | 11 |

# TABLE OF CONTENTS

|   |   |   | Page |
|---|---|---|---|
| | C. | Supreme Court Establishment of the Power of Judicial Review. [§ 20] | 11 |
| | | 1. Judicial Review of Congressional Laws and Executive Acts. [§ 21] | 11 |
| | | 2. Supreme Court Review of State Court Cases. [§ 22] | 12 |
| | D. | Limitations on Judicial Review. [§ 23] | 12 |
| | | 1. Federal Courts May Not Issue Advisory Opinions. [§ 24] | 13 |
| | | 2. Political Questions are Non–Justiciable. [§ 25] | 13 |
| | | 3. Qualifications Clauses. [§ 33] | 17 |
| | | 4. Adequate and Independent State Grounds. [§ 37] | 18 |
| | | 5. Ripeness, Standing, and Mootness: The "Big Three" Limitations on Federal Judicial Power. [§ 40] | 20 |
| | | 6. Eleventh Amendment. [§ 99] | 38 |
| | | 7. Abstention. [§ 123] | 46 |
| V. | National Legislative Power: Sources of and Limitations on Congressional Power | | 53 |
| | A. | Any Act of Congress Must Be Grounded in a Specific Provision of the Constitution. [§ 141] | 53 |
| | B. | Two Notes on Government Power. [§ 142] | 53 |
| | | 1. Government Power as Sword and Shield. [§ 143] | 53 |
| | | 2. Two Ways to Invalidate a Statute. [§ 144] | 54 |
| | C. | Specific Congressional Powers. [§ 145] | 54 |
| | | 1. Necessary and Proper Clause. [§ 146] | 55 |
| | | 2. Commerce Power. [§ 147] | 56 |
| | | 3. Taxing Power. [§ 173] | 66 |
| | | 4. Spending Power. [§ 179] | 68 |
| | | 5. War Power. [§ 184] | 70 |
| | | 6. Foreign Affairs Powers. [§ 185] | 71 |
| | | 7. Property Power. [§ 196] | 74 |
| | | 8. Power to Regulate Immigration and Naturalization. [§ 199] | 75 |
| VI. | Separation of Powers: Relationships Between and Among Branches of the Federal Government | | 79 |
| | A. | Overview of Separation of Powers. [§ 206] | 79 |
| | | 1. Enumerated Powers of the Branches of the Federal Government. [§ 207] | 80 |
| | | 2. Implied Powers of the Branches of the Federal Government. [§ 208] | 80 |
| | B. | Executive and Legislative Powers. [§ 209] | 81 |
| | | 1. The Specific Powers of the President. [§ 210] | 81 |
| | | 2. Presidential Action Affecting the Powers of Congress. [§ 211] | 82 |

# TABLE OF CONTENTS

|  |  |  |  | Page |
|---|---|---|---|---|
|  |  | 3. | Congressional Action Affecting the Powers of the President. [§ 214] | 83 |
|  |  | 4. | Executive Privilege. [§ 233] | 94 |
|  |  | 5. | Executive Immunity. [§ 237] | 96 |
|  |  | 6. | Legislative Immunity. [§ 241] | 98 |
|  | C. | Congressional Action Affecting the Judiciary. [§ 245] | | 99 |
|  |  | 1. | Congress' Ability to Determine the Scope of Federal Judicial Power. [§ 246] | 99 |
|  | D. | Judicial Review of the Detention of Detainees in the War on Terrorism. [§ 249] | | 101 |
|  |  | 1. | Detention of Citizen Enemy Combatants. [§ 250] | 101 |
|  |  | 2. | Alien Detainees Imprisoned at Guantanamo Bay Have a Right to Challenge Their Detentions in U.S. Courts. [§ 251] | 102 |
|  |  | 3. | Restrictions on Military Commissions Used to Try Enemy Combatants. [§ 252] | 104 |
| VII. | State Power to Regulate Commerce: Constitutional Limitations | | | 107 |
|  | A. | Introduction. [§ 253] | | 107 |
|  | B. | Dormant Commerce Clause—Negative Implications of the Commerce Clause. [§ 254] | | 107 |
|  |  | 1. | State Discrimination Against Interstate Commerce. [§ 255] | 108 |
|  |  | 2. | State Laws That Only Burden Interstate Commerce. [§ 279] | 115 |
|  |  | 3. | Market Participant Exception to Dormant Commerce Clause Analysis. [§ 291] | 119 |
|  | C. | The Privileges and Immunities Clause of Article IV. [§ 297] | | 122 |
|  |  | 1. | Standard of Review in Privileges and Immunities Clause of Article IV Cases. [§ 298] | 122 |
|  |  | 2. | Application of Article IV Privileges and Immunities Clause Analysis. [§ 299] | 123 |
|  |  | 3. | Article IV Privileges and Immunities Clause Does Not Apply to Non–Basic Rights. [§ 308] | 125 |
|  | D. | Congressional Power to Authorize State Discrimination Against Interstate Commerce. [§ 309] | | 126 |
|  | E. | State Power to Tax Interstate Commerce. [§ 312] | | 127 |
|  |  | 1. | Dormant Commerce Clause Limitations on a State's Power to Tax Interstate Commerce. [§ 313] | 127 |
|  |  | 2. | Due Process Limitations on a State's Power to Tax Interstate Commerce. [§ 327] | 131 |
|  |  | 3. | Equal Protection Limitations on a State's Power to Tax Interstate Commerce. [§ 329] | 132 |

# TABLE OF CONTENTS

|  |  |  |  | Page |
|---|---|---|---|---|
|  |  | 4. | State–Imposed Compensating Use Taxes Are Constitutional Despite Their Impact on Interstate Commerce. [§ 330] | 132 |
| VIII. | Federal Preemption of State Laws | | | 135 |
|  | A. | Introduction. [§ 333] | | 135 |
|  |  | 1. | A Preemption Question Exists When Both Congress and a State Have Regulated the Same Activity. [§ 334] | 135 |
|  |  | 2. | Preemption May Occur in Three Ways. [§ 335] | 136 |
|  | B. | Conflicting Laws. [§ 336] | | 136 |
|  |  | 1. | Southland Corp. v. Keating, 465 U.S. 1 (1984). [§ 337] | 136 |
|  |  | 2. | Foster v. Love, 522 U.S. 67 (1998). [§ 338] | 136 |
|  |  | 3. | Hines v. Davidowitz, 312 U.S. 52 (1941). [§ 339] | 137 |
|  | C. | Express Statement of Congress' Intent to Preempt. [§ 340] | | 137 |
|  | D. | Pervasive Regulation by Congress. [§ 341] | | 138 |
|  | E. | A State may not Divest its Courts of Jurisdiction in 42 U.S.C. § 1983 Cases. [§ 342.1] | | 139 |
| IX. | State Action Requirement for the Application of Certain Constitutional Protections | | | 141 |
|  | A. | Introduction. [§ 343] | | 141 |
|  | B. | General Analysis of State Action Questions. [§ 344] | | 141 |
|  | C. | Reliance on Governmental Assistance and Benefits. [§ 345] | | 142 |
|  |  | 1. | Symbiotic Relationship Between Government and Private Actor. [§ 346] | 142 |
|  |  | 2. | Government Involvement in a Racially Discriminatory Bequest. [§ 347] | 142 |
|  |  | 3. | State Constitutional Authorization of Racial Discrimination. [§ 348] | 143 |
|  |  | 4. | Liquor License. [§ 349] | 143 |
|  |  | 5. | Relationships Between a State and a Private School. [§ 350] | 143 |
|  |  | 6. | State Help in Executing an Attachment. [§ 351] | 144 |
|  |  | 7. | United States Olympic Committee Is Not a State Actor. [§ 352] | 144 |
|  |  | 8. | National Collegiate Athletic Association Is Not a State Actor. [§ 353] | 144 |
|  |  | 9. | Tennessee Secondary School Athletic Association Is a State Actor. [§ 354] | 145 |
|  | D. | Performing an Exclusive, Traditional Governmental Function. [§ 355] | | 145 |
|  |  | 1. | Elections. [§ 356] | 145 |

# TABLE OF CONTENTS

|   |   |   |   | Page |
|---|---|---|---|---|
|   |   | 2. | Company Town. [§ 359] | 146 |
|   |   | 3. | Privately–Owned Shopping Center. [§ 360] | 146 |
|   |   | 4. | Peremptory Challenges to Jurors. [§ 361] | 147 |
|   |   | 5. | Public Defenders. [§ 362] | 147 |
|   |   | 6. | State–Granted Monopolies. [§ 363] | 147 |
|   |   | 7. | Statutory Warehouseman's Lien. [§ 364] | 148 |
|   | E. | State–Court Intervention Which Aids Private Discrimination. [§ 365] | | 148 |
|   |   | 1. | State–Court Injunction. [§ 366] | 148 |
|   |   | 2. | State–Court Award of Money Damages. [§ 367] | 149 |
|   | F. | No State Action When Injuries Are Inflicted by Private Parties. [§ 368] | | 149 |
|   | G. | A Corporation That Is Created and Controlled by the Government Is Subject to Constitutional Restrictions. [§ 369] | | 149 |
| X. | Congressional Enforcement of Civil Rights | | | 153 |
|   | A. | Introduction to Civil Rights Legislation. [§ 370] | | 153 |
|   |   | 1. | Guarantee of Individual Rights. [§ 371] | 153 |
|   |   | 2. | Congressional Enforcement of Rights Guaranteed by the Civil War Amendments. [§ 372] | 154 |
|   | B. | Congressional Implementation of the Civil War Amendments. [§ 373] | | 155 |
|   |   | 1. | Congressional Regulation of Private Actions Under the Thirteenth Amendment. [§ 374] | 155 |
|   |   | 2. | Congressional Enforcement of the Fourteenth Amendment. [§ 380] | 157 |
|   |   | 3. | Congressional Enforcement of the Fifteenth Amendment. [§ 387] | 160 |
| XI. | Retroactive Legislation | | | 165 |
|   | A. | Constitutional Status of Laws That Operate Retroactively. [§ 392] | | 165 |
|   | B. | Due Process Clause. [§ 393] | | 165 |
|   | C. | Ex Post Facto Laws. [§ 394] | | 166 |
|   |   | 1. | Non–Violations. [§ 395] | 166 |
|   |   | 2. | Violations. [§ 396] | 169 |
|   | D. | Bills of Attainder. [§ 397] | | 170 |
|   |   | 1. | Factors to Determine if a Law Is a Bill of Attainder. [§ 398] | 171 |
|   |   | 2. | Laws That Are Bills of Attainder. [§ 399] | 171 |
|   |   | 3. | Laws That Do Not Constitute Bills of Attainder. [§ 400] | 172 |
|   | E. | Contracts Clause. [§ 401] | | 172 |
|   |   | 1. | Contracts Clause Analysis. [§ 402] | 173 |

# TABLE OF CONTENTS

|   |   |   |   | Page |
|---|---|---|---|---|
|   |   | 2. | Application of Contracts Clause Analysis. [§ 403] | 174 |
| XII. | The Takings Clause | | | 179 |
|   | A. | Introduction. [§ 408] | | 179 |
|   |   | 1. | The Takings Clause Is Not an Independent Source of Legislative Power. [§ 409] | 179 |
|   |   | 2. | Key Concepts in Takings Clause Analysis. [§ 410] | 179 |
|   | B. | "Public Use" Requirement. [§ 411] | | 180 |
|   |   | 1. | Eliminating Urban Blight. [§ 412] | 181 |
|   |   | 2. | Dispersing Land Ownership. [§ 413] | 181 |
|   |   | 3. | Transfer of Property From One Private Owner to Another. [§ 414] | 181 |
|   | C. | When Should a Regulation Be Treated as a Taking? [§ 415] | | 182 |
|   |   | 1. | Physical Occupation or Invasion of Property Will Be Considered a Taking. [§ 416] | 182 |
|   |   | 2. | Denial of All Economically Beneficial Use of the Property Constitutes a Taking. [§ 419] | 183 |
|   |   | 3. | Conditions of the Granting of Building Permits. [§ 429] | 186 |
|   |   | 4. | Temporary Takings Are Compensable for the Period When Use of the Property Was Deprived. [§ 432] | 187 |
|   |   | 5. | A Temporary Moratorium on Land Development Does Not Effect a Per Se Taking of Property Requiring Compensation Under the Takings Clause. [§ 433] | 187 |
|   |   | 6. | Coal Companies Cannot Be Forced to Assume Retroactive Liability for Funding Health Care Benefits for Coal Industry Retirees and Their Families. [§ 434] | 188 |
|   | D. | "Just Compensation" Equals Fair Market Value at the Time of the Taking. [§ 435] | | 188 |
|   | E. | Interest Earned on Client Funds Held by an Attorney in a Trust Account. [§ 436] | | 189 |
| XIII. | Procedural Due Process | | | 191 |
|   | A. | Introduction. [§ 437] | | 191 |
|   |   | 1. | Main Requirements of a Procedural Due Process Analysis. [§ 438] | 191 |
|   |   | 2. | Three–Prong Balancing Analysis. [§ 439] | 192 |
|   | B. | Government Action Requirement. [§ 440] | | 192 |
|   | C. | Intentional Deprivation. [§ 441] | | 192 |
|   | D. | Deprivation of Liberty or Property. [§ 442] | | 192 |
|   |   | 1. | Liberty Interests. [§ 443] | 193 |
|   |   | 2. | Property Interests. [§ 454] | 196 |
| XIV. | Substantive Due Process and Fundamental Rights | | | 205 |
|   | A. | Introduction. [§ 467] | | 205 |

viii

# TABLE OF CONTENTS

|  |  |  | Page |
|---|---|---|---|
|  | B. | Summary of Steps in a Substantive Due Process Analysis. [§ 469] | 208 |
|  | C. | Levels of Scrutiny Under Substantive Due Process. [§ 470] | 209 |
|  | D. | Substantive Due Process Review of Economic Legislation. [§ 471] | 210 |
|  |  | 1. Early Substantive Due Process Cases Dealing With Economic Interests. [§ 472] | 210 |
|  |  | 2. The Modern Hands–Off Approach to Cases Dealing with Economic Interests. [§ 475] | 211 |
|  | E. | Substantive Due Process Review of Social Legislation. [§ 483] | 212 |
|  |  | 1. Choice of Hairstyle | 212 |
|  |  | 2. Registration of Prescription Drug Users | 213 |
|  |  | 3. Attorney's Right to Practice Law | 213 |
|  | F. | Substantive Due Process Review of Fundamental Rights. [§ 484] | 213 |
|  |  | 1. Two Types of Fundamental Rights—Enumerated or Unenumerated. [§ 485] | 213 |
|  |  | 2. Alternative to Substantive Due Process: Fundamental Rights Strand of Equal Protection. [§ 486] | 214 |
|  |  | 3. Specific Fundamental Rights. [§ 487] | 215 |
| XV. | Equal Protection | | 241 |
|  | A. | Introduction. [§ 533] | 241 |
|  |  | 1. Class of One. [§ 534] | 243 |
|  | B. | Levels of Scrutiny. [§ 535] | 243 |
|  |  | 1. Rational Basis Review. [§ 536] | 243 |
|  |  | 2. Intermediate Scrutiny. [§ 537] | 244 |
|  |  | 3. Strict Scrutiny. [§ 538] | 244 |
|  | C. | Intent Required to Make an Equal Protection Argument. [§ 539] | 245 |
|  |  | 1. Examples of Cases Dealing With the Intent Requirement. [§ 540] | 245 |
|  |  | 2. Intent in Jury Selection Cases. [§ 545] | 246 |
|  |  | 3. Intent in Racial Gerrymandering Cases. [§ 548] | 248 |
|  | D. | Review of Laws That Discriminate on the Basis of Race or Ethnicity. [§ 553] | 250 |
|  |  | 1. Separate but Equal. [§ 554] | 251 |
|  |  | 2. Post–*Brown* Remedies for School Segregation. [§ 559] | 252 |
|  |  | 3. Affirmative Action. [§ 573] | 258 |
|  |  | 4. Interracial Sexual Relations. [§ 586] | 265 |
|  | E. | Review of Laws That Discriminate on the Basis of Alienage. [§ 591] | 266 |

# TABLE OF CONTENTS

|   |   | Page |
|---|---|---|
| | 1. Federal Laws That Discriminate Against Aliens. [§ 592] | 267 |
| | 2. State Laws That Discriminate Against Aliens. [§ 595] | 268 |
| | 3. Interplay Between Preemption and Alienage Analysis. [§ 602] | 269 |
| F. | Review of Laws That Discriminate on the Basis of Gender. [§ 605] | 270 |
| | 1. Tracing the Development of Gender Analysis Under Equal Protection. [§ 606] | 270 |
| | 2. Discrimination Based on Pregnancy Is Not Gender Discrimination Under the Equal Protection Clause. [§ 614] | 273 |
| | 3. Remedial Discrimination in Favor of Women. [§ 615] | 273 |
| | 4. In Some Cases, Women and Men Are Not Similarly Situated in Relation to the Purpose of a Law. [§ 619] | 274 |
| G. | Review of Laws That Discriminate on the Basis of Illegitimacy. [§ 624] | 276 |
| | 1. An Illegitimate Child Suing for His or Her Mother's Wrongful Death. [§ 625] | 276 |
| | 2. The Mother of an Illegitimate Child Suing for Her Child's Death. [§ 626] | 276 |
| | 3. Intestacy. [§ 627] | 277 |
| | 4. Worker's Compensation Recovery. [§ 628] | 277 |
| | 5. Denial of Welfare Benefits. [§ 629] | 277 |
| | 6. Denying Illegitimate Children a Presumption of Dependency for Inheritance Purposes. [§ 630] | 277 |
| | 7. Restrictions on Inheritance From an Intestate Father. [§ 631] | 278 |
| | 8. Permissible Limitations on Inheritance From an Intestate Father. [§ 632] | 278 |
| | 9. Right to Veto an Illegitimate Child's Adoption. [§ 633] | 278 |
| | 10. Father's Inability to Sue for the Wrongful Death of An Illegitimate Child. [§ 634] | 279 |
| | 11. Time Limit to Sue for Parental Support. [§ 635] | 279 |
| | 12. Time Limit to Establish Paternity. [§ 636] | 279 |
| | 13. Different Statutes of Limitation for Legitimate and Illegitimate Children. [§ 637] | 279 |
| | 14. Citizenship Requirements for Illegitimate Children Born Outside the United States. [§ 638] | 280 |
| H. | Review of Laws That Discriminate on the Basis of Age. [§ 639] | 280 |
| | 1. Mandatory Retirement Age. [§ 640] | 280 |
| | 2. Different Retirement Ages for Different Workers. [§ 641] | 281 |

# TABLE OF CONTENTS

|  |  |  | Page |
|---|---|---|---|
| I. | | Review of Laws That Discriminate on the Basis of Mental Status. [§ 642] | 281 |
| | 1. | Group Homes for the Mentally Retarded. [§ 643] | 282 |
| | 2. | Different Treatment of the Mentally Ill and the Mentally Retarded. [§ 644] | 282 |
| J. | | Review of Laws That Discriminate on the Basis of Sexual Orientation. [§ 645] | 282 |
| K. | | Review of Laws That Discriminate on the Basis of Social or Economic Interests. [§ 646] | 283 |
| | 1. | Selective Restrictions on Advertising. [§ 647] | 283 |
| | 2. | Selective Ban on Push–Cart Vendors. [§ 648] | 284 |
| | 3. | Exclusion of Methadone Users From Government Employment. [§ 649] | 284 |
| | 4. | Federal Retirement Law. [§ 650] | 284 |
| L. | | Irrebuttable Presumptions Used to Deprive a Person of a Governmental Benefit or the Exercise of a Right. [§ 651] | 285 |
| | 1. | Presumption That Unmarried Fathers Are Unfit Parents. [§ 652] | 285 |
| | 2. | Presumption That Certain College Students Are Not State Residents. [§ 653] | 285 |
| | 3. | Presumption of Ineligibility for Food Stamps. [§ 654] | 286 |
| | 4. | Presumption That Pregnant Teachers Cannot Teach Beyond a Certain Time. [§ 655] | 286 |
| | 5. | Presumption That Spouses of Stepchildren Do Not Qualify for Death Benefits. [§ 656] | 286 |
| | 6. | Presumption That Certain Workers Are Disabled. [§ 657] | 287 |
| | 7. | Presumption That a Child Born to a Married Woman Is a Child of Her Marriage. [§ 658] | 287 |
| XVI. | | Freedom of Speech | 291 |
| | A. | Overview of Free Speech Analysis. [§ 659] | 291 |
| | | 1. Procedural Issues. [§ 660] | 291 |
| | | 2. Is the Government Prohibiting Speech or Merely Channeling It? [§ 664] | 292 |
| | B. | Due Process Concerns That Arise With Laws That Regulate Speech. [§ 665] | 292 |
| | | 1. Vagueness. [§ 666] | 292 |
| | | 2. Overbreadth. [§ 672] | 294 |
| | C. | Prior Restraints. [§ 677] | 297 |
| | | 1. Injunctive Orders Imposing Prior Restraints. [§ 678] | 297 |
| | | 2. Licensing Systems as Prior Restraints: Cases Involving Review of Films Before Exhibition. [§ 683] | 299 |
| | | 3. "Informal" Prior Restraints. [§ 687] | 300 |

# TABLE OF CONTENTS

|  |  | Page |
|---|---|---|
| | 4. Contractually Agreed Upon Prior Restraints. [§ 688] ... | 301 |
| D. | Time, Place, or Manner Restrictions. [§ 689] ............ | 301 |
| | 1. Requirements for a Valid Time, Place or Manner Restriction. [§ 690] ........................ | 302 |
| | 2. Time, Place, or Manner Restrictions in a Public Forum. [§ 697] ................................... | 304 |
| | 3. Time, Place, or Manner Restrictions Imposed Through an Injunction, Rather Than a Generally Applicable Ordinance. [§ 712] ........................ | 310 |
| E. | Content–Based Restrictions on Speech. [§ 715] .......... | 312 |
| | 1. Clear and Present Danger Analysis. [§ 716] ......... | 313 |
| | 2. Fighting Words, Offensive Speech, Hate Speech. [§ 728] . | 318 |
| | 3. Obscenity. [§ 745] ........................... | 326 |
| | 4. Commercial Speech. [§ 763] ................... | 333 |
| F. | Symbolic Speech. [§ 782] ......................... | 341 |
| | 1. Prohibition of Symbolic Speech. [§ 783] ........... | 341 |
| | 2. Time, Place, or Manner Restrictions on Symbolic Speech. [§ 784] ................................... | 342 |
| | 3. Application of Symbolic Speech Analysis. [§ 785] ..... | 342 |
| G. | Speech in Public Schools. [§ 791] ................... | 345 |
| | 1. Non–School–Sponsored Speech. [§ 792] ........... | 345 |
| | 2. School–Sponsored Speech. [§ 793] ............... | 345 |
| | 3. Removal of Books From a School Library. [§ 794] .... | 347 |
| H. | Public Forum Analysis. [§ 795] ..................... | 347 |
| | 1. Traditional Public Forum. [§ 796] ................ | 348 |
| | 2. Designated Public Forum. [§ 797] ................ | 348 |
| | 3. Commandeered Public Forum. [§ 800] ............ | 349 |
| | 4. Application of Public Forum Analysis. [§ 801] ....... | 350 |
| | 5. Designated Forums and Religious Speakers. [§ 812] .... | 353 |
| I. | The First Amendment and the Electoral Process: Regulation of Ballot Access, and Limitations on Contributions and Expenditures. [§ 817] ......................... | 356 |
| | 1. Restrictions on Voting and Becoming a Candidate. [§ 818] ................................... | 356 |
| | 2. Limitations on Campaign Contributions and Expenditures. [§ 819] ................................... | 357 |
| J. | Restrictions on Speech of Government Employees. [§ 829] .. | 363 |
| | 1. Loyalty Oaths. [§ 830] ........................ | 364 |
| | 2. Political Activity and Political Patronage in Public Employment Situations. [§ 831] ................ | 365 |
| K. | The Right Not to Speak: Freedom From Government Coercion, Subsidies, or Taxes. [§ 842] ................ | 370 |

# TABLE OF CONTENTS

|  | Page |
|---|---|
| 1. The Right to Be Free From Compelled Speech. [§ 843] | 370 |
| 2. Government Subsidies of Speech. [§ 849] | 372 |
| 3. Tax Exemptions as De Facto Subsidies for Certain Kinds of Speech. [§ 856] | 375 |

- L. Freedom of Association. [§ 857] .................. 375
    1. Association for Business Purposes. [§ 858] .......... 375
    2. Association for Personal Reasons. [§ 859] .......... 375
    3. Association for First Amendment Purposes. [§ 860] .... 376
    4. Right Not to Associate, or Be Associated With, Certain Ideas. [§ 861] ............................... 376
    5. Cases Involving the Right of Association, and the Right Not to Associate. [§ 862] ....................... 376

XVII. Freedom of the Press ............................ 387
- A. Introduction. [§ 875] ........................... 387
- B. Freedom of the Press and the Right to a Fair Trial. [§ 876] .. 387
    1. Pretrial Publicity. [§ 877] ...................... 387
    2. Prior Restraints to Ensure Fairness of Trials. [§ 878] ... 388
- C. Access of the Press to Prisoners and Courtrooms. [§ 879] ... 388
    1. Access to Prisons or Inmates. [§ 880] ............. 388
    2. Access to Jails. [§ 881] ....................... 388
    3. No Sixth Amendment Right of Access to a Criminal Trial. [§ 882] ..................................... 389
    4. First Amendment Right of Access to Criminal Trials. [§ 883] ..................................... 389
    5. Closed Proceedings Involving Minors. [§ 884] ........ 389
    6. First Amendment Right of Access to Voir Dire. [§ 885] . 389
- D. No Reporter's Privilege. [§ 886] ..................... 390
    1. Grand Jury Testimony. [§ 887] .................. 390
    2. Search Warrants. [§ 888] ...................... 390
    3. Deposition Testimony. [§ 889] .................. 391
    4. Breach of Promise of Confidentiality. [§ 890] ........ 391
- E. Access by Individuals to the Mass Media. [§ 891] ........ 391
    1. Federally–Mandated Reply Time on Television or Radio. [§ 892] ..................................... 392
    2. No Right to Reply in Newspapers. [§ 893] .......... 392
    3. Paid Editorial Advertisements. [§ 894] ............. 392
    4. Help–Wanted Advertisements. [§ 895] ............. 393
    5. Cable Television Franchises. [§ 896] .............. 393
- F. Special Taxes on the Press. [§ 897] .................. 393
    1. Discriminatory Taxes on the Press. [§ 898] .......... 393
    2. Sales Tax. [§ 899] ........................... 394
    3. Crime Victim Compensation. [§ 900] .............. 394

# TABLE OF CONTENTS

|  |  | Page |
|---|---|---|
| XVIII. | The Religion Clauses of the First Amendment | 397 |
| A. | Introduction. [§ 901] | 397 |
| B. | The Establishment Clause. [§ 902] | 397 |
|  | 1. Establishment Clause Tests. [§ 903] | 397 |
|  | 2. Religion and Schools. [§ 906] | 399 |
|  | 3. Religious Symbols During the Holiday Season. [§ 940] | 412 |
|  | 4. Tax Exemptions and Deductions for Religious Organizations. [§ 943] | 413 |
|  | 5. Delegation of Sovereign Power to a Church. [§ 946] | 414 |
|  | 6. Resolving Church Disputes on the Basis of Church Doctrine. [§ 947] | 414 |
|  | 7. Grants to Religious Social Welfare Agencies. [§ 948] | 415 |
|  | 8. Establishment Clause Issues in a Designated Public Forum. [§ 949] | 415 |
|  | 9. Government Preference for One Religion Over Another. [§ 955] | 417 |
|  | 10. Religious Land Use and Institutionalized Persons Act. [§ 956] | 418 |
| C. | The Free Exercise Clause. [§ 957] | 418 |
|  | 1. Overview of Free Exercise Analysis. [§ 958] | 418 |
|  | 2. What Counts as "Religion" for Free Exercise Clause Purposes? [§ 975] | 425 |
|  | 3. Religion and Political Office. [§ 980] | 426 |
|  | 4. Taxes on Religious Institutions. [§ 983] | 427 |
|  | 5. Sunday Closing Laws. [§ 987] | 428 |
|  | 6. Laws Affecting the Free Exercise Rights of Native Americans. [§ 990] | 429 |
|  | 7. State Refusal to Fund Scholarships for Theology Majors. [§ 994] | 430 |
| D. | Accommodation Between the Religious Beliefs of Employees and the Interests of Employers: Tension Between the Free Exercise Clause and the Establishment Clause. [§ 995] | 431 |
|  | 1. Refusal to Work on the Sabbath. [§ 996] | 431 |
|  | 2. Exemption of Religious Organizations from Laws Banning Discrimination Based on Religion. [§ 997] | 431 |
| XIX. | The Constitution of the United States | 435 |
| **Table of Cases** | | 455 |
| **Index** | | 465 |

# CHAPTER I

## INTRODUCTION

About the Author—

Professor Philip J. Prygoski has taught Constitutional Law at the Thomas M. Cooley Law School since 1977. He has also taught at the University of Wisconsin Law School, the University of Tennessee College of Law, and the University of Oklahoma College of Law. Professor Prygoski has received numerous teaching awards at Cooley, and was awarded the Outstanding Professor Award by the Student Bar Association at Tennessee. He has written a number of law review articles on Constitutional Law, and is a frequent lecturer to lawyers and judges. Professor Prygoski received his J.D. and LL.M. degrees from the University of Michigan Law School. Professor Prygoski is a member of the American Law Institute.

# CHAPTER II

# ANALYTICAL AND EXAM APPROACH

## A. ANALYSIS OF CONSTITUTIONAL QUESTIONS. [§ 1]

To prepare yourself to discuss any Constitutional Law question, either in class, or on an exam, you should follow these three suggestions.

1. **Read the Constitution.**

    **First of all, read the Constitution.** You should do this before reading the cases. The reason is to become familiar with the specific powers, limitations on power, and individual rights enumerated in the document. It is also important to get a sense of the structure of the document and of the system of government it establishes. You must have some sense of the "big picture" to effectively engage in the balancing of interests analysis that your professor will inevitably require.

2. **Read the Assigned Cases in the Casebook.**

    **Constitutional law, as taught in law school, is primarily the study of United States Supreme Court cases.** While reading the cases in your casebook, you must come to know both "the words and the music." What I mean is that you must know the rule of the case, as well as the theory underlying the rule. Knowing the rule is important in reaching the correct result when analyzing a fact pattern. Knowing the theory is important in explaining why a court ruled a particular way, and in trying to determine what it might do in subsequent cases with different facts.

3. **Consider the "Real–Life" Implications of the Case.**

    **In addition to knowing the legal theory of a case, consider what would happen in the real world if the Supreme Court ruled a certain way.** The primary job of the Court is to decide the case before it. However, a Supreme Court ruling on a constitutional question is controlling on all other federal or state courts which might hear a case involving the same issue. As a result, a Supreme Court ruling on a particular constitutional

# CHAPTER II

question might have the effect of invalidating all state laws dealing with that question. The wide-ranging implications arising from the effect of a Supreme Court ruling are factors which you should consider when analyzing why the Court ruled a certain way in a given case. Also consider the historical, political, social, or military context of a case. These factors may also influence how a court decides a case. In trying to understand why the Court ruled the way it did, a very important question to ask is: "What if the Court ruled the other way?"

## B. BASE ALL YOUR ARGUMENTS IN THE CONSTITUTION. [§ 2]

**Every constitutional argument must be grounded in the Constitution.** If you are asserting that Congress has the power to pass a law, that law must fall within some constitutional power of Congress. If the President takes some action, it must be based in a constitutional power of the President. If a federal court hears a particular lawsuit, that exercise of judicial power must be based in the Constitution. If a state takes action, that action must be within the constitutional power of the state. If a person asserts an individual right as a defense to government action, that right must be based in the Constitution.

1. **The Constitution Is the Supreme Law of the Land.**

    **The Constitution is the supreme, overriding law of the United States.** The Supreme Court has made it clear that any statute or other governmental action that conflicts with the Constitution cannot stand. If Congress or the President engages in action that conflicts with or contravenes the Constitution, the Court will invalidate such action. Under the Supremacy Clause of Article 6 of the Constitution, the Constitution takes precedence over any conflicting state law.

2. **The Supreme Court Is the Ultimate Arbiter of the Constitution.**

    **Under our system of constitutional law, the Supreme Court is the ultimate arbiter of the Constitution.** In the landmark decision of *Marbury v. Madison* (see § 21), Chief Justice John Marshall asserted for the Court the ultimate power to interpret the Constitution. This power has come to be accepted by the other branches of the federal government and by the states.

# CHAPTER III

# OVERVIEW OF CONSTITUTIONAL LAW: A SUMMARY OF THE MAJOR AREAS OF CONSTITUTIONAL LAW

### A. TYPES OF CONSTITUTIONAL QUESTIONS. [§ 3]

**In general terms, any constitutional analysis is likely to fall into one or more of four general categories: judicial review, separation of powers, federalism, or individual rights.** While each of these will be discussed more fully later in this book, here are some general issues to consider in each area.

### B. JUDICIAL REVIEW. [§ 4]

**The first issue in this area is whether a federal court has jurisdiction to hear a case.** Under Article III of the Constitution, a federal court may hear a case only if it involves a "case or controversy," which means that the party seeking to invoke the jurisdiction of a federal court must have suffered (or be imminently in danger of suffering) an injury-in-fact which is fairly traceable to the government action complained of. An injury-in-fact will be fairly traceable to the government action complained of if a court can issue an order which will directly eliminate the injury-in-fact. If there is no Article III case or controversy, a federal court cannot hear the case.

The next inquiry is whether a federal court will decline to hear a case even though the case technically falls within its jurisdiction. The Supreme Court has created a number of "prudential" rules, under which a federal court will decline to exercise its powers. Some of these prudential rules are: a federal court will not allow a person to have standing to file a lawsuit simply because that person is a citizen who is dissatisfied with a certain government act; a federal court generally will not allow a federal taxpayer to file a lawsuit challenging an expenditure of money by Congress; and a federal court generally will not get involved in sensitive cases of foreign relations, such as declaring or conducting a war, or recognizing a particular government in a foreign country. Prudential rules do not involve constitutionally-based barriers to the exercise of a federal court's jurisdiction, but simply focus on whether it is a "bad idea" for a court to hear a case. In general, these rules reflect the idea that a federal court should decline to hear a case out of deference to another branch of the federal government or to a state. These prudential rules governing a federal court's refusal to hear a case present a prime example of the importance of understanding the theory and basic structure of our constitutional form of government, and of having a grasp of the political, social, historical, or military context of the case.

## C. SEPARATION OF POWERS. [§ 5]

**A separation of powers question involves the relationships between branches of the federal government.** This "horizontal" analysis (involving co-equal branches of the same government) will arise when one branch of the federal government takes some action which interferes with an attribute or power of another branch. The analysis focuses on whether the branch that has acted has unduly interfered with what the Court has deemed to be an essential function of another branch of the federal government. This balancing approach will require answers to two questions: 1) which attribute or power of the affected government has been infringed? and; 2) has there been an "undue interference" with that attribute? In a pure separation of powers question, there will be no mention of a state, or of any individual right being abridged.

## D. FEDERALISM. [§ 6]

**A federalism question involves the relationship between the federal government and the states.** In the typical federalism question, Congress passes a law which interferes with a state's ability to function as an independent sovereign. This "vertical" analysis (involving two separate governments, each having its own sphere of sovereignty) will frequently ask you to balance the federal interests advanced by the congressional statute against the Tenth Amendment police powers of the state. The Tenth Amendment has been interpreted to be the primary source of state power. In general terms, the police power of a state includes the state's power to regulate for the health, safety, welfare, or morals of its citizens. You may be asked to figure out which attribute or power of a state is being abridged, and whether the abridgement is so severe as to be unconstitutional.

**If both the federal government and a state regulate the same subject matter, there may be an issue of preemption.** Under the Supremacy Clause of Article 6, the Constitution and any federal laws passed pursuant to it take precedence over any state law that conflicts with the federal law or frustrates its purpose. A preemption question is easy to identify, because there will always be both a federal and a state law in the fact pattern.

# OVERVIEW OF CONSTITUTIONAL LAW

## E. INDIVIDUAL RIGHTS. [§ 7]

**These questions typically involve a government, federal or state, taking some action which abridges a right of an individual.** This "government action" requirement will be present in all individual rights cases, except those involving the Thirteenth Amendment, which prohibits slavery whether engaged in by government actors or private persons. An individual rights analysis should include the following steps:

1. **Which Government Is Acting?**

   Identify whether it is the federal government or a state which has passed the law which allegedly abridges someone's right. This is important because different constitutional provisions limit the federal government, as opposed to those which restrict states. For example, if Congress deprived someone of due process, the plaintiff's argument would be based or the Fifth Amendment due process clause. If, on the other hand, a state deprived someone of due process, the plaintiff's argument would fall under the due process clause of the Fourteenth Amendment.

2. **Identify the Interest That Has Been Abridged.**

   Describe in layperson's terms the interest that has been abridged. For example, if a state law imposes a two-year educational requirement before someone may be licensed to drive an eighteen-wheel truck, the plaintiff would be complaining about his or her inability to pursue an occupation. Or, if a state law said that aliens may not attend college within the state, the plaintiff would be complaining about exclusion from college based on the trait of lack of U.S. citizenship.

3. **Place the Abridged Interest in the Constitution.**

   The ability to pursue an occupation would be an aspect of liberty under the Fourteenth Amendment due process clause. The right not to be excluded from a benefit based upon individual or group status falls within the Equal Protection Clause of the Fourteenth Amendment.

4. **Ascribe Constitutional Weight to the Interest Abridged.**

   If a right is abridged, you must decide whether it is a fundamental right (such as freedom of speech), or simply some low-level liberty interest under the due process clause (such as the interest of police officers in wearing their hair as they choose). If a class has been disadvantaged, you must then determine whether the class is "suspect," "quasi-suspect," or "non-suspect."

5. **Set the Appropriate Level of Scrutiny for a Court to Use.**

   The level of scrutiny used by a reviewing court corresponds to the importance of the governmental interest needed to justify the law.

# CHAPTER III

Whenever a court reviews a case in the individual rights area, it will look at the purpose of the law, and the means chosen to effectuate that purpose. When the government abridges an important right, or disadvantages a suspect class of people, it will have to show a very important interest to justify the law. If only a relatively unimportant interest is affected, the law may be upheld if it advances any legitimate government interest.

**6. Balance.**

Once you have identified the interest abridged, placed it in the Constitution, ascribed its appropriate constitutional weight, and set the level of scrutiny to be used by a court, the final step in the analysis is to balance the government interest against the intrusion into the individual's constitutional interest. For example, if a very important individual right, such as free speech, is being abridged, the government will have to show a very important or compelling reason for the abridgement. If some relatively unimportant interest is abridged, the law may be good if the government has any legitimate reason for the law.

**LAW SCHOOL EXAM TIP:** Your exam will probably have essay questions, multiple choice questions, or a combination of both. Think about what kinds of issues are testable under each format. With essay questions, you are most likely to be tested on the "gray areas" of law. In this instance the professor tries to draft questions which will distinguish those students who know the theory, as well as the black-letter rules, from those who don't. If that is the goal of the exam, it makes little sense to give a question which has a clear-cut right answer. Such questions are not good evaluative tools, because they result in top-heavy grading curves. Essay questions are used to test the depth of a student's knowledge. Multiple choice questions, on the other hand, are frequently used to test the breadth of a student's knowledge. Multiple choice questions are much more likely to test rules than theory. This is where specific constitutional requirements are likely to show up (i.e., how many Senators does it take to ratify a treaty). As you go through the semester, be sensitive to what material is susceptible to each of these testing techniques.

# CHAPTER IV

# JUDICIAL REVIEW AND LIMITATIONS ON JUDICIAL REVIEW: THE CONSTITUTIONAL BASIS FOR THE EXERCISE OF FEDERAL JUDICIAL POWER

## A. ARTICLE III OF THE CONSTITUTION ESTABLISHES FEDERAL COURTS. [§ 8]

**Article III of the Constitution provides the basis for and the scope of federal judicial power.** Under Article III, "[t]he judicial power of the United States shall be vested in one Supreme Court, and in such inferior Courts as the Congress may from time to time ordain and establish. . . ."

1. Original Jurisdiction of the Supreme Court. [§ 9]

   **Under Article III, the Supreme Court has original jurisdiction in all cases ". . . affecting Ambassadors, other public Ministers and Consuls, and those in which a State shall be a party. . . ."** Under present statutes, the Supreme Court has exclusive original jurisdiction only when a state sues a state; in all other cases involving the Supreme Court's original jurisdiction, Congress, under its power to ordain and establish inferior federal courts, has conferred concurrent original jurisdiction on federal district courts. The original jurisdiction of the Supreme Court can be neither expanded nor diminished by statute.

2. Appellate Jurisdiction of the Supreme Court. [§ 10]

   **Under Article III, the Supreme Court has original jurisdiction in a very limited category of cases. (See § 21) In all cases other than those listed under its Article III original jurisdiction, the Supreme Court has appellate jurisdiction, with such exceptions and regulations as Congress shall make.** Under this grant of appellate jurisdiction, the Court has appellate jurisdiction over all cases coming from lower federal courts, and from cases coming from state courts, as long as those state-court cases involve a federal question.

# CHAPTER IV

3. **Ways to Appeal to the Supreme Court. [§ 11]**

   By statute, the Supreme Court is authorized to review some lower court decisions as a matter of right (by appeal) and others as a matter of judicial discretion (by writ of certiorari).

   a. Appeal. [§ 12]

      **Under present statutes, an appeal as a matter of right may only be taken to the Supreme Court from decisions of three-judge courts.** Federal law allows such appeals in only a small number of cases. 28 U.S.C.A. §§ 2281 and 2284.

   b. Certiorari. [§ 13]

      All federal cases not brought in three-judge courts go to **the Supreme Court by a petition for a writ of certiorari.** All cases from state courts go to the Supreme Court via a petition for a writ of certiorari. The Supreme Court will only review a final order of the highest appellate court of a state. The theory underlying the exceptionally broad scope of the certiorari jurisdiction of the Supreme Court is to give the Court the discretion to control its own docket. The Court's refusal to grant a petition for a writ of certiorari is of no precedential value, and should not be cited as precedent.

B. **DOES A FEDERAL COURT HAVE JURISDICTION? WILL IT EXERCISE IT? [§ 14]**

Under Article III, a court must have jurisdiction over a case before it may act. However, in some cases where a court has jurisdiction, it may choose not to exercise it out of deference to another branch of the federal government or to a state.

1. Determine Jurisdiction Exists. [§ 15]

   The first thing to do when analyzing a constitutional law question is to make sure that a federal court has jurisdiction to hear the case.

   a. Federal Question Jurisdiction. [§ 16]

      **Under Article III, federal courts have jurisdiction to hear cases involving a federal question.** Article III says that the jurisdiction of federal courts shall extend to all cases, in law and equity, arising under the Constitution, the laws of the United States, and treaties entered into by the United States.

   b. Diversity Jurisdiction. [§ 17]

      **Under federal statutes, federal courts have jurisdiction in diversity cases—those involving a dispute between citizens of different**

# JUDICIAL REVIEW AND LIMITATIONS ON JUDICIAL REVIEW

states, or between a citizen of a state and an alien. The idea behind diversity jurisdiction is to provide a litigant with access to a federal forum so as to escape the possible prejudices that might come into play in state court, such as elected state court judges being overly concerned with their re-election, or with the political interests of their respective states.

c. **Case or Controversy Requirement. [§ 18]**

**A lawsuit must meet the Article III definition of a "case or controversy" to fall within the jurisdiction of a federal court.** For there to be a case or controversy, there must be an actual dispute before the court, brought by a plaintiff who has suffered (or is about to suffer) a specific injury as a result of an identified government action.

2. **Even if Jurisdiction Exists, Should a Federal Court Refuse to Hear a Case? [§ 19]**

Even if a case presents a justiciable case or controversy, there are some "prudential" doctrines that a court may use to avoid taking such a case. These prudential rules usually concern separation of powers or federalism issues; the court deems it wise to defer to another branch of the federal government or to the states for a decision. For example, as a practical matter, it may be unwise for a federal court to hear a lawsuit challenging the constitutionality of U.S. military action in a foreign country. While there may be serious constitutional issues involved, the question becomes whether there is anything a federal court can (or should) do about the allegedly unconstitutional commitment of troops to a foreign country. Will the President, as Commander-in-Chief, be subject to deposition during the course of the military action? Should a federal court order the termination of hostilities by a certain date, and the return of all American troops? There are some constitutional questions which are better decided by the political (elected) branches of government, rather than by the courts.

## C. SUPREME COURT ESTABLISHMENT OF THE POWER OF JUDICIAL REVIEW. [§ 20]

**In a number of cases in the early 1800's, the Supreme Court established for the judicial branch of the federal government the power to review acts of other branches of the federal government, as well as decisions from state courts.** The Court declared that the judiciary is the ultimate arbiter of constitutional powers and rights.

1. **Judicial Review of Congressional Laws and Executive Acts. [§ 21]**

In *Marbury v. Madison*, 5 U.S. 137 (1803), the Court established for the federal judiciary the power to review and, when appropriate, invalidate acts of Congress, as well as the power to issue mandatory writs (such as a writ of mandamus) to members of the Executive branch. Right before leaving office, President John Adams appointed William Marbury to be a justice of the peace. Marbury's commission was not delivered before Adams left office, and Thomas Jefferson, the new President, directed his Secretary of State, James Madison, not to deliver the commission to Marbury. Marbury sued Madison, seeking a writ of mandamus forcing Madison to deliver the commission. Marbury relied on § 13 of the Judiciary Act of 1789, which, as Chief Justice Marshall interpreted it, purported to give the Supreme Court original jurisdiction to issue writs of mandamus. Analyzing Marbury's argument, Chief Justice John Marshall ruled, "It is emphatically the province and duty of the judicial department to say what the law is." Applying this principle, the Court invalidated § 13, on the basis that it was a congressional attempt to enlarge the constitutionally-prescribed original jurisdiction of the Supreme Court. This part of *Marbury* established the power of the judiciary to invalidate acts of Congress.

In another part of the opinion, Chief Justice Marshall declared that an appropriate federal court could issue a writ of mandamus ordering a federal executive branch official to perform a duty that he or she had a legal duty to perform. The result of *Marbury* is that the federal judiciary has review power over the other branches of the federal government.

2. **Supreme Court Review of State Court Cases. [§ 22]**

**In two other cases, *Martin v. Hunter's Lessee*, 14 U.S. 304 (1816), and *Cohens v. Virginia*, 19 U.S. 264 (1821), the Supreme Court asserted its power to review both civil and criminal cases coming out of state courts, so long as a federal question was presented on appeal.**

After *Marbury, Martin*, and *Cohens*, the power of judicial review was established in relation to other branches of the federal government, as well as to state courts.

## D. LIMITATIONS ON JUDICIAL REVIEW. [§ 23]

**There are both constitutional and prudential limitations on the exercise of judicial power by a federal court.** Constitutional limitations derive from the document itself; certain constitutional provisions establish specific requirements for the exercise of federal judicial power. For example, under Article III, a federal court can only hear a "case or controversy." If none exists (because no one has been injured by any government action), a federal court cannot hear the case. Prudential limitations, however, are judge-made rules of

# JUDICIAL REVIEW AND LIMITATIONS ON JUDICIAL REVIEW

restraint or avoidance, whose main purpose is to show respect for other branches of the federal government or for the states. Prudential limitations are not constitutionally required, but reflect the Court's view of the proper role of the judiciary in the federal system. An example of a prudential limitation is the Court's unwillingness to exercise its power to determine the constitutionality of a war overseas, even though the constitutional rights of soldiers may be implicated.

1. **Federal Courts May Not Issue Advisory Opinions. [§ 24]**

   An advisory opinion is an opinion requested by an executive official, or by a legislature, asking a court to rule on the constitutionality of some proposed government action before the law has been applied to anyone. There is no party who has been adversely affected by the law, so the opinion is merely advisory in nature. **Advisory opinions are not within the Article III definition of a "case or controversy," so federal courts may not issue such opinions.** *Muskrat v. U.S.*, 219 U.S. 346 (1911).

   As a corollary, federal courts will not hear collusive suits because they also fail to meet the Article III requirement of a case or controversy involving parties who are truly adverse, and who have a concrete stake in the outcome of the lawsuit. Collusive suits are those in which the parties do not have conflicting interests, but are acting in concert to test the constitutionality of a law.

2. **Political Questions are Non–Justiciable. [§ 25]**

   **Some disputes are not justiciable (they are not able to be resolved in a court of law). Rather, they are to be decided by the political (elected) branches of the federal government.** A political question ultimately involves separation of powers issues; a branch of the federal government other than the judiciary is the appropriate forum for resolution of a given issue. There are two kinds of political questions: Those which the Constitution explicitly gives to Congress or the President for resolution; and those which a court could hear, but are simply "too hot to handle" for some reason. With the first kind of political question, look for a specific constitutional provision which gives the decisionmaking power to Congress or the President. With the second kind, look for some separation-of-powers reason why a federal court should not hear a case, such as respect for a decision already made by Congress or the President, or risk of embarrassment to the federal government by the Court overruling some political decision made by Congress or the President (such as a decision to commit troops overseas).

# CHAPTER IV

a. **Political Questions to Be Decided by Congress or the President.** [§ 26]

   (1) **Guarantee Clause Cases.** [§ 27]

      Article IV, § 4 of the Constitution says, "The United States shall guarantee to every State . . . a Republican Form of Government. . . . " **Cases involving the Guarantee Clause are not within the jurisdiction of federal courts.** In *Pacific States Telephone & Telegraph Co. v. Oregon*, 223 U.S. 118 (1912), the Court refused to rule on the constitutionality of an Oregon law which allowed its citizens to pass laws through the initiative and referendum process. The Court said this issue was a political question to be decided by Congress.

   (2) **Expulsion of a Member of Congress.** [§ 28]

      **Either house of Congress may, upon a two-thirds vote, expel a member.** Expulsion is the removal of a legislator after he or she has been elected, taken the oath, and taken his or her seat. As a general matter, the Constitution gives either House the power to expel one of its members (Article I, § 5, cl. 2), provided that the expulsion is properly done. An interesting issue would arise if the House, for instance, exercised its power to expel a member, but did so for a constitutionally suspect reason, such as racial discrimination. The injection of an individual rights issue would then change that dispute from a political question into a justiciable one.

   (3) **Procedures for Impeachment.** [§ 29]

      **Article 1, § 3, cl. 6 gives the Senate the power to try impeachments. The Court has ruled that the Constitution gives to the Senate the exclusive power to determine the exact procedures it will use in impeachment cases.**

      In *Nixon v. U.S.*, 506 U.S. 224 (1993), a federal district judge who had been convicted of perjury and given a prison sentence challenged the procedure used by the Senate in his impeachment trial. Specifically, Judge Nixon asserted that the Senate violated the Constitution by having a committee of Senators take evidence against him, and having the full Senate decide his case on the basis of a report filed by the committee. The Court held the Constitution gives the Senate, rather than the courts, the power to decide the rules for an impeachment trial.

# JUDICIAL REVIEW AND LIMITATIONS ON JUDICIAL REVIEW

(4) **President's Power to Terminate a Treaty. [§ 30]**

**The issue of whether the President has the power to unilaterally terminate a treaty is a political question.**

In *Goldwater v. Carter*, 444 U.S. 996 (1979), the Court summarily vacated the judgment of the Court of Appeals and directed that the case be dismissed. The case involved a dispute between the Senate and the President as to whether the President has the power to unilaterally terminate a treaty without the advice and consent of the Senate. Although Art. II § 2 of the Constitution provides for the creation of treaties by the President, with the advice and consent of the Senate, the Constitution is silent as to the termination of treaties. A plurality of the Court held that the case was a nonjusticiable political question, because it involved a dispute about the extent of Presidential authority in foreign affairs and was best left for resolution by the Executive and Legislative Branches of the Government.

(5) **Political Gerrymanders. [§ 31]**

**Courts have no manageable standards by which to judge the constitutionality of political gerrymanders.**

*Vieth v. Jubelirer*, 541 U.S. 267 (2004). A four-Justice plurality concluded that political gerrymandering claims are nonjusticiable because no judicially manageable standards exist by which to tell when partisan political gerrymanders of voting districts violate the Equal Protection Clause. Plaintiffs claimed the redrawing of certain congressional voting districts constituted political gerrymandering and violated the one-person, one-vote requirement of Article I, § 2, and the Equal Protection Clause of the Fourteenth Amendment. The plurality rejected the Court's previous decision in *Davis v. Bandemer*, 478 U.S. 109 (1986), which had held that the Equal Protection Clause mandates judicial control of political gerrymandering. A fifth Justice (Kennedy) concurred, but, disagreed about political gerrymandering cases being categorically nonjusticiable. Justice Kennedy said that a manageable standard might emerge in some future case. The four dissenters would have held such disputes to be justiciable. Thus, even though a plurality of the Court in *Vieth* would have held challenges to political gerrymanders to be nonjusticiable political questions, a majority declined to do so.

*League of United Latin American Citizens v. Perry*, 548 U.S. 399 (2006). The Court rejected a challenge to a partisan redistricting of Texas' congressional map, holding that it was not an unconstitutional political gerrymander. At issue was a mid-decade redistricting plan that was passed by Republicans who had gained control of both house of the Texas legislative in 2003. In the 2004 Congressional elections, the Republicans won 21 seats, and the Democrats 11. The Court focused on whether the challenges offered a manageable, reliable measure of fairness for determining whether a partisan gerrymander is unconstitutional. A majority of the Court concluded that the plaintiffs had not provided a reliable standard for identifying unconstitutional political gerrymanders. The Court rejected the argument that a decision to effect mid-decennial redistricting, even when solely motivated by partisan objectives, presumptively violates equal protection because it serves no legitimate public purpose and burdens one group because of its political opinions and affiliation. Justice Kennedy said that a successful test for identifying unconstitutional partisan gerrymandering must show a burden, as measured by a reliable standard, on the plaintiffs' representational rights.

b. **Political Questions That Are "Too Hot to Handle." [§ 32]**

**Some disputes are deemed political questions even though the Constitution does not specifically commit these issues to the executive or legislative branch for decision. These "prudential" political questions reflect a judicial deference to decisions made by other branches of the federal government.**

In *Baker v. Carr*, 369 U.S. 186 (1962), the Court lists the following factors as guidelines in determining whether a dispute is a "prudential" political question which a court should avoid hearing. Each of these factors involves the Court showing respect for a coordinate branch of the federal government:

(1) The lack of judicially discoverable or manageable standards for resolving it;

(2) The impossibility of a court deciding the case without an initial policy decision by some other branch of government;

(3) The need for a court to show proper respect for the decisions of another branch of government;

(4) The need to adhere to a political decision already made; and

(5) The potential embarrassment from multiple pronouncements on the same issue.

Issues to watch for in the "too hot to handle" area are 1) foreign relations (whether or not a treaty has been terminated), 2) dates and duration of military activities (litigating the constitutionality of Desert Storm), and 3) validity of enactments (ratification periods for proposed amendments to the Constitution).

3. **Qualifications Clauses. [§ 33]**

   **Neither Congress nor a state may add requirements to the exclusive list of qualifications for members of Congress contained in the Qualifications Clauses of the Constitution.** Article I, § 2, clause 2, which applies to the House of Representatives, provides:

   "No person shall be a Representative who shall not have attained to the Age of twenty five Years, and been seven Years a Citizen of the United States, and who shall not, when elected, be an Inhabitant of that State in which he shall be chosen".

   Article I, § 3, clause 3, which applies to the Senate, provides:

   "No person shall be a Senator who shall not have attained to the Age of thirty Years, and have been nine Years a Citizen of the United States, and who shall not, when elected, be an Inhabitant of that State for which he shall be chosen."

   a. **Congressional Attempts to Add to the Constitutionally Prescribed Requirements for Membership in Congress. [§ 34]**

   **Congress may not add requirements for membership over and above those listed in the Constitution.**

   In *Powell v. McCormack*, 395 U.S. 486 (1969), the Court invalidated a decision by the House of Representatives to prohibit Adam Clayton Powell from taking his seat, even though he had been elected and had met the age, citizenship, and residency requirements of the Constitution. The House voted to exclude Powell because of allegations of lying about travel expenses and making illegal salary payments to his wife. The Court reasoned that the House was, in effect, adding a "good citizenship" requirement to those listed in the Constitution. This case did not involve a political question, because the House was not expelling a member, but was excluding a properly elected person from taking his seat.

## CHAPTER IV

b. **State Attempts to Add to the Constitutionally Prescribed Requirements for Membership in Congress. [§ 35]**

**A state may not impose limits on the number of terms that the state's congressional delegation may serve.**

In *U.S. Term Limits, Inc. v. Thornton*, 514 U.S. 779 (1995), the Court invalidated a provision of the Arkansas Constitution which prohibited a candidate's name from being on the ballot for a congressional election if that person had already served three terms in the House of Representatives or two terms in the Senate. The Court ruled that the Arkansas provision violated the Qualifications Clauses of the U.S. Constitution, and that state limitations could not be justified under either the Tenth Amendment state police powers provision or under the Elections Clause of the Constitution (Article I, § 1) that gives states the power to regulate the "Times, Places and Manner of holding Elections."

c. **State Attempts to Direct the Activities of Their Representatives in Congress. [§ 36]**

**A State's Constitution May Not Direct its U.S. Congressional Delegates to Support a Federal Constitutional Amendment for Congressional Term Limits.**

In *Cook v. Gralike*, 531 U.S. 510 (2001), the court held that it was not within the 10th amendment powers reserved to the states for Missouri to pass a state constitutional amendment requiring that congressional representatives pledge to work for term limits. The amendment stated that if they did not, they would have "disregarded voters instruction on term limits" or "declined to pledge to support term limits" beside their name on the ballot. The Court held this exceeded the state's 10th amendment power to regulate the manner of holding federal elections.

4. **Adequate and Independent State Grounds. [§ 37]**

**The adequate and independent state grounds analysis is a judicially-imposed limitation on the ability of the Supreme Court to review decisions by the highest appellate courts of states. The adequate and independent state grounds doctrine arises when the highest appellate court of a state decides a case involving both state and federal issues. The Supreme Court will not review such a case if the state court based its decision solely on state law, and the Supreme Court cannot change the result of the case.** This is true despite the presence of a federal issue in the case. The key question in determining whether the state decision is based on adequate and independent state grounds is whether the Supreme Court can change the result of the case. If it can, by ruling on the federal question, it will take the case. If it cannot change the result, it will not take the case because its ruling would then be very much like an advisory opinion—clarifying a federal question, but with no impact on the litigants. *Michigan v. Long*, 463 U.S. 1032 (1983).

a. **Steps in an "Adequate and Independent State Grounds" Analysis. [§ 38]**

   Here are the factors to look for in an adequate and independent state grounds issue:

   (1) Has the highest appellate court of a state ruled on the case;

   (2) Does the case involve questions of both federal and state law; and

   (3) Can the Supreme Court change the result of the case by ruling on the federal question? (Remember that the Supreme Court has no business ruling on questions that solely address state law.)

   If the answer to all three questions is "yes," there is no adequate and independent state basis for decision, and the Supreme Court may take the case.

b. **State Constitution Confers Greater Protection Than the Federal Constitution. [§ 39]**

   The common scenario in an "adequate and independent state grounds" case is that the state constitution grants a person more rights than the federal Constitution. The litigant wins under state law, and there is nothing the Supreme Court can do about it.

   Assume that a defendant is prosecuted in state court for possession of drugs. The defendant moves to exclude the drugs from evidence because the search by the police violated the Fourth Amendment to the U.S. Constitution (applied to the states through the Fourteenth Amendment), as well as the search and seizure provision of the state constitution. The state supreme court rules that the search violated the state constitution; therefore the drugs are excluded from evidence. In its opinion, however, the state supreme court misinterprets U.S. Supreme Court precedent on the Fourth Amendment, holding the drugs inadmissible under the Fourth Amendment, when they should

# CHAPTER IV

have been admitted under federal case law. The state seeks to appeal to the U.S. Supreme Court. The Court should not take the case because its cannot change the result—the drugs are still excluded based solely on the state constitution.

## SUMMARY: ADEQUATE AND INDEPENDENT STATE GROUNDS

**NOTE: In each of these cases, the plaintiff is challenging some state action on both state and federal constitutional grounds.**

|  | Did the state court find the state action valid under the state constitution? | Did the state court find the state action valid under the federal constitution? | Who won in state court? | Will the Supreme Court take this case? |
|---|---|---|---|---|
| Case 1 | Yes | Yes | State | Yes |
| Case 2 | Yes | No | Individual | Yes |
| Case 3 | No | No | Individual | No |
| Case 4 | No | Yes | Individual | No |

In cases 1 and 2, the state law or action was permissible under the state constitution. That means the only remaining question (and the dispositive one), is whether the state law or action was permissible under the federal constitution. Since the federal question is the one that will ultimately determine the outcome of the case, the U.S. Supreme Court will take the case and decide the federal question. In cases 3 and 4, the state law or action is unconstitutional under the state constitution. That means that the federal constitutional question is irrelevant to the outcome, and the U.S. Supreme Court will not take the case because it cannot change the outcome.

5. **Ripeness, Standing, and Mootness: The "Big Three" Limitations on Federal Judicial Power. [§ 40]**

    **There are a number of rules which limit the exercise of federal judicial power in both trial courts and appellate courts. These rules reflect both constitutional and judge-made limitations on the exercise of judicial power.** The three areas of justiciability tested most frequently in law school are ripeness, standing, and mootness. These are not necessarily separate, distinct areas of analysis. Be aware that some questions may call for a discussion of more than one of these doctrines.

    a. **Ripeness. [§ 41]**

        **The main question in the area of ripeness is whether anyone has suffered actual or threatened harm by the application of a statute. If there is no one who has suffered an actual injury, or a specific threat of injury, the case will not be ripe for decision.**

# JUDICIAL REVIEW AND LIMITATIONS ON JUDICIAL REVIEW

**(1)** **The Supreme Court in** *Poe v. Ullman*, **367 U.S. 497 (1961), [§ 42],** refused, on ripeness grounds, to hear a challenge to a Connecticut law which prohibited the use of contraceptives, as well as the giving of advice about contraceptives. In over seventy-five years of the law being on the books, only one prosecution (a test case eventually dismissed at the government's request) was brought under the statute. The Court reasoned that the mere abstract, generalized threat of enforcement of the law did not create a ripe controversy.

**(2)** **In** *United Public Workers v. Mitchell*, **330 U.S. 75 (1947), [§ 43],** again on ripeness grounds, the Court refused, to hear a challenge by federal civil service employees to the Hatch Act, which prohibited federal executive branch employees from participating in political campaigns. Since none of the employees (save one, whose case was accepted) had actually suffered any injury other than a subjective "chilling effect on their speech," the Court refused to hear the case, asserting that to do so would be tantamount to issuing an advisory opinion.

b. **Standing. [§ 44]**

**Standing has to do with whether the proper party is seeking to raise an issue in federal court.** For a plaintiff, the question is whether he or she is able to invoke the jurisdiction of a court to hear a case. For a defendant, who is already in court, as in a criminal case, the question is whether he or she can raise an issue as part of a defense (does a defendant in a criminal case have standing to object to the introduction of evidence that was allegedly illegally seized?).

(1) **Constitutional Aspects of Standing. [§ 45]**

**There are two requirements of standing that must always be met to satisfy the "case or controversy" requirement of Article III.**

(a) **Injury-in-fact. [§ 46]**

The would-be litigant must have suffered, or be imminently threatened with suffering, an injury-in-fact as a result of the defendant's actions. In constitutional cases (because of the fact that the government is the defendant), this means that a government agent or entity must be the cause of the actual or threatened injury.

(b) **Traceability. [§ 47]**

The injury-in-fact must be fairly traceable to the government action complained of. In other words, the court must

# CHAPTER IV

be able to issue a decree which will directly redress the injury asserted by the plaintiff.

(2) **Prudential Aspects of Standing. [§ 48]**

**In addition to the constitutional requirements for standing, there are also judge-made, "prudential" barriers to standing.** These prudential barriers reflect institutional concerns such as docket control and judicial insistence on the parties having a personal stake in the outcome of the controversy. Two examples of judge-made prudential barriers to standing are the bar to a federal taxpayer challenging a spending measure by Congress, and the bar to third-party standing. As a general matter, a federal taxpayer will not have standing to challenge a spending measure by Congress. Too many lawsuits would result, and the absence of any particularized injury would detract from the vigor with which the issues would be presented to a court. Under third-party standing, a plaintiff asserts the rights of another person to acquire standing (a doctor-plaintiff may assert the abortion rights of patients in order to challenge the cessation of welfare payments for abortions). The problem with third-party standing is that if the right-holder is not suing to vindicate his or her own right, the issues may not be litigated as vigorously as if the right-holder were the plaintiff.

(3) **Examples of Injuries in Fact. [§ 49]**

**The Court has held that it will recognize certain kinds of injuries for standing purposes, but that other asserted injuries will not qualify as meeting the case or controversy requirement of Article III.** For example, a specific economic or aesthetic injury is usually sufficient to meet Article III requirements, whereas injury to some generalized interest (such as concern about how the federal government is functioning) will not suffice to confer standing.

(a) **Injuries That Do Qualify Under Article III. [§ 50]**

(i) **Economic Injury. [§ 51]**

**An economic injury clearly meets the injury-in-fact requirement of Article III.** A doctor has been able to assert lost payments as the injury resulting from a government decision to stop funding abortions for indigent women. *Singleton v. Wulff*, 428 U.S. 106 (1976).

# JUDICIAL REVIEW AND LIMITATIONS ON JUDICIAL REVIEW

**(ii) Standing to Assert a Non–Economic Injury. [§ 52]**

**A non-economic injury may qualify to confer standing if the injury is specific to the plaintiff.** If the plaintiff personally is adversely affected by a government action, the injury asserted may be to an aesthetic, environmental, religious, or other non-economic interest.

a) **Standing to Assert Aesthetic or Environmental Injuries. [§ 53]**

A specific claim that members of an environmental group use a certain recreational area, and that their use will be harmed by government action (by polluting rivers or despoiling forests), will qualify as an injury-in-fact. *Sierra Club v. Morton*, 405 U.S. 727 (1972).

b) **Standing to Assert a Religious Injury. [§ 54]**

An injury to a religious interest may qualify as an Article III injury-in-fact. In *School District of Abington v. Schempp*, 374 U.S. 203 (1963), the Court held that parents had standing to challenge Bible reading in their children's public school classrooms as a violation of the Establishment Clause of the First Amendment. The Court did require that the plaintiff be personally affected by the challenged practice.

c) **Standing to Assert an Informational Injury. [§ 55]**

In *Federal Election Commission v. Akins*, 524 U.S. 11 (1998), the Court ruled that both prudential and constitutional standing requirements were met by voters who brought a lawsuit challenging a Federal Election Commission decision that a certain lobbying group was not subject to disclosure requirements under federal law. The voters asserted as their injury-in-fact their inability to obtain information from the lobbying group that would help them make informed political decisions and exercise their right to vote. The Court ruled that the voters met the requirement of being

# CHAPTER IV

an aggrieved party under the Federal Election Campaign Act, and that their informational injury was an injury-in-fact for Article III purposes. The Court also said that the voters' injury was fairly traceable to the Federal Election Commission's decision not to force disclosure, and that a federal court could redress this injury.

**(b) Injuries That Do Not Qualify Under Article III. [§ 56]**

**(i) General Citizen Standing. [§ 57]**

**A person will not have standing to challenge a government action solely because he or she is a citizen who is unhappy about how the government is functioning.** The remedy for such a grievance is through the ballot box. The Court has said that the interest of a citizen in constitutional governance is too abstract an injury to confer standing. *Schlesinger v. Reservists Committee to Stop the War*, 418 U.S. 208 (1974); *Lujan v. Defenders of Wildlife*, 504 U.S. 555 (1992).

**(ii) Legislative Standing. [§ 58]**

**Individual Members of Congress do not have standing to challenge the constitutionality of an Act on the basis that it dilutes their legislative power.** An abstract institutional injury is not sufficiently concrete to meet the requirement of an injury-in-fact.

In *Raines v. Byrd*, 521 U.S. 811 (1997), the Court ruled that six members of Congress did not have standing to challenge the constitutionality of the Line Item Veto Act. The Act gave the President the power to cancel specific spending and tax benefit measures of Bills after he signed them into law. The injury the members of Congress asserted was that the Act diluted their voting power, and they claimed that the Act was an unconstitutional expansion of Presidential power. The legislators did not assert a personal, particularized injury, but rather an institutional injury that affected all members of Congress equally. The Court distinguished this case from *Coleman v. Miller*, 307 U.S. 433 (1939), where standing was granted to

# JUDICIAL REVIEW AND LIMITATIONS ON JUDICIAL REVIEW

state legislators claiming an institutional injury when the Lieutenant Governor cast a tie-breaking vote to ratify a proposed federal Constitutional Amendment. There, the votes had been overidden when they were sufficient to prevent ratification, but in this case, the legislators' votes were given full effect and they simply lost the vote.

(iii) **Standing of Public Interest Organizations. [§ 59]**

**Public interest organizations will not have standing unless the organization itself or at least one of its members has suffered an injury.**

In *Sierra Club v. Morton*, 405 U.S. 727 (1972), the Court denied standing to the Sierra Club when it tried to challenge the construction of a recreation area in a national forest. The Sierra Club had failed to assert that it or any of its members had suffered any specific injury by the proposed construction. It was not enough to assert that the organization had an interest in the environment and that the government action would adversely affect that interest.

In *Summers v. Earth Island Institute*, 129 S.Ct. 1142 (2009), The Court reiterated many of the rules of standing to dismiss a lawsuit filed by a number of environmental organizations against the U.S. Forest Service (USFS). Environmental groups sued to stop the USFS from enforcing regulations that exempt small fire-rehabilitation and timber-salvage projects (including the Burnt Ridge Project) from the notice, comment, and appeal process used for more significant land management decisions. The Court reaffirmed that the "Case or Controversy" requirement of Article III restricts courts to redressing or preventing actual or imminently threatened injury to persons caused by violation of law. The Court added that an organization may assert standing on behalf of its members, including any recreational or esthetic injury the members might have suffered. The Court emphasized that, in environmental cases, generalized harm to the forest or the environment will not suffice to confer standing; there must be some imminent and concrete threat to the members' interests. The plaintiffs' claim of standing in relation to the Burnt Ridge Project failed because they voluntarily settled the part of the lawsuit relevant to Burnt Ridge, and their members are no longer threatened with any injury in relation to that project. In addition, the groups failed to establish that any member has specific plans to visit a forest where the challenged regulations are being applied.

- (iv) **Standing to Assert Stigmatic Injury to a Racial Group. [§ 60]**

   **A court will not grant standing if plaintiffs assert a stigmatic injury suffered by all members of a racial group.**

   In *Allen v. Wright*, 468 U.S. 737 (1984), parents of black school children challenged federal tax exemptions for racially discriminatory private schools. The Court refused to recognize as an Article III injury-in-fact a claim of stigmatic injury or denigration suffered by all members of a racial group. Its rationale was that to recognize such an injury would create a cause of action on behalf of any member of the racial group throughout the country. This came too close to a grant of general citizen standing.

- (v) **There Is No Standing to Challenge a State Legislative Redistricting Plan When the Plaintiffs Do Not Live in the District. [§ 61]**

   **Voters who do not live in a congressional district that is the primary focus of their racial gerrymandering claim do not have standing to challenge a statewide reapportionment scheme as being violative of the Equal Protection Clause.**

   In *U.S. v. Hays*, 515 U.S. 737 (1995), the Court ruled that Hays and other plaintiffs lacked standing to challenge Louisiana's congressional redistricting plan because they did not live in the specific district which they claimed had been drawn along racial lines. The Court treated their claim as a generalized grievance against allegedly illegal governmental conduct which did not meet the Article III requirement of a specific injury-in-fact suffered by the plaintiffs.

(4) **The Traceability Requirement. [§ 62]**

   **To meet the Article III requirements, an injury-in-fact must be fairly traceable to the government action complained of.**

**To that end, the injury-in-fact must be redressable by a decree of the Court.** Be very careful of any fact pattern in which the entity causing the injury-in-fact is not a party to the lawsuit. In that scenario, a court cannot direct the injury-causer to do anything, so there is no traceability.

   (a) In *Simon v. Eastern Kentucky Welfare Rights* **Organization, 426 U.S. 26 (1976), [§ 63]** the Court refused to find standing on behalf of persons who had been denied hospital services because of their indigency. The plaintiffs challenged an IRS ruling which continued to grant tax-exempt status to hospitals, despite their failure to treat indigents. The reason for the finding of no standing was that the entity actually causing the injury, the hospital, was not a party to the law suit, so the Court could not direct the hospital to treat indigents. In other words, regardless of the Court's decree, it was still speculative as to whether the hospital would change its behavior.

   (b) In *Allen v. Wright*, **468 U.S. 1250 (1984), [§ 64]** the Court again refused to find standing, this time, on behalf of parents of black children who challenged an IRS ruling which gave tax-exempt status to racially discriminatory private schools. Since the private schools were not parties to the lawsuit, an order of a court could not directly change the behavior of the entity causing the injury. The white private schools could still, if they chose, exclude black children, despite the loss of their tax-exempt status.

   (c) In *Linda R.S. v. Richard D.*, **410 U.S. 614 (1973), [§ 65]** the Court again found no traceability. In that case, a mother sued to challenge a state law which authorized the prosecution of husbands who failed to pay child support, but did not authorize prosecution of non-husband fathers who did not pay child support. The Court concluded that Linda's injury (no money for her child) was not traceable to the state's not prosecuting the child's father for non-payment of support. The idea was that, even if he were prosecuted, Richard could still decide not to give Linda any money. Even if the Court ordered the state to treat both classes of fathers the same, there was no guarantee that Linda's injury would be alleviated.

(5) **Federal Taxpayer Standing. [§ 66]**

   **First of all, be careful about whether a federal taxpayer is challenging a tax, or is challenging a spending measure.** A

# CHAPTER IV

federal taxpayer has standing to challenge an incorrect tax bill, or to attempt to recover taxes paid under protest. The usual law school discussion, however, focuses on whether a federal taxpayer has standing to challenge how Congress spends his or her money.

(a) **Federal Taxpayer Standing to Challenge a Spending Measure. [§ 67]**

**The general rule is that federal taxpayers do not have standing to challenge expenditures of money by Congress.** *Frothingham v. Mellon*, 262 U.S. 447 (1923). The reason for this rule is that the interest of any one federal taxpayer in how Congress spends money is too remote and speculative to qualify as the specific injury-in-fact required for standing.

(b) **Federal Taxpayer Standing to Challenge a Spending Measure That Establishes Religion. [§ 68]**

**The Court has ruled that a federal taxpayer does have standing to challenge a congressional expenditure on the basis that it violates the Establishment Clause of the First Amendment.** (In general, a government may not pass a law which has the purpose or effect of endorsing or establishing religion. See § 919 for a full discussion of the Establishment Clause.)

In *Flast v. Cohen*, 392 U.S. 83 (1968), federal taxpayers challenged federal expenditures for parochial schools. The Court reasoned that the Establishment Clause is a specific limitation on the taxing and spending powers of Congress. Remember that for the *Flast* exception to apply, a plaintiff must assert three things: 1. Congress is acting; 2. under the spending power; 3. to establish religion. If a plaintiff does not establish all three elements, there will be no standing.

  (i) **The Court Has Refused to Extend Flast Beyond the Area of Congressional Exercise of the Spending Power. [§ 69]**

  A federal taxpayer will not have standing based on that status unless he or she is challenging an exercise of the spending power by Congress.

  (ii) **Federal Taxpayer Standing to Challenge an Exercise of the Property Power. [§ 70]**

  In *Valley Forge Christian College v. American United for Separation of Church and State*, 454 U.S. 464

(1982), taxpayers did not have standing to challenge an action by the Secretary of Health, Education, and Welfare ("HEW") in giving a $500,000 piece of federal property to a church college. The Court reasoned that the taxpayers failed the *Flast* test in two respects. First, there was no congressional action (the Secretary of HEW is an executive official). Second, this was not an exercise of the spending power, but rather of Congress' Article IV, § 3, clause 2 power to dispose of federal property. In other words, the plaintiffs did not go three-for-three under *Flast*, so they did not have standing.

(iii) **Federal Taxpayer Standing to Challenge Presidential Expenditures to Establish Faith-Based Centers Within Federal Agencies. [§ 71]**

*In Hein v. Freedom From Religion Foundation, Inc.*, 551 U.S. 587 (2007), a majority of the Court ruled that federal taxpayers did not have standing to challenge Presidential orders creating centers within federal agencies to help direct federal aid to faith-based community groups. Writing for himself and two other justices, Justice Alito said that the expenditures were not made pursuant to any congressional act, but were simply general appropriations to the Executive Branch to fund everyday executive activities. To grant standing would allow federal courts to oversee virtually any executive action. The plurality refused to extend *Flast* to cover executive, rather than congressional actions.

(c) **State Taxpayers. [§ 72]**

State taxpayers are treated the same as federal taxpayers in that they do not have standing in federal court to challenge expenditures of money by their state legislature. *ASARCO v. Kadish*, 490 U.S. 605 (1989). Presumably, under *Flast*, a state taxpayer would have standing in federal court to challenge a state legislature's expenditure of money to establish religion.

(d) **Municipal Taxpayers. [§ 73]**

A municipal taxpayer, on the other hand, is treated differently from a state or federal taxpayer. In *Frothingham*, (see

§ 67) the Court said that a municipal taxpayer's interest in the expenditure of his or her money by a municipal legislative body is direct and immediate, unlike the interests of a state or federal taxpayer. As a result, a municipal taxpayer does have standing in federal court to challenge a municipal expenditure.

(e) **State and Local Taxpayers. [§ 74]**

In *DaimlerChrysler Corp. v. Cuno*, 547 U.S. 332 (2006), a group of state and local taxpayers sued to challenge local property tax exemptions and a state franchise tax credit offered to the DaimlerChrysler Corporation (DC) by the city of Toledo and the state of Ohio. On the merits, the taxpayers claimed that the tax breaks violated the Commerce Clause. The taxpayer plaintiffs claimed that they were injured because the tax breaks depleted the state and local treasuries to which they contributed. The Court held that the state taxpayers had no standing under Article 3 of the Constitution to challenge state taxing or spending decisions based solely on their status as state taxpayers. The interest of a state taxpayer in the moneys in the state treasury is shared with millions of others, is minute and indeterminable, and the effect of any tax or expenditures is so remote, fluctuating and uncertain, that there is no basis on which to confer standing. The Court also said that municipal taxpayers did have standing to challenge the illegal use of a city's funds, but that in the instant case, the plaintiffs' status as municipal taxpayers does not give them standing to challenge the state franchise tax credit at issue.

(6) **Third–Party Standing. [§ 75]**

**The general rule in federal court is that a person may not acquire standing by asserting the rights of a person not in court as a party to the lawsuit.** The theory underlying this rule is that the party whose rights are endangered should be in court as the most effective advocate of those rights. The bar to third-party standing is only a prudential rule, with the following exceptions.

(a) **Requirements for Individual Third–Party Standing. [§ 76]**

If certain requirements are met, an individual plaintiff (as opposed to an association) may get standing by asserting the rights of another person. The requirements are:

— A relationship between the plaintiff and the right-holder;

— A genuine obstacle to the right-holder asserting his or her own rights; and

— The right-holder's rights will be diluted if not asserted by the plaintiff.

**(i) In *Barrows v. Jackson*, 346 U.S. 249 (1953), [§ 77]** a case involving a restrictive covenant entered into by white homeowners, the Court said that a white seller did have standing to assert the equal protection rights of unidentified potential future black buyers as a defense to a breach-of-contract suit by other white homeowners. The buyer-seller relationship was close enough to persuade the Court to grant standing to the white defendant. In *Barrows*, there was no black purchaser in court, so there was a genuine obstacle to the rightholder asserting his or her own rights. Also, if the white seller was not able to assert the rights of potential black purchasers, those rights would be diluted by the decree of a court enforcing the restrictive covenant.

**(ii) In *Griswold v. Connecticut*, 381 U.S. 479 (1965), [§ 78]** the Court recognized third-party standing on behalf of doctors who were convicted of violating a state criminal statute by giving information about contraceptives to married couples. The doctor-patient relationship qualified for third-party standing purposes. The married couples were not parties to the criminal prosecution, so there was a genuine obstacle to their asserting their own rights. In addition, the privacy rights of the married couples would be diluted if the doctor were unable to assert their rights.

**NOTE:** In a case like *Griswold*, the criminal defendant wants to assert the fundamental privacy rights of the married couple to persuade the Court to raise the level of scrutiny it will use in reviewing the

# CHAPTER IV

case. (See § 506, below). Put simply, the doctor has a much better chance of prevailing if he or she can inject an important constitutional interest into the case.

**(iii) In *Craig v. Boren*, 429 U.S. 190 (1976), [§ 79]** sellers of beer were granted third-party standing to assert the equal protection rights of 18–20 year-old males who were unable to buy beer in a state where females could buy beer at the age of 18. The commercial relationship was enough to grant standing.

**(iv) In *Powers v. Ohio*, 499 U.S. 400 (1991), [§ 80],** the Court held that a white defendant had standing to challenge racial discrimination against black persons in the use of peremptory challenges. The Court said that the racially discriminatory use of peremptory challenges by the prosecution endangers the fairness of a criminal trial and thus causes a cognizable injury to the defendant. The Court also found that the excluded juror and the defendant have a common interest in excluding racial discrimination from the courtroom, thus satisfying the "relationship" requirement for third-party standing. Finally, the Court said that, as a practical matter, the excluded jurors face serious barriers (primarily economic) to bringing suit on their own behalf, thus meeting the "genuine obstacle" requirement.

**(vi)** *In Elk Grove Unified School District v. Newdow*, **542 U.S. 1 (2004), [§ 81]** a case in which an atheist father challenged the constitutionality of the words "under God" in the Pledge of Allegiance, the Court ruled that the father did not have standing to assert the Establishment Clause rights of his daughter. The Court relied on the fact that California domestic relations law deprives Newdow of the right to sue as his daughter's next friend, and that a state family court gave sole legal custody to the girl's mother. Expressing a reluctance to intervene in state domestic relations

# JUDICIAL REVIEW AND LIMITATIONS ON JUDICIAL REVIEW

law, the Court refused to grant third-party standing to the father to pursue a claim which was contrary to the wishes of the custodial parent and potentially injurious to the daughter.

**(b) Associational Standing to Represent Members. [§ 82]**

**An association may have standing to assert the rights of its members.** Even if an association has not suffered any injury to itself (for example, a fine levied directly against the association in its corporate capacity), it may have standing to represent its members if certain requirements are met.

**(i)** The association can only represent members who have not filed suit on their own behalf. To do otherwise would allow for duplicative suits, and would be a waste of time, money, and judicial resources.

**(ii)** Any member who is to be represented must have suffered, or be imminently in danger of suffering, an injury-in-fact. **Remember that any time you see a standing question, someone must have an injury-in-fact to meet the Article III case-or-controversy requirement.**

**(iii)** Joinder of the individual members is not necessary to the disposition of the lawsuit. Generally, the members are necessary parties when they would be entitled to differing monetary damages (for e.g., Member A gets $10,000, Member B gets $30,000). The members are not necessary or indispensable parties when all the association seeks is a declaration that the law is invalid, plus an injunction against its application. The theory is that, with a declaration or injunction, all members benefit equally, and are not needed to provide any individualized proofs as to damages.

**(iv)** The interests of the members are germane to the purpose of the organization. A State Carpenter's Association would not be able to challenge a restrictive state abortion law on behalf of its female carpenter members. However, the same group could assert the

# CHAPTER IV

rights of its members to challenge a state law which set certain requirements for licensing of carpenters.

(7) **Associational Standing to Represent Itself. [§ 83]**

**An association may have standing to represent its own interests. An association (corporation, association, partnership) may have standing to vindicate an injury-in-fact suffered by the association itself.** *Warth v. Seldin*, 422 U.S. 490 (1975). An association can be injured in two ways.

(a) **The Government Acts Directly Against the Association. [§ 84]**

For instance, a fine levied by the Environmental Protection Agency against a polluting corporation injures the corporation because it must be paid out of the corporate funds. This is clearly an injury-in-fact that is fairly traceable to government action.

(b) **Government Action That Causes Members to Quit the Organization. [§ 85]**

In *NAACP v. Alabama*, 377 U.S. 288 (1958), the NAACP challenged a state law which required the organization to turn its membership list over to the state. For our purposes assume that members started to drop out of the organization to avoid having their names disclosed to state officials. This adverse effect on the associational ties of its members would, in turn, hurt the NAACP through a reduction in contributions, dues, and volunteers. There would be a cognizable injury suffered by the NAACP that flows directly from the impact of the law on its members.

(8) **Congressional Power to Create Standing. [§ 86]**

**Congress does have the power to confer standing on parties who meet the Article III injury-in-fact requirement, and who are within the zone of interests to be protected by the statute or constitutional provision in question.** *Association of Data Processing v. Camp*, 397 U.S. 150 (1970). The "zone of interests" language is a term of art which applies only to congressional grants of standing. The interests protected by Congress are not only economic ones; aesthetic, recreational, conservational, or religious values may also be protected.

(a) In *Trafficante v. Metropolitan Life Insurance* **Co.,** 409 U.S. 205 (1972), [§ 87] the Court granted standing to tenants of an apartment complex to challenge the racially discriminatory leasing practices of the owner of the complex. The plaintiffs sued under the Civil Rights Act of 1968, which gave "persons aggrieved" the right to sue in federal court. The Court recognized the plaintiffs' asserted injuries of lost social benefits of living in an integrated community, missed business and professional opportunities, and embarrassment from being stigmatized as residents of a racially exclusive housing complex.

**(b)** *United States v. SCRAP,* 412 U.S. 669 (1973), [§ 88] is one of the strangest cases in which the Court granted standing. SCRAP was a group of five law students who were interested in a clean environment. They sued under the federal Administrative Procedures Act (APA) to challenge a surcharge on railroad freight rates imposed by the Interstate Commerce Commission (ICC). According to SCRAP, its members used the outdoor recreational areas in the Washington metropolitan area for hiking, camping, and other outdoor activities. The increase in freight rates, they claimed, would increase the use of non-recyclable goods, requiring more trees to be cut in certain forests to provide the raw material for the non-recyclable goods. Then, some of the non-recyclable products might be thrown away in the forests SCRAP members visit, thus ruining the beauty of the forests. The Court said this argument was sufficient to meet the standing requirements of Article III and the APA. Keep in mind that the SCRAP case is an extreme example of a fairly traceable injury, and the case is hard to reconcile with other standing cases.

**(c) Friends of the Earth, Inc., v. Laidlaw Environmental Services,** 528 U.S. 167 (2000). [§ 89], involved the Clean Water Act's (CWA) authorization of a citizen suit against the holder of a CWA discharge permit. The permit holder came into compliance with the permit after the citizen suit was filed and asserted that the case was moot and that the citizen-suit plaintiffs lacked standing at the outset of the lawsuit. Ruling against this permit-holder, the Court said that the ongoing pollutant discharges directly affected the citizen-suit plaintiffs' recreational, athletic, and economic interests, thereby creating a redressable injury-in-fact under Article III. The Court also said that the permit-holder's voluntary cessation of illegal activity did not moot the case

# CHAPTER IV

out (see § 98). A case might become moot only if subsequent events make it absolutely clear that the allegedly wrongful behavior could not reasonably be expected to recur, and the party asserting mootness has a heavy burden of persuading a court that the challenged conduct cannot reasonably be expected to recur.

c. **Mootness. [§ 90]**

**Under the mootness doctrine, an Article III case or controversy must exist throughout the entire litigational process. If the plaintiff's injury-in-fact ever goes away, the case will be dismissed as moot because there is nothing more the court can do for the plaintiff.**

(1) Theory Underlying the Mootness Doctrine. [§ 91]

**The idea here is that a federal court will exercise its jurisdiction only if it is able to provide relief to a litigant in a contested lawsuit.** If a court cannot redress the injury of a litigant before the court, the court's decree is tantamount to an advisory opinion.

In *DeFunis v. Odegaard*, 416 U.S. 312 (1974), a white law student challenged the University of Washington's affirmative action admissions program as a violation of his equal protection rights. His asserted injury-in-fact was his failure to be admitted to law school. However, during his lawsuit, a state court ordered him admitted to law school. When his case got to the Supreme Court, he had registered for his final term of law school. Since his only asserted injury, failure to be admitted to law school, had been taken care of, the Court dismissed his case as moot. There was nothing the Court could do for him because he had already achieved the result he sought.

**STUDY TIP:** What if a plaintiff such as DeFunis had asserted another injury-in-fact, such as having to spend money to treat the depression he suffered from having failed to gain admission to law school? This injury-in-fact would not be rectified by his having been admitted to law school; thus the case would not be moot under these facts. The moral of the story is to be careful about the injury alleged and the relief requested. As they change, so may a court's decision as to the mootness of a case.

# JUDICIAL REVIEW AND LIMITATIONS ON JUDICIAL REVIEW

(2) **Exceptions to the Mootness Doctrine. [§ 92]**

There are three main exceptions to the mootness doctrine:

— **Capable of repetition, yet evading review.**

— **Voluntary cessation of illegal activity.**

— **Collateral consequences.**

(a) **Capable of Repetition, Yet Evading Review. [§ 93]**

Under this exception, a court will not declare a dispute moot if the controversy is **capable of repetition, yet evading review, in relation to the plaintiff or a member of his or her certified class.** These cases always involve controversies of short duration, such as abortion, elections, or age laws. The idea is that the injury-in-fact will always go away before the lawsuit winds its way through the court system.

(i) In *Roe v. Wade*, 410 U.S. 113 (1973), [§ 94] the Court ruled that Jane Roe's challenge to Texas abortion laws was not moot, even though she was no longer pregnant. The Court reasoned that if the fact of non-pregnancy moots a case out, challenges to restrictive abortion laws will never survive the appellate review process.

(ii) In *Moore v. Ogilvie*, 394 U.S. 814 (1969), [§ 95] the plaintiffs, who were candidates for presidential and vice-presidential electors, challenged a state statute requiring a certain number of signatures on petitions from throughout the state. By the time the case got to the Supreme Court, the election was over. The Court invoked the "capable of repetition" exception because it was likely that the controversy would recur, but would never be resolved before the contested election was over.

(iii) Assume that an 18–year-old college student wants to challenge a state law setting the minimum drinking age at 21. By the time this case can get through the appellate courts, the dispute would be moot as to the plaintiff (he or she would be old enough to buy

# CHAPTER IV

alcohol), but would be capable of repetition in relation to the other members of the plaintiff's certified class.

(b) **Voluntary Cessation of Illegal Activity. [§ 96]**

**Voluntary cessation of illegal activity by the alleged wrongdoer is usually insufficient to make a case moot.**

In *U.S. v. W.T. Grant Co.*, 345 U.S. 629 (1953), the federal government filed an antitrust suit to break up interlocking directorates among several companies. Interlocking directorates exist when a number of the same people are on the boards of directors of different companies. The Justice Department frowns on such arrangements, and sought to stop this practice. After the U.S. government sued, the interlocking directors resigned, and then argued that the case was moot. The Court disagreed, refusing to grant these defendants the power to have their case dismissed, then rejoin other boards of directors. The Court did say, however, that the case would be moot if there were no reasonable expectations that the wrong would be repeated.

(c) **Collateral Consequences. [§ 97]**

**A claim is not moot if some collateral consequences of court action will continue even though the main issue has been resolved.**

(i) *Sibron v. New York*, 392 U.S. 40 (1968) [§ 98] A person may attack the constitutionality of his or her criminal conviction even if the entire sentence has been served, because the conviction may cause that person to be denied the right to vote, or to be subjected to a recidivist statute at some time in the future.

6. **Eleventh Amendment. [§ 99]**

**The Eleventh Amendment limits the ability of federal courts to hear cases in which an individual sues a state.** Eleventh Amendment analysis involves some of the most arcane rules in all of constitutional law. You should focus on what the Court says the Eleventh Amendment means, rather than on what the Eleventh Amendment actually says.

a. **A State May Sue Another State in Federal Court for Money Damages. [§ 100]**

A state may recover monetary damages from another state in an original action in the Supreme Court without running afoul of the Eleventh Amendment.

# JUDICIAL REVIEW AND LIMITATIONS ON JUDICIAL REVIEW

In *Kansas v. Colorado*, 533 U.S. 1 (2001), the Court ruled that the Eleventh Amendment does not bar Kansas from suing Colorado for monetary damages for violation of a compact designed to prevent the depletion of water from the Arkansas River. Even though Kansas based its claim on losses suffered by individual water users in the state, the Court reasoned that Kansas' own interest in preventing upstream diversion justified the exercise of the Court's original jurisdiction, and vitiated Colorado's Eleventh Amendment argument.

b. **An Individual Cannot Sue a State in Federal Court. [§ 101]**

**In general, the Eleventh Amendment prohibits an individual (not a state or federal government) from suing a state in federal court.** It does not matter whether the individual plaintiff is or is not a resident of the state he or she is suing. The Eleventh Amendment applies in either case.

c. **How to Get Around the Eleventh Amendment Bar to the Exercise of Federal Court Jurisdiction When an Individual Sues a State. [§ 102]**

These rules were created because it would not be acceptable for a state to be able to violate an individual's federal rights and be totally immune from federal court supervision. *Ex Parte Young*, 209 U.S. 123 (1908).

(1) **Name the state officer as an individual, not as an officer of the state.** For instance, if Tom Smith, the Attorney General of State A, has violated your federal rights, you should name Tom Smith as the Defendant in his individual capacity, not as Attorney General. The fiction here is that you are not suing the state, but just an individual named Tom;

(2) **Allege that the state officer acted outside the scope of his authority by violating your rights.** This "authority stripping" is needed to maintain the fiction that you are not suing a state. In other words, for purposes of the Eleventh Amendment, Tom is just an individual who abridged your rights; and

(3) **Allege that the state officer violated your federal rights.** If you are only able to argue that Tom violated your state rights, the Eleventh Amendment will bar the federal court from hearing your case. *Pennhurst State School and Hospital v. Halderman*, 465 U.S. 89 (1984).

d. **Relief Available Against a State. [§ 103]**

If you are able to jump through these hoops, you are now in federal court with a lawsuit against a state official. The next question is what

# CHAPTER IV

relief is available once these requirements are met. The Court has given the following rules regarding the relief available when a plaintiff has successfully met the requirements for suing a state official in federal court.

(1) **No Retroactive Money Damages. [§ 104]**

**A plaintiff cannot receive any retroactive money damages from the state.** Recovery of past debts, for instance, is totally barred by the Eleventh Amendment. The theory here is that a state could be bankrupted if ordered by federal courts to pay retroactive money damages.

(2) **Prospective Injunctive Relief Permissible. [§ 105]**

**Prospective injunctive relief is permissible to force a state official to comply with federal law in the future.** Under this rule, it is also permissible for a federal court to order a state to pay, in the future, any money that is needed to comply with the injunctive order.

> (a) In *Edelman v. Jordan*, 415 U.S. 651 (1974), [§ 106] a plaintiff sued a state official, arguing that welfare benefits were withheld in violation of federal regulations. The plaintiff requested retroactive money damages (the welfare payments not received in the past), as well as a prospective injunctive order compelling state officials to pay him the correct amount in the future. The Court denied the request for retroactive money damages, but granted the injunction, despite the fact that the state would have to pay more money in the future by way of increased welfare payments.

> (b) In *Milliken v. Bradley*, 418 U.S. 717 (1974), [§ 107] the Court upheld a lower court ruling which ordered the desegregation of Detroit public schools. The Detroit schools would have to spend $5.8 million to comply with the court's order. This future expenditure was permissible because it operated prospectively, giving the government a chance to plan for the expenditure.

> (c) If a plaintiff is able to point to specific pieces of property (artifacts from a sunken Spanish galleon) which have been unconstitutionally taken into possession by a state official, a federal court may order the state official to turn those pieces of property over to the plaintiff. *Florida Dept. of State v. Treasure Salvors, Inc.*, 458 U.S. 670 (1982). [§ 108]

# JUDICIAL REVIEW AND LIMITATIONS ON JUDICIAL REVIEW

e. **The Eleventh Amendment Only Applies in Federal Court. [§ 109]**

**The Eleventh Amendment does not apply in state court.** *Nevada v. Hall*, 440 U.S. 410 (1979). The Eleventh Amendment only bars federal courts from hearing suits by an individual against a state; it does not apply to the exercise of judicial power by a state court. If an individual sues a state in state court, the state will assert sovereign immunity as its defense. *Mt. Healthy City School District v. Doyle*, 429 U.S. 274 (1977).

f. **Congress Cannot, Under Article 1, Abrogate a State's Immunity From Suit in Its Own Courts. [§ 110]**

**Congress cannot authorize private actions against States in their own courts.**

*Alden v. Maine*, 527 U.S. 706 (1999). The Court ruled that Congress, pursuant to the Fair Labor Standards Act (FLSA), could not force states to submit to suit in their own courts. The FLSA, passed pursuant to Congress' Article I Commerce Power, contravened a state's constitutional immunity from suit in its own courts. The Court reasoned that history, practice, precedent, and the Constitution's structure precluded such a result.

g. **The Eleventh Amendment Only Protects States and Statewide Departments. [§ 111]**

**The Eleventh Amendment does not protect political subdivisions of a state (cities counties, school boards) from being sued for damages in federal court.**

For the inapplicability of the Eleventh Amendment to cities, see *Monell v. Dept. of Social Services*, 436 U.S. 658 (1978). For counties, see *Lincoln County v. Luning*, 133 U.S. 529 (1890). For school boards, see *Mt. Healthy City School District v. Doyle*, 429 U.S. 274 (1977).

h. **Congress May Abrogate a State's Eleventh Amendment Immunity by Acting Under Section 5 of the Fourteenth Amendment. [§ 112]**

**Congress may, by a plain and clear statement of its intent to do so, take away a state's Eleventh Amendment immunity.** This means that a state may then be sued directly in federal court for retroactive money damages. Congress may take away a state's

# CHAPTER IV

immunity by acting under § 5 of the Fourteenth Amendment, *Fitzpatrick v. Bitzer*, 427 U.S. 445 (1976).

**(1) Congress May Not Abrogate a State's Eleventh Amendment Immunity by Acting Under Section 5 of the Fourteenth Amendment if It Has No Underlying Constitutional Power to Do So. [§ 113]**

Title I of the Americans with Disabilities Act allowed the disabled to sue States for discrimination in federal court for monetary damages. As the disabled are not a suspect or quasi-suspect class, state regulation regarding the disabled is only subject to rational basis scrutiny. Congress, in passing the ADA, did not identify a pattern of irrational state discrimination against the disabled. As no such discrimination could be found, § 5 of the Fourteenth Amendment did not apply and thus Congress did not have a valid power source to abrogate the State's immunity under Title 1. *Board of Trustees of the University of Alabama v. Garrett*, 531 U.S. 356 (2001).

However, in *Tennessee v. Lane*, 541 U.S. 509 (2004), the Court upheld Title II of the Americans with Disabilities Act, which prohibits public entities from discriminating against persons with disabilities in relation to their physical access to state courts, and which abrogates a state's Eleventh Amendment immunity from private suits in federal court in such cases. Unlike *Garrett* (above), Congress, in passing Title II, had before it ample evidence of exclusion of persons from courthouses and court proceedings because of their disabilities, and Title II is therefore a valid exercise of Congress' power under § 5 of the 14th Amendment to abrogate state immunity.

In *United States v. Georgia*, 546 U.S. 151 (2006), the Court held that Title II of the Americans with Disabilities Act (ADA) validly abrogates states' sovereign immunity insofar as it creates a private cause of action for money damages against states for actual violations of 14th Amendment rights. Goodman sued state defendants to challenge the conditions of his confinement in a Georgia prison. He alleged violations of 42 U.S.C. § 1983 and Title II of the ADA. The Court, assuming that the Circuit Court correctly found that Goodman had alleged actual Eighth Amendment violations that would, if substantiated, violate Title II of the ADA, ruled that Goodman's claims were based on conduct that violated § 1 of the 14th Amendment. As such, Congress has the power, acting under § 5 of the 14th Amendment, to abrogate state sovereign immunity by authorizing private suits for money damages against states.

### (2) Congress May Only Abrogate a State's Eleventh Amendment Immunity if It Is Acting to Remediate or Prevent a Constitutional Violation. [§ 114]

The court has made it clear that if Congress acts to abrogate a state's Eleventh Amendment immunity the object of such a law must be the remediation or prevention of constitutional violations. In *College Savings Bank v. Florida Prepaid Postsecondary Education Expense Board*, 527 U.S. 666 (1999), the Court held that Congress had not abrogated a state's Eleventh Amendment immunity under the Trademark Remedy Clarification Act (TRCA) because no protected property interest was involved in the case. Plaintiff sold certificates of deposit to help finance college costs. When the state of Florida got in the business, plaintiff accused it of false and misleading advertising. The Court ruled that Florida did nothing to abridge any constitutionally cognizable property interest, so Congress could not have acted under the TRCA to remedy any constitutional violation. *See*, also *Florida Prepaid Postsecondary Education Expense Board v. College Savings Bank*, 527 U.S. 627 (1999).

### i. Congress May Not Abrogate a State's Eleventh Amendment Immunity by Acting Under the Commerce Clause. [§ 115]

Congress may not take away a state's Eleventh Amendment immunity by acting under the Interstate Commerce Clause or the Indian Commerce Clause.

### *Seminole Tribe of Florida v. Florida*, 517 U.S. 44 (1996), [§ 116]

The Court invalidated a provision of the federal Indian Gaming Regulatory Act (IGRA) which allowed Indian tribes to sue states in federal court to enforce the IGRA. **The Court ruled that section 5 of the Fourteenth Amendment is the only constitutional provision under which Congress may unilaterally abrogate a state's Eleventh Amendment immunity from suit in federal court.** In so ruling, the Court overruled *Pennsylvania v. Union Gas Co.*, 491 U.S. 1 (1989), in which the Court said that Congress could abrogate a state's Eleventh Amendment immunity by acting under the Commerce Clause.

# CHAPTER IV

j. **The Bankruptcy Clause of the Constitution Acts as a Limitation on State Sovereignty. [§ 117]**

**States, in ratifying the Constitution's Bankruptcy Clause, surrendered any sovereign immunity in relation to federal bankruptcy proceedings.**

In *Central Virginia Community College v. Katz*, 546 U.S. 356 (2006), the Court held that a bankruptcy trustee's proceeding to set aside a debtor's preferential transfers to state agencies is among the proceedings necessary to effectuate the in rem jurisdiction of bankruptcy courts. The state agencies asserted the Eleventh Amendment as a defense against the recovery of the transfers. The Court held that the Bankruptcy Clause itself abrogated states' sovereign immunity, giving Congress the power to authorize limited subordination of state sovereign immunity in the bankruptcy area. The Court pointed out that the Framers' primary goal in adopting the Bankruptcy Clause was to prevent competing sovereigns from interfering with discharges from bankruptcy. The Bankruptcy Clause contemplates a uniform federal response to the problems of divergent and uncoordinated bankruptcy laws that existed in the American Colonies. The Court made it clear that the issue in the case was not one of statutory abrogation of states' sovereign immunity, but rather an abrogation that was effected in the plan of the Constitution as envisioned by the Framers.

k. **A State May Waive Its Eleventh Amendment Immunity. [§ 118]**

**A state may, by making a plain and clear statement of its intent to do so, waive its Eleventh Amendment immunity in federal court.** *Port Authority Trans–Hudson Corp. v. Feeney*, 495 U.S. 299 (1990).

l. **State Waiver of Eleventh Amendment Immunity by Removing a Case From State Court to Federal Court. [§ 119]**

**A State waives its Eleventh Amendment immunity when it removes a case from state court to federal court.**

In *Lapides v. Board of Regents of the University System of Georgia*, 535 U.S. 613 (2002), a professor filed a state-court lawsuit against the board of regents and university officials in their individual capacities, alleging a violation of state tort law and 42 U.S.C. § 1983. The state officials removed the case to federal court, and then moved to dismiss the lawsuit. The state conceded that a state statute had waived Georgia's sovereign immunity from state-law suits in state court, but it then asserted Eleventh Amendment immunity from suit in federal court. The Court applied the general principle that a state's voluntary appearance in federal court amounts to a waiver of its Eleventh Amendment immunity. Even though Georgia was involuntarily brought into this case as a defendant in state court, it then voluntarily removed the case to federal court, thus invoking federal court jurisdiction, and waiving any Eleventh Amendment immunity it might have had.

m. **The Eleventh Amendment Does Not Apply When the Federal Government Sues a State in Federal Court. [§ 120]**

**The Eleventh Amendment only applies when an individual sues a state in federal court; it does not bar the exercise of federal judicial power when the United States sues a state in federal court.** *United States v. Texas*, 143 U.S. 621 (1892).

n. **An Individual May Sue a Public Official in Federal Court if the Official Will Pay the Damages Out of His or Her Personal Assets. [§ 121]**

**The Eleventh Amendment bars a plaintiff from seeking damages from the public treasury, but damages are a permissible remedy against individual public office-holders if the damages are to be paid out of their assets.** *Scheuer v. Rhodes*, 416 U.S. 232 (1974).

o. **The Eleventh Amendment Provides No Immunity to Entities Created Pursuant to the Compact Clause. [§ 122]**

**The Eleventh Amendment does not protect an entity created pursuant to the Compact Clause unless the states intended to confer immunity on that entity.** (Under Article I, § 10, clause 3, "No State shall, without the consent of Congress, . . . enter into any Agreement or Compact with another State . . . " This provision is intended to prevent agreements between states that will increase the political power of one or both states or diminish the power of the federal government). In *Hess v. Port Authority Trans–Hudson Corp.*, 513 U.S. 30 (1994), the Court held that two injured railway workers could sue the Port Authority railway in federal court. The Court reasoned that even though the Port Authority was created pursuant to a compact between New York and New Jersey, those states did not structure the railway so as to confer on it the Eleventh Amendment immunity of the states. The Court focused on the fact that the railway is financially independent, and any judgment against it would not be paid out of state funds.

# CHAPTER IV

7. **Abstention. [§ 123]**

   The abstention doctrine deals with the relationship between the federal and state court systems. An abstention issue arises when a federal court has jurisdiction to hear a case, because a federal question is present, but declines to do so out of respect for state courts. Abstention is an example of a judicially-imposed limitation on the exercise of federal judicial power. The idea here is that, except in extreme circumstances, a federal court should defer to a state court for the resolution of an issue which also falls within the state court's jurisdiction.

   **There are two kinds of abstention that you should know:**

   a. *Pullman* **Abstention. [§ 124]**

   *Pullman* **abstention arises when 1) a lawsuit is filed in federal court, 2) the case involves issues both of federal and state law, and 3) the issue of state law is ambiguous, uncertain, or unsettled.** If it chooses, the federal court may abstain from hearing this case and allow the parties to seek a state-court clarification of the unclear question of state law. The state-court ruling on the state-law question may obviate the need for a return to federal court for a ruling on the federal constitutional issue. In other words, if the plaintiff wins in state court, based on the state law issue, there is no need to return to federal court. As a matter of fact, the federal court then would not be able to entertain the federal question because to do so would be to issue an advisory opinion.

   In *Railroad Commission v. Pullman Co.*, 312 U.S. 496 (1941), railroads filed suit in federal court challenging an order of the Railroad Commission of Texas that all sleeping cars in Texas be under the control of a Pullman conductor, as opposed to a Pullman porter. The railroads argued that the order was not authorized by state law, and that it was unconstitutional. If the Commission order was not valid, the result would be that more positions would be available for Pullman porters than for Pullman conductors. At the time, Pullman conductors were white and Pullman porters were black. Pullman porters intervened in the case, claiming that the order violated their equal protection rights. The federal district court heard the case, and decided that the Commission order was not authorized by the laws of Texas. The Supreme Court reversed and remanded, on the theory that the federal district court should have abstained on the question of state law and allowed the Texas courts to decide the issue. The federal district court was to retain jurisdiction, but allow the parties to go to state court for clarification of the power of the Commission.

# JUDICIAL REVIEW AND LIMITATIONS ON JUDICIAL REVIEW

(1) **Once in State Court, the Plaintiff May Litigate All Claims in State Court. [§ 125]**

**Under *Pullman* abstention, the plaintiff who is sent to state court for a ruling on the state-law issue may decide to litigate the entire package (both state and federal claims) in state court.** The reason to do so would be to save the time and money that would be required to return to federal court after the state-court proceedings have run their course.

(2) **Once in State Court, the Plaintiff Must Reserve the Right to Return to Federal Court to Litigate the Federal Issues in the Case. [§ 126]**

A plaintiff who has been sent to state court to clear up a state-law issue has a right to return to federal court for a resolution of the federal constitutional question. However, once in state court, the plaintiff must specifically reserve, on the record, the right to return to federal district court to litigate his or her federal claims. *England v. Louisiana State Board of Medical Examiners*, 375 U.S. 411 (1964).

b. *Younger* **Abstention. [§ 127]**

Under *Younger v. Harris*, 401 U.S. 37 (1971), abstention, in its classic form, arises when a defendant in a pending state criminal proceeding files a lawsuit in federal court seeking to enjoin the pending state criminal proceeding. **The general rule is that a federal district court will not enjoin a pending state criminal proceeding unless the prosecution is brought for purposes of bad faith or harassment.**

(1) **Theory Underlying *Younger* Abstention. [§ 128]**

The federal district court will abstain in such a case to show respect for state courts, as well as to avoid the unworkable result of having to decide a huge number of requests for injunctions by state defendants who believe their federal rights have been violated. It would wreak havoc on both the federal and state court systems if federal district courts were routinely to interfere with ongoing state criminal proceedings. Another part of the justification for *Younger* abstention is that the state criminal defendant may assert his federal constitutional rights in the state courts. As long as the state criminal defendant has a forum in which to assert his or her constitutional arguments, there is no overriding need for a federal court to get involved.

# CHAPTER IV

(2) **Exceptions to *Younger* Abstention. [§ 129]**

A federal court may choose not to abstain, even if there is a pending state criminal proceeding, if there is serious danger to the rights of the state criminal defendant. For e.g.;

(a) **Bad Faith. [§ 130]**

A bad-faith prosecution is one which has no reasonable chance of success. *Allee v. Medrano*, 416 U.S. 802 (1974). A federal court may decide to enjoin such a state-court prosecution.

(b) **Harassment. [§ 131]**

A prosecution brought only to harass or retaliate against a person may be enjoined, despite the general rule of *Younger.*

In *Dombrowski v. Pfister*, 380 U.S. 479 (1965), a civil rights organization, and a number of its officers sued to enjoin enforcement of two Louisiana laws regulating the activities of subversive organizations. Under these state laws, it was a felony to participate in the formation or management, or to contribute to the support, of any subversive organization. The plaintiffs asserted that the state authorities were threatening prosecution simply to harass them, and that there was no reasonable chance of a valid conviction. The Court ruled that the plaintiffs were entitled to injunctive relief to prevent their prosecution under state laws that were so vague and overbroad as to chill their right to free speech.

(3) **Reversal of Usual Order of Filing. [§ 132]**

In the typical *Younger* case, the first lawsuit is the pending state criminal proceeding, and the second is the federal request for injunctive relief. Federal courts usually abstain in these circumstances because it would wreak havoc on state criminal justice systems for federal courts to routinely enjoin pending state criminal proceedings. However, *Younger* may apply even if the order of the lawsuit is reversed.

*Hicks v. Miranda*, 422 U.S. 332 (1975). The Court held that *Younger* abstention may apply when a state prosecution is begun shortly after a federal lawsuit is filed. The fact pattern under

# JUDICIAL REVIEW AND LIMITATIONS ON JUDICIAL REVIEW

*Hicks* invloves a person who is specifically threatened with prosecution under a state criminal law and files a lawsuit in federal court to enjoin the threatened prosecution. Before anything of substance on the merits (swearing-in of witnesses, taking testimony) takes place in federal court, the state prosecutes. The state may then, under *Younger*, ask the federal court to abstain from hearing the federal lawsuit pending the outcome of the state criminal trial. The rule allows a state to pull the federal plaintiff out of federal court by filing criminal charges soon after the federal lawsuit is filed.

**(4) Younger Abstention Has Been Applied to Some Non-Criminal Cases. [§ 133]**

*Younger* abstention has been extended to some, but not all, state civil and administrative proceedings. **The general principle is that *Younger* will apply to any pending civil or administrative proceeding in which an important state interest is involved.** As a result, a federal court will abstain from hearing lawsuits in which the federal plaintiff has a state forum in which to assert his or her federal constitutional rights. The Court has ruled that federal courts should abstain, under *Younger*, when the following state proceedings are pending at the time of the filing of the federal lawsuit.

(a) The application of a state public nuisance statute to a theater that allegedly showed obscene movies. *Huffman v. Pursue Ltd.*, 420 U.S. 592 (1975). [§ 134]

(b) An action by a state to recover fraudulently obtained welfare funds. *Trainor v. Hernandez*, 431 U.S. 434 (1977). [§ 135]

(c) A state contempt proceeding for failure to pay civil judgments. *Juidice v. Vail*, 430 U.S. 327 (1977). [§ 136]

(d) State child abuse proceedings. *Moore v. Sims*, 442 U.S. 415 (1979). [§ 137]

(e) State bar disciplinary hearings. *Middlesex County Ethics Committee v. Garden State Bar Association*, 457 U.S. 423 (1982). [§ 138]

(f) State administrative agency hearing involving an alleged civil rights violation. *Ohio Civil Rights Commission v. Dayton Christian Schools*, 477 U.S. 619 (1986). [§ 139]

# CHAPTER IV

(g) State lien provisions in support of civil judgment. *Pennzoil Co. v. Texaco, Inc.*, 481 U.S. 1 (1987). [§ 140]

## REVIEW PROBLEMS—JUDICIAL REVIEW AND LIMITATIONS ON JUDICIAL REVIEW

**PROBLEM 1.** The City of Id has a criminal trespass ordinance which prohibits anyone from going onto someone else's private property, for any reason. Members of a certain religious group are upset about the employment practices of a store in a privately-owned shopping mall. They would like to go into the mall to protest, but are afraid that they might be arrested. They want to file suit to challenge the ordinance. Should a court hear this lawsuit?

**Answer:** No. This is not a ripe controversy. The generalized threat of enforcement of a law is not enough to create a ripe controversy under Article III. If the members of the religious group had been arrested or been specifically threatened with arrest, a ripe controversy would exist and a federal court would hear their lawsuit. See §§ 40–43 for review.

**PROBLEM 2.** The State of Oz passed a law allowing 18, 19, and 20–year old women to buy beer, but prohibiting males from buying beer until they were 21 years of age. Paul Pubmeister is the owner of a local tavern whose business is hurt by not being able to sell beer to 18, 19, and 20 year-old males. Paul wants to challenge the Oz law on behalf of his 18, 19, and 20–year-old male customers. Does he have standing?

**Answer:** Yes. Under third-party standing rules, a seller of a product has standing to assert the rights of his or her customers in order to obtain standing to sue in federal court. See §§ 75, 76, 79 for review.

**PROBLEM 3.** Jane Jones is pregnant and wants an abortion. The State of Oz has a law which requires an adult woman to notify a doctor of her intent to have an abortion, and then to wait seventy-two hours before having the abortion. Jane files a class action lawsuit challenging the state law. Shortly after filing the lawsuit, Jane has a miscarriage. Should the court dismiss the case as moot?

**Answer:** No. A case will not be declared moot if the controversy is capable of repetition, yet evading review, in relation to the plaintiff or a member of her certified class. Jane may become pregnant again, or, even if she may not, another woman in the class may become pregnant and want an abortion. See §§ 90–94 for review.

**PROBLEM 4.** Joe Jones is the parent of a boy attending the City of Id School District. Joe and his son, Bob, are members of the Sikh religion. Due to his religious

## JUDICIAL REVIEW AND LIMITATIONS ON JUDICIAL REVIEW

beliefs, Bob wears a small dagger, called a kirpan, to school. The school has a "no-weapons" policy, and suspends Bob when he refuses to take off his kirpan. Joe and Bob sue the City of Id School District in federal court. Does the Eleventh Amendment bar this suit?

**Answer:** No. The Eleventh Amendment is irrelevant to these facts. The Eleventh Amendment is a bar to an individual suing a state in federal court. Political subdivisions of states, such as cities, counties, or school boards, are not protected by the Eleventh Amendment. See § 111 for review.

# CHAPTER V

# NATIONAL LEGISLATIVE POWER: SOURCES OF AND LIMITATIONS ON CONGRESSIONAL POWER

## A. ANY ACT OF CONGRESS MUST BE GROUNDED IN A SPECIFIC PROVISION OF THE CONSTITUTION. [§ 141]

**Congress does not have a general power to pass laws for the general welfare; congressional legislation must fall within a constitutional provision which provides specific justification for the law.** To analyze the constitutional validity of any law passed by Congress, ask two questions: 1) what is the specific constitutional provision which justifies the law; and 2) what is the scope of that constitutional provision (what people or activities fall within the reach of that constitutional power). For example, if Congress passes a law making carjacking a federal crime, first ask what constitutional provision might provide a basis for that law. Arguably, carjacking is within the scope of Congress' power to regulate interstate commerce. Once the Commerce Clause is identified as the provision which arguably justifies the federal carjacking law, ask whether the specific activity regulated under the statute is in interstate commerce. For instance, may Congress, under its commerce power, criminalize the theft of a car that was built, sold, stolen, and recovered, all in the same state?

## B. TWO NOTES ON GOVERNMENT POWER. [§ 142]

There are two principles that should be applied when analyzing the constitutionality of an exercise of government power.

1. **Government Power as Sword and Shield. [§ 143]**

    **Any provision of the Constitution which is a source of power for a particular government may also serve as a defense against action by another government or branch of government.** For instance, the Tenth Amendment is a source of power for a state when it passes a law (such as

# CHAPTER V

a criminal law). However, when Congress passes a law which arguably abridges a state's powers, the state may assert the Tenth Amendment as a defense against that congressional action (such as the argument that a federal law requiring local police to investigate and report on purchasers of handguns violates a state's ability to decide how to deliver police services to its citizens).

2. **Two Ways to Invalidate a Statute. [§ 144]**

    **When analyzing the constitutionality of congressional action, there are two ways for a court to invalidate the action: 1) Eliminate the power source, or; 2) Balance.**

    a. **Eliminate the Constitutional Power Source Relied on by Congress to Justify the Law.**

        **Under this approach, the plaintiff asserts that the legislature exceeded the scope of the constitutional provision on which it relied to pass a law.** For example, the Court has ruled that Congress exceeded its commerce power when it passed a federal criminal statute prohibiting the possession of a firearm in or within 1,000 feet of a school.

    b. **Balance.**

        **Under the balancing approach, the law is presumptively within a constitutional power source, but it is invalid if it contravenes some other provision of the Constitution.** For example, the Court ruled that the commerce power was broad enough to allow Congress to regulate the wages and hours of state employees, but that federally-mandated wage and hour laws unduly abridged a state's Tenth Amendment power to decide how to deliver police services to its citizens.

## C. SPECIFIC CONGRESSIONAL POWERS. [§ 145]

**Whenever Congress passes a law, you must be able to identify the specific provision in the Constitution which justifies that law.**

The powers of Congress are dispersed throughout the Constitution, but the main list, for law school purposes, is in Article I, § 8. Here is a list of the main congressional powers listed in that section:

1. Power to Tax;

2. Power to Spend for the General Welfare;

# NATIONAL LEGISLATIVE POWER

3. Power to Regulate Commerce Among the Several States, With Foreign Nations, and With the Indian Tribes;

4. Power to Regulate Immigration and Naturalization;

5. Power to Pass Uniform Laws Dealing With Bankruptcy;

6. Power to Coin Money;

7. Power to Establish a Postal Service;

8. Power to Set Up a System of Copyrights;

9. Power to Set Up Federal Courts (This Power Is Also Based in Article III, § 1);

10. Power to Declare War;

11. Power to Raise and Maintain Armies;

12. Power to Regulate and Dispose of Federal Property;

13. Power to Acquire Private Property for a Public Use, As Long as Just Compensation Is Paid;

14. Power to Pass Regulations for the District of Columbia.

**STUDY TIP:** Be careful about this last power. **Congress has no enumerated power to regulate for the general welfare of the country as a whole (it has no general police power), but it does have a specific power to pass police power regulations for the District of Columbia.** If Congress wants to regulate for the general welfare of the entire country, it usually does so under the Commerce Power.

1. **Necessary and Proper Clause. [§ 146]**

   **Under Article I, § 8, Clause 18, Congress has the power to pass laws to enable itself or any branch or officer of the federal government to carry out any constitutional power.** Congress may, as a result, legislate for the executive and judicial branches, as well as for itself.

   a. **Must Be Used With Another Constitutional Provision.**

      **The Necessary and Proper Clause cannot be used by itself as a source of power.** It must be coupled with some other constitutional provision.

# CHAPTER V

(1) When Congress passes laws regulating the conditions under which aliens may become citizens, it is acting pursuant to the Necessary and Proper Clause and its Article I power to establish a uniform rule of naturalization.

(2) When Congress passes a law making it a crime to threaten the President's life, the law is based on the Necessary and Proper Clause and Article II (which establishes the office of the Presidency).

(3) When Congress passes a law setting up a system of federal magistrates, the law is based on the Necessary and Proper Clause and Article III (which establishes the federal judiciary).

b. **Congress May Choose Any Reasonable Means.**

The Supreme Court has interpreted the Necessary and Proper Clause to mean that Congress may choose whatever means it deems convenient to carry out some power of government. *McCulloch v. Maryland*, 17 U.S. 316 (1819). Thus, "necessary" does not require that the only, or even least drastic, means to achieve a congressional goal be used.

In *U.S. v. Comstock*, 130 S.Ct. 1949 (2010), the Court, in a 7–2 ruling held that federal law allows a district court to order the civil commitment of a mentally ill, sexually dangerous federal prisoner beyond the date of his release from federal prison. Taking a very broad view of the Necessary and Proper Clause, the Court ruled that the civil commitment statute is reasonably adopted to the furtherance of Congress' power to act as a responsible federal custodian of people who have been in the federal penal system. The Court says that there must be a means-end rationality between the enacted statute and the federal power, and that the civil commitment statute is rationally related to protecting the mentally ill and society from evils that may have resulted from incarceration of mentally ill prisoners in the federal system. Justice Thomas (joined by Justice Scalia) dissents, arguing that the Necessary and Proper Clause must be directly related to the effectuation of an enumerated power, and that any connection to a constitutional power is simply too attenuated in this case.

2. **Commerce Power. [§ 147]**

**Under Article I, § 8, Clause 3, Congress has the power "to regulate Commerce with foreign Nations, and among the several States, and**

# NATIONAL LEGISLATIVE POWER

with the Indian Tribes." Law school courses focus on Congress' ability to regulate commerce among the several states.

a. **Two Main Issues That Arise in the Commerce Clause Area. [§ 148]**

(1) **What Is the Scope or Reach of the Commerce Power?**

What people or activities fall within the definition of "interstate commerce," and are thus regulable by Congress under that power? If a person or activity is not in interstate commerce, Congress may not regulate that person or activity under its Commerce Clause power.

(2) **Does a Congressional Act Unduly Abridge States' Rights?**

Even if the regulated person or activity is in interstate commerce, Congress may not regulate so as to contravene essential attributes of state sovereignty.

b. **Scope of the Commerce Power. [§ 150]**

In the *Lopez* case (§ 164), the Court has said that there are three categories of activity that Congress may regulate under the commerce power. First, Congress may regulate the use of the channels of interstate commerce. Second, Congress may regulate the instrumentalities of interstate commerce. Finally, Congress may regulate people or activities that have a close and substantial relation to interstate commerce.

(1) **Pre–1937 Examples of Local Activities That Were Not Within the Commerce Power. [§ 151]**

(a) **Manufacturing. [§ 152]**

The Court held that Congress' Commerce Power was not broad enough to reach the manufacture of refined sugar within a state. Thus, the Sherman Antitrust Act could not be used to break up a 98% monopoly of sugar refineries. *U.S. v. E.C. Knight Co.*, 156 U.S. 1 (1895).

(b) **Child Labor. [§ 153]**

The Court held that the Congress could not impose standards for the employment of children within the various states. Again, the idea was that production of goods, even by children, is a purely local matter, the

# CHAPTER V

regulation of which is solely reserved to the states under the Tenth Amendment. *Hammer v. Dagenhart*, 247 U.S. 251 (1918).

### (c) Wage and Hour Restrictions. [§ 154]

The Court held that Congress could not require certain bituminous coal producers to comply with federal minimum-wage and maximum-hour requirements. The mining of coal was a purely local activity that fell outside the reach of the Commerce Power. *Carter v. Carter Coal Co.*, 298 U.S. 238 (1936).

## (2) Post–1937 Expansion of the Commerce Power: The Switch in Time That Saved Nine? [§ 155]

Up through 1936, the Supreme Court consistently invalidated congressional legislation designed to help pull the country out of the Depression. President Roosevelt, frustrated by the Court's rulings, proposed his famous Court Packing Plan in February 1937. Under this plan, the President would be given authority by Congress to appoint one new Justice for each Justice who was 70 years old, and had served as a judge for at least ten years. The Plan would have set the maximum member of Justices at fifteen, a number that would have been reached because there were six Justices over the age of 70 at the time of the proposal by President Roosevelt. Shortly after the proposed Court Packing Plan, the Court began to use a broader Commerce Clause analysis which gave much greater power to Congress to regulate activities or people within the states.

## (3) Judicial Justifications for an Expanded Commerce Power. [§ 156]

### (a) Close and Substantial Effect on Commerce. [§ 157]

**Congress can, under the Commerce Power, reach intrastate activities if those activities have a close and substantial effect on interstate commerce.** Thus, Congress could restrict the ability of a steel company to discharge employees because of union activity. The Commerce Clause was held to be a sufficient basis for the National Labor Relations Act which Congress passed to deal with labor-management issues. *NLRB v. Jones & Laughlin Steel Corp.*, 301 U.S. 1 (1937).

# NATIONAL LEGISLATIVE POWER

(b) **Aggregation Theory. [§ 158]**

**Congress can, under the Commerce Power, reach an intrastate activity which, by itself, has a minimal impact on interstate commerce, if that activity, taken together with all other examples of that activity, has a substantial impact on interstate commerce.** In *Wickard v. Filburn*, 317 U.S. 111 (1942), the Court upheld, as applied to a small farmer, a federal law limiting the amount of wheat that could be grown by one person. Even though Filburn's activity, by itself, had a negligible impact on commerce, Congress could regulate him because, in the aggregate, Filburn's activity, together with that of other farmers across the country, had a substantial impact on interstate commerce.

(c) **Regulation of Class of Activities. [§ 159]**

**Where a class of activities is within the reach of the Commerce Power, Congress may regulate any particular actor or activity within the class.**

In *Perez v. United States*, 402 U.S. 146 (1971), the Court upheld Congress' ban on purely intrastate extortionate credit transactions because they may affect interstate commerce. The federal Consumers Credit Protection Act legitimately was applied to local loan sharks because Congress could reasonably conclude that loan sharking is an integral part of organized crime which, in the aggregate, affects interstate commerce. The Court said that where a class of activities is within the Commerce Power, courts have no power to excise, as trivial, individual instances of the class.

(d) **Congressional Finding of Effect on Commerce. [§ 160]**

**The Court will defer to a congressional finding that a regulated activity or person affects interstate commerce if there is any rational basis for such a finding.** If Congress meets this de minimis standard, the only remaining question for the Court is whether the means chosen is rationally related to achieving the legitimate congressional goal. *Hodel v. Virginia Surface Mining and Reclamation Association*, 452 U.S. 264 (1981).

# CHAPTER V

**(4) Examples of the Modern Scope of the Commerce Power. [§ 161]**

### (a) Civil Rights. [§ 162]

The Court upheld the ability of Congress to pass Title II of the Civil Rights Act of 1964 which forbade discrimination by race or color in hotels, motels, or restaurants that are in interstate commerce. The Court upheld the application of Title II to Ollie's Barbecue, a small restaurant in Birmingham, Alabama, on the theory that the discrimination by Ollie's Barbecue was representative of many other discriminations across the country, and was therefore within the reach of Congress' Commerce Power. *Katzenbach v. McClung*, 379 U.S. 294 (1964).

### (b) Intrastate Noncommercial Use of Marijuana. [§ 163]

*Gonzales v. Raich*, 545 U.S. 1 (2005). The Court upheld, under the Commerce Clause, Congress' power to proscribe the intrastate, noncommercial cultivation and use of marijuana, even when done in compliance with state law. In 1996, the State of California enacted the Compassionate Use Act which authorized limited marijuana use for medicinal purposes. Pursuant to doctors' recommendations, two California residents used marijuana for serious medical conditions. One plaintiff grew and ingested marijuana on her private property. Federal Drug Enforcement Administration (DEA) agents seized and destroyed six marijuana plants pursuant to the federal Controlled Substance Act (CSA). Relying heavily on *Perez* (§ 159) and *Wickard* (§ 158), the Court ruled that Congress can regulate purely intrastate activity that is not itself commercial if it concludes that failure to regulate that class of activity would undercut the regulation of the interstate market in that commodity. The Court reasoned that the CSA was appropriately applied in this case because growing marijuana for home consumption has a substantial effect on supply and demand in the national market for that commodity. In determining whether Congress' Commerce Clause authority reaches an activity in the aggregate, the Court need not independently determine whether the activity has a substantial effect on interstate commerce, but only whether Congress had a rational basis for so concluding. Here, Congress had a rational basis for believing that regulation of home-grown marijuana was

# NATIONAL LEGISLATIVE POWER

related to enforcement problems with the CSA, such as diversion of home-grown marijuana into illicit channels.

(5) **The Commerce Power Does Not Allow Congress to Regulate Purely Local Activities. [§ 164]**

**Congress may not use the Commerce Clause as a justification to criminalize local activity when that activity does not, even when aggregated with similar activity across the country, have a substantial effect on interstate commerce.** In *U.S. v. Lopez*, 514 U.S. 549 (1995), the Court invalidated a federal criminal law that prohibited the possession of a firearm within 1,000 feet of a school. The Court, 5–4, reasoned that gun possession in a school zone is not an economic activity that, even when considered along with similar activity nationwide, has a substantial impact on interstate commerce. In *Lopez*, the Court said that the federal law is invalid because it did not provide for any case-by-case determination that a particular act of gun possession had a direct relationship with interstate commerce. In *Lopez*, the Court said that there are three categories of activity that Congress may regulate under the commerce power. First, Congress may regulate the use of the channels of interstate commerce. Second, Congress may regulate the instrumentalities of interstate commerce. Finally, Congress may regulate people or activities that have a close and substantial relation to interstate commerce.

In *U.S. v. Morrison*, 529 U.S. 598 (2000), the Court, by a 5–4 vote, invalidated a provision of the 1994 Violence Against Women Act (VAWA) that created a civil cause of action for crimes motivated by gender bias. The plaintiff alleged that she was raped by three students at Virginia Tech, and she filed a federal lawsuit under VAWA. The Court ruled that Congress exceeded the scope of its commerce power by criminalizing what was a purely local, noneconomic activity. The Court, applying *Lopez* (previous case), refused to aggregate the effects of localized criminal activity, reasoning that to do so would allow Congress to regulate virtually any local activity whose combined impact affected commerce, such as family law, marriage, divorce, and childrearing.

In *Jones v. U.S.*, 529 U.S. 848 (2000), the Court unanimously held that a federal arson statute that applies to any building used in interstate commerce or in any activity affecting interstate commerce does not cover an owner-occupied private residence that is not being used for commercial purposes. Jones tossed a Molotov cocktail into a home owned and occupied by his cousin as a dwelling place for everyday family living. He was convicted for violating the federal arson statute. Applying the principles of *Lopez* (see above), the Court refused to construe the statute to include a private residence within the definition of "an activity affecting commerce." The Court rejected, as too attenuated, the arguments that the house was in interstate commerce because it was used as collateral to obtain a mortgage from an out-of-state lender, that it was used to obtain an out-of-state insurance policy, or that it was used to receive natural gas from outside the state.

In *Pierce County v. Guillen*, 537 U.S. 129 (2003) the Court upheld a federal statute which prohibited certain materials collected by a state or local government from being admitted into evidence in state or federal court. As an exercise of its Spending Power, Congress passed a statute which provides state and local governments with funding to improve dangerous sections of their roads. Fearing that the collection of data under this statute would increase the liability rate for accidents that happened at hazardous locations, Congress passed a law providing that materials collected for purposes of reporting under the funding measure shall not be admitted into evidence in state or federal court. Relying on *Lopez* (above), a unanimous Court upheld the evidentiary law as a proper exercise of Congress' Commerce Clause authority to regulate the channels and instrumentalities of interstate commerce.

c. **Commerce Power and Federalism. [§ 165]**

**When Congress, acting under its Commerce Power, passes a law which interferes with some attribute of state sovereignty, a state may assert the Tenth Amendment as a defense against that congressional action.**

(1) **Tenth Amendment. [§ 166]**

Under the Tenth Amendment, "[t]he powers not delegated to the United States by the Constitution, nor prohibited by it to the States, are reserved to the States respectively, or to the people." **The Court has interpreted the Tenth Amendment to mean that there are certain aspects of sovereignty that a state must have to function as a state and to occupy its proper place in a federal system.** Judicial interpretation of the Tenth Amend-

# NATIONAL LEGISLATIVE POWER

ment has changed over time, but today the Court focuses on whether a federal law impairs a state's ability to structure itself (determine which forms and procedures to use) or to provide services to its citizens (police, fire, schools). The Tenth Amendment serves as a source of power for the states (also referred to as a state's police power), as well as a defense asserted by a state against congressional action (a federal law impairs the ability of a state to provide adequate police services).

**(2) Major Cases in the Development of the Commerce Power and the Tenth Amendment. [§ 167]**

In a case where Congress regulates under the Commerce Clause, be very careful about who is regulated. Is Congress regulating just states, or is it regulating both states and private entities (such as a minimum-wage law that applies to all employers)? If Congress is regulating both states and private entities, the only protection states have from congressional impingement on states' rights is their participation in the national political process. The Court defers to congressional decisions as reflecting the will of the States. If Congress regulates just states, the Court will determine if the federal law unduly interferes with an essential attribute of state sovereignty, such as the delivery of police services.

**(a) National League of Cities v. Usery, 426 U.S. 833 (1976). [§ 168]**

The Court, by a 5–4 vote, overruled *Maryland v. Wirtz*. The Court ruled that, while the general subject matter of wages and hours is within the scope of the Commerce Power, Congress may not regulate the wages and hours set by a state as an employer because the federal law operated to directly displace the States' freedom to structure integral operations in areas of traditional governmental functions. The Court reasoned that the added obligations of the federal wage and hour provisions deprived a state of the power to deliver essential police services to its citizens.

**(b) Garcia v. San Antonio Metropolitan Transit Authority, 469 U.S. 528 (1985). [§ 169]**

The Court overruled *National League of Cities v. Usery*, and adopted a new Commerce Clause analysis for cases in which Congress regulated both private and governmental actors. The Court said that it would not assert the Tenth

# CHAPTER V

Amendment on behalf of the states as a defense against congressional action. In other words, the Court rejected the balancing approach of earlier cases. In its place the Court said that states were protected by their participation in the national political process. If a state has Senators and Representatives who participate in the national political process, the Court will presume that the state's interests are protected against undue congressional interference. If the legislative process works properly, the Court will not involve itself in changing the result of any given congressional vote. Under *Garcia*, the Court is extremely deferential to any congressional action which regulates both states and private entities. *Garcia* is the current analysis for cases in which Congress, acting within the scope of the commerce power, regulates both private and governmental actors.

**(c) New York v. U.S., 505 U.S. 144 (1992). [§ 170]**

The Court invalidated part of a congressional Commerce Clause law which required certain states to take title to all low-level radioactive waste generated in the state, take possession of the waste, and be liable in damages suffered by the owner or generator of the waste. The Court, by a 6–3 vote, distinguished this case from *Wirtz*, *National League of Cities*, and *Garcia* on the basis that those cases involved generally applicable laws (both states and private entities were regulated by the laws in those cases), whereas this law regulated only state governments. The Court said that the federal law commandeered state legislative processes by directly forcing them to enact and enforce a federal regulatory program. The Court said that the law overstepped the boundary between federal and state authority, regardless of whether one concludes that the law is outside the scope of the Commerce Power, or infringes on some aspect of state sovereignty. In other words, the Court refused to say which method of analysis it was using: eliminating the Commerce Clause as the constitutional provision justifying the law; or asserting that the Tenth Amendment right of the state to set its legislative agenda had been unduly abridged by the federal law.

**(d) Printz v. U.S., 521 U.S. 898 (1997). [§ 171]**

The Court, by a 5–4 vote, invalidated a provision of the Brady Handgun Violence Prevention Act (the Act) that

# NATIONAL LEGISLATIVE POWER

required the chief law enforcement officer of each local jurisdiction in the country to conduct background checks on prospective handgun buyers and to perform other ministerial tasks related to the purchase of handguns. The Court ruled that, similar to *New York v. U.S.*, (previous case), Congress' commandeering of state executive officers violated the system of dual sovereignty mandated by the structure of the Constitution. Compelling state officers to execute federal laws, especially without the states' consent, violates longstanding, constitutional practice and contravenes the Court's prior holdings, which make clear that Congress may not compel states to enact or administer a federal regulatory program. The Act also contravenes principles of separation-of-powers in that it transfers the President's power to execute federal laws to local law-enforcement officers throughout the country.

(e) **Reno v. Condon, 528 U.S. 141 (2000). [§ 172]**

The Court upheld the federal Driver's Privacy Protection Act (DPPA) which restricts disclosure by state motor vehicle departments and private parties of certain personal information about any person contained in motor vehicle records. The Court held that because drivers' information is an article of commerce, the law is within the scope of Congress' commerce power. The Court also ruled that the DPPA did not run afoul of the anti-commandeering rule of *New York* and *Printz* (previous cases) because it did not require the South Carolina legislature to enact any laws or regulations, nor did it require state officials to assist in the enforcement of federal statutes regulating private individuals.

**STUDY TIP:** If you see a federal law based on the Commerce Clause, determine who is regulated. If both private and governmental actors are subject to the law, *Garcia* applies, and the only protection a state receives is from its participation in the national legislative process. If only a state is regulated, and Congress is effectively commandeering a state legislature or a state executive officer, the federal law will be invalid because Congress cannot force state officials to perform federal functions. This kind of law violates the principle of "dual sovereignty," under which states must be free to structure themselves and their essential activities in accordance with the wishes of the state electorate.

# CHAPTER V

3. **Taxing Power. [§ 173]**

   Article I, Section 8 gives Congress the power to lay and collect taxes, imposts, and excises, but requires that all duties, imposts, and excises be uniform throughout the United States. This uniformity limit pertains to geographical uniformity, requiring uniform application (no discrimination) among the several states. The uniformity requirement is not violated if a tax is not uniform in relation to individual persons.

   a. **Two Ways a Tax Can Be Valid. [§ 174]**

   **A taxing measure passed by Congress can be valid in one of two ways: as a revenue-raising measure, or as a means to achieve a valid regulatory goal of Congress.**

   (1) **Tax as Revenue–Raiser.**

   As long as the purpose of a taxing measure is to raise revenue, it will be upheld, even if the amount of the tax is oppressive or even destructive. *Bailey v. Drexel Furniture Co.*, 259 U.S. 20 (1922).

   (2) **Tax as a Means to Achieve a Valid Regulatory Goal of Congress.**

   A taxing measure will also be valid if it is a means to achieve a valid regulatory goal of Congress. If Congress can regulate something under its commerce power, it may tax that activity as a means to achieve its permissible regulatory purpose. The theory is that if Congress may regulate or even prohibit an activity under its commerce power, it certainly may employ the less intrusive means of taxing that activity. Because of the broad scope of the modern commerce power (See §§ 150–164, above), it is not surprising that, since the late 1930's, the Court has upheld every federal tax attacked as a regulation.

   b. **Constitutional Limitations on the Taxing Power. [§ 175]**

   Even though virtually every tax would be upheld today, you should be aware that a federal tax measure may be overturned if it contravenes other constitutional protections.

   (1) **Fifth Amendment Privilege Against Self–Incrimination. [§ 176]**

   A federal tax may be invalid if, as one of its ancillary reporting provisions, it requires a taxpayer to file a return which reveals illegal sources of income, thereby forcing the taxpayer to incriminate himself or herself in violation of the privilege against self-incrimination. *Marchetti v. U.S.*, 390 U.S. 39 (1968).

In *Massachusetts v. U.S.*, 435 U.S. 444 (1978), the Court upheld a federal registration tax on all civil aircraft, including police aircraft, used by the State of Massachusetts. Justice Brennan, writing for four members of the Court, voted to uphold the tax, but said that two issues raised by a tax imposed on an instrumentality of a state are whether the tax unduly impairs a state's ability to deliver traditional governmental services, and whether the sovereignty of the state-regulatee is protected by the state's participation in the national political process. The crux of the second issue is whether the Senators and Representatives of the allegedly aggrieved state had an opportunity, as part of the national legislative process, to protect the interests of the state through lobbying and voting.

In *South Carolina v. Baker*, 485 U.S. 505 (1988), the Court upheld afederal law which removed the federal income tax exemption for interest earned on certain state and local bonds, unless the bonds were registered in the owner's name. South Carolina had argued that the federal law was invalid because it, in effect, commandeered the state legislative process by forcing states to pass laws authorizing a certain form of bond registration. Relying on *Garcia* (See § 169), the Court upheld the law on the basis that South Carolina participated in the national political process and thus had no Tenth Amendment challenge to the federal law.

**(2) State's Ability to Tax the Federal Government. [§ 177]**

A state may not directly tax (or burden) an instrumentality or agent of the federal government. For instance, in ***Johnson v. Maryland,*** 254 U.S. 51 (1920), the Court held that a state could not require a federal postal employee to obtain a state driver's license before performing his federal duties.

However, the Court has held that a state's taxation of a federal employee's salary is a sufficiently indirect burden on the federal government to be permissible. In ***Jefferson County v. Acker,*** 527 U.S. 423 (1999), the Court upheld an occupational tax imposed by an Alabama county on the salaries of federal judges sitting in the county. The Court held that the tax was a nondiscriminatory income tax on the judges' wages and, as such, did not violate the doctrine of intergovernmental tax immunity.

### (3) Compensation Clause Restricts the Government's Ability to Tax Federal Judges. [§ 178]

The Compensation Clause (Art. III, § 1) guarantees that the compensation of federal judges shall not be diminished during their terms of office. Congress cannot reduce judicial salaries, nor can it impose certain taxes on the salaries of judges. In *U.S. v. Hatter*, 532 U.S. 557 (2001), the Court held that the Compensation Clause does not forbid Congress from applying a generally applicable, nondiscriminatory tax to the salaries of federal judges, whether or not the judges were appointed before enactment of the tax. Applying this rule, the Court upheld the imposition of the Medicare tax on the salaries of federal judges. However, the Court invalidated the imposition of the Social Security tax on the salaries of federal judges because it discriminated against judges by singling them out for unfavorable treatment in relation to other federal employees. This discriminatory treatment of judges undercut the central purpose of the Compensation Clause, which is to protect judicial independence by shielding judges from retaliatory salary reductions.

## 4. Spending Power. [§ 179]

**Under the Spending Power, Congress has the power to spend "for the general welfare."** Remember that Congress does not have any explicit constitutional power to **regulate** for the general welfare (even though it may do so under the Commerce Power). In other words, Congress has no general police power similar to that of the states. Remember that Congress does have a constitutionally-based police power over the District of Columbia. **The issue of what is "for the general welfare" belongs to Congress, and the Court will uphold a spending measure if there is any rational basis to support Congress' conclusion that the law will advance the general welfare.**

*Sabri v. U.S.*, 541 U.S. 600 (2004). The Court upheld a federal statute which made it a crime to bribe state or local officials whose agency received more than $10,000 per year in federal funding. The Court held that Congress's authority to designate federal monies to promote the general welfare is accompanied by a corresponding authority under the Necessary and Proper Clause to ensure that taxpayer dollars are in fact spent for the general welfare.

# NATIONAL LEGISLATIVE POWER

a. **Regulation Through the Spending Power. [§ 180]**

   **When Congress imposes conditions on the receipt of federal money, the Court will uphold the spending measure so long as the recipient is free to reject the federal money and exercise his or her rights (in the case of an individual) or powers (in the case of the state).** There are three issues to look for when analyzing a congressional spending measure to see if it is constitutional:

   (1) **Is the Law Voluntary? [§ 181]**

   If the law leaves the recipient with a theoretical choice to accept or reject the federal "strings" accompanying the grant, the law will be upheld. The last time the Court invalidated a spending measure on the basis that it was coercive rather than voluntary was in 1936. In *United States v. Butler*, 297 U.S. 1 (1936), the Court struck down a federal law under which the government contracted with farmers to limit the number of acres of specified crops they planted. The Court ruled that the regulation was not voluntary because, due to the Depression, the farmers had no choice except to agree to the terms offered by the government.

   (2) **Is the Condition on the Receipt of Money Related to the General Purpose of the Federal Grant? [§ 182]**

   Although the Court has never invalidated a law on the basis that a condition on the receipt of federal funds was unrelated to the general purpose of the federal expenditure, it has raised the possibility that conditions on federal grants may be invalid if unrelated to the federal purpose in passing the spending measure. *South Dakota v. Dole*, 483 U.S. 203 (1987). For example, this issue would arise if Congress conditioned the receipt of federal highway funds on a state's willingness to pass a restrictive abortion law.

   (3) **Are There Any Other Constitutional Provisions Which Would Limit Congress' Ability to Impose a Condition on the Receipt of Money? [§ 183]**

   Other provisions of the Constitution may serve as possible limitations on the Spending Power.

   (a) **Tenth Amendment.**

   Since the *Butler* case in 1936, the Court has not invalidated any spending measure on the basis that it violates the Tenth Amendment rights of states.

# CHAPTER V

### (b) Individual Rights.

Congress may not spend money in a way that violates the constitutional rights of individuals.

#### (i) Establishment Clause.

Congress may not spend money so as to establish religion in contravention of the First Amendment. (See, for example, § 911, below).

#### (ii) Equal Protection.

Congress may not spend in a way that violates the equal protection principle of the Due Process Clause of the Fifth Amendment. In *Califano v. Goldfarb*, 430 U.S. 199 (1977), the Court struck down a provision of the Social Security Act which granted benefits to widows but not widowers, thus discriminating on the basis of gender.

#### (iii) Other Constitutional Rights.

Congress may not grant or withhold federal funds on any conditions it chooses. The conditions themselves must be constitutionally valid. For example, Congress could not validly condition housing assistance money to states on the adoption of a state policy restricting public housing solely to white people, or to Christians, or to married couples. The condition itself would violate individual rights to equal protection, religion, and privacy.

## 5. War Power. [§ 184]

**Under Article I, Section 8 of the Constitution, Congress has the power to declare war, raise armies and navies, and provide for the national defense.** When used together with the Necessary and Proper Clause, Congress may exercise this power in peacetime as well as in wartime. Not only may Congress declare war, it may also prepare for future wars, wage war once it has begun, and deal with the social and economic consequences of past wars.

*Woods v. Cloyd W. Miller Co.*, 333 U.S. 138 (1948). The Court upheld the continuation of federal rent control after the end of World War II. The Court said that the war power does not necessarily end with the cessation of hostilities; Congress must be able to remedy conditions created by the

# NATIONAL LEGISLATIVE POWER

mobilization of persons and materials for war. As long as the effects of war continue to be felt in society and are reasonably traceable to the war, Congress may use the war power to alleviate problems which flowed from the hostilities.

6. **Foreign Affairs Powers. [§ 185]**

   Congress and the President have very broad powers in the area of foreign affairs. As an element of its intrinsic sovereignty, the United States has the power to deal with foreign nations, even if the congressional or presidential action is not specifically authorized by a provision of the Constitution.

   a. **Congress May Delegate to the President the Power to Act in Foreign Affairs. [§ 186]**

   **As part of the government's power to deal in foreign affairs, Congress may vest discretion in the President to implement congressional policy on foreign affairs.** Such a delegation need not be based in a specific constitutional provision; it is justified under Congress' intrinsic powers to deal in foreign affairs.

   *U.S. v. Curtiss–Wright Export Corp.* 299 U.S. 304 (1936). The Court upheld the power of Congress to pass a Joint Resolution authorizing the President to place an embargo on the sale of arms to countries involved in armed conflict in South America. The President issued a proclamation imposing such an embargo. The Court rejected the argument that the Joint Resolution was an unconstitutional delegation of power to the President, emphasizing that the federal government's powers to deal in foreign affairs do not depend on specific affirmative grants from the constitution; they are necessary elements of a country's sovereignty.

   b. **Treaties and Executive Agreements. [§ 187]**

   (1) **Treaties. [§ 188]**

   **Under Article II, Section 2, Clause 2, the President has the power to enter into treaties with other countries. A treaty must be ratified by two-thirds of the Senate.** There are two kinds of treaties: self-executing, and non-self-executing. Self-executing treaties do not need implementing legislation; they contain all the details of the agreement between the countries and have the force of law as soon as they are ratified by the Senate. Non-self-executing treaties need to be implemented by legislation passed by Congress. They do not have the force of law until the implementing legislation is passed.

# CHAPTER V

*Medellin v. Texas*, 552 U.S. 491 (2008). In a case involving federalism, separation of powers, and treaty obligations, the Court ruled that state courts were not obligated to reconsider their convictions and sentences of 51 Mexican nationals, despite a holding by the International Court of Justice (ICJ) that the Vienna Convention rights of the nationals were violated, coupled with a directive from President Bush that state courts give effect to the ICJ ruling by reopening the cases of the Mexican nationals. Medellin was convicted of the rape and murder of two girls without being informed of his Vienna Convention rights to seek assistance from Mexican diplomats. When he finally raised this issue, Texas courts ruled that the claim was time-barred. The question was whether President Bush, in an attempt to enforce a treaty could order state courts to reopen cases. The Court ruled that neither the ruling of the ICJ nor the directive of the President constituted directly enforceable federal law that would preempt state limitations on courts reopening cases. The Court ruled that the ICJ ruling was not directly enforceable because the Vienna Convention is a non-self executing treaty that requires implementing legislation to have the force of law. Since Congress never passed such legislation, the treaty does not have the force of law, and the President's directive was not supported by any treaty obligation. In addition, the Court said that President Bush's directive does not independently require states to provide reconsideration of the claims of the Mexican nationals without regard to state procedural default rules. Citing Justice Jackson's concurrence in *Youngstown Sheet & Tube* (§ 212), the Court ruled that the responsibility for transforming an international obligation arising from a non-self executing treaty into domestic law falls to Congress, not the President. Since there was no explicit or implicit authorization by Congress, the Vienna Convention remains a non-self executing treaty. The Court ruled that the President may not rely on a non-self executing treaty to establish binding rules of decision that preempt contrary state law.

**(2) Executive Agreements. [§ 189]**

**An executive agreement is an agreement between the President and the chief executive of another country.** Senate ratification of executive agreements is unnecessary. Executive agreements are not mentioned in the Constitution, but have become an accepted practice, reflecting the President's intrinsic powers in the area of foreign affairs (irrespective of any enumerated

# NATIONAL LEGISLATIVE POWER

powers, the President, as the head of the Executive branch of the federal government, has the power to deal in foreign affairs).

c. **Relationships Among Treaties, Executive Agreements, Federal Statutes, and State Laws. [§ 190]**

   (1) **Under the Supremacy Clause of Article VI, Treaties and Executive Agreements Always Take Precedence Over Conflicting State Laws. [§ 191]**

   An individual state cannot have the power to contravene a federal enactment in the area of foreign affairs.

   (2) **Operative Treaties Are on a Parity With Federal Statutes. [§ 192]**

   An operative treaty is a self-executing treaty (no legislation required), or a non-self-executing treaty plus its implementing legislation. **If there is a conflict between an operative treaty and a federal statute, the most recent enactment wins.** The result is that a treaty may supersede a prior federal law, or a federal law may supersede a prior treaty.

   (3) **An Operative Treaty or a Federal Statute Take Precedence Over a Conflicting Executive Agreement. [§ 193]**

   Treaties and statutes are enacted by specific constitutional procedures, requiring the participation of Congress and the President. These enactments trump an executive agreement entered into by the President with no congressional participation.

   (4) **A Treaty May Be a Source of Legislative Power. [§ 194]**

   **The ability of Congress to pass a law to implement a treaty constitutes an independent source of congressional power, over and above any enumerated powers the Constitution gives to Congress.** The Court has treated Congress' power to pass laws to implement treaties as necessary and proper to the effectuation of the President's treaty power.

   *Missouri v. Holland*, 252 U.S. 416 (1920). The Court upheld the federal Migratory Bird Treaty Act, implementing a treaty between the United States and Canada which regulated the taking of migratory birds. The Court ruled that a treaty may confer on Congress the power to legislate in an area over which

# CHAPTER V

it otherwise has no power; Congress may pass legislation necessary and proper for the implementation of a treaty. The Court also ruled that the Tenth Amendment is not a limitation on the treaty power of Congress.

### (5) A Treaty or Executive Agreement Cannot Violate the Constitutional Rights of Individuals. [§ 195]

**The Constitution is the supreme law of the land, and its protection of individual rights cannot be contravened by a treaty or executive agreement.**

*Reid v. Covert*, 354 U.S. 1 (1957). The Court ruled that court-martial jurisdiction over civilian dependents of American soldiers abroad cannot be justified by an international executive agreement giving the armed forces jurisdiction to try such civilians for crimes. A treaty or executive agreement cannot authorize the violation of constitutional rights, such as the rights to an indictment and trial by jury, guaranteed by Article III and the Fifth Amendment.

## 7. Property Power. [§ 196]

**Under Article IV, Section 3, Clause 2, Congress has the power to dispose of and make all necessary rules and regulations respecting any property belonging to the United States.** Pursuant to this provision, Congress may exercise almost unlimited power over federally owned lands and other property, including the power to control the occupancy and use of such lands, impose restrictions against trespass or injury to the land, and forbid exploitation of the natural resources of the land. Congress also has power to sell, lease, give away, or otherwise dispose of surplus government property upon whatever terms and conditions it chooses to impose.

### a. Congress May Regulate Wild Animals on Federal Property. [§ 197]

Congress may regulate wild animals on federal land, and can, under its Necessary and Proper Power, regulate them if they wander off federal land.

*Kleppe v. New Mexico* 426 U.S. 529 (1976). The Court upheld a federal statute which prohibited the shooting or capture of wild horses roaming free on federal lands located within the boundaries of one state. Any conflicting state statutes (permitting destruction of such animals to protect private ranchers) are invalid under the Supremacy Clause.

## NATIONAL LEGISLATIVE POWER

**b. Congress Has the Power to Pass Laws to Govern the Territories of the United States. [§ 198]**

The Property Power provides the basis for Congress to govern territories of the United States, such as Guam, American Samoa, or the Virgin Islands. *Hooven & Allison Co. v. Evatt*, 324 U.S. 652 (1945).

**8. Power to Regulate Immigration and Naturalization. [§ 199]**

Article I, Section 8, Clause 4 gives Congress the power to establish a uniform, national rule of naturalization. This is an exclusive power of Congress, and one that can be exercised on whatever terms Congress sets. Under this power, Congress may determine the process by which a person gains or loses citizenship, and the criteria under which those decisions are made. Congress also has a plenary, exclusive power to regulate immigration, including the power to determine the status and conditions of aliens in the country (such as the criteria under which aliens may enter and remain in the country). Congress also has the power to set the terms and conditions for deportation. (The issue of classifications based on alienage is treated in § 590.)

**a. Immigration Laws Receive Rationality Review. [§ 200]**

The Court consistently defers to congressional action regarding the terms and conditions of immigration. Under rational basis review, the Court only requires that a law be rationally related to achieving a legitimate government interest. Under this standard, it is extremely unlikely that a court will invalidate a law.

**b. Congress' Power Over Immigration May Trump First Amendment Rights. [§ 201]**

Congress' power to regulate immigration is a compelling government interest which may justify an abridgement of individual rights.

*Kleindienst v. Mandel*, 408 U.S. 753 (1972). The Court upheld a provision of the Immigration and Nationality Act of 1952 making foreign Communists ineligible to receive visas for travel in the United States. The Act was applied to exclude a Belgian scholar who had been invited to lecture at American universities. The free speech concerns were outweighed by the power of Congress to exclude aliens on any grounds related to national policy.

**c. Loss of Citizenship. [§ 202]**

Congress may impose some conditions on the retention of citizenship, but may not involuntarily revoke a person's citizenship.

# CHAPTER V

(1) **A Citizen Must Voluntarily and Intentionally Relinquish Citizenship. [§ 203]**

The government must prove a voluntary relinquishment of citizenship. *Vance v. Terrazas*, 444, U.S. 252 (1980). The Court ruled that a citizen of the United States cannot lose that citizenship unless the government can prove, by a preponderance of the evidence, that the person voluntarily engaged in some action for which he or she could be expatriated, and that the person intended to give up U.S. citizenship when he or she took that action. Terrazas, who was a citizen of both the United States and Mexico at birth, took an oath of allegiance to Mexico and expressly renounced his United States citizenship. The Court ruled that the government must prove that Terrazas had a specific intent to renounce his citizenship.

(2) **Congress May Not Involuntarily Revoke Citizenship. [§ 204]**

**Congress may not override the requirement that a person must voluntarily relinquish citizenship.**

In *Afroyim v. Rusk*, 387 U.S. 253 (1967), Afroyim, who was a naturalized American citizen, went to Israel and voluntarily voted in an election for the Israeli legislature. The Court invalidated a federal statute which revoked Afroyim's U.S. citizenship as a penalty for voting in the foreign political election. Such an act did not evidence an intent to voluntarily relinquish citizenship.

(3) **Congress May Impose Some Conditions on Retention of Citizenship. [§ 205]**

**Congress' power over naturalization is broad enough to justify the imposition of some conditions on the grant of citizenship to persons who were not born in the United States or eventually naturalized in the United States.**

*Rogers v. Bellei*, 401 U.S. 815 (1971). The Court upheld a federal statute under which persons born abroad, who acquired citizenship by having a parent who was a U.S. citizen, would lose their citizenship if they did not return to the United States and reside here for five years continuously between the ages of 14 and 28.

# NATIONAL LEGISLATIVE POWER

## REVIEW PROBLEMS—NATIONAL LEGISLATIVE POWER: SOURCES OF AND LIMITATIONS ON CONGRESSIONAL POWER

**PROBLEM 1.** Congress passes a new crime bill by which it imposes certain reporting requirements on state and local police agencies. One provision requires state police officers to fill out a detailed set of forms and notify the nearest U.S. Attorney's Office whenever someone is arrested with an automatic weapon. The purpose of the law is to keep track of these weapons, and to coordinate the federal government's response to the crime problem. Discuss the ability of Congress to pass this law, and a state's constitutional arguments against it.

**Answer:** The issue of crime clearly has a close and substantial effect on interstate commerce, so Congress may reach this activity under the Commerce Clause and the Necessary and Proper Clause. The state will claim that the law violates its Tenth Amendment power to decide how to utilize its police officers. The state would also argue that its citizens would receive less police protection because of the federal requirement that the local police spend their time performing federally-mandated tasks. This case is like *New York v. U.S.* (see § 170) in that only state and local governments are regulated. It is different from *New York v. U.S.* in that the federal law does not commandeer the state legislature, but rather imposes requirements on local police officers. In *Printz v. U.S.* (see § 171), the Court invalidated a law such as this one, asserting that Congress' commandeering of state executive officers (local police) violated the system of dual sovereignty required by the Constitution.

**PROBLEM 2.** As part of a treaty with the country of Freedonia, the United States has agreed that the citizens of each country, regardless of which country they are living in, shall receive only those constitutional protections to which they are entitled under the Constitution of their native country. As a result, Freedonians living in the United States are not entitled to protection against unreasonable searches and seizures, or compelled self-incrimination. Is this provision constitutional?

**Answer:** No. The Constitution is the supreme law of the land, and a treaty may not violate its provisions. Constitutional protections of individual rights cannot be abridged by a treaty or executive agreement. (See § 195)

**PROBLEM 3.** As part of an "Energy Conservation Act," Congress provides that states will be entitled to federal money if they agree to pass legislation ensuring that three-time felons receive life in prison with no parole. Is this condition on the receipt of money constitutional?

**Answer:** Maybe, but maybe not. (That's another way of saying that you better discuss both sides of the issue.) The general rule is that any condition on

# CHAPTER V

the receipt of federal money is constitutional. However, in *South Dakota v. Dole* (§ 182), the Court said that it might violate the Constitution for Congress to impose a condition on the receipt of money that is unrelated to the purpose of the federal grant. In this case, life imprisonment for three-time felons does not appear to fall within the purposes of a federal energy conservation law, so the argument is that this particular condition on the receipt of this federal money is unconstitutional.

**PROBLEM 4.** Congress passes a law which provides housing and education benefits for soldiers who participated in the Gulf War. What constitutional provision(s) would Congress cite to support such action?

**Answer:** Congress may pass such a law under its War Power coupled with the Necessary and Proper Clause. The War Power gives Congress the power to prepare for war, wage war, and deal with the after effects of war. (See § 184.)

# CHAPTER VI

# SEPARATION OF POWERS: RELATIONSHIPS BETWEEN AND AMONG BRANCHES OF THE FEDERAL GOVERNMENT

## A. OVERVIEW OF SEPARATION OF POWERS. [§ 206]

**The doctrine of separation of powers involves the relationships between and among the branches of the federal government. The first three Articles of the Constitution set forth the powers of the respective branches: Article I deals with the powers of Congress; Article II deals with the powers of the President and the Executive Branch; and Article III deals with the powers of the Judiciary.** You should read these Articles to get some sense of the powers of each branch of the federal government and how the Articles work together to create our basic constitutional structure. In a separation of powers case, one branch of the federal government has impinged on the power of another branch. In such a case, you must consider the constitutional basis for the action taken by the branch of government that has acted, as well as the constitutional basis for the argument the affected branch uses to challenge the law. For example, what if Congress were to pass a law authorizing the appointment of a special prosecutor to investigate alleged executive wrongdoing, and the law prohibited the President from firing the special prosecutor? Assume that the President challenges the part of the law prohibiting the President from removing the special prosecutor from office. The President's contention is that the Constitution prohibits Congress from imposing any restrictions on the President's power to remove an executive official such as a special prosecutor. The first step in analyzing the constitutionality of the restrictions on the President's removal power would be to see what constitutional provisions justified the law; the Necessary and Proper Clause and Article II provide the answer (Congress has the power to pass laws for the executive branch). Second, you must ask what is the constitutional basis for the President's challenge to this law. The Article II basis is that the law unduly interferes with the power of the President to remove executive branch officials (allegedly an essential part of the President's power

# CHAPTER VI

as head of the executive branch). For each step, the essence of the analysis is to tie the argument to some enumerated or implied power of each branch of government involved in the dispute.

**As a general matter, you should follow these steps in any separation of powers analysis:**

**1.** Determine which branch of the federal government is acting and which branch is being affected by the law. Who is doing what to whom?

**2.** Determine whether the challenge to the law is based on a specific provision of the Constitution which sets forth required rules or procedures. If such a provision exists, apply the rules given in the Constitution. For instance, under Article I, § 7, before a bill may become law, it must be presented to the President for signature. If the House and the Senate passed a resolution which was supposed to operate as law, but was never presented to the President for signature, the argument against the law would be that it violated the specific requirement of presentment in Article 1, § 7.

**3.** If no specific constitutional provision applies, a balancing approach is called for. On the side of the acting government, you must identify the constitutional power asserted as a basis for the action taken. On the side of the branch of government affected by the law, you must identify the essential attribute or power of that branch that is adversely affected, and determine whether the intrusion effected by the law is too great. By way of example, if Congress imposed restrictions on the President's power to fire an executive branch official, there is no specific constitutional prohibition of such action. To determine whether such a restriction violated separation of powers principles, the Court would ask whether the Congressional restrictions unduly interfered with the President's power as the head of the executive branch.

1. **Enumerated Powers of the Branches of the Federal Government. [§ 207]**

    **Articles I, II, and III of the Constitution set forth certain specific powers of each of the branches of the federal government; these are the enumerated powers of Congress, the President, and the Judiciary respectively.**

2. **Implied Powers of the Branches of the Federal Government. [§ 208]**

    **In addition to those powers specifically listed in the Constitution, the Court recognizes certain unenumerated (or implied) powers of each**

# SEPARATION OF POWERS

**of the branches. These unenumerated powers are necessary to carry out the enumerated powers.** For instance, Congress' enumerated powers to tax, spend, and coin money give rise to an unenumerated power to charter a national bank. The President's enumerated power as head of the executive branch gives rise to the unenumerated power to hire and fire executive branch officials. The Court's enumerated power to hear cases involving constitutional rights gives rise to the unenumerated power to create procedural rules to protect those rights (such as the exclusionary rule, under which evidence obtained in violation of the Constitution is not admissible into evidence).

## B. EXECUTIVE AND LEGISLATIVE POWERS. [§ 209]

**The President's main enumerated powers are to execute the laws, act as Commander-in-Chief, enter into treaties, appoint officers of the federal government, veto congressional acts presented for the President's signature, and grant pardons for federal offenses.** In addition, the President has implied powers, especially in the area of foreign affairs. The main congressional powers are set forth in Article I, § 8, and are discussed at § 145. Remember that Congress, under the Necessary and Proper Clause, Article 1, § 8, cl. 18, has the power to make laws not only for itself, but for the President and the courts.

1. **The Specific Powers of the President. [§ 210]**

    a. The President is vested with the executive power; specifically, the power to take care that the laws of the country are faithfully executed. Under Article II, all executive power is vested in the President.

    b. The President is Commander-In-Chief of the Armed forces.

    c. The President has the power to make treaties, with the advice and consent of the Senate.

    d. The President has the power, with the advice and consent of the Senate, to appoint Ambassadors, Ministers, Consuls, and Justices of the Supreme Court. However, Congress may vest the appointment of Inferior Officers in the President alone, Courts of Law, or Heads of Departments.

    e. The President has the power to veto Congressional enactments. Congress may override a presidential veto by a two-thirds vote of those present, if the number present in each house constitutes a quorum.

    f. The President has the power to grant pardons or reprieves for federal offenses, except in cases of impeachment. Remember that The President

# CHAPTER VI

has no power to pardon someone who has violated state law. Such an attempt would raise tenth amendment problems of the President interfering with a state's sovereignty.

2. **Presidential Action Affecting the Powers of Congress. [§ 211]**

   **Generally, the President may not take action unless it is within one of the powers granted to the President by the Constitution.** This rule does not apply as stringently when the President acts in the area of foreign affairs. As the representative of the United States, the President's actions in foreign affairs need not be based in a specific Article II power; they may be justified by the President's intrinsic power to represent and protect the sovereign interests of the country.

   a. **The President Does Not Have the Power to Seize Private Property. [§ 212]**

      **Under the Fifth Amendment, it is Congress that has the power to take private property for public use, as long as just compensation is paid to the property owner.** The President does not have any constitutional power to seize private property, nor to compensate the property owner for the seizure (again, it is Congress is the branch of the federal government authorized to spend money).

      In *Youngstown Sheet & Tube v. Sawyer*, 343 U.S. 579 (1952), the Court reviewed President Truman's order to his Secretary of Commerce, Sawyer, to seize and operate most of the country's steel mills in order to avert a strike in the industry. President Truman argued that a steel strike would jeopardize the safety and effectiveness of troops engaged in the Korean police action. The Court invalidated the President's action as not being justified by either the President's power as Commander-in-Chief, or by his power to take care that the laws be faithfully executed. The Commander-in-Chief power was too attenuated a basis for the seizure of private property, and there was no law that the President was executing when he ordered the steel mills to be seized. Since Congress is the only branch of the federal government that may take and pay for private property (see § 412, below), the President was violating separation of powers by performing what was essentially a congressional function.

      Justice Jackson wrote an important concurrence in this case, in which he described his vision of how a court should analyze presidential action that arguably crosses the line into congressional powers. The three scenarios he posits are:

      (1) When the President acts pursuant to an express or implied authorization from Congress, presidential power is at its maximum;

# SEPARATION OF POWERS

(2) When the President acts in the absence of either a congressional grant or denial of authority, the President's action is in a "twilight zone" of concurrent presidential and congressional authority, and the result of the case may depend more on the imperatives of events, rather than abstract theories of law;

(3) When the President acts contrary to the express or implied will of Congress, presidential power is at its minimum.

**STUDY TIP:** Be aware of how the role of a reviewing court would change as we go through Justice Jackson's three fact patterns. If the President's power is at its maximum, the Court will be very deferential to presidential action. If the President's power is at its minimum, the Court will scrutinize the presidential action very carefully. If the presidential action falls within the "twilight zone" of concurrent presidential and congressional authority, the Court will have to balance the competing interests of the President and Congress. Should the role of the court change as a function of presidential and congressional agreement or disagreement?

b. **Congress May Explicitly or Implicitly Authorize Presidential Action. [§ 213]**

**Congress may, by statute or resolution, authorize the President to take certain action. Even without specific authorization, congressional acquiescence to presidential action may create an inference of congressional authorization.**

In *Dames & Moore v. Regan*, 453 U.S. 654 (1981), the Court upheld Executive Orders implementing an Executive Agreement between the United States and Iran. The Executive Orders terminated all litigation between each government and nationals of the other country, set up a Claims Tribunal to settle any claims that might exist, nullified prejudgment attachments against Iran's assets, and ordered transfer to Iran of all its assets held in U.S. banks. Specifically, the Court ruled that the President's actions nullifying attachments and ordering the transfer of assets were authorized by a specific congressional statute. The President's suspension of claims was not authorized by statute, but was implicitly authorized by a congressional history of acquiescence to presidential claims settlements.

3. **Congressional Action Affecting the Powers of the President. [§ 214]**
**Congress may not take any action which unduly interferes with an enumerated or unenumerated power of the President.** Generally, the

# CHAPTER VI

Court determines which power of the President is being abridged, whether that power is central to the functioning of the Presidency, and whether Congress has unduly invaded presidential prerogatives.

a. **Legislative Vetoes. [§ 215]**

Under the Constitution, it is for Congress to pass laws, and for the executive branch to implement them. It has become an accepted practice, however, for Congress to delegate to executive branch agencies or officials the power to promulgate regulations which have the force of law. Congress must provide specific standards for the executive official to follow, and must not retain control over the execution of the laws by the executive branch official. **A legislative veto exists when Congress purports to give power to an executive agency or official, but keeps for itself the power to invalidate the ensuing executive action.** In other words, a congressional delegation to the executive branch must be clean, with no strings attached.

(1) **Delegation of Power to the Executive Branch. [§ 216]**

**As a general matter, Congress may delegate to the President, other officers in the executive branch, or an independent regulatory commission, the power to promulgate rules and regulations to implement congressional goals.** A delegation of power will be valid if:

(a) Congress has not attempted to give away some non-delegable power (declare war, consent to the appointment of a Justice);

(b) Congress has stated the objective of the law; and

(c) Congress has provided specific standards for the executive branch official or independent commission to follow. *Yakus v. U.S.*, 321 U.S. 414 (1944).

The Court has upheld every congressional delegation since 1935.

(2) **A Legislative Veto May Invalidate an Otherwise Valid Delegation. [§ 217]**

**Whenever Congress passes a law, or takes action that is the equivalent of passing a law, it must meet both the bicameralism and presentment requirements of Article I, section 7.** Bicameralism means that both the House and the Senate must

# SEPARATION OF POWERS

pass the bill. Presentment means that the bill must be presented to the President for signature. For presentment purposes, it does not matter if the President does nothing or vetoes the bill; all that matters is that the President has been given an opportunity to sign it. For purposes of legislative veto analysis, the Court considers to be a "law" any bill that has gone through the normal legislative process, or any congressional action that has the effect of altering the legal rights, duties, and relations of persons.

**(a) In *INS v. Chadha*, 462 U.S. 919 (1983), [§ 218]** the Court invalidated a provision of the Immigration and Nationality Act of 1952 which authorized the Attorney General to suspend deportation of an alien under certain circumstances, but allowed either house of Congress to override the Attorney General's suspension and force the alien to be deported. The Court said that the House resolution requiring the deportation of Chadha was an exercise of legislative power (tantamount to a law) because it changed Chadha's legal rights and relations. This legislative action was therefore subject to the bicameralism and presentment requirements of the Constitution, both of which it failed. The House acted without its resolution being submitted to the Senate (no bicameralism) or to the President for signature (no presentment). If the law had not provided that either house could override the Attorney General's decision, the delegation to the executive branch would have been constitutional. The veto provision, however, allowed Congress to retain control of the ultimate outcome even after it attempted the delegation to the executive branch.

**(b) Metropolitan Washington Airports Authority v. Citizens for the Abatement of Aircraft Noise, Inc., 501 U.S. 252 (1991). [§ 219]**

The Court relied in large part on legislative veto analysis to invalidate a federal law under which Virginia and the District of Columbia agreed to transfer authority over two local airports to the Airports Authority, which was subject to the control of a review board made up entirely of members of Congress. The effect of the law was to give Congress, through its representatives, control (veto power) over the decisions of the Airport Authority. If Congress

# CHAPTER VI

wanted to delegate power to the Authority, it had to do it cleanly, without retaining control.

### (c) War Powers Resolution. [§ 220]

Under the War Powers Resolution, passed by Congress on November 7, 1973, Congress attempted to ensure that it would have an important role in the commitment of American troops to hostilities in foreign countries. An obvious response to the American experience in Vietnam, Section 5 (c) of the War Powers Resolution provides that " . . . at any time that United States Armed Forces are engaged in hostilities outside the territory of the United States, . . . without a declaration of war or specific statutory authorization, such forces shall be removed by the President if the Congress so directs by concurrent resolution." Under this law, bicameralism is present (there must be a concurrent resolution), but there is no presentment. This is a legislative veto under *Chadha* because the specific constitutional requirement of presentment is not met.

## b. Line Item Veto. [§ 221]

**It is unconstitutional for Congress to give the President the power to cancel an item of new direct spending after the President has already signed the spending measure into law.** Such a line item veto violates the Presentment Clause.

*Clinton v. City of New York*, 524 U.S. 417 (1998). The Court invalidated the Line Item Veto Act which gave the President the power to cancel any item of new spending or any limited tax benefit which had already been signed into law. This Act violated the Presentment Clause because it authorized the President to unilaterally amend Acts of Congress by repealing selected sections of the statutes. Under the Presentment Clause, Article I, § 7, after a bill has passed both Houses of Congress, it must be presented to the President. If the President signs the bill it becomes law. If the President does not approve (sign) the bill, he or she shall return it to the House where it originated. This return of the bill is commonly known as the veto of the bill, and may be overridden by a two-thirds vote of each House of Congress. The line item veto procedure differs from the constitutionally prescribed procedure for passing a law in that a normal Presidential veto occurs before the bill becomes law, whereas the line item veto is used after the bill has become a law. Also, the normal veto is of the entire bill, but the line item veto is

# SEPARATION OF POWERS

used on only a part of the law. The Court concluded that upholding the Line Item Veto Act would authorize the President to create a law that was not voted on by either House or presented to the President for signature.

c. **Appointment Power of the President. [§ 222]**

**Under Article II, the President nominates, and with the advice and consent of the Senate, appoints, all principal officers of the United States, including ambassadors and members of the Judiciary. The President must also nominate, and with the advice and consent of the Senate, appoint all inferior officers, unless Congress has vested the appointment of specific inferior officers in the President alone, courts of law, or heads of departments.**

STUDY TIP: On a law school exam, it would make little sense to test an appointments issue in which the President nominates someone and the Senate confirms that person. That kind of appointment is always constitutional, and is therefore not very effective as a testing device. What is likely to be tested is the kind of appointment in which Congress vests the appointment of an **inferior** officer in some court or person in the federal government. The two issues you should be careful about are whether the appointee is an inferior officer (if not, the President must nominate and the Senate confirm), and whether Congress has vested the appointment in an appropriate person or court. You may be asked to analyze a law under which Congress gives the Speaker of the House or the President pro tem of the Senate the power to appoint members of a federal commission. You must know that the commission members are inferior officers, and that Congress may not vest the appointment of such officers in anyone other than the President, a court of law, or the head of an executive department.

(1) **Buckley v. Valeo, 424 U.S. 1 (1976). [§ 223]**

The Court invalidated a section of the Federal Election Campaign Act which provided for appointment of the members of the Federal Election Commission. Under the law, two commissioners were appointed by the President pro tem of the Senate, two by the Speaker of the House, and two by the President. This scheme violated the Appointments Clause of Article II because Congress vested the appointment of four of the six commissioners in the wrong persons. Under the Appointments Clause, Congress may vest the appointment of **inferior** officers in the President alone, a court of law, or a head of a department. The Speaker of the House and the President pro tem of the Senate are not on the list; therefore, the appointments they made were invalid, at least in terms of the enforcement powers of the Federal Election Commission. The four commissioners who were appointed by the wrong persons may still perform investigative and informative functions (simple legislative tasks) but may not perform any executive, enforcement functions.

### (2) Weiss v. U.S., 510 U.S. 163 (1994). [§ 224]

The Court ruled that the appointment process of military judges complies with the requirements of the Appointments Clause. Two marines were court-martialed and convicted for various violations of the Uniform Code of Military Justice. They appealed, in part on the basis that military judges lack the authority to convict because the manner in which they are appointed violates the Constitution. The Court said that all the military judges in this case were commissioned officers, and that all commissioned officers are appointed by the President with the advice and consent of the Senate. Their subsequent assignment to the position of military judge is not an appointment to a new position (it is simply an assignment of a military officer to another job within the armed forces), therefore the requirements of the Appointments Clause are irrelevant when a commissioned officer is assigned to the position of military judge.

### d. Congressional Restrictions on the President's Power to Remove Executive Branch Officers. [§ 225]

**There is no specific constitutional provision which gives the President the power to remove executive branch officials. However, as a necessary incident of the office (an implied power), the President must be able to make personnel decisions within the executive branch, including removing some executive officers.** A problem arises when Congress attempts to impose restrictions on the President's power to remove executive branch officials. While the Constitution has no explicit provision giving Congress the power to limit the President's removal power, Congress arguably possesses such a power under the Necessary and Proper Clause and Article II

# SEPARATION OF POWERS

of the Constitution. Combining these clauses, Congress has power to legislate for the executive branch, presumably including the power to impose restrictions on the President's removal power.

**(1) Analysis of Congressional Restrictions on the President's Power to Remove an Executive Branch Officer. [§ 226]**

**The Court will determine if the restrictions on removal imposed by Congress unduly interfere with an essential attribute or power of the Presidency.** Under this approach, the Court must identify which power of the President is being abridged, and whether Congress has interfered too greatly with that power. A minority view on the Court (see Justice Scalia's opinion in *Morrison v. Olson* at § 231) is that Article II gives all executive power to the President, and **any** diminution of that power by Congress violates the Constitution. Justice Scalia does not believe it appropriate for the Court to decide "how much is too much" when it comes to congressional abridgment of the President's power to remove an executive branch officer.

**(2) Evolution of Case Law Dealing With Congress Restricting the President's Removal Power. [§ 227]**

**When Congress imposes restrictions on the President's power to remove an executive branch official, the Court focuses on the functions performed by that official, and whether the President must have unfettered power to remove that person from office.** Supreme Court analysis in removal cases has evolved from a categorical approach (focusing exclusively on the nature of the person whom the President is trying to remove), to a balancing approach which looks at whether the removal restrictions impermissibly interfere with presidential power. The Court determines which attribute of presidential power is affected by the removal restriction, and whether the restriction unduly interferes with that presidential power.

**(a) Early Case Law. [§ 228]**

**The President Has Almost Unlimited Power to Remove Officials Who Perform Purely Executive Functions.**

In *Myers v. U.S.*, 272 U.S. 52 (1926), the Court broadly ruled that the President had the power to remove executive branch officials. The Court struck down a statute that allowed the removal of first-class postmasters only if the President had the consent of the Senate.

# CHAPTER VI

(b) **Rise of the Administrative State. [§ 229]**

**Congress May Restrict the President's Power to Remove Officials Who Perform Quasi–Legislative or Quasi–Judicial Functions.**

*Humphrey's Executor v. U.S.*, 295 U.S. 602 (1935). This case came down in the post-Depression era when administrative agencies were starting to proliferate. The Court ruled that the President had unrestricted power to remove an official who performed purely executive functions, but Congress could impose restrictions on the President's power to remove officials who perform quasi-legislative or quasi-judicial functions. The theory was that the administrative agency officials were to be independent from presidential influence, and therefore could not be subject to removal at will by the President. *Humphrey's Executor* still reflected a categorical approach under which the scope of the power of the President to remove an executive official was a function of the nature of the position held by that employee.

(c) **Modern Case Law. [§ 230]**

**The Court Asks Whether Removal Restrictions Imposed by Congress Unduly Interfere With An Essential Attribute of the Presidency.**

(i) In *Morrison v. Olson*, 487 U.S. 654 (1988), [§ 231] the Court upheld the Ethics in Government Act of 1978. Under this law, Congress created a Special Division of the Court of Appeals which could, under certain circumstances, appoint a special prosecutor to investigate alleged wrongdoing in the executive branch. Congress also limited the President's power to fire the special prosecutor. *Morrison* deals with issues of removal restrictions, the Appointments Clause, and a general separation of power analysis. Each of these issues in *Morrison* will be discussed separately.

**Removal. Removal restrictions imposed by Congress will be valid unless they unduly interfere with an essential attribute of the Presidency.** The law in *Morrison* provided for the appointment of a special prosecutor (or independent counsel) to investigate and, if indicated, prosecute wrongdoing by certain executive branch officials. Obviously, Congress thought it unwise to allow the President free rein to fire an independent counsel who was investigating high-level executive officials. As a result, Congress said that the Attorney General could only remove the independent counsel for "good cause," as defined in the statute. This restriction on the Attorney General also restricts the President, who constitutionally has the power to control the Justice Department. The Court, 7–1, upheld the removal restrictions. Chief Justice Rehnquist reasoned that the imposition of a "good cause" standard for removal of the special prosecutor did not unduly trammel on executive authority. While the majority in *Morrison* used a balancing analysis to determine the constitutionality of the removal restrictions, Justice Scalia, in dissent, said that the Constitution had already decided this issue by giving all executive power to the President. He argued that the Court should not be deciding when a congressional intrusion into presidential power is excessive; any intrusion is too much.

**Appointments.** Under the Ethics in Government Act, the independent counsel is appointed by a Special Division of the Court of Appeals of the District of Columbia. This court is made up of three Court of Appeals judges or Supreme Court Justices, to be appointed by the Chief Justice of the United States for two-year terms. The appointment of the independent counsel by the Special Division of the Court of Appeals was upheld as consistent with the Appointments Clause of Article II. The Court in *Morrison* determined that the independent counsel was an inferior officer, due primarily to the nature and scope of her charge and her jurisdiction, and that Congress legitimately vested the appointment of this inferior officer in a court of law—the Special Division of the Court of Appeals.

**General Separation of Powers Analysis.** The Court in *Morrison* also held that the Ethics in Government Act, as a whole did not violate the separation of powers doctrine because it in no way unduly interfered with the functions of the executive branch. Congress

# CHAPTER VI

did not attempt to increase its own powers at the expense of the President, and there was no judicial usurpation of presidential power because the Special Division's role was basically limited to appointing the independent counsel.

**(ii) In** *Bowsher v. Synar***, 478 U.S. 714 (1986), [§ 232]** the Court reviewed a federal law designed to balance the budget and eliminate the federal deficit by 1991. Under the law, the Comptroller General of the United States was to receive reports from selected government officials and then give the President his recommendations on where to cut expenditures to help balance the budget. The Court declared that the Comptroller General was performing an executive function by engaging in the budget-cutting process. The issue in *Bowsher* was whether Congress could delegate executive functions to a government officer (the Comptroller General) who is removable by Congress. **Congress may not have removal power over an executive official, whether a person is an executive official by status (under the President on the organizational chart) or by function (given executive functions by statute).** The only way that Congress may remove an executive officer is by impeachment. Thus, the delegation by Congress to the Comptroller General in *Bowsher* was unconstitutional. The court also characterized Congress' power to remove the Comptroller General as a legislative veto. The power to remove is the power to control; Congress may not delegate executive functions to someone whom it can fire.

**(iii) In** *Free Enterprise Fund and Beckstead and Watts, LLP v. Public Company Accounting Oversight Board,* **130 S.Ct. 3138** (2010), [§ 232.1], The Court reviewed provisions of the Sarbanes–Oxley Act of 2002 which created the Public Company Accounting Oversight Board (PCAOB) and provided for the appointment and removal of its members. The PCAOB is composed of five members appointed by the Securities and Exchange Commission (SEC). The SEC can remove members of the PCAOB only for good cause. The SEC Commissioners, in turn, cannot

## SEPARATION OF POWERS

themselves be removed by the President except for "inefficiency, neglect of duty, or malfeasance in office." The plaintiffs in this case sued the PCAOB to prevent it from investigating the plaintiffs, alleging that the PCAOB was unconstitutional and should be enjoined from any investigatory or disciplinary actions. The plaintiffs made two arguments: first, that the law contravened separation-of-powers limitations, and second, that the law violated the Appointments Clause. The Court, 5–4, held that separation-of-powers principles were violated by the removal scheme, and that the Appointments Clause requirements were met by the statute. The separation-of-powers argument was that PCAOB members were insulated from Presidential control by two layers of tenure protection: PCAOB members could only be removed by the SEC for good cause, and the SEC Commissioners could only be removed by the President for good cause. The Court held that the dual for-cause limitations on the removal of PCAOB members violated the Constitution. The rationale of the Court was that the dual for-cause system destroys any accountability the President might have in the removal of PCAOB members. The Court has upheld the power of Congress to create independent agencies run by principal officers whom the President can remove only for good cause. The Court has also upheld similar for-cause removal restrictions on the power of principal executive officers to remove their own inferior officers. However, this dual for-cause scheme is different because it protects PCAOB members from removal except for good cause, while taking away from the President any decision about whether such good cause exists. The scheme destroys the President's accountability because, without the ability to oversee the decision to remove a PCAOB member for cause, the President cannot ensure that the laws are faithfully executed—an essential function of the President under our constitutional scheme.

The Court also held that the appointment of the PCAOB members is consistent with the Appointment Clause, which says that Congress may vest the appointment of inferior officers in the President alone, courts of law, or heads of departments. The Court said that the PCAOB members are inferior officers, and that the SEC is a department under the Appointment Clause. The Court went on to say that the several Commissioners of the SEC, not its Chairman, are the SEC's "Head" for purpose of the Appointment Clause. Thus, when Congress vested the appointment of the PCAOB members (inferior officers) with the SEC (a collective "Head" of a department), it complied with Appointment Clause requirements.

4. **Executive Privilege. [§ 233]**

**Executive privilege means that a President has a presumptive right to refuse to disclose materials, documents, or communications that are generated during that President's tenure in office. It is a presumptive privilege (the burden is on the party seeking disclosure to justify the production of the materials) which may be overridden by a sufficiently weighty reason for disclosure.** The privilege is based on the need of the President to be able to conduct the affairs of office free from excessive public scrutiny. Any analysis of an executive privilege question must include the following steps:

    a. Someone, such as a litigant in a criminal or civil trial, subpoenas a president to testify or turn over documents, tapes, or other materials;

    b. The President opposes production, and asserts executive privilege as a bar to turning over the requested items;

    c. The Judge Decides whether the requested material is relevant evidence in the proceeding for which it is requested. If irrelevant, The President need not disclose it;

    d. If the material is relevant, The District Court, in an in camera proceeding, balances the need for disclosure against The President's reasons for keeping the material secret; and

    e. The District Court will decide whether the material requested will be disclosed.

**STUDY TIP:** Be as specific as possible about the precise reason for the assertion of executive privilege and about the need for disclosure. As these interests change, the

# SEPARATION OF POWERS

**ultimate balance will change.** For instance, it is a relatively weak argument for the President to assert a general, undifferentiated need for secrecy (forced disclosure would impair the ability of the President to communicate with subordinates). It is much better for the President to assert that forced disclosure of documents would endanger some specific, compelling government interest, such as foreign affairs (a President would be able to successfully assert executive privilege to block a subpoena requesting sensitive military documents during wartime). The reason for disclosure will vary with the nature of the proceeding in which disclosure is sought. For instance, presidential documents may be subpoenaed in a criminal case to protect the fundamental rights of the defendants, or they may be requested by the Senate Judiciary Committee during a judicial confirmation hearing to help the Senate carry out its advise and consent function in the appointment of judges.

(1) **In *U.S. v. Nixon*, 418 U.S. 683 (1974), [§ 234]** the Court unanimously upheld a subpoena duces tecum issued in a criminal trial of seven of President Nixon's political associates which directed President Nixon to turn over certain tapes and materials which were generated during his Presidency and which pertained to the Watergate burglary. The Court held that a presumptive executive privilege existed as a function of the separation-of-powers doctrine. The Court reasoned that the checks and balances inherent in our constitutional structure required some degree of secrecy regarding presidential communications. On balance, the Court ruled that President Nixon's generalized claim of privilege (no national security or foreign affairs argument was advanced) was outweighed by the fundamental due process rights of the parties in a criminal prosecution.

(2) **Nixon v. Administrator of General Services, 433 U.S. 425 (1977). [§ 235]**

On the day he was pardoned, President Nixon and the Administrator of General Services (GSA) entered into an agreement which provided rules of access to President Nixon's presidential materials. Neither President Nixon nor GSA could have access to the materials without the other's consent, and President Nixon could withdraw or order the destruction of any materials after a certain number of years. In response to this agreement, Congress passed the Presidential Recordings and Materials Preservation Act, which provided new guidelines for review and release of these materials. Under the statute, GSA had control over President Nixon's materials, and was to formulate regulations to ensure public access to them. President Nixon objected, in part on the basis that executive privilege protected his materials from forced disclosure in the manner prescribed by Congress. The Court upheld the law on its face, but ruled that a former President is able to assert executive privilege for any materials generated during his or her time in office. President Nixon argued that non-disclosure was necessary to protect the President's ability to receive candid advice from aides and advisors. The Court ruled that the interest asserted by President Nixon was outweighed by Congress's interest in preserving the materials for historical and archival purposes, restoring public confidence in our political processes, and the importance of the materials for pending or future civil or criminal litigation.

(3) **Cheney v. U.S. District Court, 542 U.S. 367 (2004). [§ 236]**

The Court ruled that Vice President Cheney did not have to respond to discovery orders seeking the identities of participants in the National Energy Policy Development Group (NEPDG) that he chairs. Public interest groups filed suit under the Federal Advisory Committee Act, a government disclosure statute, seeking information about the members and activities of NEPDG. The District Court ordered extensive discovery and invited the government to assert executive privilege as to whatever materials it deemed sensitive. The Circuit Court denied the government's petition for a writ of mandamus to vacate the discovery order and to dismiss Vice President Cheney as a party because of separation-of-powers principles. The Supreme Court remanded the case to the Circuit Court for reconsideration. Noting that the discovery orders in this case were overly broad, the Court rejected the position taken by the District Court that the Executive had the burden of asserting executive privilege before the discovery order could be challenged. The Court said that when district courts are asked to enforce unnecessarily broad subpoenas, they should first explore alternatives to forcing the executive to invoke executive privilege. Thus, the assertion of executive privilege is not a necessary precondition to the Executive asserting separation-of-powers objections to the disclosure orders.

5. **Executive Immunity. [§ 237]**

Executive immunity means that the President is immune from liability for damages in a civil suit for any official act performed while the President

# SEPARATION OF POWERS

is in office. As with executive privilege, there is no constitutional provision conferring such immunity, but the Court has recognized it as a necessary incident of the powers of the President.

a. **Absolute Immunity for the President. [§ 238]**

   **The Court has ruled that a President has absolute immunity from civil damages liability for his or her official acts, as long as the President was acting within the outer perimeter of the duties of the office.** As long as the President was arguably performing the duties of the office, the President is protected by absolute immunity.

   In *Nixon v. Fitzgerald*, 457 U.S. 731 (1982), the Court affirmed a summary dismissal of a lawsuit against President Nixon by a former employee of the Department of the Air Force whose job was terminated after he testified before Congress about cost overruns on an airplane. The Court refused to subject the President to potential liability on every employment decision which could be traced back to the President as head of the executive branch.

b. **No Temporary Immunity From Civil Damages Litigation for Events That Occurred Before the President Took Office. [§ 239]**

   **Separation-of-powers principles do not require federal courts to stay all civil damages litigation against a sitting President until he leaves office.** The Constitution does not require temporary immunity from a civil damages lawsuit during a President's term in office.

   In *Clinton v. Jones*, 520 U.S. 681 (1997), the Court refused to stay a civil lawsuit against President Clinton for actions that allegedly occurred before he became President. Paula Corbin Jones sued President Clinton under federal and state law, alleging that, while he was Governor of Arkansas, Mr. Clinton made "abhorrent" sexual advances toward her, and that her rejection of those advances had adverse consequences on her government employment. The Court, ruling that the Constitution does not require that a lawsuit for civil damages against a sitting president be deferred until the President leaves office, rejected the President's argument that defending such a lawsuit would necessarily interfere too greatly with the President's ability to carry out the duties of the office.

c. **Qualified Immunity for Presidential Aides and Advisors. [§ 240]**

   **Executive branch officials other than the President have qualified immunity from civil damages liability. To determine whether qualified immunity applies, ask whether a reasonable person in**

an official capacity knew or should have known that his or her actions were violating clearly established constitutional rights. If the U.S. Attorney General were to authorize what was clearly an illegal wiretap of a political enemy, the Attorney General would be subject to a suit for civil damages because the Attorney General knew or should have known that such action violated the Fourth Amendment rights of the person subject to the wiretap.

*Harlow v. Fitzgerald*, 457 U.S. 800 (1982). In this companion case to *Nixon v. Fitzgerald* (above at § 238), the Court set forth the general rule of qualified immunity for presidential aides or advisors—an executive branch official other than the President will be immune from civil damages liability unless the official, judged by a reasonableness standard, knew or should have known that he or she was violating clearly established constitutional rights. **However, the Court said that if a presidential aide were entrusted with discretionary authority in a highly sensitive national security or foreign affairs position, that aide might be entitled to absolute immunity to protect the performance of functions vital to our national interest.** Absolute immunity for presidential aides would require a fact-specific finding of the importance of the job performed by the aide, and would clearly be an exception to the general rule of qualified immunity.

6. **Legislative Immunity. [§ 241]**

   **Under the Speech or Debate Clause, Article 1, section 6, clause 1, Senators and Representatives are immune from civil or criminal suit for any words or conduct that are an integral part of the legislative process.**

   a. **U.S. v. Brewster, 408 U.S. 501 (1972). [§ 242]**

      The Court ruled that the Speech or Debate Clause does not protect a Senator from criminal prosecution if the prosecution can reasonably be deemed to be based on words or conduct that were not an essential part of the legislative process. The Speech or Debate Clause did not protect a Senator from prosecution for solicitation and acceptance of bribes in exchange for favorable votes on future legislation.

   b. **Gravel v. U.S., 408 U.S. 606 (1972). [§ 243]**

      Senator Gravel was protected by the Speech or Debate Clause when he read into the Congressional Record a stolen "Top Secret-Sensitive" copy of the Pentagon Papers (a history of American decisionmaking in Vietnam). However, private republication of the

# SEPARATION OF POWERS

Pentagon Papers in the Beacon Press was not protected under the Speech or Debate Clause because republication was not essential to the deliberations of the Senate. The Court in *Gravel* also ruled that a legislative aide or assistant is entitled to the same immunity as his or her boss under the Speech or Debate Clause.

    c.   **Hutchinson v. Proxmire, 443 U.S. 111 (1979). [§ 244]**

Senator Proxmire used to give a "Golden Fleece Award" to publicize what he considered wasteful government spending. Giving the award on the floor of the Senate was protected activity, but republication through a press release, newsletters, a television show, and phone calls to government agencies was not protected under the Speech or Debate Clause.

## C. CONGRESSIONAL ACTION AFFECTING THE JUDICIARY. [§ 245]

**Whenever Congress takes an action that affects the judiciary, ask whether the law is unduly interfering with an essential attribute of the judiciary or undermining the integrity of the judicial branch.** The main attribute of the federal judiciary is to hear cases which fall within the Article III jurisdiction of federal courts—cases involving a federal question, or cases in which there is diversity of citizenship between the parties.

    1.   **Congress' Ability to Determine the Scope of Federal Judicial Power. [§ 246]**

**Under Article III, there must be a Supreme Court. Its original jurisdiction, which is set by the Constitution, includes all cases affecting Ambassadors, other public Ministers and Consuls, and those in which a State shall be a party. The Supreme Court has appellate jurisdiction in all other cases (as long as a federal question or diversity of citizenship is present) with such exceptions and regulations as Congress shall make.** Under Article III, and Article I, section 8, clause 9, Congress has the power to establish lower federal courts.

        a.   **Jurisdiction Stripping. [§ 247]**

**With the exception of the constitutionally-mandated original jurisdiction of the Supreme Court, Congress has the power to set the original jurisdiction of federal district courts, and the appellate jurisdiction of the U.S. Courts of Appeals and the Supreme Court.** There is a question whether there are any constitutional limits on Congress' ability to set the appellate jurisdiction of the

# CHAPTER VI

Supreme Court or the jurisdiction of lower federal courts. This issue may arise if Congress attempts to excise certain kinds of cases from a court's jurisdiction. What if Congress said, for instance, that the Supreme Court does not have appellate jurisdiction to review lower federal court decisions involving the constitutionality of a federal school prayer law? This kind of "jurisdiction-stripping" case present a specific kind of constitutional balance. On one side of the scale is the explicit constitutional power of Congress to determine the appellate jurisdiction of the Supreme Court (or the jurisdiction of lower federal courts). On the other side is an implied separation-of-powers concept and two individual rights arguments. Take the law mentioned above, eliminating Supreme Court appellate jurisdiction to review school prayer cases coming from lower federal courts. Congress would argue that it has an unlimited Article III power to make exceptions to the appellate jurisdiction of the Supreme Court. To attack the law, you would argue that the jurisdiction-stripping statute violates separation of powers because it removes the Supreme Court from the system of checks and balances. With no ultimate Court review of such a law, we go from a three-branch system of government to a two-branch system (or even one branch if Congress overrides a presidential veto to pass the school prayer law). The next argument would be that a litigant has a procedural due process right to a federal judicial forum, and that the jurisdiction-stripping statute deprives the litigant of the right to have the Supreme Court hear the case. The last argument is that the jurisdiction-stripping statute effectively deprives the litigant of the substantive right involved in the case—here the First Amendment right to be free from the establishment of religion.

*Ex Parte McCardle*, 74 U.S. 506 (1869). During the post-Civil War Reconstruction era, Congress passed a statute giving federal circuit courts the power to hear petitions for writs of habeas corpus from persons who thought they were imprisoned in violation of federal law. Under the jurisdiction-granting statute in *McCardle*, if a petition were denied by a federal circuit court, appeal could be taken to the Supreme Court. McCardle, imprisoned by the military government of Mississippi, sought a petition for habeas corpus from a federal circuit court, and the court denied his request. He appealed to the Supreme Court, which accepted his case and held oral arguments. After oral arguments, but before the case was decided, Congress withdrew appellate jurisdiction from the Supreme Court in this kind of case. The Court dismissed McCardle's case for want of jurisdiction. Be careful not to read *McCardle* too broadly. McCardle could still file his petition for habeas corpus directly with the Supreme Court and possibly get Supreme Court review. There has never been a Supreme Court decision dealing with, let alone upholding, complete withdrawal by Congress of the Court's ability to hear a particular kind of case. All *McCardle* stands for is that Congress, under its power to make exceptions to the appellate jurisdiction of the Supreme Court, was able to withdraw one avenue of appeal to the Supreme Court.

b. **Developing Sentencing Guidelines. [§ 248]**

**It does not violate the Constitution for federal judges to sit on a commission which develops sentencing guidelines for federal courts.**

In *Mistretta v. U.S.*, 488 U.S. 361 (1989), the Court upheld the Sentence Reform Act of 1984 which created the U.S. Sentencing Commission as an independent commission and placed it in the judicial branch of the federal government. The commission was made up of seven voting members appointed by the President (no Appointments Clause problem—see § 227, above), three of whom were to be federal judges. The Court asked two questions: Did Congress give the commission powers that are more appropriately performed by other branches of the federal government and; does the inclusion of judges on the commission and its placement in the judicial branch undermine the integrity of the judiciary? The Court answered both questions "NO". On the first, the Court said that judges are the ones who sentence criminals every day, so they are uniquely able to contribute to a sentencing commission's deliberations. Secondly, the integrity of the judiciary was not affected because the power of the judiciary was not expanded (it was in fact reduced by limiting a judge's discretion in the sentencing process), and it has become accepted practice to ask judges to engage in rulemaking.

## D. JUDICIAL REVIEW OF THE DETENTION OF DETAINEES IN THE WAR ON TERRORISM. [§ 249]

**The Court has jurisdiction under federal habeas corpus statutes to review the detentions of persons, whether citizens or foreign nationals, detained by the government in the war on terrorism.** A plurality of the the Court used a flexible due process analysis to analyze these cases.

1. **Detention of Citizen Enemy Combatants. [§ 250]**

    **A U.S. citizen who is detained as an enemy combatant is entitled to notice of the charges against him and some sort of hearing to contest those charges with the assistance of counsel.**

# CHAPTER VI

*Hamdi v. Rumsfeld*, 542 U.S. 507 (2004). The Court ruled that a U.S. citizen who is detained as an enemy combatant has a Fifth Amendment due process right to notice of the charges against him and a hearing to contest those charges with the assistance of counsel. There was no majority ruling on the precise nature of the required hearing, or whether a military tribunal might meet the requirements of due process. Justice O'Connor, writing for four Justices, said that a citizen detainee must receive meaningful and timely notice of the factual basis for his designation as an enemy combatant, and a fair opportunity to rebut the Government's factual assertions before a neutral decisionmaker, with the right to counsel being protected as part of the process. Justices Souter and Ginsburg concurred on the due process issues. According to a Department of Defense affidavit, Hamdi was affiliated with a Taliban unit in Afghanistan, and was subsequently classified as an enemy combatant. He was originally detained at Guantanamo Bay, and was then transferred to a stateside military prison where he was held incommunicado. His father filed a habeas corpus petition on his behalf. The plurality said that even when the detention of enemy combatants is legally authorized (as it was here by a Congressional resolution passed after the September 11 terrorist attacks), a court must decide what process is due a citizen who challenges his enemy combatant status. The plurality applied the balancing test of *Mathews v. Eldridge* (§ 439) to decide what process is constitutionally required. Given the exigencies of an ongoing war, the plurality opted for a flexible due process approach, saying that enemy combatant proceedings may be tailored to alleviate burdens on the Executive branch during a continuing military conflict. A majority of the Court emphasized that, unless Congress moves to suspend the writ of habeas corpus (which it had not done), the Judiciary has an obligation to serve as an important check on the Executive's discretion in relation to the detention of citizen enemy combatants.

2. **Alien Detainees Imprisoned at Guantanamo Bay Have a Right to Challenge Their Detentions in U.S. Courts. [§ 251]**

*Rasul v. Bush*, 542 U.S. 466 (2004). The Court ruled that alien detainees imprisoned at Guantanamo Bay Naval Base must be given access to U.S. courts. The Court left open the question of what substantive rights the detainees might assert. The petitioners were Australian and Kuwaiti citizens who were captured in Afghanistan and Pakistan during hostilities between the United States and the Taliban regime in Afghanistan, and were being held incommunicado at Guantanamo Bay. Pursuant to a treaty with Cuba, the United States exercises plenary and exclusive jurisdiction, but not ultimate sovereignty, one Guantanamo Bay. The Court focused on the extensive control that the United States exercises over Guantanamo Bay, along with the facts that these alien detainees were not nationals of countries at war with the United States, had never been given access to any tribunal, and had never been charged with and convicted of any crimes.

*Boumediene v. Bush,* 128 S.Ct. 2229 (2008). The Court ruled, 5–4, that aliens detained as enemy combatants at Guantanamo Bay are entitled to the right of habeas corpus to challenge the legality of their detention. The Court, through Justice Kennedy, reaffirmed the finding in *Rasul v. Bush* (previous case) that, although Cuba retains technical sovereignty over Guantanamo Bay, the United States has total military and civilian control over the military base there. Specifically, the Court ruled that § 7 of the Military Commisions Act of 2006 (MCA) was unconstitutional because it denied federal courts jurisdiction to hear habeas actions that were pending at the time of its enactment. A central issue in the case was whether the Suspension Clause of the Constitution applies to Guantanamo Bay. The Suspension Clause reads ". . . [t]he Privilege of the Writ of Habeas Corpus shall not be suspended, unless when in Cases of Rebellion or Invasion the public Safety may require it." The Court ruled that the Suspension Clause has full effect at Guantanamo Bay, and that Congress, in the Detainee Treatment Act of 2005 (DTA), (and the MCA, which applied removal of habeas jurisdiction to cases already in the judicial pipeline), did not provide an adequate and effective substitute for the habeas writ. The DTA gave detainees access to a federal appeals court to challenge their designation as enemy combatants, but the Court ruled that Congress did not provide a "meaningful opportunity" for a detainee to demonstrate that he is being held pursuant to an erroneous application of relevant law. The Court ruled that the Combatant Status Review Tribunals (CSRTs) set up by the Defense Department to determine a person's enemy combatant status were deficient, primarily because of constraints imposed on a detainee's ability to rebut the factual basis for the government's assertion that he is an enemy combatant. Pursuant to the DTA, a reviewing court could only assess whether the CSRT complied with the standards and procedures prescribed by the Secretary of Defense. The CSRT proceedings were potentially defective in that the detainee has limited means to find or present evidence to challenge the government's argument that he is an enemy combatant, does not have the assistance of counsel, may not be able to confront witnesses against him, and may not even be aware of all the allegations relied on by he government to order his detention. The Court said that risk of error was too great, and that the consequence of error may be detention for the duration of hostilities that may last a generation or more.

# CHAPTER VI

3. **Restrictions on Military Commissions Used to Try Enemy Combatants. [§ 252]**

   **Military commissions used to try enemy combatants at Guantanamo Bay must comply with federal law and principles of international law.**

   *Hamdan v. Rumsfeld*, 548 U.S. 557 (2006). The Court rejected the Bush administration's plan to try Guantanamo Bay detainees before military commissions because those tribunals were unauthorized by federal statute and violated international law. Salim Ahmed Hamdan, a Yemeni who was a former driver for Osama Bin Laden, was captured in Afghanistan and taken to Guantanamo Bay. Hamdan was declared eligible for trial by a military tribunal, and his military trial began, only to be halted by a federal district court which ruled that his trial violated military law and the Geneva Conventions. The Court of Appeals, with a panel including now-Chief Justice Roberts, reversed, allowing the tribunal to proceed. The Supreme Court reversed and remanded, with the result being that the administration must go back to Congress to get approval for the military commissions.

   The Court first ruled that the Detainee Treatment Act of 2005, which provides that ". . . no court shall have jurisdiction to hear or consider an application for habeas corpus filed by an alien detained at Guantanamo Bay," does not apply to cases such as Hamdan's, which were pending at the time Congress passed the Act. The Court then ruled that the Uniform Code of Military Justice (UCMJ), the Authorization for the use of Military Force (AUMF) (passed after the attacks on September 11, 2001 and authorizing the President to "use all necessary and appropriate force against those nations, organizations, or persons he determines planned, authorized, committed or aided" the September 11th attacks), and the Detainee Treatment Act (DTA), merely acknowledge a general Presidential authority to convene military commissions when justified under the Constitution and laws, including the law of war. The Court said that the structure and procedures of Hamdan's military commission violate the UCMJ. The commission's procedures included the right of the presiding officer to preclude the defendant from learning what evidence had been introduced against him, and to admit any evidence that the presiding officer determined would have probative value to a reasonable person. The Court said that UCMJ Article 36 was violated because, under that provision the rules that the President promulgates for military commissions must be the same as those governing courts-martial, and there was nothing in the record to demonstrate why it would be impracticable to apply court-martial rules to Hamdan.

   The Court also ruled that Common Article 3 of the Geneva Conventions applies to Guantanamo Bay detainees and is enforceable in federal courts.

# SEPARATION OF POWERS

Common Article 3 requires humane treatment of captured combatants and prohibits trials except by a regularly constituted court affording all the judicial guarantees which are recognized by civilized people. Common Article 3 does not require all the protections of a civilian court or a court martial, but it does require some protections missing from the procedures used in Hamdan's military commission. For instance, the rules governing Hamdan's commission failed to guarantee the defendant the right to attend the trial, and the prosecution was able to introduce hearsay evidence, unsworn testimony, and coerced testimony. The Court, ruling that conspiracy is not a recognized violation of the law of war under the Geneva conventions, the Hague Conventions or any other source of international law, concluded that the government, by charging Hamdan with conspiracy, had not charged Hamdan with an offense that may be tried by military commission under the law of war.

## REVIEW PROBLEMS—SEPARATION OF POWERS: RELATIONSHIPS BETWEEN BRANCHES OF THE FEDERAL GOVERNMENT

**PROBLEM 1.** As part of an executive agreement with the country of Someko, the President of the United States has agreed to return certain Somekon prisoners who are in jail in the State of Oz (a state of the United States) for having violated numerous state laws. The President issues pardons for all the prisoners, and demands their release. Does the Constitution give the President the power to take this action with regard to the prisoners?

**Answer:** No. The Constitution only gives the President the power to pardon federal offenses. There is no presidential power to pardon someone who has violated state law. (See § 210 for review.)

**PROBLEM 2.** The legislature of the State of Oz has delegated to state administrative agencies the power to promulgate rules for the operation of those agencies. Before the rules go into effect, they must be approved by a joint committee composed of three members of the State Senate and three members of the State House of Representatives. Is this system constitutional? Assume that all rules of United States constitutional law apply in Oz.

**Answer:** No. This is a legislative veto. The joint committee has a veto power over the decisions of the administrative agencies. This would violate presentment because the action of the joint committee is not presented to the Governor for approval. It would also probably violate bicameralism because, even though there are members of both houses on the commission, the Constitution contemplates the participation of the full House and the full Senate in any lawmaking. (See § 217 for review.)

# CHAPTER VI

**PROBLEM 3.** President Jefferson Hope is sued for firing state employees based on their race while he was the governor of the State of Oz. The plaintiffs seek monetary damages under appropriate federal statutes. The alleged discrimination occurred before the President took office. In his defense, the President asserts executive immunity. Will the President prevail?

**Answer:** No. The Constitution does not require a federal court to stay all civil damages litigation against a sitting President until he leaves office. See § 239.

**PROBLEM 4.** Congress has given the Secretary of State the power to appoint ambassadors and deputy ambassadors to foreign countries. Pursuant to this power, Jane Jones, the Secretary of State, appointed Helen Hale to be ambassador to the Ukraine, and appointed Bob Brown to be deputy ambassador. Are these appointments constitutional?

**Answer:** No, and Yes. Under the Appointments Clause, principal officers must be nominated by the President and confirmed by the Senate. Helen is a principal officer, so she cannot be appointed by the Secretary of State. Bob, on the other hand, is an inferior officer whose appointment can be vested in the head of a department, such as the Secretary of State. (See § 222 for review.)

# Chapter VII

# STATE POWER TO REGULATE COMMERCE: CONSTITUTIONAL LIMITATIONS

## A. INTRODUCTION. [§ 253]

The Tenth Amendment states that, "[t]he powers not delegated to the United States by the Constitution, nor prohibited by it to the States, are reserved to the States respectively, or to the people." The Court has interpreted the Tenth Amendment to be the basis of a state's "police power"—the state's ability to regulate for the health, safety, welfare, and morals of its citizens. **A law passed pursuant to a state's police power is presumptively valid, but may run into problems if it interferes with the flow of interstate commerce or treats out-of-staters differently from the way it treats instaters.** For instance, a state law which prohibits the instate disposal of toxic waste that was generated out of state obviously interferes with interstate commerce, and is probably invalid. A state law which restricts the ability to practice law to state residents interferes with the right of persons to travel from state to state to pursue an occupation. If you see a state law which interferes with interstate commerce or treats out-of-staters worse than it treats instaters, you should consider the following analyses as possible methods of finding the law unconstitutional.

    1. Dormant Commerce Clause

    2. Privileges and Immunities Clause of Article IV (Not the Fourteenth Amendment)

    3. Equal Protection Clause.

## B. DORMANT COMMERCE CLAUSE—NEGATIVE IMPLICATIONS OF THE COMMERCE CLAUSE. [§ 254]

The Commerce Clause serves not only as a source of power for congressional action, but also serves as a limitation on state action that impedes the free flow

# CHAPTER VII

of commerce. **The dormant commerce clause doctrine (the Commerce Clause is "dormant" because Congress has not acted under it) applies when a state, in the absence of any preempting federal action, passes a law which interferes with interstate commerce. (Interstate commerce is any interstate transaction involving access to, sale, or purchase of any good, service, or natural resource).** In the absence of congressional action, the Court applies the Commerce Clause as a limitation on state action. Keep in mind that Congress, as the ultimate holder of the commerce power, may "overrule" a Court decision interpreting the Commerce Clause as a limiter of state action. There are two ways that a state may interfere with the free flow of commerce: discriminate against interstate commerce, and burden interstate commerce.

1. **State Discrimination Against Interstate Commerce. [§ 255]**

    **To use the discrimination analysis, you must be able to show that the state law, by purpose or effect, treats out-of-staters differently from instaters.** The main rationale for the rule against a state discriminating against out-of-staters is to prohibit local economic protectionism and the economic balkanization of the country through retaliatory laws passed by the various states. For instance, if the Court upheld a state law prohibiting the importation of solid waste into the state, other states might pass the same kind of law, with the cumulative result being the destruction of the interstate market in waste disposal.

    a. **Analysis of a State Law That Discriminates Against Out-of-Staters. [§ 256]**

    (1) **Identify the Discrimination. [§ 257]**

    **You must show that the law, by purpose or effect (facially or as applied), classifies along state lines—that instaters are treated better than out-of-staters.** The discrimination may take the form of a disadvantage imposed on out-of-staters (denial of access to an instate market), or a benefit given to instaters (exemption of an instate business from an otherwise generally applicable tax).

    (2) **Identify the Reason for the Discrimination. [§ 258]**

    You have two choices: local economic protectionism; or some valid police power reason such as health or safety. **Discrimination against interstate commerce for the purpose of favoring local business or investment interests is per se invalid.** It is not a legitimate state interest for a state to try to secure an economic advantage for local business interests. If the discrimina-

# STATE POWER TO REGULATE COMMERCE: LIMITATIONS

tion is justified by a valid police power interest unrelated to economic protectionism, and there are no other means to achieve that interest, the law may be valid.

**b. Aspects of Discrimination Analysis Under the Dormant Commerce Clause. [§ 259]**

**(1) Strict Scrutiny of Facially Discriminatory Laws. [§ 260]**

**Facial discrimination against out-of-staters invokes judicial strict scrutiny.** Under strict scrutiny, a state must show that it has a compelling reason for its discrimination against out-of-staters, and that the discrimination effected by the state law is narrowly tailored to achieving the state's goal.

**(a) Hughes v. Oklahoma, 441 U.S. 322 (1979). [§ 261]**

The Court invalidated an Oklahoma ordinance that banned the exportation for sale outside the state of minnows that were procured within the waters of Oklahoma. The Court said that such facial discrimination invokes the strictest scrutiny of any purported legitimate purpose and of the absence of nondiscriminatory alternatives.

**(b) Maine v. Taylor, 477 U.S. 131 (1986). [§ 262]**

The Court upheld a law that discriminated on its face against out-of-staters. Maine prohibited the transfer into Maine of live baitfish from out of state. The Court upheld the ban even though it would benefit Maine's baitfish industry. The Court was persuaded by Maine's argument that its unique population of wild fish would be threatened by parasites that might be brought in with out-of-state fish, and that there was no less discriminatory means to protect against the importation of the parasites.

**(c) Oregon Waste Systems, Inc. v. Dept. of Environmental Quality of Oregon, 511 U.S. 93 (1994). [§ 263]**

The court invalidated an Oregon law that imposed a $2.50 per ton surcharge on the disposal of solid waste generated in other states, but only an $0.85 per ton fee on solid waste generated within the state. The Court said that Oregon's restrictions failed to pass the "strictest scrutiny" indicated by the facial discrimination against out-of-staters.

**(2) Risk of Multiple Burdens. [§ 264]**

If a state law creates a risk of multiple burdens, it may be unconstitutional. Ask what would happen if other states had the

# CHAPTER VII

same kind of law. **The cumulative impact of a number of states each passing a law which prohibited out-of-staters from doing business instate would severely hurt the interstate market.** The question under the multiple burdens doctrine is "What if everybody did it?" If the answer is that everybody doing it would severely impair interstate commerce, the law is invalid.

*Baldwin v. Seelig*, 294 U.S. 511 (1935). The Court invalidated a New York law that prohibited the sale in New York of milk bought outside New York below a price set by New York law. This law created too great a risk of multiple burdens. If other states passed the same kind of law, the national market would be fragmented.

(3) **Reciprocity Requirements. [§ 265]**

**Reciprocity requirements violate the dormant commerce clause because they create too great a risk of multiple burdens on interstate commerce.** For dormant commerce clause purposes, a reciprocity requirement is a law which allows residents of State B to do business in State A only if State B grants the same privilege to residents of State A. If such a law were upheld, the result would be the balkanization of the national market.

(a) **Great A. & P. Tea Co. v. Cottrell, 424 U.S. 366 (1976). [§ 266]**

The Court invalidated a reciprocity requirement under which Mississippi said that milk from another state could be sold in Mississippi only if Mississippi milk could be sold in the other state.

(b) **Sporhase v. Nebraska, 458 U.S. 941 (1982). [§ 267]**

The Court invalidated a Nebraska reciprocity requirement that denied a permit to withdraw and transport Nebraska water for use in another state unless the other state granted reciprocal rights to transfer its water into Nebraska.

(4) **Requiring Business to Be Performed Instate. [§ 268]**

**A state cannot require business to be performed instate if that business could be performed more efficiently out of state.**

# STATE POWER TO REGULATE COMMERCE: LIMITATIONS

*Pike v. Bruce Church*, 397 U.S. 137 (1970). The Court invalidated an Arizona law requiring that growers of Arizona cantaloupes pack them in Arizona. The court noted that it would view with particular suspicion state statutes that required business operations to be performed instate that could more efficiently be performed out of state. The Court said that this kind of law is virtually **per se** illegal, even if it has a legitimate purpose.

(5) **Discrimination by Political Subdivision of a State; Less Drastic Means. [§ 269]**

**It is discrimination against interstate commerce for a political subdivision of a state (such as a city or a county) to exclude out-of-staters from doing business within their boundaries.** If a city or county discriminates against people who reside outside the city or county boundaries, that will count as a discrimination against out-of-staters even though some instaters are also excluded from doing business inside the city or county.

*Dean Milk v. Madison*, 340 U.S. 349 (1951). The Court invalidated a Madison, Wisconsin ordinance that prohibited the sale of any milk in Madison that was not pasteurized within five miles of the town square. The Court ruled that this law discriminated against interstate commerce even though some people within Wisconsin (those outside the five-mile limit) were also disadvantaged. The Court also ruled that the law was unconstitutional because Madison had less drastic means available to achieve its goal of ensuring healthy milk.

*Fort Gratiot Sanitary Landfill, Inc. v. Michigan Dept. of Natural Resources*, 504 U.S. 353 (1992). The Court invalidated a state law which prohibited private landfill owners from accepting any solid waste that originated outside the county where the landfill was located, unless the county specifically approved such importation. The Court relied on *Dean Milk v. Madison* (see § 262), to conclude that such a ban by a county discriminates against interstate commerce even though some in-staters may also be hurt by their inability to transfer waste into a particular county.

(6) **Subsidy for Instate Economic Interests. [§ 270]**

**A state may not set up a system under which it subsidizes instate economic interests at the expense of out-of-state economic interests.**

# CHAPTER VII

*West Lynn Creamery v. Healy*, 512 U.S. 186 (1994). The Court invalidated a Massachusetts pricing order which imposed an assessment on all fluid milk sold by dealers to Massachusetts retailers. Most of the milk is produced out of state, but the entire assessment is paid into a fund to be distributed to Massachusetts dairy farmers. The Court ruled that the law discriminated against interstate commerce because it benefited the local dairy industry at the expense of out-of-state interests. The disbursements from the fund amounted to a subsidy of instate dairy interests.

(7) **Protecting Privacy Rights of Residents. [§ 271]**

**A municipality may protect the privacy rights of its citizens, even if interstate commerce is indirectly affected by the regulation.**

*Breard v. Alexandria*, 341 U.S. 622 (1951). The Court upheld a local ordinance which prohibited door-to-door solicitation, even though the ordinance may have had the effect of discriminating against interstate commerce. The Court upheld the ordinance because its purpose was to protect the privacy rights of homeowners, not to provide an economic advantage to local businesses.

(8) **Waste Disposal Cases. [§ 272]**

There are a number of waste disposal cases which illustrate the non-discrimination principles of dormant commerce clauses analysis.

(a) **Banning the Importation of Solid Waste. [§ 273]**

**A state may not prohibit the importation of waste into the state.**

*Philadelphia v. New Jersey*, 437 U.S. 617 (1978). The Court invalidated a New Jersey law which prohibited the importation into New Jersey of any solid or liquid waste which originated or was collected outside New Jersey. New Jersey attempted to use health and environmental concerns in support of the law. **The Court said that if simple economic protectionism is effected by the law, a virtual *per se* rule of invalidity applies.** It also said that whatever the purpose of the law, a state may not choose a means which discriminates against articles coming from out of

# STATE POWER TO REGULATE COMMERCE: LIMITATIONS

state unless there is some reason other than their place of origin to treat them differently. **The Court also reiterated the rule that a state may not give its residents a preferred right of access over out-of-staters to natural resources located within the state's borders.** A big factor in the Court's decision was the issue of multiple burdens. **If the Court upheld this law, it would be an invitation for every state to pass a law prohibiting the importation of solid, hazardous, or nuclear waste, thereby destroying the interstate market for the sale and processing of these items.**

(b) **Extra Fee on Out-of-State Waste. [§ 274]**

**A state may not charge out-of-staters an extra fee for dumping waste.**

*Chemical Waste Management v. Hunt*, 504 U.S. 334 (1992). The Court invalidated an Alabama law which imposed an extra fee of $72 per ton on the disposal of hazardous waste from out of state when the waste was disposed of in privately-owned landfills in Alabama. The Court said that even if the law were aimed at health, safety, or environmental concerns of Alabama, it could not employ a means which facially discriminated against the interstate market. Less drastic means were available, such as a per-mile tax on all vehicles transporting hazardous waste in the state.

(c) **Higher Fee for Dumping Out-of-State Waste. [§ 275]**

**A higher fee for out-of-state dumpers of waste fails strict scrutiny.**

*Oregon Waste Systems, Inc. v. Dept. of Environmental Quality of Oregon*, 511 U.S. 93 (1994). The court invalidated an Oregon law that imposed a $2.50 per ton surcharge on the disposal of solid waste generated in other states, but only an $0.85 per ton fee on solid waste generated within the state. The Court said that Oregon's restrictions failed to pass the "strictest scrutiny" indicated by the facial discrimination against out-of-staters. The Court said that even if landfill space could be considered a natural resource, a state may not accord its own citizens a preferred right of access over consumers in other states to natural resources located within the state's borders.

# CHAPTER VII

**(d) Requiring Waste to Be Processed Locally. [§ 276]**

**A town cannot require waste to be processed locally when it could be processed more cheaply elsewhere.**

*C & A Carbone v. Town of Clarkstown, New York*, 511 U.S 383 (1994). The Court invalidated a local ordinance which authorized a private contractor to build, within town limits, a solid waste transfer station for the purpose of separating recyclable from non-recyclable waste. To finance the operation, the town guaranteed a minimum waste flow to the transfer station. The operator of the station was authorized to charge a "tipping fee," which was higher than the cost of disposing of unsorted waste in the private market. To meet the waste flow guarantee, the town passed an ordinance requiring all nonhazardous solid waste within the town limits to be disposed of at the transfer station. Carbone received solid waste at his own sorting station and separated it into recyclable and non-recyclable items. Carbone was then required to take the sorted materials to the transfer station and pay the tipping fee, even though the trash had already been sorted. Carbone was also prohibited from shipping its sorted trash directly; it had to go through the transfer station. The court ruled that the town ordinance discriminated against interstate commerce, and that the article of commerce here was not so much the trash itself as the service of processing and disposing of it. The Court said that the town had less drastic means available to achieve its goals, such as uniform safety regulations.

**(9) No Distinction Between Nonprofit and For-profit Enterprises. [§ 277]**

**For purposes of Commerce Clause analysis, the Court will not treat nonprofit and for-profit enterprises differently.** Discrimination against interstate commerce in a nonprofit area violates the Commerce Clause.

In *Camps Newfound/Owatonna, Inc. v. Harrison*, 520 U.S. 564 (1997), the Court struck down a Maine property tax that exempted property owned by charitable organizations, unless the organization operated primarily for the benefit of nonresidents. A church camp, 95% of whose campers were from outside the state, challenged the tax law. The Court held that the camp was engaged in commerce because it both purchased and provided goods and services, and the tax law was facially discriminatory against interstate commerce. The Court refused to treat nonprofit organizations any differently for purposes of Dormant Commerce Clause analysis, concluding that there is no reason why the nonprofit character of an enterprise should exclude it from either affirmative or negative Commerce Clause analysis.

(10) **Direct Wine Sales to Instate Consumers. [§ 278]**

**State laws that allow instate wineries to sell wine directly to instate consumers but limit out-of-state wineries from doing so discriminate against interstate commerce in violation of the Commerce Clause.**

*Granholm v. Heald,* 544 U.S. 460 (2005). The Court struck down regulatory schemes in Michigan and New York that allowed instate, but not out-of-state wineries to make direct sales to consumers. These laws violated the anti-discrimination principle of the Commerce Clause and were not saved by § 2 of the Twenty-first Amendment which gives a state the power to regulate the importation of intoxicating liquors into the state. Michigan and New York had regulatory schemes which required separate licenses for producers, wholesalers, and retailers of wine. Michigan allowed instate wineries to ship directly to consumers, subject only to a licensing requirement, but out-of-state wineries had to go through a wholesaler and a retailer, thus increasing their costs. New York allowed direct sales to consumers by instate wineries, but required out-of-state wineries to open up a New York branch office and warehouse. The Court ruled that, under the Commerce Clause, the states' schemes did not advance the legitimate local purpose that could not be adequately served by reasonable nondiscriminatory alternatives. Other means exist to protect the states' interests in preventing minors from purchasing wine over the Internet, avoiding the evasion of taxes, and protecting public health and safety. The Court also ruled that § 2 of the Twenty-first Amendment does not supersede other provisions of the Constitution, and does not displace the rule that States may not give a discriminatory preference to their own producers.

2. **State Laws That Only Burden Interstate Commerce. [§ 279]**

A state law affecting commerce that treats instaters and out-of-staters the same will be considered merely a burden on interstate commerce and will be analyzed under a balancing test. The fact that instaters are subject to the

# CHAPTER VII

same burdens as out-of-staters makes it less likely that the law will violate the central commerce clause principle that there should be one national market, not a number of regional or state markets. **A nondiscriminatory state law that interferes with interstate commerce is constitutional if it is supported by a legitimate state interest and only incidentally affects interstate commerce, unless the burden on interstate trade is clearly excessive in relation to the local benefits.** *Pike v. Bruce Church*, 397 U.S. 137 (1970).

a. **Steps to Follow in Determining the Constitutionality of a State Law That Burdens Interstate Commerce. [§ 280]**

   (1) Make sure there is no discrimination, by purpose or effect, against out-of-staters. Instaters and out-of-staters are subject to the same burdens and regulations.

   (2) Identify the local interest advanced by the law. Economic protectionism is never a valid state interest, so the state should assert some police power goal such as health or safety.

   (3) See if the law only incidentally affects interstate commerce. The primary purpose and effect of the law must be to advance the state's police power interest.

   (4) Balance the adverse impact on interstate commerce against the extent to which the state's goals are advanced by the law.

   (5) See if there are any less drastic means by which the state could achieve its goals.

   (6) See if the law, if upheld, would create too great a risk of multiple burdens.

b. **Issues to Look for When Applying Dormant Commerce Clause Analysis to a State Law That Burdens Interstate Commerce. [§ 281]**

   (1) **Determine Whether the Subject Matter Regulated Is Local or National in Nature. [§ 282]**

   **In conducting a Dormant Commerce Clause balance, consider the nature of the subject matter regulated. If the subject matter is national in scope, thus requiring uniform regulation, a state law will be harder to uphold.** For example, what

# STATE POWER TO REGULATE COMMERCE: LIMITATIONS

if Chicago passed its own laws and regulations for air-traffic controllers. This is the kind of subject matter that had better be regulated in one, uniform way by the federal government. However, if a state or city is regulating something local in nature, the Court will be more disposed to uphold the law.

### (a) Cooley v. Board Of Wardens, 53 U.S. 299 (1851). [§ 283]

The Court upheld a Pennsylvania law that required ships using the local harbor to take on a local pilot. The Court focused on the nature of the subject matter regulated, concluding that the specific needs of local harbors required diverse, local regulations rather than a uniform, national scheme of regulation.

### (b) Southern Pacific v. Arizona, 325 U.S. 761 (1945). [§ 284]

The Court invalidated an Arizona law that limited the length of trains in the state to seventy freight cars. The Court said that the Arizona law imposed too great a burden on an aspect of interstate commerce that is national in scope (interstate rail transportation), and thus required uniformity of regulation.

### (c) Kassel v. Consolidated Freightways Corp., 450 U.S. 662 (1981). [§ 285]

The Court invalidated an Iowa law that prohibited 65-foot double trailers from operating in the state. The Court alluded to the strong presumption in favor of state highway regulations, but said that Iowa failed to present any persuasive evidence that 65-foot double trailers are any more dangerous than 55-foot single trailers.

## (2) Determine Whether the Law Creates a Risk of Multiple Burdens. [§ 286]

**If a state law creates the potential for conflicting laws to be enacted by other states, that may be enough to invalidate the law under the Dormant Commerce Clause.**

*Bibb v. Navajo Freight Lines*, 359 U.S. 520 (1959). The Court invalidated an Illinois law requiring that special mudguards be welded onto all trucks operating within the state. This law

# CHAPTER VII

caused long delays for trucks entering Illinois from other states. State highway safety regulations carry a strong presumption of validity, but the Illinois law imposed too great a burden on interstate commerce. There were less drastic means by which Illinois could have achieved its safety goals, and the law created too great a risk of multiple burdens.

If the Illinois law were upheld, any number of other states could pass laws requiring their own kind of contoured mudguards, thereby causing a multiplicity of burdens on interstate commerce.

### (3) Determine Whether a Price Affirmation Law Has Extraterritorial Effects. [§ 287]

**A state may not pass a law which effectively sets prices in other states.**

*Healy v. Beer Institute*, 491 U.S. 324 (1989). The Court invalidated a Connecticut law that required out-of-state shippers of beer to affirm that the prices they would charge Connecticut wholesalers were no higher at the time of affirmation than the prices charged in the four states bordering Connecticut. The Court focused on the extraterritorial effect of the law, asserting that a state may not pass a law which has the practical effect of setting a price scale for use in other states. The Court also cited the multiple-burdens problem, asking what would happen if a number of other states passed this kind of law.

### (4) Determine Whether the State Law Causes Business to Shift From One Out-of-Stater to Another. [§ 288]

**It is not unconstitutional for a state law to cause some interstate business to shift from one interstate supplier to another, as long as the total flow of goods in interstate commerce is not diminished.**

*Exxon Corp. v. Maryland*, 437 U.S. 117 (1978). The Court upheld a Maryland law that prohibited petroleum producers (such as Exxon) from operating retail gas stations in the state. The purpose was to avoid the situation in which, during a gas shortage, big producers would supply their own retail stations and shut out independent gas station owners. **There was no discrimination against the interstate market because all petroleum sold in the state would continue to come from out**

# STATE POWER TO REGULATE COMMERCE: LIMITATIONS

of state. There is no impermissible burden on interstate commerce where a state law causes some business to shift from one interstate supplier to another.

(5) **Determine Whether the State Law Simply Prefers One Kind of Container Over Another. [§ 289]**

**It is not unconstitutional for a state to distinguish between kinds of containers, even though there may be an incidental effect on out-of-state suppliers.**

*Minnesota v. Clover Leaf Creamery*, 449 U.S. 456 (1981). The Court upheld a Minnesota law that banned nonreturnable milk containers made of plastic, but allowed other nonreturnable milk containers, such as those made of pulpwood. Since the law differentiated between the type of container rather than instate versus out-of-state producers, the Court found no discrimination against interstate commerce. The State's environmental and ecological arguments outweighed any burden on interstate commerce.

(6) **Determine Whether a Law Applies to All Carriers. [§ 290]**

**A state may impose a flat fee on all trucks that engage in intrastate activities, even if some of the carriers also engage in interstate commerce.**

*American Trucking Assoc., Inc. v. Michigan Public Service Commission*, 545 U.S. 429 (2005). The Supreme Court held that a Michigan statute that imposed a flat $100 annual fee on all trucks that engaged in intrastate deliveries did not violate the dormant Commerce Clause. The petitioners argued that the statute burdened interstate commerce because interstate carriers who for the sake of efficiency would carry not only interstate goods but also "top off" their loads with intrastate goods had to pay the same flat fee as carriers who hauled only intrastate goods. The petitioners argued that a per mile fee would be fairer. The Court held the statute did not violate the dormant Commerce Clause because it did not discriminate against interstate commerce on its face, it applied evenhandedly to all carriers making intrastate deliveries, and it was not a scheme to tax an activity that took place outside the State.

3. **Market Participant Exception to Dormant Commerce Clause Analysis. [§ 291]**

**A state is a market regulator when it acts in its sovereign capacity to regulate what other parties can do within their contractual relation-**

# CHAPTER VII

ships. **It is a market participant when it is a party to a contract and makes business decisions for itself. When a state acts as a market participant, rather than a market regulator, it may discriminate against out-of-staters for any reason, including local economic advantage, and be immune from a Dormant Commerce Clause analysis.** In such cases, a state may limit its sales to instate buyers or limit its purchases to instate sellers.

**STUDY TIP:** The "market participant exception" only frees a state from a Dormant Commerce Clause analysis. It does **not** immunize a discriminating state from an Article IV Privileges and Immunities Clause of analysis, or from an Equal Protection analysis. Under an Article IV Privileges and Immunities Clause argument, a state cannot deny to out-of-staters certain basic rights which it grants to its own citizens, unless it has an important reason for the discrimination. Under an Equal Protections argument, a state cannot treat out-of-staters worse than instaters, unless it has a legitimate reason for doing do.

### a. Examples of "Market Participant" Cases. [§ 292]

The Court has upheld the ability of a state to prefer local economic interests over those of out-of-staters.

*Department of Revenue of Kentucky v. Davis*, 128 U.S. 1801 (2008). Kentucky exempts from state income taxes interest on bonds issued by the state or its political subdivisions, but not on bonds issued by other states and their subdivisions. Plaintiffs, who paid Kentucky state income tax on out-of-state municipal bonds, sued for a refund, claiming that Kentucky's differential tax discriminated against interstate commerce. The Court ruled that Kentucky was acting as a market participant rather than a market regulator, and was therefore immune from Dormant Commerce Clause analysis. The Court said that the logic of exempting a state from Commerce Clause analysis applies with great force to laws favoring a state's municipal bonds, since issuing bonds to finance public projects is a quintessentially public function.

### (1) State–Owned Auto Salvage Business. [§ 293]

**A state may discriminate against out-of-staters in the operation of a state-owned auto salvage business.**

*Hughes v. Alexandria Scrap*, 426 U.S. 794 (1976). The Court upheld a Maryland law that was designed to rid the state of old,

# STATE POWER TO REGULATE COMMERCE: LIMITATIONS

inoperable automobiles. Under the law, a person who owned an old automobile could transfer it to a scrap processor who could claim a bounty from the state for the destruction of the automobile. Under a 1974 amendment to the law, a processor had to submit title documentation to the state to claim the bounty. The title documentation requirements were more lenient for instate processors than they were for out-of-state processors. The Court upheld the different requirements because the state had entered the auto salvage market, and could discriminate against out-of-staters if it chose to do so.

### (2) State–Owned Cement Company. [§ 294]

**A state may discriminate against out-of-staters in the sale of cement by a state-owned cement company.**

*Reeves v. Stake*, 447 U.S. 429 (1980). The Court upheld a South Dakota policy of preferring in-state buyers of cement produced at a state-owned cement plant. As a result of a cement shortage, South Dakota built and operated a cement plant. For almost 60 years, South Dakota sold cement to both in-state and out-of-state buyers. In 1978, in the midst of a cement shortage, South Dakota decided to sell cement to instaters first with out-of-staters getting what was left after in-state demand was met. The Court ruled that because South Dakota was a market participant its preference for instaters was not subject to a Dormant Commerce Clause challenge.

### (3) State as Party to Construction Contracts. [§ 295]

**A city may discriminate against non-residents of the city in the awarding of city-funded construction contracts.**

*White v. Massachusetts Council*, 460 U.S. 204 (1983). The Court upheld an executive order of the Mayor of Boston requiring that all construction projects funded by the city be performed by a work force made up of at least 50% Boston residents. For the Court's treatment of such a program under the Privileges and Immunities Clause of Article IV, see *United Building and Construction Trades Council v. Camden*, 465 U.S. 208 (1984), below, at § 305.

## b. Limits of the Market Participant Doctrine. [§ 296]

**A state will be treated as a market participant as long as it is making purchase or sales decisions in relation to a contract to**

which it is a party. As soon as it tries to control the terms of a contract to which it is not a party, it is acting as a market regulator and the Dormant Commerce Clause will restrict its actions.

*South-Central Timber Development Co. v. Wunnicke*, 467 U.S. 82 (1984). A plurality of the Court found that Alaska was not acting as a market participant when it sold state-owned timber to buyers, but required as part of the contract that the timber be processed in the state of Alaska before it could be shipped out of state. According to the plurality, the problem was that Alaska was trying to control a market transaction that occurred subsequent to the initial sale of timber by the state.

## C. THE PRIVILEGES AND IMMUNITIES CLAUSE OF ARTICLE IV. [§ 297]

**As a general rule, the Privileges and Immunities Clause of Article IV (not the Privileges or Immunities Clause of the Fourteenth Amendment) prohibits a state from denying to out-of-staters privileges that it grants to its own citizens. This clause only protects individuals, not corporations, and applies only when a state is discriminating against out-of-staters in relation to the exercise of a basic or fundamental right.** For Article IV Privileges and Immunities purposes, the basic rights protected are the right to pursue an occupation, the right to own or dispose of property within the state, the right of access to state courts, and the right to come into the state to exercise a fundamental right.

1. **Standard of Review in Privileges and Immunities Clause of Article IV Cases. [§ 298]**

    **To justify a discrimination against out-of-staters and to withstand an Article IV Privilege and Immunities attack, a state must show that it has a substantial reason for treating out-of-staters differently from its own citizens, and that the discrimination is substantially related to achieving the state's goals.** A state statute may violate the Privileges and Immunities Clause even if it does not facially discriminate against out-of-staters.

    *Hillside Dairy, Inc. v. Lyons*, 539 U.S. 59 (2003). The Court held that a state statute can still violate the Privileges and Immunities Clause even though it does not facially discriminate against out-of-staters. The Court remanded the case, saying that the absence of an express statement in the state law identifying out-of-staters as a discriminated against class is not

# STATE POWER TO REGULATE COMMERCE: LIMITATIONS

a sufficient basis for disallowing the Privileges and Immunities argument. The issue in the case was whether a system of milk price supports violated the Privileges and Immunities Clause by requiring payments into an equalization fund to be made based on purchases of milk from out-of-state as well as California milk producers.

2. **Application of Article IV Privileges and Immunities Clause Analysis.** [§ 299]

   a. **Durational Residency Requirements for Voting. [§ 300]**

   **A one-year residency requirement for voting is unconstitutional.**

   *Dunn v. Blumstein*, 405 U.S. 330 (1972). The Court said that, under the Privilege and Immunities Clause of Article IV, it is permissible for a state to require that voters be bona fide residents of the state. However, the Court, under the Equal Protection clause, invalidated a Tennessee voter registration requirement that voters live in the state for one year, and in the county for three months.

   b. **State Statute Limiting Abortions to State Residents. [§ 301]**

   **A state may not prohibit out-of-state women from coming instate to have an abortion.**

   *Doe v. Bolton*, 410 U.S. 179 (1973). The Court invalidated a Georgia statute which prohibited an abortion from being performed in the state unless the patient requesting the abortion certified in writing, under oath, that she was a legal resident of the state of Georgia. The Court ruled that a state cannot limit the medical care available within its borders to its own residents.

   c. **Elective Office Limited to Residents. [§ 302]**

   **A state may limit the right to hold elective office to state residents.**

   *Kanapaux v. Ellisor*, 419 U.S. 891 (1974). The Court upheld a South Carolina law which restricted to state residents the right to hold elective office in the state.

   d. **Higher License Fees for Out-of-Staters. [§ 303]**

   **Higher commercial license fees for out-of-staters are constitutionally suspect.** Such fees run afoul of the central purpose of the Article: IV Privileges and Immunities Clause, which is to outlaw classifications based on non-citizenship of a state unless the non-citizens constitute a particular evil at which the statute is directed.

*Toomer v. Witsell*, 334 U.S. 385 (1948). The Court invalidated a South Carolina law which charged out-of-staters $2500 for a commercial shrimp license while charging instaters only $250. This law also created a risk of multiple burdens if other states imposed the same kind of requirement.

e. **Hiring Preferences for Instaters. [§ 304]**

**A state may not require private employers to give a hiring preference to state residents.**

*Hicklin v. Orbeck*, 437 U.S. 518 (1978). The Court invalidated an Alaska law that required private employers in a number of oil and gas operations to give a hiring preference to Alaska residents over out-of-staters.

f. **Construction Set–Asides for Local Residents. [§ 305]**

**A city ordinance requiring that a certain number of jobs on city funded construction projects be set aside for city residents is subject to attack under the Privileges and Immunities Clause of Article IV.**

*United Building and Construction Trades Council v. Camden*, 465 U.S. 208 (1984). The Court held that the Privileges and Immunities Clause of Article IV is available as a challenge to a municipal ordinance that set aside a certain percentage of jobs on city-funded construction projects for city residents. The Court rejected arguments that the clause does not apply when a city (as opposed to a state) prefers its own residents. The Court remanded the case to state court for a determination as to whether there was a substantial reason for the City of Camden to reserve a percentage of city jobs for city residents.

g. **Excluding Out-of-Staters From the Practice of Law. [§ 306]**

**A state may not exclude non-residents from the practice of law within the state.**

The Court has consistently invalidated requirements that a lawyer be a resident of the state (or of the Virgin Islands) before being admitted to practice in the state. Practicing law is a basic right, and the

# STATE POWER TO REGULATE COMMERCE: LIMITATIONS

exclusions did not meet the test of being substantially related to a substantial state objective. *New Hampshire v. Piper*, 470 U.S. 274 (1985) (A resident of Vermont took and passed the New Hampshire bar examination, but was not allowed to be sworn in as a lawyer until she established a residence in New Hampshire); *Supreme Court of Virginia v. Friedman*, 487 U.S. 59 (1988) (An attorney who resided in Maryland was not allowed admission to the Virginia bar "on motion"—that is, without having to take the Virginia bar examination—even though Maryland allowed Virginia attorneys to become members of the Maryland bar on that basis); *Barnard v. Thorstenn*, 489 U.S. 546 (1989) (To be admitted to the bar of the District Court of the Virgin Islands, an attorney had to demonstrate that he or she had resided in the Virgin Islands for at least one year and intended to continue to reside and practice in the Virgin Islands if admitted to practice).

h. **Denying Out-of-Staters a Tax Deduction for Alimony Paid During the Tax Year. [§ 307]**

**The Privileges and Immunities Clause of Article IV prohibits a state from denying out-of-staters a tax deduction for alimony paid during the tax year while granting such a deduction to state residents.**

*Lunding v. New York Tax Appeals Tribunal*, 522 U.S. 287 (1998). The Court invalidated a provision of a State of New York tax law which effectively denied only non-resident taxpayers a state income tax deduction for alimony paid during the tax year. The law was challenged by a Connecticut couple who had to pay higher New York state income taxes when the State refused to allow them to deduct a pro rata share of the alimony the husband had paid to a previous spouse. Relying on the Privileges and Immunities Clause of Article IV, the Court ruled that New York had not met its burden of demonstrating that there is a substantial reason for the difference in treatment between state residents and non-residents and that the discrimination against non-residents bears a substantial relationship to any of the State's proffered objectives. The Court said that a citizen of a state has a right to move to and carry on business in another state without being subject to higher taxes than people who are residents of the second state.

3. **Article IV Privileges and Immunities Clause Does Not Apply to Non–Basic Rights. [§ 308]**

**The protections of the clause only apply when a basic right is abridged (see § 294).** If one of the basic rights is not affected, an

# CHAPTER VII

out-of-stater will not be able to assert the Article IV Privileges and Immunities Clause as a challenge against the discriminatory state law.

*Baldwin v. Fish and Game Commission of Montana*, 436 U.S. 371 (1978). The Court held that the Privileges and Immunities Clause of Article IV did not apply to a Montana law that charged out-of-staters a higher fee than instaters for a private, non-commercial hunting license. This case, unlike *Toomer* (see § 300 above), did not involve state discrimination in relation to the basic right of pursuing an occupation.

## D. CONGRESSIONAL POWER TO AUTHORIZE STATE DISCRIMINATION AGAINST INTERSTATE COMMERCE. [§ 309]

**If Congress authorizes a state to impose a discriminatory tax on out-of-state entities, such a tax will be immune from a Dormant Commerce Clause challenge, but will be invalid under the Equal Protection Clause if the only reason for the law is local economic protectionism.** Since Congress is the ultimate holder of the commerce power, it may give to states the power to discriminate against out-of-state commerce. However, Congress does not have a power to violate the Equal Protection principle of the Constitution, so it may not give such a power to the states.

**STUDY TIP:** If you see Congress passing a law which gives states the power to impose discriminatory taxes on out-of-staters, be careful about the specific constitutional challenge to the state tax. If it is only that the state tax violates the Dormant Commerce Clause, the tax is valid. If the challenge is that the state tax violates the Equal Protection Clause, the tax is unconstitutional if the state is simply promoting domestic business by discriminating against nonresident competitors.

1. **Prudential Insurance Co. v. Benjamin, 328 U.S. 408 (1946). [§ 310]**

    The Court upheld, against a Dormant Commerce Clause challenge, a South Carolina law that taxed out-of-state insurance companies at a higher rate than instate insurance companies. Congress had authorized this tax under the McCarran Act.

2. **Metropolitan Life Insurance Co. v. Ward, 470 U.S. 869 (1985). [§ 311]**

    The Court, relying on the Equal Protection Clause, invalidated an Alabama law that taxed out-of-state insurance companies at a higher rate than instate insurance companies.

# STATE POWER TO REGULATE COMMERCE: LIMITATIONS

## E. STATE POWER TO TAX INTERSTATE COMMERCE. [§ 312]

In general, states have a presumptive power to tax interstate business operating within the state. To deny states that power would force them to provide services to out-of-state businesses without being able to recoup any of the costs of providing those services. **The main limitations on a state's power to tax interstate commerce come from the Dormant Commerce Clause, the Due Process Clause, and the Equal Protection Clause.** Under the Dormant Commerce Clause, the principle is that interstate businesses should pay their fair share for services received from the state. The Court is concerned about whether the tax passes an unfair share of the tax burden onto interstate commerce, or unduly burdens interstate commerce. Under the Due Process Clause, the main concern is the fundamental fairness of the state tax; are an individual's connections with a state substantial enough to justify the state tax? Under Equal Protection Clause, the question is whether the state has a legitimate reason for discriminatory taxation of out-of-staters, and whether it has chosen rational means to achieve its goal. Remember that it is not a legitimate government interest to prefer local economic interests for purely protectionist reasons.

1. **Dormant Commerce Clause Limitations on a State's Power to Tax Interstate Commerce. [§ 313]**

    The Court has adopted a four-part test by which to analyze a state tax that is challenged under the Dormant Commerce Clause. This test comes from *Complete Auto Transit, Inc. v. Brady*, 430 U.S. 274 (1977), in which the Court upheld Mississippi's tax on the privilege of doing business within the state. The Court looked to the practical effect of the tax, rather than its label, to see if it violated the Commerce Clause. **Under the four-part test, a state tax will survive a Commerce Clause challenge if the tax: 1) is applied to an activity with a substantial nexus to the taxing state; 2) is fairly apportioned; 3) does not discriminate against interstate commerce; and 4) is fairly related to the services provided by the state.**

    a. **Cases Illustrating Each of the Elements of the Four-Part Test of Complete Auto Transit. [§ 314]**

    (1) **Substantial Nexus. [§ 315]**

    The activity taxed must have a substantial nexus to the taxing state.

    *Wisconsin v. J.C. Penney Co.*, 311 U.S. 435 (1940). The Court upheld, against a Due Process challenge, a Wisconsin tax on

# CHAPTER VII

corporations chartered out of state, but doing business instate. The test for Due Process purposes is whether the taxing power exerted by the state bears fiscal relation to protection, opportunities, and benefits given by the state; has the state given anything for which it can ask something in return.

(2) **Fair Apportionment. [§ 316]**

**A state tax which is not apportioned to the amount of business a company does in the state violates the Dormant Commerce Clause.**

*Western Live Stock v. Bureau of Revenue*, 303 U.S. 250 (1938). The Court discussed the issue of multiple (or cumulative) tax burdens being placed on interstate commerce if there were no apportionment requirement. Not only would the multiple taxes (by each state in which an entity does business) impose an unfair burden on the taxed corporation, it would discriminate against interstate commerce by virtue of local commerce being free from any cumulative tax burden.

(a) **A State's Choice of Apportionment Scheme Will Be Up-Held if at All Rational. [§ 317]**

**The Court uses rational basis scrutiny to evaluate a state's choice of an apportionment scheme.** It is difficult for a state apportionment scheme to fail this test.

(b) **Single–Factor Apportionment Scheme Valid. [§ 318]**

**It is constitutional for a state to use a single-factor apportionment scheme which compares instate sales to total gross sales.**

*Moorman Manufacturing Co. v. Bair*, 437 U.S. 267 (1978). The Court upheld an Iowa tax which used a single-factor apportionment formula which compared Iowa sales to total gross sales. The tax had been applied to an Illinios manufacturer. The Court said that the Due Process Clause imposes two restrictions on a state's ability to tax the income of an interstate business: there must be some minimal connection between the activities taxed and the taxing state, and the income attributed to the state for tax purposes must be rationally related to values connected with the taxing state.

# STATE POWER TO REGULATE COMMERCE: LIMITATIONS

(c) **Two Factors to Determine if Apportionment Scheme Is Valid. [§ 319]**

**It is constitutional for a state to use a two-factor apportionment scheme which looks at whether the apportionment formula is internally and externally consistent.**

*Container Corporation v. Franchise Tax Board*, 463 U.S. 159 (1983). The Court upheld California's tax apportionment scheme. The Court looks at two factors to see if an apportionment formula is constitutional: 1) Is it internally consistent—that is, if the same formula were applied by every jurisdiction, would it result in no more than 100% of the business' income being taxed; and 2) Is it externally consistent—that is, does the apportionment formula reflect a reasonable sense of how income is generated? The taxpayer has the burden of proving that the apportionment formula is unconstitutional because there is no rational relationship between the income attributed to the state, and the intrastate value of the enterprise taxed.

(d) **Multiple Burdens and Apportionment Schemes. [§ 320]**

**An apportionment scheme will be constitutional if it does not expose foreign corporations to impermissible multiple tax burdens.**

*Barclay's Bank PLC v. Franchise Tax Board of California*, 512 U.S. 298 (1994). The Court upheld California's "worldwide combined reporting" method of calculating the corporate franchise tax owed by unitary multinational corporations. This is the same method of taxation approved in *Container Corporation* (see previous case supra), only here it is applied to foreign corporations or domestic corporations with foreign parents. The Court found that this tax met the four-part test of *Complete Auto Transit*, and that it does not expose foreign multinational corporations to constitutionally impermissible multiple tax burdens.

(3) **Non–Discrimination Against Interstate Commerce. [§ 321]**

**The purpose of a discriminatory tax cannot be local economic advantage. A tax which applies equally to all products, regardless of their destination, is constitutional.**

# CHAPTER VII

(a) **Boston Stock Exchange v. State Tax Commission, 429 U.S. 318 (1977). [§ 322]**

The Court invalidated a New York law which reduced the tax liability on the sale of corporate shares or stock certificates if they were sold in the state of New York rather than out of state. This tax was an unconstitutional discrimination against interstate commerce because the higher tax burden on out-of-staters was for the purpose of securing an economic advantage for instate stock transactions and the New York Stock Exchange.

(b) **Commonwealth Edison v. Montana, 453 U.S. 609 (1981). [§ 323]**

The Court upheld a Montana severance tax on coal. The rate of the tax varied, but could not exceed 30% of the contract price. The tax was challenged as discriminatory against interstate commerce because 90% of Montana coal was shipped to other states. The Court said that all coal, regardless of destination, was taxed at the same rate, so there was no impermissible discrimination against out-of-staters.

(c) **South Central Bell Telephone Co. v. Alabama, 526 U.S. 160 (1999). [§ 324]**

The Court invalidated an Alabama franchise tax scheme that imposed higher tax liability on out-of-state corporations. The tax for a domestic firm is based on the par value of the firm's stock, which the firm may set at a level below its book or market value. An out-of-state firm must pay tax in the amount of capital it employs in the state, with no discretion to control its own tax base. This discriminatory treatment violated the Dormant Commerce Clause.

(4) **Relation to Services Provided. [§ 325]**

**A state tax on an interstate business must be fairly related to services provided by state.**

*General Motors v. Washington*, 377 U.S. 436 (1964). The Court, in upholding Washington's tax on doing business in the state, shed some light on the requirement that a tax must be fairly related to the services provided by the state: The question is whether the state has exerted its power in proper proportion to

# STATE POWER TO REGULATE COMMERCE: LIMITATIONS

the taxpayer's activities within the state, and to the taxpayer's consequent enjoyment of the opportunities and protections of the state.

b. **Dormant Commerce Clause as a Limitation on State Sales Taxes. [§ 326]**

**A State Sales Tax on Every Interstate Bus Ticket Sold Instate Does Not Violate the Commerce Clause.**

*Oklahoma Tax Commission v. Jefferson Lines Inc.*, 514 U.S. 175 (1995). The Court upheld an Oklahoma sales tax on bus tickets sold in Oklahoma for interstate travel. The Court applied the four-part test of *Complete Auto Transit*, and determined that the state sales tax met the requirements of the Commerce Clause: it is applied to an activity with a substantial nexus to the taxing state; it is fairly apportioned; it does not discriminate against interstate commerce; and it is fairly related to services provided by the taxing state.

2. **Due Process Limitations on a State's Power to Tax Interstate Commerce. [§ 327]**

A state law which taxes an interstate business operating within the state will withstand a Due Process challenge only if there are "minimum contacts" between the entity taxed and the taxing state, and there is a rational relationship between the income attributed to the taxing state and the intrastate values of the enterprise taxed. See *Wisconsin v. J.C. Penney Co.*, above, at § 315.

a. **Braniff Airways, Inc. v. Nebraska State Board of Equalization and Assessment, 347 U.S. 590 (1954). [§ 328]**

The Court upheld Nebraska's ad valorem tax on the equipment of Braniff, even though the airline made only eighteen stops a day in the state. The Court said that Braniff had established a taxable situs for due process purposes through its habitual use of the property in the state. The test is whether the tax in practical operation has relation to opportunities, benefits, or protection conferred by the taxing state.

**NOTE:** The Due Process "minimum contacts" test differs from the Dormant Commerce Clause "substantial nexus" test. In *Quill Corp. v. North Dakota*, 504 U.S. 298 (1992), the Court made it clear that the nexus requirements of the Due Process and Commerce Clauses are not identical. The Due Process "minimum contacts" test focuses on an individual and the fundamental fairness of the tax. The Commerce

# CHAPTER VII

Clause "substantial nexus" test looks at the structural concerns of the interstate market. A corporation may have "minimum contacts" with a taxing state for Due Process purposes, but lack the "substantial nexus" required by the Commerce Clause.

3. **Equal Protection Limitations on a State's Power to Tax Interstate Commerce. [§ 329]**

    **A state may not impose a higher tax on out-of-staters than on instaters if the only reason is to prefer local business interests.** If a state law is passed for the sole reason of securing a local economic advantage, that law fails rational basis scrutiny under Equal Protection analysis.

    *Metropolitan Life Insurance Co. v. Ward*, 470 U.S. 869 (1985). The Court invalidated, on Equal Protection grounds, a state tax on out-of-state insurance companies that was higher than the tax on instate companies. This tax was designed solely for economic protectionism, and failed rationality review.

    *Michelin Tire Corp. v. Wages*, 423 U.S. 276 (1976). The Court upheld Georgia's nondiscriminatory, general ad valorem property tax as applied to imported tires that were stored in a warehouse ready for sale or distribution. The Court said that this kind of tax, applied to goods that were no longer in transit, was not prohibited by the Import–Export Clause.

4. **State–Imposed Compensating Use Taxes Are Constitutional Despite Their Impact on Interstate Commerce. [§ 330]**

    **A state may impose a compensating use tax, up to the amount of the state sales tax, on goods purchased out of state (where there is no sales tax, or one lower than that of the state imposing the use tax), and brought into the state for use.** A compensating use tax puts instate sellers (who must charge the sales tax) on the same footing with out-of-state sellers (who do not have to charge a sales tax). A use tax is invalid if it discriminates against interstate commerce. It will be discriminatory if the use tax imposed on out-of-state goods is higher than the sales tax imposed on instate goods; that would discourage a buyer from going to another state to buy a product.

    For example, the amount of a use tax in State A cannot exceed the sales tax in State A minus the sales tax in State B. If State A has a sales tax of 4%, and State B has no sales tax, the use tax in State A may go up to 4%. If State A has a sales tax of 4%, and State B has a sales tax of 2%, State A's use tax may go as high as 2%.

# STATE POWER TO REGULATE COMMERCE: LIMITATIONS

a. **Henneford v. Silas Mason, 300 U.S. 577 (1937). [§ 331]**

The Court upheld a use tax imposed on construction equipment purchased out of state. The Court reasoned that this tax was not a tax on interstate commerce, but on the use of the product after it had become situated in the state.

b. **Associated Industries of Missouri v. Lohman, 511 U.S. 641 (1994). [§ 332]**

The state of Missouri imposed an "additional use tax" on goods purchased outside the State and stored, used, or consumed within the state. The tax was supposed to compensate local jurisdictions for lost sales tax revenue. However, local sales tax rates vary from county to county and in many jurisdictions the use tax exceeded the sales tax. The tax scheme was challenged on the ground that it violated the Commerce Clause. The Court held that the use tax discriminates against interstate commerce in those jurisdictions where the use tax exceeds the sales tax. The compensatory tax doctrine saves the use tax in the jurisdictions where the use tax does not exceed the sales tax. Therefore, the tax scheme is not altogether invalid. It is only invalid in those jurisdictions where the additional use tax imposes a greater burden on interstate commerce than the local sales tax imposes on local, intrastate commerce.

## REVIEW PROBLEMS—STATE POWER TO REGULATE COMMERCE: CONSTITUTIONAL LIMITATIONS

**PROBLEM 1.** The legislature of the State of Oz (a state of the United States) passes a law which prohibits darkened glass from being used on the windows, windshields, or rear windows of automobiles being driven within the state. The purpose of the law is to allow police officers to see what the occupants of cars are doing. Bob is from the State of Id, which allows darkened glass on cars. Bob is arrested while driving through Oz. Discuss the Dormant Commerce Clause issues that Bob would raise in challenging the Oz statute.

**Answer:** This law is similar to the one invalidated in *Bibb v. Navajo Freight Lines*, at § 286. The law treats all automobiles the same, wherever they come from, so there is no discrimination against interstate commerce. However, this law would be unconstitutional because of the great burden it imposes on commerce: cars from certain states are, in effect, prohibited from entering the State of Oz.

**PROBLEM 2.** The legislature of the State of Oz is concerned about the growing scarcity of landfill space within the state, the financial well-being of instate

# CHAPTER VII

garbage haulers, and the safety and health of its citizens. The State, under its power of eminent domain, acquires all the existing landfill space within the state. It then accepts for disposal only garbage generated within the State of Oz. Jane's Disposal Services, Inc., an out-of-state disposal company, challenges this law as violating its rights under the Dormant Commerce Clause, the Privileges and Immunities Clause of Article IV, and the Equal Protection Clause. Discuss each of these arguments.

**Answer:** Ordinarily, such blatant discrimination against out-of-staters would violate the Dormant Commerce Clause. However, based on these facts, the State of Oz has entered the market of waste disposal, so the market participant exception exempts the State of Oz from any Dormant Commerce Clause analysis. It may discriminate against out-of-staters for whatever reason, and not be subject to any Commerce Clause constraints. Jane's Disposal Services, Inc., as a corporation, is not protected by the Privileges and Immunities Clause of Article IV, so it cannot assert the argument that the State of Oz is denying it the basic right to pursue an occupation within the state. Under Equal Protection analysis, rational basis review is applied, and the discrimination will be upheld if rationally related to a legitimate government interest. Preferring local economic interests is not a legitimate government concern, so Oz's only chance of having the law upheld is if a court accepts its safety or health arguments.

# Chapter VIII

# FEDERAL PREEMPTION OF STATE LAWS

## A. INTRODUCTION. [§ 333]

**Under the Supremacy Clause of Article 6, the U.S. Constitution, federal laws, and treaties take precedence over contrary state constitutional provisions, statutes, or common law.** Federal preemption of contrary state laws is grounded in the basic constitutional structure of a national government composed of various states, with each of the states being sovereign within its own boundaries. When any branch of the federal government acts it is deriving its power from the Constitution, which is the supreme law of the land. From the standpoint of constitutional federalism, it would make no sense for one state, through its laws, to be able to frustrate the operation of federal law; the result of such a system would be to vest each state with a veto power over federal action.

1. **A Preemption Question Exists When Both Congress and a State Have Regulated the Same Activity. [§ 334]**

    **A preemption issue arises when Congress, acting under one of its constitutional powers, regulates a certain activity and a state, acting under its Tenth Amendment police power, regulates the same activity.** For preemption analysis to apply, both laws must be valid. For instance, assume that Congress and a state each passed a law regulating the construction of nuclear power plants. The first step would be to see if both laws are constitutional—that is, Congress' law as an exercise of its commerce power, and the state's law as an exercise of its police power. If both are valid, there is a preemption question—does the state law conflict or interfere with the operation of the federal law? If the answer is yes, the state law is invalid under preemption principles. If the federal law is invalid, it is out of the analysis (there is no preemption issue), and the only remaining question is whether the state law violates some implicit constitutional limitation such as the dormant commerce clause (see § 254 above).

# CHAPTER VIII

A preemption analysis has two steps:

    a.  Make Sure That The Federal And State Laws Are Valid; And

    b.  See If The State Law Interferes With The Operation Of Federal law.

2. **Preemption May Occur in Three Ways. [§ 335]**

    a.  Conflict between federal and state laws—federal law wins. A conflict may occur when it is not possible to comply with both laws, or when compliance with the state law would frustrate the purpose of the federal law.

    b.  Congress expressly says it intends to occupy an entire area of regulable activitycfederal law wins, even if there is no conflict between the federal and state laws.

    c.  Congress has regulated an area so pervasively that a court may reasonably infer that Congress intended to occupy the entire field of regulable activity.

Each of these types of preemption is illustrated below.

## B. CONFLICTING LAWS. [§ 336]

**This kind of preemption involves two distinct kinds of cases: in one, it is physically impossible to comply with both laws; in the other, it is possible to comply with both, but compliance with the state law frustrates the purpose of the federal law.** The second category usually involves a state law which imposes more stringent restrictions on a person or activity than does the applicable federal law.

1. **Southland Corp. v. Keating, 465 U.S. 1 (1984). [§ 337]**

    The Court invalidated, on preemption grounds, a California law that required certain contractual disputes to be adjudicated in court rather than sent to arbitration. The state law conflicted with a federal law which prohibited states from requiring adjudication when contracting parties had agreed to arbitration.

2. **Foster v. Love, 522 U.S. 67 (1998). [§ 338]**

    The Court invalidated, on preemption grounds, a Louisiana statute which set up an "open primary" for all congressional offices, with such elections to be held in October of a federal election year. Under this system, a candidate who receives a majority of votes in the open primary is elected to office and nothing is done on federal election day (in November of even-numbered years) to fill the office. The Court ruled that the law conflicted with federal statutes, passed pursuant to the Elections Clause of the Constitution (Article 1, § 4, clause 1), which set the date for the biennial congressional elections as the Tuesday following the first Monday in November of even-numbered years. The federal laws were passed to prevent distortion of the voting process by having some states select their congressional representatives early, and to avoid the burden of voters having to go the polls twice during presidential election years.

3. **Hines v. Davidowitz, 312 U.S. 52 (1941). [§ 339]**

The Court invalidated, on preemption grounds, a Pennsylvania law requiring aliens to register yearly, and to carry an identification card to be shown to certain specified government officials. This state law frustrated the purposes and objectives of the federal law which required aliens to register once, and did not require the carrying of an identification card.

## C. EXPRESS STATEMENT OF CONGRESS' INTENT TO PREEMPT. [§ 340]

**If Congress says that it intends to occupy an entire field of regulation, state regulation in the area is prohibited, regardless of whether the state law conflicts with the federal law.**

*Aloha Airlines, Inc. v. Director of Taxation*, 464 U.S. 7 (1983). The Court invalidated, on preemption grounds, a state tax on the annual gross income of airlines operating within the state. The Court relied on a federal statute which expressly preempted any such gross receipts tax.

**Under the doctrine of express preemption, Congress must make a plain and clear statement of its intent to preempt before it constrains traditional state authority to order its government.** *Gregory v. Ashcroft*, **501 U.S. 452 (1991).**

*Nixon v. Missouri Municipal League*, 541 U.S. 125 (2004). The Court held that a section of the 1996 Telecommunications Act, which says that no state or local law may prohibit or have the effect of prohibiting the ability of any entity to provide any interstate or intrastate telecommunications service, does not preempt state or local laws barring their political subdivisions from providing such services. The Court cited *Gregory* (above) for the proposition that if Congress is to constrain traditional state authority to order its own government, it must make a clear statement of its intent to do so. Since Congress failed to make a clear statement that the statutory term "any entity" included political

# CHAPTER VIII

subdivisions of states, the Court refused to find preemption.

**When the text of an express statutory preemption clause is susceptible to more than one plausible reading, courts ordinarily accept the reading that disfavors preemption.**

*Altria Group v. Good*, 129 S.Ct. 538 (2008). The court ruled that the Federal Cigarette Labeling and Advertising Act (the Act) neither expressly or impliedly preempted a cause of action under the Maine Unfair Trade Practices Act (MUTPA). Smokers of defendant's "light" cigarettes sued under MUTPA, asserting false advertising, namely that the "light" cigarettes delivered less tar and nicotine than defendant's regular cigarettes. The Court held that plaintiffs' state–law fraud claim was not preempted by the Act, even though lawsuits based on the health risks of smoking may be preempted by the Act.

**STUDY TIP:** When analyzing a preemption question, be careful about which specific field has been preempted by Congress. In *Pacific Gas & Electric Co. v. State Energy Resources Conservation & Development Commission*, 461 U.S. 190 (1983), the Court found no preemption of a California law that prohibited the construction of nuclear power plants until the state was satisfied that a particular project satisfied its concerns of cost and consumer need. Congress had preempted the narrow field of safety in nuclear-power production, but the state law operated in a specific area that Congress had not touched.

## D. PERVASIVE REGULATION BY CONGRESS. [§ 341]

**If Congress regulates an area very comprehensively, a court may draw the inference that Congress intended to occupy that area.**

*Burbank v. Lockheed Air Terminal, Inc.*, 411 U.S. 624 (1973). The Court invalidated, on preemption grounds, a city curfew on aircraft flights from the local airport. Despite a legitimate local interest, noise control, pervasive federal regulation of aircraft traffic led the Court to conclude that Congress had intended to preempt the field of airport regulation.

**EXAMPLE:** [§ 342] *Pennsylvania v. Nelson*, 350 U.S. 497 (1956). The Court invalidated, on preemption grounds, Pennsylvania's Sedition Act. Extensive federal regulation of the area of anti-communist laws led the Court to consider the field preempted.

# FEDERAL PREEMPTION OF STATE LAWS

## E. A STATE MAY NOT DIVEST ITS COURTS OF JURISDICTION IN 42 U.S.C. § 1983 CASES. [§ 342.1]

**A state may not divest its courts of subject-matter jurisdiction over suits seeking money damages from corrections officers.**

*Haywood v. Drown*, 129 S.Ct. 2108 (2009). The Court invalidated, on Supremacy Clause grounds, a section of New York's Correction Law which divested state courts of jurisdiction over § 1983 suits that seek money damages from corrections officers. Believing that suits for damages against correction officers were largely frivolous and vexatious, New York stripped its courts of jurisdiction to hear § 1983 actions against such officers, and substituted a state remedy in which a prisoner can sue in the State Court of Claims, a court in which the plaintiff would not be entitled to attorney's fees, punitive damages, or injunctive relief. The Court ruled that, even though States retain substantial leeway to establish the contours of their judicial systems, they do not have authority to nullify a federal right or cause of action they believe to be inconsistent with local policies. Thus, a State may not relieve congestion in its courts by declaring a whole category of federal claims to be frivolous.

## REVIEW PROBLEM—FEDERAL PREEMPTION OF STATE LAWS

**PROBLEM:** Congress passes a law which sets the standards of maturity that kiwi fruit must meet before it is shipped in interstate commerce. The State of Oz has a law which sets different standards for kiwi maturity before the fruit can be sold in the state. Is the Oz law constitutional?

**Answer:** No. The Oz law is preempted by the federal law setting minimum standards for the interstate shipment of kiwi fruit. While it may be possible to comply with both the federal and state laws, the state law certainly frustrates the purpose of the federal law, which is to balance the needs of the growers, the consumers, and the interstate market. You should think about the danger to interstate commerce that would flow from numerous state laws setting standards different from those of the federal government. See § 336 for further review.

# CHAPTER IX

# STATE ACTION REQUIREMENT FOR THE APPLICATION OF CERTAIN CONSTITUTIONAL PROTECTIONS

## A. INTRODUCTION. [§ 343]

**Most of the provisions of the Constitution which protect individual rights limit government actors, but are irrelevant when a private actor abridges someone's rights.** The Bill of Rights limits the federal government, and the Fourteenth and Fifteenth Amendments limit state governments. (The Thirteenth Amendment prohibits all slavery whether engaged in by a government or by a private actor.) **The "state action" requirement (actually "government action," since it applies to the federal government also) becomes an issue when a private actor harms someone in such a way that a constitutional issue would arise if the harm were inflicted by a government actor, and when there is some reason to impute government action to the private individual who caused the harm.** To be able to assert that a private actor violated his or her constitutional rights, a plaintiff must be able to argue that the private party's actions are sufficiently imbued with state action to make the Constitution applicable. In other words, when is there enough of a connection between the private actor and a government so that the Court will treat the private actor as if he or she is the equivalent of a government actor?

## B. GENERAL ANALYSIS OF STATE ACTION QUESTIONS. [§ 344]

There are three main factors the Court considers when deciding whether to impute state action to a private party, thus making constitutional limitations applicable to the actions of the private party:

    1. To What Extent Does The Private Actor Rely On Governmental Assistance And Benefits;

    2. Whether The Actor Is Performing A Traditional Governmental Function That Has Been Engaged In Exclusively By Government;

# CHAPTER IX

3. Whether The Injury Caused Is Aggravated In A Unique Way By Government intervention.

**STUDY TIP:** Be aware that these categories will overlap in many of the cases. For instance, the Court has found state action when an attorney in a civil case exercises a peremptory challenge based on race. (See § 356). In such case, the Court has said that state action could be imputed to the attorney because jury selection is a traditional, exclusive government function, and because the state court was significantly involved in racial discrimination by enforcing the peremptory challenge.

## C. RELIANCE ON GOVERNMENTAL ASSISTANCE AND BENEFITS. [§ 345]

This is pretty much a "kitchen-sink" kind of analysis. **The plaintiff argues every possible connection between the private actor and the state, and the Court looks at the totality of circumstances to see if there is enough of a connection between the private actor and a government to apply constitutional protections.** Be aware of the number and kinds of relationships between the private actor and the government. The Court today is not very willing to impute state action to private actors.

1. **Symbiotic Relationship Between Government and Private Actor. [§ 346]**

    **Numerous relationships between a private actor and a government may be enough to impute state action to the private actor.**

    *Burton v. Wilmington Parking Authority*, 365 U.S. 715 (1961). The Court found state action on the part of a private restaurant owner who refused to serve members of racial minorities. The Court looked at all the connections between the state and the restaurant and found the Fourteenth Amendment applicable. The restaurant was located in a state-owned parking authority, and was leased from the authority. The Court focused on the interdependence between the restaurant and the parking authority, including the fact that the restaurant would share the parking authority's tax exemption in relation to any improvements done to the restaurant.

2. **Government Involvement in a Racially Discriminatory Bequest. [§ 347]**

    **There is state action if government officials act as trustees of a racially discriminatory private will. State action may also be present if there are enough connections between a city and land devised for use as a whites-only park.**

# STATE ACTION REQUIREMENT FOR CERTAIN PROTECTIONS

*Evans v. Newton*, 382 U.S. 296 (1966). The Court found state action when Senator A.O. Bacon devised land to Macon, Georgia for use as a whites-only park. The Court had previously ruled that it was state action for government officials to act as trustees of a racially discriminatory private will. In *Evans*, the Court also found state action after private trustees had been substituted for the original public trustees. The park had long been an integral part of the city's activities, had been granted a tax exemption, and had been maintained by the city. The Court also alluded to the municipal nature of the services provided by such a park.

3. **State Constitutional Authorization of Racial Discrimination. [§ 348]**

    **State action existed when a private party, relying on a state constitutional provision (since repealed), refused to rent an apartment because of the race of the lessee.**

    *Reitman v. Mulkey*, 387 U.S. 369 (1967). The Court found state action in a private party's refusal to rent an apartment to someone because of the applicant's race. A provision of the California constitution authorized racial discrimination in the sale or rental of property. The right to discriminate based on race was a part of the basic charter of the state, and, as such, implicated the state in any refusal to sell or rent because of race. (This provision of the California Constitution was repealed in 1974.)

4. **Liquor License. [§ 349]**

    **A state granting a liquor license to a private bar or club does not make the bar or club a state actor.**

    *Moose Lodge v. Irvis*, 407 U.S. 163 (1972). The Court found no state action simply because a state grants a liquor license to an establishment. Irvis was refused service at a local Moose Lodge because of his race. He asserted state action by virtue of the lodge's liquor license.

5. **Relationships Between a State and a Private School. [§ 350]**

    **Extensive funding, heavy regulation, and large student referral by the state are not enough to confer state action on a private school.**

    *Rendell-Baker v. Kohn*, 457 U.S. 830 (1982). The Court found no state action on the part of a private school that allegedly discharged some teachers without affording them procedural due process. The Court rejected the teachers' claim under 42 U.S.C. § 1983 that their free speech rights were violated because they were fired allegedly for supporting student grievances against the school. There was no state action despite

# CHAPTER IX

nearly all the students being referred to the school by government agencies (such as the Drug Rehabilitation Division of the Massachusetts Department of Mental Health), the school being heavily regulated by the state, and public funds accounting for 90B99% of the school's operating budget.

6. **State Help in Executing an Attachment. [§ 351]**

   **Active participation by state officials in executing a prejudgment attachment will constitute state action.**

   In *Lugar v. Edmonson Oil Co.*, 457 U.S. 922 (1982), an oil company which supplied oil to the operator of a truck stop was not paid. The oil company sued on the debt in state court and, pursuant to state law, sought prejudgment attachment of certain of the debtor's property. The Court found state action because the state statute authorized a court clerk and the sheriff to authorize and execute a prejudgment attachment of a debtor's property. The active participation of these state officials distinguishes this case from *Flagg Bros. v. Brooks* (see § 364 below).

7. **United States Olympic Committee Is Not a State Actor. [§ 352]**

   **There was no government action by virtue of Congress giving the United States Olympic Committee the power to control the use of the word "Olympic."**

   *San Francisco Arts & Athletics, Inc. v. U.S. Olympic Committee*, 483 U.S. 522 (1987). The Court found no government action on the part of the U.S. Olympic Commitee (USOC), despite the fact that Congress explicitly gave the USOC power to allow or prohibit the use of the word "Olympic" by other groups. The organizers of the "Gay Olympic Games" sued, asserting that the USOC violated their equal protection rights under the Due Process Clause of the Fifth Amendment. The Court ruled that there were insufficient connections between Congress and the USOC to impute state action.

8. **National Collegiate Athletic Association Is Not a State Actor. [§ 353]**

   **The NCAA is not a government actor; it is a voluntary organization made up of both private and public institutions.**

   *NCAA v. Tarkanian*, 488 U.S. 179 (1988). The Court found no state action on the part of the National Collegiate Athletic Association (NCAA) when the University of Nevada, Las Vegas (UNLV) suspended its basketball coach (Jerry Tarkanian) under threat by the NCAA to impose sanctions on

# STATE ACTION REQUIREMENT FOR CERTAIN PROTECTIONS

UNLV if it did not take action against Tarkanian. Tarkanian sued the university and the NCAA, alleging a violation of due process. The Court ruled that the NCAA, being a private association composed of both private and public universities, was not a state actor.

9. **Tennessee Secondary School Athletic Association Is a State Actor. [§ 354]**

   **The Tennessee Secondary School Athletic Association is a state actor because it is pervasively entwined and dominated by the state public school system.**

   *Brentwood Academy v. Tennessee Secondary School Athletic Association*, 531 U.S. 288 (2001). The Court found state action when the Association, which has 84% of its members being public schools and mainly public officials on its governing body, disciplined a member school without due process. The Court held that even though it was nominally a private association, it was heavily intertwined with the public school system: its members are eligible to participate in the state retirement system, state board of education members serve as members of its governing bodies and there could be no Association but for the participation of the public school officials. The Court ruled that given the facts, the nominally private character of the Association is overcome by the pervasive entwinement of public institutions and officials in the organization, and the significant involvement between the two entities.

## D. PERFORMING AN EXCLUSIVE, TRADITIONAL GOVERNMENTAL FUNCTION. [§ 355]

**The Court will find state action when a private party is performing a function that has traditionally been performed by government. In recent years the Court has insisted that the function be one that has been exclusively performed by government.** The result has been a reluctance by the Court to find state action under this theory.

1. **Elections. [§ 356]**

   **Any pre-primary or primary election that feeds into a general election will be considered state action.**

   a. In *Smith v. Allwright*, 321 U.S. 649 (1944), [§ 357] Lonnie Smith, a black resident of Harris County, Texas, sued officials of the Democratic Party of Texas who refused to allow him to vote in a primary election of the Democratic Party. The Court found state action on the part of the Democratic Party when it excluded Smith

# CHAPTER IX

and other blacks from voting in the primary election. State delegation to a political party to set the qualifications for primary elections is a delegation of a state function which implicates the state in the party's actions. The Court dcided Smith on the basis of the Fifteenth Amendment, which prohibits a state from abridging the right to vote on account of the race of the voter.

b. In *Terry v. Adams*, 345 U.S. 461 (1953), [§ 358] the Court found state action on the part of the Texas Jaybird Democratic Association when it excluded blacks from its pre-primary elections. *Terry* was a class action brought by black citizens challenging the actions of a self-governing voluntary political association which held its own primary elections which, in effect, determined who would run as candidates in the official primary election of the Texas Democratic Party. The Jaybird Democratic Association did not allow blacks to vote or run in their pre-primary elections. the rule seems to be that any party or association activity that feeds into a general election will be deemed state action.

2. **Company Town. [§ 359]**

**If a company town performs the traditional functions of a municipality, it will be treated as a state actor.**

In *Marsh v. Alabama*, 326 U.S. 501 (1946), Grace Marsh, a Jehovah's Witness, was distributing literature on the premises of a company-owned town contrary to the wishes of the town's management. She was asked to stop, she refused, and was arrested by a Deputy Sheriff who had been hired to serve as the town's policeman. She was convicted of trespass under a state statute making it a crime to remain on the premises of another after having been asked to leave. The Court found state action, reasoning that the town was the functional equivalent of a municipality, so the First Amendment would apply there as it would in any town.

3. **Privately–Owned Shopping Center. [§ 360]**

**No state action is involved when the owner of a privately-owned shopping center excludes speakers from the shopping center.**

In *Hudgens v. NLRB*, 424 U.S. 507 (1976), union members began to picket their employer's store in a shopping center, but left when told they would be arrested for trespassing. The picketers asserted a First Amendment right to picket in the shopping center which they claimed was the functional equivalent of a municipal shopping district. The Court found no state action when the owner of the privately-owned shopping center excluded

# STATE ACTION REQUIREMENT FOR CERTAIN PROTECTIONS

the picketers from the shopping center premises. The relatively limited nature of the place distinguishes this case from the company-town case of *Marsh v. Alabama* (previous case). However, a state may, by its constitution, give speakers access to privately-owned shopping centers. *Pruneyard Shopping Center v. Robins*, 447 U.S. 74 (1980).

4. **Peremptory Challenges to Jurors. [§ 361]**

   **The use of peremptory challenges, in a criminal or civil case, involves state action.**

   In *Edmonson v. Leesville Concrete Co.*, 500 U.S. 614 (1991), Edmonson sued Leesville Concrete in federal district court, alleging that Leesville's negligence had caused him personal injury. Leesville used two of its three peremptory challenges to exclude black jurors. Edmonson, who is black, asserted that the racial exclusion of jurors violated his equal protections rights under the Fifth Amendment Due Process Clause. The Court found state action on the basis of Leesville's attorney using peremptory challenges to exclude jurors because of their race. Selecting a jury is a quintessential, exclusive governmental function, and when the court confers on a private party the power to determine who gets on a jury, the private attorney's actions will be limited by the Constitution. The Court also said that state action was present because the state court, by enforcing the peremptory challenges, significantly involved itself in invidious racial discrimination.

5. **Public Defenders. [§ 362]**

   **Public defenders are not considered state actors, even though they are paid by the state.**

   In *Polk County v. Dodson*, 454 U.S. 312 (1981), Richard Dodson, who was convicted of robbery in state court, filed a 42 U.S.C. § 1983 claim against his public defender, alleging ineffective assistance of counsel. The Court found that there is no state action on the part of a public defender when he or she is acting in the adversarial role of appointed counsel.

6. **State–Granted Monopolies. [§ 363]**

   **A public utility, even if granted monopoly status by a state, is not a state actor.**

   In *Jackson v. Metropolitan Edison Co.*, 419 U.S. 345 (1974), Catherine Jackson filed a 42 U.S.C. § 1983 action against Metropolitan Edison, claiming violation of her due process rights. The Court found no state action when the heavily regulated electric company discontinued Jackson's service without providing her with notice, a hearing, and an opportunity to pay her bills. The Court said even if the company had been granted a monopoly by the state, that fact would not be dispositive of the state action issues. The Court ruled that supplying electricity was not traditionally the exclusive prerogative of the state, so no state action could be imputed to the electric company.

### 7. Statutory Warehouseman's Lien. [§ 364]

**No state action exists when a state authorizes an owner of a warehouse to sell the belongings of someone who did not pay his or her bill.**

*Flagg Bros., Inc. v. Brooks*, 436 U.S. 149 (1978). The Court found no state action when a state statute authorized the owner of a warehouse to sell the belongings of someone who had not paid her storage bill. Shirley Brooks sued under 42 U.S.C. § 1983, alleging an unconstitutional deprivation of property when the owner of a warehouse threatened to sell her property pursuant to the statutory authorization. The Court emphasized that the activity sought to be characterized as state action must be an exclusive governmental function, and that this self-help remedy was simply one means among many to resolve this kind of dispute.

## E. STATE–COURT INTERVENTION WHICH AIDS PRIVATE DISCRIMINATION. [§ 365]

**The Court has used this kind of state action analysis exclusively where a white homeowner breaches a restrictive covenant with other white homeowners not to sell a house to a black buyer.** In these cases, the Court has found state action whether the plaintiff seeks injunctive relief (enforcement of the restrictive covenant), or attempts to recover money damages from the breaching party.

### 1. State–Court Injunction. [§ 366]

The Court has found sufficient state action. In the case where the plaintiff seeks an injunction forcing the white seller to comply with the terms of the restrictive covenant, the white homeowner has sold his or her house to a black buyer, and the buyer will move in unless the state court enforces the restrictive covenant. In other words, the state-court injunction will directly cause the discrimination against the black buyer to take place. The Court has found state action in such a case.

*Shelley v. Kraemer*, 334 U.S. 1 (1948). The Court found state action when a state court issued an order enforcing a restrictive covenant in which

# STATE ACTION REQUIREMENT FOR CERTAIN PROTECTIONS

white homeowners agreed not to sell property to black buyers. State action was present by virtue of the state-court judge ordering the white seller to comply with the terms of the restrictive covenant; in effect, the decree of the state court directly prevented the black buyer from moving into the house.

2. **State–Court Award of Money Damages. [§ 367]**

In the second case, where the plaintiff seeks money damages from the white homeowner who breached the restrictive covenant, the Court found state action because a state-court award of money damages against the white seller would be tantamount to imposing a penalty against the white seller for refusing to discriminate on racial grounds in the sale of a house.

*Barrows v. Jackson*, 346 U.S. 249 (1953). The Court found state action in a state-court suit for monetary damages for breach of a racially restrictive covenant. While this suit would not have resulted in judicially enforced discrimination (as in *Shelley v. Kraemer*), the practical effect of an award of money damages would be that the state would be enforcing a penalty against a seller who chose not to discriminate against a buyer because of race.

## F. NO STATE ACTION WHEN INJURIES ARE INFLICTED BY PRIVATE PARTIES. [§ 368]

**A State's failure to protect an individual from violence by a private party does not constitute a violation of the Due Process Clause. The government has no obligation to protect a person from harm by another person.** There will be state action, however, if a person is injured while under the custody or control of the state.

*DeShaney v. Winnebago Dept. of Social Services*, 489 U.S. 189 (1989). The Court found no state action when a state social worker investigated allegations of child abuse, found some corroborating evidence, but left the little boy in his home where he was severely beaten by his father. The boy suffered brain damage and, as a result of the beatings, became profoundly retarded. The Court rejected the argument that the social worker's failure to act deprived the boy of due process. A state's failure to protect a person from private violence does not involve state action unless the state takes a person into custody and holds that person there involuntarily.

## G. A CORPORATION THAT IS CREATED AND CONTROLLED BY THE GOVERNMENT IS SUBJECT TO CONSTITUTIONAL RESTRICTIONS. [§ 369]

**A corporation is a government actor when it is created by a special congressional statute which establishes detailed goals for the corporation,**

# CHAPTER IX

sets forth is structure and powers, and gives the President the power to appoint a majority of its board of directors.

*Lebron v. National Railroad Passenger Corp.*, 513 U.S. 374 (1995). Lebron, a creator of billboard displays that comment on public issues, sued the National Railroad Passenger Corporation (Amtrak), claiming that Amtrak violated his First Amendment rights by rejecting a billboard display he designed because of the political nature of the billboard's message (criticizing the Coors beer company for supporting the Nicaraguan Contras and other right-wing causes). The Court held that Amtrak is a government actor, despite the fact that the congressional statute creating Amtrak provided that Amtrak was not an agency of the U.S. Government. The Court noted that Amtrak was created by a special authorizing statute, the statute set forth the structure and powers of Amtrak, and the President had the power to appoint a majority of Amtrak's board of directors.

## REVIEW PROBLEMS—STATE ACTION REQUIREMENT

**PROBLEM 1.** Pat Jones filed a civil lawsuit against Christine Smith, alleging that Christine engaged in gender discrimination by refusing to promote Pat because he is a man. During jury selection, the attorney for Christine uses all her peremptory challenges to exclude male jurors. Pat claims that the use of peremptory challenges to exclude male jurors violates the Fourteenth Amendment's prohibition against gender discrimination. Is there sufficient state action for Pat to have an equal protection argument?

**Answer:** Yes. The Court has ruled that picking a jury is an exclusive, traditional sovereign function, and that state action exists whenever an attorney, in a civil or criminal case, exercises peremptory challenges. See § 361.

**PROBLEM 2.** The Lizard Lounge, which is a bar owned by the Mayor of Id, has a liquor license issued by the State of Oz. The Mayor has instructed the doorkeepers (a politically correct term for bouncers) to admit to the bar only those persons who voted for the Mayor in the last election. Jane and Bob, vocal political opponents of the Mayor, are refused admission because they voted against him in the last election. They want to file a civil rights lawsuit against the Mayor, arguing that his policy violated their rights to free speech and political association. Do they have a case?

**Answer:** No. The mere granting of a liquor license does not turn the bar owner into a state actor. For Jane and Bob to have any chance of proceeding with their lawsuit, they would have to show a number of significant relationships between the government and the Lizard Lounge, such as a lease agreement, maintenance and protection by the city, and location

# STATE ACTION REQUIREMENT FOR CERTAIN PROTECTIONS

within a city-owned building. (See *Moose Lodge v. Irvis* § 349, and *Burton v. Wilmington Parking Authority* § 346.)

**PROBLEM 3.** The State of Oz, through its Racing Commission, grants franchises to operate off-track betting (OTB) establishments, where a person may go to place a bet on horse races occurring all over the state. Betty's Betting Parlor, which has a state-granted franchise, restricts access to U.S. citizens. Bob, a citizen of Canada, sues, claiming that Betty is violating his equal protection rights. Does Bob have a case?

**Answer:** Probably not. In *Jackson v. Metropolitan Edison Co.*, the Court said that even if a state had granted a monopoly to a utility company, that alone would not constitute state action. Presumably, the granting of a franchise by the state would not be state action either. See § 363 for further review.

# CHAPTER X

# CONGRESSIONAL ENFORCEMENT OF CIVIL RIGHTS

## A. INTRODUCTION TO CIVIL RIGHTS LEGISLATION. [§ 370]

**Following the Civil War, the Constitution was amended three times in an attempt to eliminate not only slavery as an institution, but also the vestiges of slavery (disabilities imposed because of a person's race or color).** The Civil War Amendments provide, in pertinent part:

**Thirteenth Amendment (1865):** Section 1. "Neither slavery nor involuntary servitude . . . shall exist within the United States. . . . "

Section 2. "Congress shall have power to enforce this article by appropriate legislation." (Note: There is no state action requirement in the Thirteenth Amendment.)

**Fourteenth Amendment (1868):** Section 1. ". . . No State shall have or enforce any law which shall abridge the privileges or immunities of citizens of the United States; nor shall any State deprive any person of life, liberty, or property, without due process of law; nor deny to any person within its jurisdiction the equal protection of the laws."

Section 5. "The Congress shall have power to enforce, by appropriate legislation, the provisions of this article."

**Fifteenth Amendment (1870):** Section 1. "The right of citizens of the United States to vote shall not be denied or abridged by the United States or by any state on account of race, color, or previous condition of servitude."

Section 2. "The Congress shall have power to enforce this article by appropriate legislation."

1. **Guarantee of Individual Rights. [§ 371]**

    The first section of each of the Civil War Amendments provides a guarantee that states (and under the Thirteenth Amendment, private parties

# CHAPTER X

as well) will not abridge the individual rights of persons covered by the Amendments. In other words, each amendment creates a right that is assertable against a state (or private party with the Thirteenth Amendment) if the state abridges the specific activity protected by the amendments. An individual may use section 1 of any of these amendments as the basis of a constitutional claim against a state.

2. **Congressional Enforcement of Rights Guaranteed by the Civil War Amendments. [§ 372]**

   The enabling clauses of the Civil War Amendments (section 2 of the Thirteenth and Fifteenth Amendments, and section 5 of the Fourteenth Amendment) give Congress the power to pass laws effectuating the guarantees of these amendments. Under the enabling clauses, Congress is able to pass legislation which directly limits the ability of states to engage in activity which might abridge the rights protected under the amendments. In other words, Congress may create statutory causes of action against states that violate the rights protected by the amendments. Congress has passed various statutes under these enabling clauses. The most important are:

   —42 U.S.C. § 1981 (1866) "Equal rights under the law. All persons . . . shall have the same right in every State . . . to make and enforce contracts, to sue, be parties, give evidence, and to the full equal benefit of all laws and proceedings for the security of persons and property as is enjoyed by white citizens. . . . "

   —42 U.S.C. § 1982 (1866) "Property rights of citizens. All citizens of the United States shall have the same right, in every State . . . , as is enjoyed by white citizens thereof to inherit, purchase, lease, sell, hold and convey real or personal property."

   —42 U.S.C. § 1983 (1871) "Civil action for deprivation of rights. Every person who, under color [of state law], subjects . . . any citizen of the United States or other persons within the jurisdiction thereof to the deprivation of any rights, privileges or immunities secured by the Constitution and laws, shall be liable to the person injured in an action of law, suit in equity or other proper proceeding. . . . "

   —42 U.S.C. § 1985 (1871) "Conspiracy to interfere with civil rights. . . . If two or more persons in any State . . . conspire . . . for the purpose of depriving, either directly or indirectly, any person or class of persons of the equal protection of the laws, or of equal privileges and immunities under the laws; . . . the party so injured or deprived may have an action for the recovery of damages, . . . against any one or more of the conspirators."

# CONGRESSIONAL ENFORCEMENT OF CIVIL RIGHTS

## B. CONGRESSIONAL IMPLEMENTATION OF THE CIVIL WAR AMENDMENTS. [§ 373]

When Congress enacts legislation under an enabling clause of one of the Civil War Amendments, it is protecting the substantive rights guaranteed by the specific amendment. For example, if Congress, acting under the enabling clause of the Thirteenth Amendment, prohibits private schools from excluding students based on their race, it is necessarily saying that such racial exclusion is a badge or incident of slavery which Congress may prohibit under its constitutional power to enforce the guarantees of the Thirteenth Amendment. The Court has given Congress great leeway to legislate under the enabling clauses of the Civil War Amendments. For instance, the Court has ruled that Congress, acting under section 5 of the Fourteenth Amendment, may prohibit literacy tests as a prerequisite for voting, even though the Court has never ruled that literacy tests are unconstitutional under section 1 of the Fourteenth Amendment. In this chapter, we deal with congressional interpretation of the guarantees of the Civil War Amendments. In subsequent chapters, we deal with the Court's interpretation of the substantive guarantees of those amendments.

1. **Congressional Regulation of Private Actions Under the Thirteenth Amendment. [§ 374]**

    **The Thirteenth Amendment does not require state action; all slavery is prohibited, whether engaged in by private or governmental entities.**

    a. **Congress May Prohibit Private Racial Discrimination in the Sale or Lease of Property. [§ 375]**

        **Refusal to sell or lease property based on race is a badge of slavery, and is actionable under 42 U.S.C. § 1982.**

        *Jones v. Alfred H. Mayer Co.*, 392 U.S. 409 (1968). The Court upheld the constitutionality of 42 U.S.C. § 1982. A black couple was not allowed to purchase a home because of their race. All the defendants were private parties, and no state action was involved. The Court relied on the Thirteenth Amendment as the basis for § 1982's prohibition of racial discrimination in private actions regarding the sale of property. The Court held that refusal to sell or lease property based on someone's race is a badge or incident of slavery under the Thirteenth Amendment and, as such, is an activity that Congress has the authority to prevent.

    b. **Congress May Prohibit Private Racial Discrimination in Contractual Relationships. [§ 376]**

        **Racial discrimination in private contracts is actionable under 42 U.S.C. § 1981.**

*Runyon v. McCrary*, 427 U.S. 160 (1976). The Court ruled that 42 U.S.C. § 1981 prohibits private, commercially operated, non-sectarian schools from excluding qualified children solely because of their race. The statute prohibits racial discrimination in the making and enforcement of private contracts, including the general offer by the school to attract qualified students. The Court said it was not considering the question of a religious school practicing racial discrimination for religious reasons; this was simply a private contractual situation.

c. **Congress May Prohibit Private Racial Discrimination in Commercial Relationships. [§ 377]**

**Racial discrimination by private employers is actionable under 42 U.S.C. § 1981.**

*McDonald v. Santa Fe Trial Transportation Co.*, 427 U.S. 273 (1976). The Court ruled that 42 U.S.C. § 1981 prohibits private employers from discriminating on the basis of race. Two white employees who were fired for theft sued on the basis that a black employee who had done the same thing was not fired. The Court ruled that whites, as well as blacks, have a cause of action under § 1981.

d. **Congress May Prohibit Private Racially–Motivated Conspiracies Depriving Someone of Civil Rights. [§ 378]**

**Private Race-based Conspiracies to Deprive Someone of Civil Rights are Actionable under 42 U.S.C. § 1985.**

In *Griffin v. Breckenridge*, 403 U.S. 88 (1971), the white defendants, acting under a mistaken belief that the black plaintiffs were workers for a civil rights organization, stopped the plaintiffs' car on a public highway in Mississippi and assaulted them. The Court ruled that 42 U.S.C. § 1985 provides a cause of action for private conspiracies to deprive a person of the right to interstate travel, so long as the plaintiff can show some racial or class-based motivation for the interference with the right. The Court based its ruling on both the Thirteenth Amendment and Congress' power to protect the exercise of the right to interstate travel, which is guaranteed against both private and governmental intrusion.

e. **Congress May Not Regulate Absent Racial Motivation. [§ 379]**

**Private conspiracies must be racially motivated to be actionable under 42 U.S.C. § 1985.**

# CONGRESSIONAL ENFORCEMENT OF CIVIL RIGHTS

In *United Brotherhood of Carpenters v. Scott*, 463 U.S. 825 (1983), a group of men protesting a construction company's practice of hiring nonunion workers assaulted two of the company's employees and destroyed some construction equipment. The group consisted of several truckloads of local union members who were part of a protest meeting two days prior to the assault, and who had planned the assault on the nonunion workers. The Court ruled that 42 U.S.C. § 1985 does not protect against a private conspiracy to infringe free speech rights, as long as there was no racial motivation for the conspiracy. The Court distinguished *Griffin* (previous case) as a case involving Thirteenth Amendment rights, plus the right to travel—neither requiring state action for abridgement to occur. First Amendment rights, on the other hand, are only protected from state action.

2. **Congressional Enforcement of the Fourteenth Amendment. [§ 380]**

   **Under section 1 of the Fourteenth Amendment, a state may not deprive a person of equal protection of the laws, or of life, liberty, or property without due process of law. Section 1 of the amendment does not apply to the actions of private parties.** Accordingly, Congress may regulate only state action when it legislates under section 5 of the Fourteenth Amendment.

   a. **Generally, Congress May Only Prohibit State Deprivations of Individual Rights. [§ 381]**

      **When legislating under section 5 of the Fourteenth Amendment, Congress is limited to remedying state action.**

      *Civil Rights Cases*, 109 U.S. 3 (1883). The Court ruled that § 5 of the Fourteenth Amendment did not give Congress the power to pass the Civil Rights Act of 1875, which prohibited racial discrimination in places of public accommodation. The Court held that the Fourteenth Amendment deals only with state action; invasion of individual rights by private persons is not within the scope of the amendment, and therefore Congress may not reach such activity under § 5.

   b. **Congress May Prohibit Deprivations of Civil Rights Engaged in Jointly by Private and State Actors. [§ 382]**

      **Joint action by private and governmental actors meets the state action requirement of the Fourteenth Amendment.**

      *U.S. v. Price*, 383 U.S. 787 (1966). Under 18 U.S.C. §§ 241 and 242, it is a crime to conspire to deprive a person of his or her civil rights. In *Price*, several indictments alleged that three police officers and

# CHAPTER X

fifteen private citizens murdered three civil rights workers, thereby depriving them of their due process rights. The Court ruled that indictments could be brought against the private parties because a private person is deemed to be "acting under color of state law" for purposes of civil rights statutes if he or she is jointly engaged with state officials in the prohibited activity.

c. **Congress May Criminalize a Private Conspiracy to Deprive a Person of the Right to Interstate Travel. [§ 383]**

**The right to interstate travel is a fundamental right of national citizenship which Congress may protect from even private interference.**

In *U.S. v. Guest*, 383 U.S. 745 (1966), the defendants were indicted under a federal civil rights law (42 U.S.C. § 241) for conspiring to interfere with a black citizen's right to travel freely to and from the State of Georgia. The Court held that the indictment was proper, because the right to interstate travel is fundamental, and Congress may criminalize even private conspiracies engaged in with the specific intent to deprive a person of that right. For a discussion of the constitutional basis for the right to interstate travel, see *Saenz v. Roe*, § 513, *supra*.

d. **Congress May Prohibit Literacy Tests for Voting. [§ 384]**

**A person may not be denied the right to vote because of an inability to read or write the English language.**

*Katzenbach v. Morgan*, 384 U.S. 641 (1966). The Court upheld a provision of the Voting Rights Act of 1965 which provided that no person who has completed the sixth grade in a Puerto Rican school in which instruction was in a language other than English shall be denied the ability to vote in any election because of an inability to read or write English. The federal law nullified New York literacy tests for voting. The Court held that Congress, acting under § 5 of the Fourteenth Amendment, may prohibit literacy tests as a prerequisite for voting, even though the Court has not ruled them to be unconstitutional.

e. **Congress Does Not Have the Power to Set the Voting Age in State and Local Elections. [§ 385]**

**States have the power to set the qualifications for voters in state, county, and municipal elections.**

*Oregon v. Mitchell*, 400 U.S. 112 (1970). Seven Justices, in a fragmented set of opinions, cut back on the *Morgan* (previous case) dictum that Congress has unlimited power to define substantive equal protection guarantees. The Justices invalidated a section of the 1970 amendments to the Voting Right Act which lowered the minimum voting age in state and local elections from 21 to 18 years of age. (The decision resulted in the passage of the Twenty–Sixth Amendment in 1971, accomplishing that result.) *Morgan* was distinguished as being limited to cases involving congressional protection of racial or ethnic minorities. In *Mitchell*, the Justices focused on the importance, from a state's rights perspective, of a state being able to determine the qualifications of its own voters for state, county, and municipal offices.

f. **Congress Does Not Have the Power Under § 5 of the Fourteenth Amendment to Define Substantive Rights. [§ 386]**

**Congress can only remedy violation of rights defined by the Court; it may not create substantive rights.**

In *Boerne v. Flores*, 521 U.S. 507 (1997), the Court by a 6–3 vote, held that the Religious Freedom Restoration Act (RFRA) exceeded Congress' enforcement power under § 5 of the Fourteenth Amendment. In *Boerne*, the Catholic Archbishop of San Antonio applied for a building permit to enlarge a church. The local zoning authorities denied the permit on the basis of a historic preservation ordinance which the zoning authorities said applied to the church. The Archbishop challenged the zoning ordinance, relying in part on RFRA, which would require the city to show a compelling reason for the permit denial and that it had chosen the least restrictive means to achieve the purposes of the historic preservation ordinance. RFRA applied to any branch of federal or state government, to all federal or state officials, and to all federal or state laws. § 5 of the Fourteenth Amendment gives Congress the power to enforce the equal protection and due process guarantee of the Fourteenth Amendment. The Court said that Congress does not have the power to define substantive rights under the Fourteenth Amendment; it only has the power to remedy violations of rights that have been defined by the Court under its power to interpret the Constitution. For Congress to define (not simply protect) substantive rights would violate separation-of-powers principles. The Court also said that RFRA, by defining substantive rights enforceable against states, violates the states' traditional prerogatives to regulate for the health and safety of its citizens.

In *Kimel v. Florida Board of Regents*, 528 U.S. 62 (2000), the Court held that, although Congress unequivocally expressed its intent to

# CHAPTER X

abrogate states' Eleventh Amendment immunity from suits under the Age Discrimination in Employment Act (ADEA), the attempted abrogation was unconstitutional as an attempt by Congress to decree the substance of the Equal Protection Clause's restrictions on states. As in *Boerne* (previous case), the Court said that it was the province of the judiciary to define the protections of the Fourteenth Amendment, and that the ADEA prohibited substantially more state employment decisions and practices than would likely be held unconstitutional under the applicable equal protection standard of rationality review.

3. **Congressional Enforcement of the Fifteenth Amendment. [§ 387]**

   **To enforce the Fifteenth Amendment's prohibition against discrimination in voting based on race, Congress passed the Voting Rights Act of 1965.** The Act is directed at forcing governmental entities (such as cities or counties) to comply with congressional mandates requiring fairness in the voting process; it does not provide a private cause of action for a person who might be aggrieved by some governmental action that abridged his or her right to vote, such as a state literacy test.

   a. **Congressional Prohibition of Literacy Tests for Voting is Constitutional. [§ 388]**

   **Congress may prohibit literacy tests as a means of eliminating racial discrimination in voting.**

   *South Carolina v. Katzenbach*, 383 U.S. 301 (1966). The Court upheld provisions of the Voting Rights Act of 1965 which prohibited states from using discriminatory literacy tests and other devices as a means of denying the right to vote on racial grounds. The main provision suspended the use of literacy tests (as a qualification for voting) for a period of five years from the last occurrence of substantial voting discrimination. This provision of the Act automatically applied to any state or political subdivision of a state which used a literacy test as a qualification for voting, and in which fewer than 50% of its voting-age residents were registered to vote on November 1, 1964. South Carolina challenged the act as exceeding congressional authority and encroaching on an area reserved to the states by the Constitution. The Court held that, even in light of the Tenth Amendment powers of the states, Congress may use any rational means to effectuate the prohibition of racial discrimination in voting as set forth in the Fifteenth Amendment.

## CONGRESSIONAL ENFORCEMENT OF CIVIL RIGHTS

b. **Use of Racial Criteria in Drawing Voting Districts Is Constitutional When Done to Comply With the Voting Rights Act. [§ 389]**

A state may create or maintain a black-majority voting district to comply with federal law.

*United Jewish Organizations v. Carey*, 430 U.S. 144 (1977). A majority of the Justices (seven Justices agreed in the judgment, but there was no majority opinion) upheld, against Fourteenth and Fifteenth Amendment challenges, provisions of a New York state legislative apportionment statute which used racial criteria to change the size of nonwhite majorities in some districts. To attain a 65% nonwhite majority in one district, a Hasidic Jewish community was split between two districts. A state may create or maintain black majorities in certain districts to ensure that its apportionment plan complies with the Voting Rights Act.

c. **Congress May Ban Electoral Changes That Have a Discriminatory Effect, Even if There Is No Intent to Discriminate. [§ 390]**

Congress' remedial power under § 2 of the Fifth Amendment is broad enough to allow it to prohibit even non-intentional racial discrimination that affects a person's right to vote.

*Rome v. U.S.*, 446 U.S. 156 (1980). The Court upheld the Attorney General's refusal, under § 5 of the Voting Rights Act, to approve certain electoral changes on the basis that the changes had a racially discriminatory effect. (The changes involved reducing the number of electoral wards in the city, changing the terms of government officials, and adopting ward-based residency requirements). The Court ruled that the Voting Rights Act ban on electoral changes with a discriminatory effect is constitutional, even if there is no showing that the governmental unit ever intended to discriminate. While § 1 of the Fifteenth Amendment prohibits only intentional discrimination in voting, Congress may, under § 2, prohibit any practice that has a nonintentional discriminatory effect.

d. **Application of Preclearance Requirements to a Covered County When Voting Changes Are Mandated by a State That Is Not Covered. [§ 391]**

The Voting Rights Act's preclearance requirements apply to measures mandated by a noncovered State to the extent that these measures will effect a voting change in a covered county.

# CHAPTER X

*Lopez v. Monterey County*, 525 U.S. 266 (1999). Section 5 of the Voting Rights Act (VRA) requires designated States and political subdivisions to obtain federal preclearance before changing their voting laws. Monterey County (a covered jurisdiction) changed its laws regarding the election of judges. The State of California (a noncovered jurisdiction) had passed laws requiring the very changes effected by Monterey County. The Court ruled that the VRA's preclearance requirements apply to any measures mandated by a covered jurisdiction, even if they were required by a noncovered jurisdiction such as a state. The Court also ruled that the VRA requirements, passed pursuant to the Fifteenth Amendment, did not interfere with a state's rights to structure its own voting system.

e. **Bailout Provision of the Voting Rights Act Applies to a Small Utility District With an Elected Board. [§ 391.1]**

   **All political subdivisions, including a utility district that does not register its own voters, are eligible to seek to bail out from the preclearance requirements of the Voting Rights Act.**

*Northwest Austin Municipal Utility District Number One v. Holder*, 129 S.Ct. 2504 (2009). The Court dealt with the issue of whether a small utility district is a "political subdivision" which is eligible under § 4(a) of the Voting Rights Act (VRA) to seek a bailout from the preclearance requirements of the VRA. The district has an elected board, and, because it is located in Texas, is required by § 5 of the VRA to seek preclearance whenever it makes any change regarding its elections. The District Court ruled that a § 4 (a) bailout is available only to counties, parishes, and subunits that register voters. The Court ruled that the VRA permits all political subdivisions, including the water district at issue in the case, to seek bailout from the preclearance requirements.

The Court invoked the rule that if a court can decide a case on statutory grounds, it will not reach the constitutional issue. However, in dicta, the Court opined that the VRA currently raises serious constitutional concerns because it intrudes on traditional areas of state and local responsibility, and differentiates between States in ways that may no longer be justified.

## REVIEW PROBLEMS—CONGRESSIONAL ENFORCEMENT OF CIVIL RIGHTS

**PROBLEM 1.** While driving down the street in the City of Id, Ben Jaines was stopped by two city police officers. The police asked Ben to get out of his car, and

## CONGRESSIONAL ENFORCEMENT OF CIVIL RIGHTS

when Ben refused, the officers pulled him from the vehicle. While making racial slurs (Ben was not of the same race as the officers), the officers began to hit and kick Ben. Two young men came by, and, while not actually participating in the beating of Ben, stood by threateningly, and prevented Ben from escaping. The police officers and the two young men were indicted under federal laws making it a crime to conspire to deprive a person of his or her Fourteenth Amendment rights. Are the indictments of the two young men valid?

**Answer:** Yes. If private parties are engaged in a joint endeavor with government officials to deprive someone of his or her civil rights, indictments may be brought against the private individuals. See § 378 for further review.

**PROBLEM 2.** The Court has ruled that, as a general matter, literacy tests for voting do not violate the Fourteenth Amendment. May Congress, acting under its enforcement power from § 5 of the Fourteenth Amendment, prohibit literacy tests as a prerequisite to voting in state elections?

**Answer:** Yes. Congress may, under its § 5 enforcement power, go beyond what the Court rules in terms of protecting individual rights. When a person sues under § 1 of the Fourteenth Amendment, he or she is arguing that his or her individual rights have been violated. When Congress acts under § 5, it is trying to remediate institutional problems by imposing requirements on entire political subdivisions. See § 384 for further review.

**PROBLEM 3.** May Congress pass a law prohibiting racial discrimination in the sale or lease of real property? Discuss.

**Answer:** Yes. Racial discrimination in the sale or lease of real property falls under the Thirteenth Amendment's prohibition of slavery. A refusal to sell or lease property is a badge or incident of slavery, and Congress may prohibit such activity under its enforcement power flowing from § 2 of the Thirteenth Amendment. Remember that there is no state action requirement under the Thirteenth Amendment; slavery is prohibited, whether engaged in by private or governmental actors. See § 370 for further review.

# CHAPTER XI

# RETROACTIVE LEGISLATION

## A. CONSTITUTIONAL STATUS OF LAWS THAT OPERATE RETROACTIVELY. [§ 392]

**The Constitution has a number of provisions that prohibit the state and federal governments from passing laws that retroactively impair substantive rights.** Fundamental fairness prohibits a government from imposing a civil or criminal penalty on someone who engaged in conduct which was not criminal or otherwise objectionable at the time it occurred. Retroactive laws also create notice problems; a person is entitled to know that certain activity is punishable before he or she has engaged in it. The three specific kinds of retroactive legislation studied in Constitutional Law classes are ex post facto laws, bills of attainder, and laws which impair the obligations of contracts.

## B. DUE PROCESS CLAUSE. [§ 393]

**The Due Process Clauses impose limitations on a court's ability to retroactively change the criminal law in such a way as to harm a defendant.** The Ex Post Facto Clauses apply only to legislative acts; they do not apply to court rulings having retroactive effect. If a court retroactively construes a criminal statute or a common law doctrine to the detriment of a defendant, the Due Process Clause may be the defendant's only argument.

In *Rogers v. Tennessee*, 532 U.S. 451 (2001), the Court held that the Tennessee Supreme Court did not deny due process by retroactively applying to a criminal defendant the abolition of the common law rule that a criminal defendant cannot be convicted of murder unless his victim dies within a year and a day. The Court said that only judicial acts which are unexpected and indefensible in reference to law that existed prior to the conduct at issue would violate the Due Process Clause. The Court found that the abolition of the rule was not unexpected and indefensible because advances in medical science have rendered the rule obsolete, and it has been legislatively or judicially abolished in many jurisdictions.

# CHAPTER XI

## C. EX POST FACTO LAWS. [§ 394]

**An ex post facto law imposes criminal punishment for an act that was not a crime when it was done, or increases the punishment for a crime over and above the punishment prescribed at the time the crime was committed.** There are two Ex Post Facto provisions in the Constitution. Article 1, § 10 prohibits states from passing Ex Post Facto laws, and Article 1, § 9 prohibits the federal government from doing so. For a law to be an ex post facto law, it must operate to the detriment of the defendant; any retroactive changes in the criminal law which do not hurt the defendant do not fall within the definition of an ex post facto law. As a general rule, these provisions limit only the power of legislatures to adopt new statutes; they do not limit the power of a court to overrule precedent and apply that ruling retroactively.

1. Non–Violations. [§ 395]

   **The following laws do not violate the Ex Post Facto provisions of the Constitution.**

   a. **Sentencing of Habitual Offenders.**

      **Increased punishment for recidivists does not violate the prohibition against Ex Post Facto laws.**

      In *Gryger v. Burke*, 334 U.S. 728 (1948), the State of Pennsylvania imprisoned Francis Gryger for life as a habitual offender. One of the convictions on which his life sentence was based occurred before enactment of the Pennsylvania Habitual Criminal Act. The Court held that the Pennsylvania law did not violate the prohibition against Ex Post Facto laws because his sentence as a habitual offender is not to be viewed as additional punishment for earlier crimes; it is simply a stiffened penalty for the latest crime.

   b. **Deportation of Aliens.**

      **Deportation of aliens has been held not to constitute punishment for purposes of the Ex Post Facto Clause.**

      In *Harisiades v. Shaughnessy*, 342 U.S. 580 (1952), the Court dealt with the question of whether the United States constitutionally may deport legally resident aliens because of membership in the Communist Party which ended before enactment of the federal law under which the aliens were deported. The Court held that the Ex Post Facto provisions of the Constitution only apply to penal laws which increase criminal punishment for previously lawful conduct. Deportation is a civil procedure which does not fall within the reach of the Ex Post Facto Clause.

# RETROACTIVE LEGISLATION

c. **Reducing a Sentence. Reducing the penalty for a crime does not violate the Ex Post Facto Clause because it does not hurt the defendant.**

*Rooney v. North Dakota*, 196 U.S. 319 (1905). A legislature may retroactively reduce the penalty for a crime. This does not violate the Ex Post Facto law ban because the defendant is not hurt by the change in the law.

d. **Retroactive Lengthening of Parole Reconsideration Hearings.**

**A states's retroactive application of a rule that lengthens the time for an inmate's reconsideration for parole does not violate the Ex Post Facto Clause.**

In *Garner v. Jones*, 529 U.S. 244 (2000), the Court held that the Georgia parole board's retroactive application of an amendment that lengthened the time for an inmate's reconsideration for parole did not violate the Ex Post Facto Clause. The amended Georgia rule did not create a significant risk of prolonging an inmate's incarceration. The focus is to determine whether the procedural change increases the penalty by which a crime is punishable. If the rule, by its own terms, fails to show such a risk, then it is the inmate's burden to show that the rule's practical implementation and its retroactive application results in a longer period of incarceration than under the earlier rule.

e. **Involuntary Civil Commitment of Dangerously Mentally Ill Persons.**

**Involuntary commitment of a mentally ill person has been held not to constitute punishment for purposes of the Ex Post Facto Clause. Such a commitment after a person has already served a prison sentence for a crime does not violate the Ex Post Facto Clause because it is not imposing additional punishment for the crime.**

In *Kansas v. Hendricks*, 521 U.S. 346 (1997), the Court upheld Kansas' Sexually Violent Predator Act, which established procedures for the civil commitment of sexually violent offenders who suffer from a mental abnormality or personality disorder which makes the person likely to engage in the predatory acts of sexual violence. Leroy Hendricks, who was imprisoned for a sexual offense involving two 13–year-old boys and was diagnosed as a pedophile, was committed under the Act, after his release from prison. He argued that the Act was an Ex Post Facto law, since it retroactively increased the punishment for his crime. A 5–4 majority of the Court held that the Act did not establish criminal proceedings because its purpose was the protection of the public from harm, not punishment or deterrence, and was limited to persons who suffered from a volitional impairment rendering them dangerous beyond their control. Since restricting the freedom of the dangerously mentally ill is a legitimate nonpunitive governmental objective, and since the Act does not impose punishment, it does not violate the Ex Post Facto Clause.

In *Kansas v. Crane*, 534 U.S. 407 (2002), the Court ruled that *Hendricks* did not require a total or complete lack of control as a prerequisite to imposing civil commitment on a dangerous sexual offender. However, the Constitution does not permit such commitment under *Hendricks* without any lack-of-control determination. The Court reasoned that an absolutist approach is not feasible, and would risk barring the civil commitment of some highly dangerous individuals who suffer severe mental abnormalities.

In *Smith v. Doe*, 538 U.S. 84 (2003), the Court upheld Alaska's Sex Offender Registration Act (SORA) against the argument that it violated the Ex Post Facto Clause. SORA requires any sex offender or child kidnapper to register with the state. Some information is kept confidential, but much important information about the offender is published on the Internet. SORA's registration and notification requirements are retroactive. Plaintiffs in the case were convicted of aggravated sex offenses before SORA was passed, but were covered by its provisions. Following *Hendricks* (above), the Court ruled that, because SORA is nonpunitive, its retroactive application does not violate the Ex Post Facto Clause. The Court said that the determinative question is whether the state intended to establish civil proceedings. If the intent of the legislature was to impose punishment, the law is invalid under the Ex Post Facto Clause. If the intent was to enact a regulatory scheme that is civil and nonpunitive, the Court must ask whether the law is so punitive either in purpose or effect as to negate the state's intention to deem it civil.

f. **An act found to be civil cannot be deemed punitive for purposes of an "as applied" challenge to a law which allegedly violates the Ex Post Facto Clauses.**

In *Seling v. Young*, 531 U.S. 250 (2001), the Court heard an as-applied challenge to a Washington state statute authorizing the civil commitment of sexually violent predators. The statue, patterned after the one upheld by the Court in *Kansas v. Hendricks* (See § 395), had been held by the Washington Supreme Court to be civil. Young had been convicted of six rapes. One day before Young was to be released from prison, the State filed a petition to commit him as a sexually violent predator. Young asserted that the conditions under which he was confined made the Act punitive as applied to him, thus giving rise to an Ex Post Facto argument. The Court rejected his argument, holding that once an act is found to be civil, it cannot be deemed punitive as applied to any individual so as to give rise to an Ex Post Facto argument.

2. **Violations. [§ 396]**

The following laws violate the Ex Post Facto Clause.

a. **Reduction of "Good Time" a Prisoner May Earn.**

**Reducing the amount of "Good Time" a prisoner may earn violates the Ex Post Facto Clause because it adversely affects the prisoner's rights.**

*Weaver v. Graham*, 450 U.S. 24 (1981). A state law, passed after a prisoner was convicted and sentenced, which reduced the amount of good time deductible from his sentence, was invalid as an Ex Post Facto law because it lengthened the amount of time the prisoner would be incarcerated.

b. **Retroactive Cancellation of Early Release Credits.**

**Retroactively cancelling a prisoner's early release credits, regardless of the reason the credits were awarded, violates the Ex Post Facto Clause because it retroactively increases the prisoner's punishment.**

In *Lynce v. Mathis*, 519 U.S. 433 (1997), the Court held that the retroactive application of a state law to cancel early release credits awarded to inmates convicted of murder and attempted murder violated the Ex Post Facto Clause. The fact that the credits were awarded solely because of concerns of prison overcrowding, and not for good behavior, was irrelevant to the Ex Post Facto inquiry. The law clearly operated retroactively, and also resulted in increased punishment (the petitioner had already been released from prison, so the law resulted in his rearrest and reincarceration).

c. **Revising a Sentencing Statute.**

**Application of a revised sentencing statute to pre-revision crimes violates the Ex Post Facto Clause where the result is an increased sentence.**

*Miller v. Florida*, 482 U.S. 423 (1987). Application of a state's revised sentencing statute to a defendant for crimes committed before the statute's revisions became effective violated the Ex Post Facto Clause. At the time the defendant committed the crime, the original statute provided a range of 3½ to 4½ years as a sentence. After the crime was committed, the statute was changed to provide for 5½ to 7 years in prison.

    d.  **Reducing the Quantum of Evidence Needed to Convict.**

        **A state may not reduce the quantum of evidence needed to convict after the time of the commission of the offense.**

*Carmell v. Texas*, 529 U.S. 513 (2000). An amendment to a Texas statute authorized convictions of certain sexual offenses on a victim's testimony alone. Prior to this amendment, a victim's testimony plus other corroborating evidence was necessary for such a conviction. The State of Texas applied the amendment retroactively to Carmell, who was subsequently convicted. The Court held that such an amendment governed the sufficiency of evidence needed for meeting the burden of proof. Moreover, the law affects the quantum of evidence required to convict. The Court held that Texas's amendment, which altered the legal rules of evidence, and received less, or different, testimony than the law required at the time of the commission of the offense, violated the Ex Post Facto Clause.

    e.  **Reviving a Time–Barred Prosecution.**

        **A state may not pass a law which allows prosecution for an offense which was time-barred at the time of the law's enactment.**

*Stogner v. California*, 539 U.S. 607 (2003). In 1993, California enacted a new criminal statute of limitations permitting prosecution for sex-related child abuse where the prior limitations period has expired, if the prosecution is begun within one year of a victim's reporting the crime to the police. Stogner was indicted for sex-related child abuse allegedly committed between 1955 and 1973. At the time those crimes were committed, the statute of limitations was three years. The Court held that it violates the Ex Post Facto Clause for a law enacted after expiration of a previously applicable statute of limitations to be used to revive a time-barred prosecution.

## D.  BILLS OF ATTAINDER. [§ 397]

**A Bill of Attainder is a legislative act imposing punishment on an individual or an easily identifiable group of individuals without the benefit**

# RETROACTIVE LEGISLATION

**of a judicial trial.** A Bill of Attainder punishes on the basis of a past or unalterable trait, and is aimed at named individuals or a small class of individuals who engaged in some specific conduct. If the legislature defines the class of individuals based on their having engaged in specific conduct, the law will qualify as a Bill of Attainder. There are two Bill of Attainder clauses in the Constitution: Article 1, § 10 limits states, and Article 1, § 9 limits the federal government.

1. **Factors to Determine if a Law Is a Bill of Attainder. [§ 398]**

    The Court has identified three questions to ask in deciding whether a law is a bill of attainder. If you can answer these questions in the affirmative, the law will likely be held invalid as a bill of attainder.

    1. Does the law fall within the historical meaning of legislative punishment? The court has included within this definition imprisonment, banishment, the punitive confiscation of property, and the legislative prohibition of individuals or groups from employment or vocational opportunities;

    2. Can the law reasonably be said to further only punitive legislative purposes? The court looks at the nature and severity of the burden imposed to see if the law is directed to punishment, or to the accomplishment of some nonpunitive goals; and

    3. Does the legislative record reveal a legislative intent to punish? The Court looks to the legislative history, legislative record, and pattern of laws dealing with a specific subject to discern the motivation of the legislature in passing the law (did they intend to punish?). *Selective Service System v. Minnesota Public Interest Research Group*, 468 U.S. 841 (1984).

2. **Laws That Are Bills of Attainder. [§ 399]**

    a. **Forbidding Salary Payments.**

    **A federal law that forbade salary payments to named federal employees has been held to violate the prohibition against Bills of Attainder.**

    In *U.S. v. Lovett*, 328 U.S. 303 (1946), the Court reviewed a federal law which, motivated by a congressional intent to purge the federal government of subversive employees, prohibited salary payments to three named federal employees. The Court invalidated this law as a bill of attainder, reasoning that the law operated as a perpetual exclusion from government employment, which qualified as punishment under the Ex Post Facto Clause.

    b. **Exclusion of Communists From Union Positions.**

**Prohibiting communists from being union officers violates the prohibition against Bills of Attainder.**

*U.S. v. Brown*, 381 U.S. 437 (1965). The Court invalidated, as a bill of attainder, a federal law prohibiting anyone who had been a member of the Communist Party during the last five years from being a labor union officer. Under this law, a person would be punished based on past, unalterable characteristics.

3. **Laws That Do Not Constitute Bills of Attainder. [§ 400]**

    a. **Disposition of Presidential Papers.**

**A federal law taking custody of presidential materials does not constitute a Bill of Attainder.**

*Nixon v. Administrator of General Services*, 433 U.S. 425 (1977). The Court rejected a bill of attainder argument against a federal law which provided for the custody and disposition of the papers and materials of former President Nixon. The law was not a Bill of Attainder for two reasons: it did not inflict punishment on former President Nixon, and it was not aimed at him as an individual (although he was the only one affected by the law), but rather at him as a "legitimate class of one."

    b. **Denial of Education.**

**Denial of education grants for failure to register for the draft was held not to constitute a Bill of Attainder.**

*Selective Service System v. Minnesota Public Interest Research Group*, 468 U.S. 841 (1984). The Court rejected a Bill of Attainder argument against a federal law which denied federal higher education money to male students who had not registered for the draft. The law was not a Bill of Attainder for two reasons: denial of educational benefits was not punitive, and the law did not unalterably hurt male students because they could register late and still receive benefits.

## E. CONTRACTS CLAUSE. [§ 401]

**The Constitution prohibits a state from passing a law which impairs the obligations of existing contracts. The Contracts Clause has nothing to do**

**with a state passing a law which affects someone's ability to contract in the future.** The Contracts Clause, which is part of Article 1, § 10, only limits states; if the federal government passes a law impairing the obligations of a contract, an attack on the law would be based on the Due Process Clause of the Fifth Amendment. If the federal government passes a law impairing the obligations of an existing contract, rational basis scrutiny applies, and the plaintiff has the burden of showing either that there is no legitimate reason for the law, or that the government has chosen means that are not rationally related to achieving its goals.

1. **Contracts Clause Analysis. [§ 402]**

   Not all modifications of the obligations of existing contracts will violate the Contracts Clause. In Contracts Clause cases, the Court has balanced the constitutional prohibition of a state impairing the obligations of contracts against the exercise of the state's police power. In 1983, the Court summarized existing Contracts Clause law as follows: If a state passes a law which impairs the obligations of an existing contract, the Court uses a three-part test to determine the constitutionality of that law. The Court asks:

   a. Has The Law Substantially Impaired An Obligation Of An Existing Contract;

   b. Does The Government Have A Significant And Legitimate Reason For The Impairment; And

   c. Is The Law Based On Reasonable Conditions And Is It Appropriate To The Public Purpose Underlying The Law?

   *Energy Reserves Group v. Kansas Power & Light Co.*, 459 U.S. 400 (1983).

   **EXAMPLE:** For instance, assume that a state passes a no-fault divorce law, replacing its old law which required a showing of some statutorily-defined reason for granting a divorce (cruelty, abandonment, adultery). To determine whether the no-fault divorce law would survive a Contracts Clause challenge, apply the three-part test from *Energy Reserves Group*. First, ask whether the new no-fault divorce law substantially impairs an obligation of existing marriage contracts. The party challenging the law would argue that the basis on which marriage contracts could be terminated is an important part of the contracts, and the passage of a

# CHAPTER XI

no-fault divorce law substantially impairs that obligation. Second, discuss the state's reasons for switching to a no-fault divorce system. The state would argue that no-fault is a more civil, less destructive method of terminating marriages than requiring a husband or wife to get on the witness stand and testify about the shortcomings of his or her spouse. Third, discuss whether the change in the state's divorce law is appropriate to achieving the state's purpose. If the state's interest is avoiding the effects of spouses testifying against each other, along with the unpleasant consequences of such testimony, adoption of a no-fault system seems appropriate, and the law would be held constitutional.

2. **Application of Contracts Clause Analysis. [§ 403]**

   a. **Mortgage Moratorium Law. [§ 404]**

   **A state law imposing a temporary moratorium on mortgage foreclosures does not violate the Contracts Clause.**

   *Home Building & Loan Association v. Blaisdell*, 290 U.S. 398 (1934). The Court upheld, against a Contracts Clause challenge, a post-Depression mortgage moratorium law which postponed the exercise of the contractual right of banks to foreclose on home mortgages within the state. The underlying mortgage indebtedness was not affected by the law. Important factors were: the Depression created an emergency need for such a law; no special group was advantaged—society in general benefited; and the relief was appropriately tailored and limited to the duration of the emergency. While this case was decided prior to the codification of Contracts Clause law in *Energy Reserves Group* (see § 403), the Court looked at precisely the same factors. The state law in *Blaisdell* substantially impaired an obligation of existing mortgage contracts—when a bank could foreclose on home mortgages for non-payment. However, ameliorating the effects of the Depression was certainly a significant state interest. Finally, the temporary postponement of the banks' right to foreclose was an appropriate response to a broad-based societal problem. After considering these factors, the Court held that the Minnesota law did not violate the Contracts Clause.

   b. **Altering a State's Own Obligation. [§ 405]**

   **A state law altering the obligations of a contract to which the state is a party may violate the Contracts Clause.**

# RETROACTIVE LEGISLATION

*U.S. Trust v. New Jersey*, 431 U.S. 1 (1977). The Court invalidated a New Jersey statute which impaired the obligations of earlier contractual obligations of New York and New Jersey with Port Authority bondholders. New York and New Jersey had statutorily-based commitments to Port Authority bondholders not to use certain revenues for any railroad facility that was not self-supporting. The states passed statutes repealing the existing commitments to the bondholders, thereby enabling the Port Authority to use those revenues for previously prohibited purposes. The Court balanced the prohibitive language of the Contracts Clause against the collective police powers of the two states, but emphasized that complete deference to a legislature's decision to change contractual obligations was not appropriate when the state's self-interest may be advanced by the change in contract terms. The Court held that the New Jersey statute violated the Contracts Clause.

c. **Adding Obligations to a Contract. [§ 406]**

**A state law adding obligations to a contract is subject to contracts clause analysis.**

*Allied Structural Steel Co. v. Spannaus*, 438 U.S. 234 (1978). The Court invalidated a Minnesota law which imposed additional pension obligations on a company, over and above what it had agreed to in labor negotiations. The state law required the company to pay full pensions to employees who had worked ten years or more for the company, even though the labor-management agreement set varying, and usually longer, periods for company contribution to a pension plan. The Court focused on the severe impact on the company (clearly a substantial impairment of a contractual obligation), the company's reliance on the original plan, and the very narrow focus of the law (unlike the broad societal interest in *Blaisdell*, above). The fact that specific companies were singled out to bear the cost of protecting the economic interest of retiring workers led the Court to conclude that the means chosen by the state to deal with the problem of retirees having no pension benefits were not appropriately tailored to ameliorating any broad-based societal problem. As a result, the Minnesota law was held violative of the Contracts Clause.

d. **Limiting Prices. [§ 407]**

**A state law limiting price increases which a natural gas supplier could charge a public utility under a price-escalator clause of a pre-existing contract does not violate the Contracts Clause.**

In *Energy Reserves Group, Inc. v. Kansas Power & Light Co.*, 459 U.S. 400 (1983), the Court upheld a state law which prohibited the

# CHAPTER XI

price that a supplier of natural gas could charge to a public utility from rising to a level set by a previous contract between the supplier and the utility. The Court reasoned that the state had a substantial reason for the law: protecting consumers of natural gas from increases in the cost of natural gas caused by federal deregulation of the industry. The Court held that the state law did not violate the Contracts Clause.

**STUDY TIP:** Usually, a Contracts Clause challenge is raised when a state impairs the obligations of a contract between two private parties. Be careful about a state impairing the obligations of a contract between itself and a private party. The danger in such a case is that the state may be changing the terms of the contract to benefit itself rather than to address some broad-based societal problem. If a state changes the obligations of its own contract, the same three-part test applies, but a court will apply it more stringently to protect against a state advancing its own interests by trying to get out from under unfavorable contract obligations.

## REVIEW PROBLEMS—RETROACTIVE LEGISLATION

**PROBLEM 1.** Randy Rowdy was arrested on June 1, 1994, for violation of a state criminal law making it a misdemeanor to sell under 50 grams of cocaine. If convicted under this statute, Randy could get a prison term of two to five years. On August 30, 1994, the state legislature made the sale of over 25 grams of cocaine a felony, punishable by a prison term of fifteen to twenty-five years. After Randy's conviction for selling 40 grams of cocaine, the state trial judge applied the new felony sentencing guidelines, and gave Randy fifteen years in prison. Is the sentence constitutional?

**Answer:** No. It is in violation of the constitutional prohibition against ex post facto laws for a sentencing statute to be applied to a crime that was committed before the statute went into effect.

**PROBLEM 2.** Assume that the United States is involved in a very long, costly, and deadly war with the county of Freedonia. As a result, many people are protesting the war, some by joining radical, subversive groups whose purpose is to overthrow the U.S. government by force or violence. In response, Congress passes a law which prohibits any person who has ever been a member of a subversive group from joining the armed forces of the United States. This law also precludes these persons from ever being eligible for student loans which are available for ex-members of the

# RETROACTIVE LEGISLATION

military. Fred Frag had been a member of a subversive group, but saw the error of his ways and quit. He tries to enlist in the Air Force, but is refused because of his past membership in the subversive group. Does Fred have a bill of attainder argument?

**Answer:** Yes. This law is designed to punish someone for past, unalterable traits. To have the law upheld, Congress would have to show that the law furthers some nonpunitive purpose, and that Congress did not intend to punish former members of subversive groups. See §§ 397–399 for further review.

**PROBLEM 3.** The legislature of the State of Oz is concerned about the widespread use of automatic weapons in the state. To combat the problem, the State passes a law which prohibits the sale of certain weapons in the state. Gunther's Guns, a very successful gun shop, has a contract with Barb's Ballistics, Inc., to purchase three hundred automatic weapons over the next two years. Under the new state law, any future sales or purchases of automatic weapons would be illegal. Does Gunther have an argument that the Oz law violates his rights under the Contracts Clause?

**Answer:** Yes. A state has impaired the obligations of an existing contract, so Gunther does have an argument. This law substantially impairs the obligations of his contract by prohibiting any sale of these weapons. The question then is whether the state has a significant reason for the law (reducing crime) and whether the means are appropriately tailored to achieving that goal. Obviously, the state has a significant interest in reducing crime, so the analysis devolves to the appropriateness of the means chosen by the state. This law imposes a great burden on gun dealers who have existing contracts to purchase certain weapons, and might, on balance, violate the Contracts Clause. See §§ 401–407 for further review.

# CHAPTER XII

# THE TAKINGS CLAUSE

## A. INTRODUCTION. [§ 408]

The Fifth Amendment provides that the federal government may take private property for a public use only if just compensation is paid to the property owner. This protection against governmental appropriation of private property has been incorporated through the Due Process Clause of the Fourteenth Amendment to apply to the states.

1. **The Takings Clause Is Not an Independent Source of Legislative Power. [§ 409]**

    The Takings Clause is not an independent source of power. **It must be exercised in conjunction with some other enumerated power of Congress, or in conjunction with the Tenth Amendment police power if a state is taking property.** For instance, if Congress takes private property so that it may build a post office, that congressional action is based in part on Congress' postal power, coupled with its power under the Takings Clause.

2. **Key Concepts in Takings Clause Analysis. [§ 410]**

    a. **Eminent Domain.**

    Eminent domain is an inherent power of the federal government and of the states. **The power of eminent domain is the power of a government to force the owner of real or personal property to transfer that property to the government.**

    b. **Taking of Private Property.**

    In a classic "taking" case, the government expressly exercises its power of eminent domain and offers compensation for the property taken. The questions then arise whether the taking is for a "public use," and whether the compensation offer is fair.

    However, a plurality of the Court has asserted that the Takings Clause applies to all branches of government and that there may be actions

# CHAPTER XII

by courts that constitute an unconstitutional taking. In *Stop the Beach Renourishment v. Florida Department of Environmental Protection*, 130 S.Ct. 2592 (2010), the Court dealt with the question of whether the Florida Supreme Court took property without compensation in violation of the Takings Clause. Responding to the erosion of certain ocean beaches, Florida passed a law which added sand to the seabed in various locations and gave title to the new waterfront land to the state. A group of private landowners sued, claiming that the state took their property rights to exclusive access to the water, to have as unobstructed view of the water, and to have certain accretions to their beachfront property. The Florida Supreme Court ruled that, under state law, there was no unconstitutional taking of property. The court affirmed the ruling of the Florida Supreme Court. Four Justices (Scalia, Roberts, Thomas, and Alito) concluded that if a court declares that what was once an established right of private property no longer exists, it has taken that property in violation of the Takings Clause. The plurality opined that the Takings Clause is not confined to a specific branch of government, and that takings effected by the judicial branch are also susceptible to attack under the Takings Clause. Justice Kennedy and Sotomayor thought that any restrictions on a court's ability to alter property rights should come from the Due Process Clause rather than the Takings Clause.

**c. Public Use.**

Under the Takings Clause, private property may only be taken for a public use. **A public use is any use that advances a legitimate power of the government and accrues to the benefit of the general public.** The Court will virtually always accept the government's contention that a taking is for a public use.

In most Constitutional Law classes, two issues predominate in Takings Clause discussions: what is a "public use"; and when does a government regulation (which is not compensable) so severely diminish a property owner's use of the property that the regulation should be treated as a taking (which is compensable)?

## B. "PUBLIC USE" REQUIREMENT. [§ 411]

When a legislature exercises its power of eminent domain, it must be for a public use. In public use cases, the issue is not whether there has been a taking—there has. The issue is why the government condemned the property. **If a legislature says a taking is for a public use, a court will almost always agree, even if the condemned property is transferred to another private party.**

# THE TAKINGS CLAUSE

1. **Eliminating Urban Blight. [§ 412]**

   **Condemnation of private property in an effort to eliminate urban blight will be considered a public use.**

   *Berman v. Parker*, 348 U.S. 26 (1954). The Court found that a public use existed when Congress authorized a federal agency to condemn property in the Washington, D.C. area for the purpose of eliminating urban blight. (Most of the condemned property was substandard housing and rundown commercial establishments). The Court upheld the "public use" aspect of the taking even though the condemned property at issue, a department store, did not itself pose any problem of blight. The Court recognized that Congress' plan required the development of a large part of the Washington, D.C. area, rather than proceeding by a piecemeal approach. When a legislature declares that a taking is for a public use, the court's review role is extremely narrow; if the taking arguably advances the public use asserted by the legislature, the taking will meet the public use requirement.

2. **Dispersing Land Ownership. [§ 413]**

   **A transfer of private property from one party to another in an effort to reduce the concentration of land ownership will be considered a public use.**

   *Hawaii Housing Authority v. Midkiff*, 467 U.S. 229 (1984). The Court found a public use when Hawaii, in an effort to break up an extremely high concentration of land ownership, used the power of eminent domain to transfer land from a small group of wealthy private owners to their former tenants. The Court found that the State had a legitimate interest in reducing the perceived economic and social evils of concentrated land ownership.

3. **Transfer of Property From One Private Owner to Another. [§ 414]**

   **A condemnation may be for a public use even though the property is transferred from one private party to another.**

   *Kelo v. New London, Connecticut*, 545 U.S. 469 (2005). The Court held that the "public use" requirement is met if a local government, acting pursuant to an integrated development plan designed to revitalize its ailing economy, takes the property of private landowners and, in turn, conveys it to private developers. The city of New London, Connecticut enacted a development plan that was projected to create over 1,000 jobs, increase tax and other revenues, and revitalize an economically distressed city. Land purchased from willing owners and land acquired by eminent domain from unwilling owners would be transferred to, among others, the Pfizer Corporation, real estate developers, and commercial builders. The unwilling landowners claimed that such uses did not fall within the definition of a "public use" under the Fifth and Fourteenth Amendments. Relying heavily on *Berman* and *Midkiff* (preceding cases), the Court ruled, 5–4, that the disposition of this property was a "public use" under the Takings Clause. The Court said that a city could not take one person's property simply to convey a private benefit on another private party. The takings in this case, however, served the legitimate public purposes of creating new jobs and generating additional tax revenues. The Court rejected the argument that the condemned land had to be open for use by the general public (as residences or specific office buildings would not be), and adopted the interpretation hat the public use requirement is satisfied if the land will be used for a public purpose. The Court also reemphasized its policy of deference to legislative judgments as to what public needs justify the use of the Takings power. The dissenters argued that the taking of private property and transferring it to another private owner, so long as the property might be upgraded, effectively nullifies the "public use" requirement by obliterating any distinction between the public and private use of property.

## C. WHEN SHOULD A REGULATION BE TREATED AS A TAKING? [§ 415]

In a typical taking case, a government takes someone's property and offers compensation in return. The burden of the taking does not fall on the public in general, nor does the benefit of the compensation accrue to the general public. However, when a government imposes a regulation (such as a zoning law) applicable to all residents or activities within its jurisdiction, no compensation is paid to those regulated. There is no specific taking of property (just a limitation on the use of property in general), so no particularized offer of compensation is made. A problem arises when the general regulation so severely affects the use of someone's property or diminishes its value that the property owner claims the regulation is tantamount to a taking, and should be compensated.

1. **Physical Occupation or Invasion of Property Will Be Considered a Taking. [§ 416]**

    **A general regulation that effects a physical occupation or invasion of property will be considered a taking.**

    a. **Permanent Physical Occupation of Property Will Be a Taking. [§ 417]**

    **Government authorization to a private party to occupy someone else's property will be treated as a taking.**

# THE TAKINGS CLAUSE

*Loretto v. Teleprompter Manhattan CATV Corp.*, 458 U.S. 419 (1982). The Court found a taking when New York City authorized a cable TV company to permanently affix their cables to the walls and roofs of certain privately-owned apartment buildings. The Court emphasized that a permanent physical occupation of property has invariably been found to be a taking.

    b. **Physical Invasion of Property Will Be a Taking. [§ 418]**

    **Government action that effectively takes an easement of a private party's airspace will be treated as a taking.**

    *U.S. v. Causby*, 328 U.S. 256 (1946). The Court found a taking when army planes flew over Causby's chicken farm, making the chickens too nervous to lay eggs. The government had taken an easement of air space, for which it was required to pay compensation.

2. **Denial of All Economically Beneficial Use of the Property Constitutes a Taking. [§ 419]**

**Government action that deprives a property owner of all economically viable use of his or her property will be treated as a taking.**

    a. **Laws Requiring Coal to Be Left in Place. [§ 420]**

    A law prohibiting a coal company from mining coal on its property will be treated as a taking if the coal company is deprived of all economically viable use of its property.

    (1) **Pennsylvania Coal Co. v. Mahon, 260 U.S. 393 (1922). [§ 421]**

    The Court found a taking when a Pennsylvania statute prohibited coal-mining companies from mining coal on its land if the mining would cause a subsidence of the surface. The coal company had sold the surface rights, but had expressly reserved the right to remove all the coal under the surface. The statute effectively destroyed the mining rights reserved under the contract, and thereby effected a compensable taking. Compare with the next case.

    (2) **Keystone Bituminous Coal Association v. Debenedictis, 480 U.S. 470 (1987). [§ 422]**

    The Court found no taking in a challenge to Pennsylvania's Subsidence Act that prohibited mining of coal so as to cause subsidence of buildings. As applied, the law required 50% of coal under protected structures to be kept in place. Distinguishing this case from *Mahon*, above, the Court said that this Pennsylvania statute advanced important public interests (safety and water supplies), and did not deprive the coal company of all economically viable use of its land since the law affected less than 2% of its coal.

b. **Restrictions on Building Imposed by Landmarks Preservation Law. [§ 423]**

**Application of a Landmarks Preservation Law will not be treated as a taking if the law applies to many buildings and the owner still has an economically viable use for the property.**

*Penn Central Transportation Co. v. New York City*, 438 U.S. 104 (1978). The Court found no taking as a result of New York's Landmarks Preservation Law being applied to prevent construction of a skyscraper office building in the airspace above Grand Central Terminal. The law applied to a large number of buildings, was designed to benefit the public generally, and did not unduly impair the owner's economically viable use of the property.

c. **Zoning Ordinance Limiting Number of Houses on Parcel of Land. [§ 424]**

**No taking is effected by a zoning ordinance limiting the number of houses an owner can put on a parcel of land.**

*Agins v. City of Tiburon*, 447 U.S. 255 (1980). The Court found no taking by the application of a zoning ordinance which limited the number of houses which the owner could put on a parcel of property. This ordinance did not prevent all economically viable use of the land, and, on balance, it was justified by the city's interest in promoting orderly land development.

d. **Rent–Control and Limitations on Terminating a Tenancy. [§ 425]**

**No taking was effected by a combination of city laws which controlled rent and limited the grounds on which a mobile home owner could terminate a tenancy.**

*Yee v. City of Escondido*, 503 U.S. 519 (1992). The Court found no taking, rejecting the argument that the combination of two laws effected a physical occupation under *Loretto*, § 423 above. Escondido had two laws that regulated mobile home parks: one was a rent-control ordinance, the other a limitation on the grounds on which the owner of a mobile-home park could terminate a mobile home owner's tenancy. Facially, these ordinances did not result in any physical invasion of the park owner's property.

e. **State-Imposed Cap on Commercial Rents. [§ 426]**

**No regulatory taking exists when a state places a cap on commercial rents.**

*Lingle v. Chevron U.S.A. Inc.*, 544 U.S. 528 (2005). The Supreme Court rejected an oil company's claim that a Hawaii statute that placed a cap on the amount of rent it could charge dealers leasing its gas stations constituted a regulatory taking in violation of the Fifth Amendment to the U.S. Constitution. The oil company argued that if the statute did not "substantially advance" a legitimate state interest, then a taking had occurred because the statute caused the oil company to receive less rent revenue. The Court denied the oil company relief and held that whether a statute substantially advances a legitimate state interest is only relevant to due process claims not takings claims.

f. **Law Prohibiting Building Houses on Seashore Lots. [§ 427]**

**The Court has remanded a case in which a state law prohibiting building any occupiable dwelling on seashore lots was challenged as effectuating a taking.**

*Lucas v. South Carolina Coastal Council*, 505 U.S. 1003 (1992). The Court remanded to state court this case challenging a state law which barred building any occupiable dwellings on seashore lots. The law was applied to two lots which were zoned for single-family dwellings and purchased two years before the law went into effect. The Court held that a State could avoid paying compensation where a regulation deprives a landowner of all economically viable use of his land only if it could show that the landowner's proposed use could have been enjoined as a private or public nuisance. It then remanded for consideration of whether principles of nuisance and property law prohibited the landowner from using the land as he intended. On remand, the South Carolina Supreme Court held that the State could not prohibit the landowner from constructing habitable dwellings on his land, and that the landowner had suffered a compensable temporary taking during the period in which he was enjoined from doing so.

# CHAPTER XII

g. **Laws Requiring Destruction of Cedar Trees. [§ 428]**

**No taking was effected by a state law requiring the destruction of cedar trees located near apple orchards; the public benefited so greatly that no compensation was required.**

*Miller v. Schoene*, 276 U.S. 272 (1928). The Court found no taking by a state law requiring destruction of red cedar trees within a stated distance of apple orchards. On balance, the destruction of one class of property to save another was of such great value to the public as not to be a compensable taking.

3. **Conditions of the Granting of Building Permits. [§ 429]**

**The Court has ruled that a government imposing conditions on the granting of building permits effects a taking.**

a. **Granting an Easement as a Condition of Receiving a Building Permit. [§ 430]**

Requiring the granting of a public easement as a condition of granting a building permit is a taking.

*Nollan v. California Coastal Commission*, 483 U.S. 825 (1987). The Court found a taking when the Commission refused to issue a building permit for beachfront property unless the landowners granted a public easement across their property to the ocean. The permit condition severely diminished the landowners' use of their property, and did not substantially advance the government interest of enhancing the ability of the public to view the ocean.

b. **Unconstitutional Conditions Attached to the Granting of a Building Permit. [§ 431]**

**A government may not condition the granting of a building permit on the property owner's dedication of part of her property for public uses.**

*Dolan v. Tigard*, 512 U.S. 374 (1994). The Court found a taking when a local planning commission conditioned the approval of Dolan's application to expand her store and parking lot upon the dedication of a portion of her land for a public greenway to minimize possible flooding, and a pedestrian/bike path to relieve traffic congestion. Dolan's request for variances from the condition was denied. The Court relied on the doctrine of "unconstitutional conditions," under which a government may not extract private property in exchange for

# THE TAKINGS CLAUSE

a discretionary benefit that the government might confer. The Court found an "essential nexus" between each permit condition and the legitimate state interest stated in each condition by the commission. However, the inquiry then turned to whether the permit conditions bear "rough proportionality" to the projected impact of the proposed development (Dolan's expansion). The government must make some individualized determination that the land sought to be extracted is related in nature and in extent to the proposed development's impact. The commission failed to show that either condition was reasonably related to the public benefits that would purportedly flow from imposing those conditions on Dolan's application.

4. **Temporary Takings Are Compensable for the Period When Use of the Property Was Deprived. [§ 432]**

   **Temporary takings of property are compensable on the same theory as are permanent takings—the property owner is deprived of all economically viable use of the property, even though temporarily.**

   *First English Evangelical Lutheran Church v. County of Los Angeles*, 482 U.S. 304 (1987). The Court found a compensable temporary taking during the period when an interim flood-control ordinance deprived a church of all economically viable use of its property. The ordinance temporarily prohibited the reconstruction of church buildings that had been destroyed by a flood.

5. **A Temporary Moratorium on Land Development Does Not Effect a Per Se Taking of Property Requiring Compensation Under the Takings Clause. [§ 433]**

   **A temporary moratorium on land development imposed during regulatory agencies' process of formulating a comprehensive land use plan does not automatically effect a per se taking of property requiring compensation under the Takings Clause.**

   *Tahoe-Sierra Preservation Council Inc. v. Tahoe Regional Planning Agency*, 535 U.S. 302 (2002). The Tahoe Regional Planning Agency imposed two moratoria, totaling thirty-two months, on development in the Lake Tahoe Basin. While the moratoria were in effect, the Agency formulated a comprehensive land use plan for the area. The plaintiffs claimed that the moratoria temporarily deprived them of all economically viable use of their land, and was thus a compensable taking under *Lucas* (§ 427) and *First English Evangelical Church* (§ 432). The Court held that the moratoria were not per se takings of property which required compensation under the Takings Clause. The Court distinguished physical

# CHAPTER XII

takings that acquire property for public use, from regulatory takings that simply prohibit private uses. Per se rules (such as temporary takings are compensable under the Takings Clause) are appropriate for physical takings. However, per se rules are not appropriate in the area of regulatory takings. In those cases, ad hoc, factual inquiries are to used. The Court cited *Penn Central* (§ 423), which looked at a number of factors, such as the property owner's reasonable investment-backed expectations and the nature of the government action. The Court ruled that the duration of the moratoria is only one factor for a court to consider is appraising regulatory takings claims.

6. **Coal Companies Cannot Be Forced to Assume Retroactive Liability for Funding Health Care Benefits for Coal Industry Retirees and Their Families. [§ 434]**

**The Court invalidated a federal law which imposed liability on coal companies, some of whom were no longer in business, for retirement benefits for former employees of the coal industry.** A four-person plurality ruled that this law violated the Takings Clause, and one Justice said that the law violated the Fifth Amendment Due Process Clause.

*Eastern Enterprises v. Apfel*, 524 U.S. 498 (1998). The Court reviewed a 1992 federal law which assessed premiums against any coal company that had signed any national collective bargaining agreement between the years of 1947 and 1978. The Commissioner of Social Security would then use statutorily prescribed formulas to assign retirees to each of the coal companies. The law was challenged by a coal company that left the coal industry in 1965, but was responsible for over 1,000 miners under the law. A plurality ruled that the liability imposed by the law constituted a taking under the Takings Clause. A fifth Justice (Kennedy) said that this kind of retroactive law violated principles of substantive due process.

## D. "JUST COMPENSATION" EQUALS FAIR MARKET VALUE AT THE TIME OF THE TAKING. [§ 435]

**The general rule is that a government must pay the property owner the fair market value of the property at the time of the taking.** The Court, taking a very pragmatic view of this concept, has focused on what a willing buyer would pay in cash to a willing seller. This issue rarely comes up in law school discussions, but is very important in real-world cases involving takings of property.

# THE TAKINGS CLAUSE

## E. INTEREST EARNED ON CLIENT FUNDS HELD BY AN ATTORNEY IN A TRUST ACCOUNT. [§ 436]

**The interest earned by client funds deposited by attorneys in bank accounts is the private property of the client for purposes of the Takings Clause.**

*Phillips v. Washington Legal Foundation*, 524 U.S. 156 (1998). The Court dealt with a Texas program under which small amounts of client money held by an attorney had to be deposited in bank accounts. The interest earned on these accounts would then be paid to legal foundations that provided legal services for low-income people. The Court ruled that the interest was the private property of the clients for purposes of the Fifth Amendment's Takings Clause.

## REVIEW PROBLEMS—THE TAKINGS CLAUSE

**PROBLEM 1.** The City of Id wanted to develop its waterfront area. The Planning Commission approved a plan for a private developer to build a marina, as well as a very large shopping mall on the waterfront. To accomplish this goal, the City had to acquire property on and near the waterfront. Exercising its power of eminent domain, the City condemned three entire blocks of residences, then sold the land to a private development company. Joe Jones, one of the former homeowners, brought suit to block the sale. He claims that transferring property from one private owner to another is not taking land "for a public use." Will Joe win on this argument?

**Answer:** No. Courts consistently hold that if a legislature says a taking is in the public interest, the taking will be for a public use. This includes taking property from one private owner and transferring it to another. See §§ 411–414 for further review.

**PROBLEM 2.** Edna Eggers owned some beautiful beachfront property which she wanted to develop. She applied to the City Planning Commission for a building permit, and was told that she could have the permit only if she would allow part of her property to be used as a walkway to allow the public to have access to the beach. Edna sues, challenging the condition on the granting of the building permit. Will she win?

**Answer:** Yes. The government may not condition the granting of a permit on a landowner's giving up private property. If the government wants a walkway, it must use its power of eminent domain, and pay Edna the fair market value of the land it has taken. See §§ 429–431 for further review.

# CHAPTER XII

**PROBLEM 3.** Over the course of a few months, there were a number of sightings of strange objects in the sky over the City of Id. Many people were convinced that UFOs were visiting the city. One night, one of the objects crashed in an area on the outskirts of town. The City of Id and the State of Oz began investigations. As part of their investigations, the City of Id passed an emergency ordinance prohibiting all activity, including building, on the suspected crash site. Beulah Bodine owned the property, and was about to start construction of a major amusement park. Beulah was not able to use her property for the nine months it took to complete the investigations. At that point, the City repealed its ordinance, and Beulah began building. Beulah sues to recover compensation for the time period when she could not use her property. Does she have a case?

**Answer:** Yes. Temporary takings are compensable as long as they meet the requirement of depriving the owner of all economically viable use of the land for a certain period of time. See § 432 for further review.

# Chapter XIII

# PROCEDURAL DUE PROCESS

## A. INTRODUCTION. [§ 437]

The Fifth Amendment prohibits the federal government from depriving a person of life, liberty, or property without due process of law. The Fourteenth Amendment imposes the same limitation on states. **The due process clauses are intended to ensure that a government uses a fair procedure when it singles out an individual for a deprivation of life, liberty, or property.** Procedural due process analysis deals with the **manner** in which a government acts; its purpose is to prevent the government from arbitrarily depriving a person of life, liberty, or property.

1. **Main Requirements of a Procedural Due Process Analysis. [§ 438]**

    **The three main requirements of procedural due process are an impartial decisionmaker, notice, and a hearing.** Decisionmakers must not have prejudged an issue before them, or have a monetary interest in the outcome of a case. Notice must be reasonably calculated, under all the circumstances, to apprise parties of the nature of the charge or action against them. Depending on the importance of the interest being affected and the competing government interests, a person's right to respond may take the form of either a pre-deprivation or post-deprivation hearing. Consider these factors as you go through the cases in this section.

    *Caperton v. A.T. Massey Coal Co., Inc.,* 129 S.Ct. 2252 (2009). The Court ruled that the Due Process Clause required recusal of a State Supreme Court Justice due to the risk of actual bias resulting from extraordinary campaign contributions received by the justice. The Supreme Court of Appeals of West Virginia reversed a trial court judgment of fifty million dollars against a coal company and its affiliates. The vote to reverse was 3–2. One of the justices voting to reverse had received a large campaign contribution from the board chairman and principal officer of the corporation found liable for the damages. It was this justice who denied a motion to recuse himself. The Court ruled that there are objective standards that require recusal when the probability of actual bias on the

# CHAPTER XIII

part of the judge or decisionmaker is too high to be constitutionally tolerable. The Court found that, in all the circumstances of this case, due process requires recusal. The Court said that the objective standards implementing the Due Process Clause do not require proof of actual bias, but, rather, the question is whether, under a realistic appraisal of psychological tendencies and human weakness, the judge's interest in the case poses such a risk of actual bias or prejudgment that the practice must be forbidden if due process guarantees are to be met.

    2.   **Three–Prong Balancing Analysis. [§ 439]**

Once you have identified the liberty or property interest that has been allegedly abridged, you must determine how much procedural protection is required. To answer that question, the Court looks at the following three factors:

    a.   The private interest affected by the government action;

    b.   The risk of erroneous deprivation of that interest through the procedure presently in place; and

    c.   The government interest, including the added fiscal and administrative burdens that the new procedure would entail. *Mathews v. Eldridge*, 424 U.S. 319 (1976).

## B. GOVERNMENT ACTION REQUIREMENT. [§ 440]

**Procedural due process guarantees apply only to government action.** There is no procedural due process issue if a private person or institution is depriving someone of liberty or property. For a discussion of how to make a "state action" argument, see Chapter IX.

## C. INTENTIONAL DEPRIVATION. [§ 441]

**Procedural due process analysis applies only to an intentional deprivation of liberty or property.** A negligent deprivation of liberty or property does not give rise to a procedural due process argument.

*Daniels v. Williams*, 474 U.S. 327 (1986). The Court rejected a 42 U.S.C. § 1983 action by an inmate who sued a jail officer for injuries suffered when the inmate slipped and fell on a pillow negligently left on a stairway by the jail officer. The Due Process Clause is not implicated by a state official's negligent act causing unintended loss of or injury to life, liberty, or property.

## D. DEPRIVATION OF LIBERTY OR PROPERTY. [§ 442]

For procedural due process analysis to apply, a government must be intentionally depriving a person of a liberty or property interest which is

# PROCEDURAL DUE PROCESS

**cognizable by a court.** If the interest is not a judicially recognized liberty or property interest, no procedural due process argument is available.

1. **Liberty Interests. [§ 443]**

   Procedural due process protects individuals when they are arrested or incarcerated. (Those issues are outside the scope of this outline.) **Procedural due process also applies in a number of civil contexts where freedom of movement or the exercise of a fundamental right is curtailed.**

   a. **Commitment to Mental Institutions. [§ 444]**

   **Involuntary commitment to a mental institution involves a cognizable liberty interest.**

   (1) **Adults.**

   Although the Court has not been specific about which procedures are required, an adult must be given fair due process protection prior to involuntary commitment to a mental institution, including a pre-commitment adversary hearing, *O'Connor v. Donaldson*, 422 U.S. 563 (1975).

   The standard of proof for involuntary civil commitment of an adult is clear and convincing evidence that the person meets the statutory commitment requirements. *Addington v. Texas*, 441 U.S. 418 (1979). [§ 448]

   (2) **Children.**

   No pre-commitment adversary hearing is required when a parent or the state commits a child to a mental institution against his or her will. However, a child is entitled to a finding by a "neutral fact-finder" that the commitment meets all statutory requirements. *Parham v. J.R.*, 442 U.S. 584 (1979).

   (3) **Inmates.**

   An inmate has a liberty interest in not being transferred from prison to a mental institution for treatment. The Court ruled that an inmate is entitled to notice, a hearing, and appointment of counsel before such a transfer. *Vitek v. Jones*, 436 U.S. 407 or 445 U.S. 480 (1980).

   *Wilkinson v. Austin*, 545 U.S. 209 (2005). Inmates who had been moved from a state penitentiary to a maximum security prison brought a class action suit and claimed that the state's procedures

# CHAPTER XIII

for moving inmates to the maximum security prison violated the due process requirements of the Fourteenth Amendment to the U.S. Constitution. The Court held that the state created the inmates' liberty interest in avoiding movement to the maximum security prison by creating and implementing policies for determining which prisoners should be moved to the maximum security facility. The Court also held that the state's procedures for moving inmates sufficiently protected the inmates' liberty interest in avoiding erroneous transfer and the state's interest in running its prison system efficiently. Thus, the state's procedures for moving inmates to its maximum security prison did not violate the inmates' due process rights.

b. **Parolees' Interests. [§ 445]**

**A parolee has a liberty interest involved when a state revokes parole.** A parolee has a liberty interest in pursuing a normal life after release from prison. If a state chooses to revoke parole, the individual is entitled to notice of the reason for revocation and a hearing to determine whether parole restrictions have been violated. *Morrissey v. Brewer*, 408 U.S. 471 (1972). The same rule applies to revocation of probation. *Gagnon v. Scarpelli*, 411 U.S. 778 (1973).

c. **Prisoners' Interests. [§ 446]**

**A prisoner has no liberty interest in not being transferred from one prison to another, or in not being placed in administrative segregation**

(1) **Prison Transfers.**

A prisoner has no liberty interest in not being transferred from prison to prison, so no notice or hearing is required before such a transfer. *Olim v. Wakinekona*, 461 U.S. 238 (1983).

(2) **Prison Segregation.**

A prisoner has no constitutionally-based liberty interest in not being placed in administrative segregation. However, if state statutes and regulations prescribe certain procedures for placing someone in administrative segregation, a prisoner does have a statutorily-based liberty interest in remaining in the general prison population. *Hewitt v. Helms*, 459 U.S. 460 (1983).

d. **Liberty Interests of Children. [§ 447]**

**Corporal punishment in public schools does involve a liberty interest of the child.** Disciplinary corporal punishment in public schools does involve a liberty interest, but there is no procedural due process right to notice or a hearing prior to imposing the punishment. Post-punishment judicial remedies for excessive punishment are sufficient to protect a child's liberty interests. *Ingraham v. Wright*, 430 U.S. 651 (1977).

e. **Termination of Parental Rights. [§ 448]**

A liberty interest is involved when a state acts to terminate parental rights.

(1) **Appointment of Counsel. [§ 449]**

**The Constitution does not require a state to appoint counsel for every indigent parent facing termination of parental rights.** A parent does not have a sufficiently important liberty interest in the parent-child relationship to automatically require the appointment of counsel for every indigent parent whose parental rights are to be terminated. *Lassiter v. Dept. of Social Services*, 452 U.S. 18 (1981).

(2) **Evidence of Unfitness to Parent. [§ 450]**

**A State must show clear and convincing evidence of unfitness to parent before it may terminate parental rights.** A state may not terminate parental rights, thereby extinguishing a parent's liberty interest in his or her child, unless it shows by clear and convincing evidence that a parent is unfit. *Santosky v. Kramer*, 455 U.S. 745 (1982).

(3) **Trial Transcripts. [§ 451]**

**An indigent person who wants to appeal a court order terminating his or her parental rights is entitled to a free trial transcript.** A state may not deny an appeal of a termination order simply on the basis that the person cannot afford the record preparation fees. *M.L.B. v. S.L.J.*, 519 U.S. 102 (1997) (see § 529).

f. **Reputation. [§ 452]**

**Injury to reputation alone is not a liberty interest protected under procedural due process. However, if injury to reputation is linked to some other interest, such as pursuing employment, there may be a liberty interest involved.** The Court rejected a due process argument by a plaintiff whose reputation was allegedly injured by police circulation to merchants of a flyer designating plaintiff an "active shoplifter." Since damage to his reputation was not tied to any other interest such as employment, there was no protectable liberty interest. *Paul v. Davis*, 424 U.S. 693 (1976).

    g.   **Sex Offender Registration Law. [§ 453]**

**Procedural due process does not entitle offenders to a hearing to determine whether they are currently dangerous before their inclusion in a publicly disseminated sex offender registry.** Connecticut's "Megan's Law" requires persons convicted of sex offenses to register with the State and requires the State to post a sex offender registry on the Internet. Plaintiff complained that he was being deprived of a liberty interest, and demanded a predeprivation hearing to determine if he was currently dangerous. The Court, relying on *Paul* (previous case), said that a mere injury to reputation does not constitute the deprivation of a liberty interest, and that, in any event, procedural due process does not entitle him to a hearing to establish a fact (current dangerousness) that is not material to the registration statute. The conviction alone is the sole material fact for purpose of the registration statute, and the defendant was provided sufficient due process to contest the conviction. *Connecticut Dept. of Public Safety v. Doe*, 538 U.S. 1 (2003).

2.   **Property Interests. [§ 454]**

**Procedural due process guarantees apply when the government intentionally deprives an individual of real or personal property.** The applicability of procedural due process analysis becomes an issue when a government deprives a person of some non-traditional form of property, such as welfare or disability payments. **The general rule is that government benefits will be considered property for procedural due process purposes if the recipient is "entitled" to receive the benefit. An entitlement (as opposed to a mere expectation) exists when, under the law granting the benefit, the recipient is entitled to receive the benefit as long as specified conditions of eligibility are met.**

    a.   **Government Employment. [§ 455]**

**Government employment will not be a property interest if the employee can be fired at will (for no reason); it will be a property interest if the employee can only be fired "for cause" (such as a tenured teacher).** A property interest in government employment may arise from express contractual language, or from the facts and circumstances surrounding a particular employment relationship (such as an oral promise by the boss to continue an employee's employment).

# PROCEDURAL DUE PROCESS

(1) **Tenure Rights Qualify as a Property Interest. [§ 456]**

   **No express or implied tenure rights in a teaching position at a public university means no property interest.**

   *Board of Regents v. Roth*, 408 U.S. 564 (1972). The Court found that a state university professor had no property interest in his teaching job. The professor had been hired for one year, and there were no express or implied tenure rights granted to him. He had no entitlement to his job, simply a unilateral expectation of continued employment. Since he had no property interest in his job, he was not entitled to a hearing, or even a formal statement of the reasons why he was not retained.

(2) **Implied Tenure Rights May Qualify as a Property Interest. [§ 457]**

   **Policies and practices of a school may create an entitlement to a job.**

   *Perry v. Sindermann*, 408 U.S. 593 (1972). The Court ruled that a state college teacher with ten years experience who had been let go without a hearing must have a chance to prove that he had an entitlement to continued employment based on the policies and practices of the institution which allegedly created an implied tenure system.

(3) **Tenured Employee Entitled to Pretermination Hearing. [§ 458]**

   **A tenured government employee is entitled to a limited pretermination hearing.**

   *Cleveland Board of Education v. Loudermill*, 470 U.S. 532 (1985). The Court held that an employee terminable only for cause was entitled to procedural due process protections prior to termination. This requires some form of a pretermination hearing, coupled with post-termination administrative procedures for review. The pretermination hearing need only be designed to determine "whether there are reasonable grounds to believe that the charges against the employee are true and support the proposed action." This satisfies the essential requirements of due process, namely, notice and an opportunity to be heard.

(4) **Suspension of Tenured Employee Without Pay. [§ 459]**

   **A tenured employee in a position of public trust and visibility who is charged with a felony is not entitled to a**

# CHAPTER XIII

**hearing prior to suspension without pay.** A prompt post-suspension hearing will suffice.

*Gilbert v. Homar*, 520 U.S. 924 (1997). The Court assumed, but did not explicitly hold, that the suspension without pay of a tenured employee infringed a protected property interest, but held that in circumstances involving an employee in a position of public trust and visibility who is charged with a felony, the employee is not entitled to a pre-suspension hearing. A police officer at a state university was suspended without pay after being charged with a felony drug offense, without a pre-suspension hearing. Prior decisions indicate that a tenured employee is entitled to a pretermination hearing to provide a check against erroneous deprivations by assuring that there are reasonable grounds for dismissal. In this case, however, because the fact that the employee was charged with a felony eliminated the risk of the suspension being an erroneous deprivation, due process would be satisfied by a prompt post-suspension hearing.

(5) **Withholding of Payments on Public Works Contracts. [§ 460]**

**A state statutory scheme that allows a public entity to withhold payment on public works contracts if the subcontractor fails to pay prevailing wages to employees, but allows the subcontractor to file an ordinary breach of contract suit against the general contractor or the public entity, does not violate the 14th Amendment's Due Process Clause.**

*Lujan v. G & G Fire Sprinklers Inc.*, 532 U.S. 189 (2001). The Court held that a state may withhold payments on a public works project without an opportunity for a hearing if a subcontractor fails to pay prevailing wages to employees, as long the state authorized the subcontractor to sue the general contractor or state officials who authorized the withholding. The Court ruled that the subcontractor had not been deprived of any existing entitlement, and that whatever property interest it had could be protected by an ordinary breach-of-contract suit.

b. **Government Benefits. [§ 461]**

**When a government seeks to terminate a benefit which it has conferred, the court will look to the importance of that benefit to the recipient; the question is whether the recipient's interest in avoiding the loss outweighs the government's interest in terminating the benefit without providing notice or a hearing.**

# PROCEDURAL DUE PROCESS

### (1) Welfare Recipients.

**Welfare recipients are entitled to a pre-termination hearing.**

*Goldberg v. Kelly*, 397 U.S. 254 (1970). The Court ruled that welfare recipients are entitled to an evidentiary hearing prior to termination of their benefits. Welfare benefits are needed for the purposes of subsistence, so the Court refused to allow a summary termination of benefits pending resolution of a recipient's eligibility.

### (2) Disability Benefits Recipients.

**Disability benefit recipients are not entitled to a pre-termination hearing.**

*Mathews v. Eldridge*, 424 U.S. 319 (1976). The Court ruled that there is no right to a hearing prior to the termination of disability benefits. The Court said that receipt of disability payments is simply not as crucial as receipt of subsistence welfare payments.

## c. Public School Education. [§ 462]

**A public school student has a property interest in his or her education which may not be taken away without due process protections.** Be sure to distinguish between a disciplinary suspension, as opposed to an academic dismissal; the Court uses a different rule in each of these cases.

### (1) Disciplinary Suspension.

**No formal hearing is required before a student receives a temporary disciplinary suspension.**

*Goss v. Lopez*, 419 U.S. 565 (1975). The Court ruled that, as a general matter, before a student is given a temporary disciplinary suspension (ten days or less) from public school, he or she must be given notice (oral or written) of the reasons for the suspension, and at least an informal opportunity to respond to the charges. A full-blown adversary hearing is not required.

### (2) Academic Dismissal.

**No hearing is required before a student is dismissed for academic reasons.**

*Board of Curators v. Horowitz*, 435 U.S. 78 (1978). The Court ruled that a medical student was not entitled to any sort of

# CHAPTER XIII

hearing or opportunity to respond before an academic dismissal. In this case, the school used a long, extensive evaluation process which the Court deemed adequate to protect the student's interests.

d. **Judicial Review of Punitive Damages Award. [§ 463]**

**Limiting judicial review of the amount of a punitive damages award may violate procedural due process guarantees.**

*Honda Motor Co. v. Oberg*, 512 U.S. 415 (1994). The Court invalidated an Oregon law barring judicial review of the amount of a jury's punitive damages award unless the court affirmatively finds that there is no evidence to support the verdict. Such a rule violates procedural due process protections because it abrogates a traditional common-law safeguard against arbitrary deprivations of property, without providing any adequate substitute.

e. **Grossly Excessive Judgments Imposed on a Tortfeasor. [§ 464]**

**Grossly excessive punitive damages awards may be a deprivation of property in violation of the Due Process Clause.**

*BMW of North America v. Gore*, 517 U.S. 559 (1996). The Court struck down a $2,000,000 punitive damages award as grossly excessive in relation to a $4,000 compensatory damages award. Gore discovered that his new BMW had been repainted before delivery. He sued BMW for fraud and the jury awarded $4,000,000 in punitive damages and $4,000 in compensatory damages. The Alabama Supreme Court reduced the punitive damages award to $2,000,000. The Supreme Court considered three factors in assessing the constitutionality of the punitive damages award: the reprehensibility of defendant's misconduct; the disparity between the actual or potential harm suffered by the plaintiff and the punitive damages award; and the difference between the punitive damages awarded and the civil penalties authorized or imposed in comparable cases. Applying these factors, the Court determined that BMW's conduct was not so egregious as to justify the punitive sanction imposed on it.

*State Farm v. Campbell*, 538 U.S. 408 (2003). The Court, applying the three factors from *Gore* (previous case), struck down a $145,000,000 punitive damages award on a $1,000,000 compensatory damages judgment. Campbell was involved in an automobile accident in which one person was killed and another injured. State Farm, Campbell's insurance company, contested liability and refused to settle the case for the $50,000 policy limit. A jury returned a verdict for over three times the policy limit, and State Farm refused to appeal. Campbell then sued State Farm for bad faith, fraud, and intentional infliction of emotional distress. The Court struck down the punitive damages award, saying that the Due Process Clause prohibits the imposition of grossly excessive or arbitrary punishment on a tortfeasor.

f. **Property Interest in Enforcement of Restraining Order. [§ 465]**

   **A person does not have a property interest in the enforcement of a restraining order unless the state legislature specifically creates one by statute.**

   *Castle Rock, Colorado v. Gonzales*, 545 U.S. 748 (2005). A wife brought a civil rights claim against Castle Rock and several police officers for failing to enforce a restraining order against her estranged husband. The wife argued that she had a property interest in the enforcement of the restraining order and that she had been deprived of that property interest in violation of the due process clause of the Fourteenth Amendment when police refused to arrest her husband for violating the restraining order. The Supreme Court held that even though the statutory language on the restraining order appeared to require the police officers to arrest the husband, similarly worded statutes had traditionally been interpreted to still allow police officers to exercise discretion whether or not to make an arrest. The Court also noted that had the Colorado legislature intended to create such a property interest it would have specifically done so. Thus, the wife did not have a property interest in the enforcement of the restraining order.

g. **Notice Required Before a State May Sell Property. [§ 466]**

   **When a government intends to abridge or terminate a property interest, it must provide notice that is reasonably designed to apprise the property owner of the proposed action and give him or her a chance to respond.**

   *Jones v. Flowers*, 547 U.S. 220 (2006). The Court held that when a mailed notice of a tax sale is returned marked "unclaimed," a state must take additional reasonable steps to try to provide notice to the property owner before selling his property, if it is practicable to do so. The Court had previously held that notice to a property owner was constitutionally sufficient if it was reasonably calculated to reach the intended recipient when sent, *Mullane v. Central Hanover Bank &*

# CHAPTER XIII

*Trust Co.*, 339 U.S. 306 (1950). The issue in this case was whether the state must take additional steps if it becomes aware that its initial notice attempt had failed. The Court balanced the state's interest against the individual's property interest, and ruled that the state failed to meet due process standards because additional reasonable steps were available to the state, given the particular circumstances of the case. Possible additional steps were resending the notice by regular mail, posting a notice on the front door of the property, or resending the notice to "occupant."

## REVIEW PROBLEMS—PROCEDURAL DUE PROCESS

**PROBLEM 1.** Timmy Toon was a second-grader at Id Elementary School, a public school within the State of Oz. One day, while Timmy's class was returning from a field trip on the school bus, Timmy was so tired that he fell asleep in the back of the bus. Dana Dancer, Timmy's teacher, herded forty second-graders off the bus, did a quick search of the seats, and left Timmy on the bus. Dana never did see Timmy in the back seat. A very frantic Timmy was rescued three hours later. Timmy's parents file a 42 U.S.C. § 1983 suit against Dana, claiming a deprivation of Timmy's liberty without due process of law. Do they have a case?

**Answer:** No. There was no intentional deprivation of Timmy's rights. Procedural due process rules apply only to intentional deprivations, and this certainly sounds like mere negligence on the part of Timmy's teacher. See § 441 for further review.

**PROBLEM 2.** Sam Soathe was a welfare recipient in the State of Oz. Sam was not the easiest person in the world to get along with, and he argued constantly with his caseworker at the state welfare office. After one of these sessions, the caseworker decided that Sam no longer met the eligibility requirements, and terminated his benefits. Sam sues, claiming a procedural due process violation. Does he have a case?

**Answer:** Yes. A welfare recipient is entitled to an evidentiary hearing prior to the termination of benefits. See § 461 for further review.

**PROBLEM 3.** The State of Oz has a law which provides that parental rights may be terminated if the State is able to show by a preponderance of the evidence that a person is an unfit parent. Does this law comport with procedural due process requirements?

**Answer:** No. A state may not terminate parental rights unless it can show by clear and convincing evidence that a person is an unfit parent. See § 450 for further review.

# PROCEDURAL DUE PROCESS

**PROBLEM 4.** Arleena Addams was an assistant professor at a very prestigious state law school. She had a one-year contract with no express tenure rights or right of renewal of the contract. Halfway through her contract, she mentioned to the Dean of the law school that she would certainly like to buy a house and establish some roots in the community. The Dean said, "Go ahead. We will have needs in your teaching areas for at least three years." Acting on this statement, Arleena bought a house. At the end of her year-long contract, she was let go by the law school. Arleena sues, claiming a deprivation of a property interest. Does she have a case?

**Answer:** Yes. A property interest may arise not only from contractual language, but also from facts and circumstances which give rise to an implied promise to continue the employment relationship. The Dean's comments were tantamount to an oral promise to retain Arleena beyond her one-year contract. See § 455 for further review.

# CHAPTER XIV

# SUBSTANTIVE DUE PROCESS AND FUNDAMENTAL RIGHTS

## A. INTRODUCTION. [§ 467]

**The Constitution protects an individual from government action which abridges fundamental personal rights.** If a state or the federal government takes action which adversely affects a person's individual rights and that person challenges the law, the challenge must be based on a specific provision of the Constitution.

An example of a case in which the Court interpreted and applied a specific conditional guarantee is *District of Columbia v. Heller*, 128 S.Ct. 2783 (2008). The Court ruled, 5–4, that the Second Amendment protects an individual right to posses a firearm unconnected to service in the militia. The Court said that the District of Columbia prohibition on usable handguns in the home violates the Second Amendment. The District of Columbia generally prohibited the possession of handguns. In addition, the District also required residents to keep their lawfully owned firearms, such as registered long guns, "unloaded and disassembled or bound by a trigger lock or similar device" unless they are located in a place of business or being used for lawful recreational facilities. Heller, a D.C. police officer authorized to carry a handgun while on duty at the Federal Judicial Center, applied for a registration certificate for a handgun he wished to keep at home. The District of Columbia refused to issue the certificate and Heller sued. The Court ruled that the District must permit him to register his handgun and must issue him a license to carry it in his home for purposes of self-defense. Justice Scalia, writing for the majority, said that the Second Amendment right is not unlimited, and that the Court's opinion should not be taken to cast doubt on laws prohibiting the possession of guns by felons, and the mentally ill, or laws forbidding the carrying of firearms in sensitive places such as schools or government building. The Court said that D.C.'s total ban on handgun possession in the home prohibits an entire class of arms that Americans overwhelmingly choose for the lawful purpose of self-defense, and that under any of the standards of scrutiny the Court has applied to enumerated constitutional rights, this ban would fail constitutional muster.

# CHAPTER XIV

The Due Process Clauses of the Fifth and Fourteenth Amendments provide potential bases for challenging government action which arguably impinges on individual rights. Under substantive due process analysis, a court is asked to determine the constitutionality of a law which abridges the rights of a class of persons (for example, a state law which prohibits any pregnant woman from having an abortion). Under procedural due process analysis (see § 439), a court is asked to determine the constitutionality of the procedures used when a government deprives an individual of life, liberty, or property (for example, a state law which terminates a specific person's welfare benefits without any pre-termination hearing).

**Under substantive due process analysis, the Court reviews the substance of legislation to see if it unduly interferes with an individual's rights or interests that are protected by the Due Process Clauses of the Constitution.** The Court protects certain individual rights (such as the right to marry, the right to procreate, or the right to refuse medical treatment) from government abridgement because those rights are aspects of liberty protected by the Due Process Clauses of the Constitution. If the federal government acts, the Fifth Amendment Due Process Clause is the appropriate provision for a plaintiff to use; if a state acts, the Fourteenth Amendment Due Process Clause is the appropriate provision. Once you identify the right or interest being abridged, you must argue that it is an aspect of liberty under the appropriate due process clause; then you must determine if it is simply a low-level liberty interest (relatively unimportant) or a fundamental right (very important). A right will be deemed fundamental if it is essential to an Anglo-American system of jurisprudence, or implicit in the concept of ordered liberty. **The importance of the right being abridged sets the level of scrutiny that a court will use to review the law. The more important the right, the higher the level of scrutiny.** Setting the level of scrutiny also determines who has the burden of proof—the plaintiff or the government. **At rationality review, the plaintiff always has the burden of proving that the law is irrational. At strict scrutiny, once the plaintiff has made a prima facie showing that a fundamental right has been abridged, the burden shifts to the government to show that it has a compelling reason for the law, and that the government has used narrowly tailored means to achieve its goal (means that are directed specifically at the source of the evil the government is trying to prevent).** For instance, a state could not deny a marriage license to a person (thus depriving him of the fundamental rights to marry) based on his failure to pay child support for his children; there are less drastic means available to achieve the state's goal of ensuring payment of child support obligations (such as initiating a lawsuit to collect the back payments). The Court will balance the abridgement of the right asserted against the preferred government justification for the law.

# SUBSTANTIVE DUE PROCESS AND FUNDAMENTAL RIGHTS

A case that bridges the gap between the doctrine of substantive due process and the Privileges or Immunities Clause of the Fourteenth Amendment is *McDonald v. Chicago*, 130 S.Ct. 3020 (2010). The Court, 5–4, ruled that the Second Amendment right recognized in *District of Columbia v. Heller* (above) is a fundamental right that is to be incorporated through the Fourteenth Amendment to apply against the states. In *McDonald*, the city of Chicago and the village of Oak Park (a Chicago suburb) passed laws banning the possession of handguns. Five Justices held that the Fourteenth Amendment, though the process of selective incorporation of certain Bill of Rights protections, made the Second Amendment applicable to the states. Extending the holding of *Heller* to states, Justice Alito held that the right to keep and bear arms is a fundamental right, and that self-defense is the central component of the Second Amendment right. Justice Alito, for four Justices, ruled that the Fourteenth Amendment's Due Process Clause is the vehicle through which the Second Amendment right gets applied to the states. Justice Alito stated that there was no need to employ the Privileges or Immunities Clause of the Fourteenth Amendment because the Court has historically used the Due Process Clause to determine if a Bill of Rights protection is protected against state infringement.

Justice Thomas, the fifth vote for incorporation, held that the right to keep and bear arms is a privilege of American Citizenship, and should be incorporated through the Fourteenth Amendment's Privileges or Immunities Clause. Justice Thomas stated that the Fourteenth Amendment's Due Process Clause, which speaks only to "process," cannot impose any substantive restraints on state legislation.

### NOTE: PRIVILEGES OR IMMUNITIES CLAUSE OF THE FOURTEENTH AMENDMENT. [§ 468]

**In addition to the Due Process Clause, the Fourteenth Amendment contains the Privileges or Immunities Clause, which precludes any state from making or enforcing any law which shall abridge privileges or immunities flowing from the federal government.** This clause is to be distinguished from the Privileges and Immunities Clause of Article IV (see § 297 above), which prohibits a state from discriminating against out-of-staters in relation to state-granted rights or privileges. Until recently, the Court has interpreted the Fourteenth Amendment Privileges or Immunities Clause so that it is a virtual nullity in terms of providing an effective challenge to a state law.

    a. *Slaughterhouse Cases*, 83 U.S. 36 (1873). The Court upheld a state law which granted a monopoly to a certain slaughterhouse to engage in the livestock business in the city of New Orleans. In rejecting an argument based on the Privileges or Immunities Clause of the Fourteenth Amend-

# CHAPTER XIV

ment, the Court held that the clause did not incorporate any of the protections of the Bill of Rights, but rather protected only those rights which flow from the relationship between a United States citizen and the federal government. The rights which theoretically are protected under the clause are: the right to petition the government for redress of grievances, the right to petition for a writ of habeas corpus, the right to use the navigable waters of the United States, the right to come to the seat of government to transact business, rights secured by treaties with foreign countries, and the rights secured by the Thirteenth and Fifteenth Amendments and by other provisions of the Fourteenth Amendment. However, remember that only once in the history of the Court has it used the clause to invalidate a state law, and that case was overruled five years later (See *Colgate v. Harvey*, 296 U.S. 404 (1935), overruled in *Madden v. Kentucky*, 309 U.S. 83 (1940)).

b. *Saenz v. Roe*, 526 U.S. 489 (1999). The Court invalidated a California statute which limited maximum welfare benefits available to a family that lived in the state for less than a year to the amount payable by the state of the family's prior residences. The Court also ruled that Congress could not authorize such discrimination by statute.

The Court identified three components of the right to interstate travel, and the constitutional bases for each of these rights:

1. The right of a citizen of one state to enter and leave a state. This right was not implicated in the case, so the Court had no need to identify a constitutional basis for it.

2. The right to be treated as a welcome visitor rather than an unfriendly alien when temporarily present in a state. The Court based this right in the Privilege and Immunities Clause of Article 4, § 2, which removes from the citizens of each State the disabilities of alienage in the other States.

3. The right of the newly arrived citizen to be treated like other residents of the state. This right is protected by the Privileges or Immunities Clause of the Fourteenth Amendment; a ruling which breathed new life into that clause, which had been dormant since the ***Slaughter-House Cases*** in 1873.

## B. SUMMARY OF STEPS IN A SUBSTANTIVE DUE PROCESS ANALYSIS. [§ 469]

**1. Identify which government is acting, federal or state.** This step is important because if a state is acting, the Fourteenth Amendment Due Process Clause applies, whereas if the federal government is acting, the Fifth

# SUBSTANTIVE DUE PROCESS AND FUNDAMENTAL RIGHTS

Amendment Due Process Clause applies.

**2. Describe in layperson's terms the interest that has been abridged.** For instance, if a state imposes a two-year training requirement for drivers of large trucks, a person challenging that law will argue that his or her interest in pursuing an occupation has been abridged.

**3. Place the abridged interest in the Constitution (assert that it is an aspect of liberty under the appropriate due process clause).** Driving a truck (or, pursuing an occupation) is an aspect of liberty under the Fourteenth Amendment Due Process Clause (if a state has passed the law), or the Fifth Amendment Due Process Clause (if the federal government has passed the law).

**4. Ascribe constitutional weight to the interest abridged—is it a low-level liberty interest or a fundamental right?** You must look to Supreme Court cases to determine whether the Court has accorded a specific interest the status of a fundamental right.

**5. Set the appropriate level of scrutiny.** Remember that, under substantive due process, a law abridging a non-fundamental right receives only rational-basis review, whereas a law abridging a fundamental right receives strict scrutiny.

**6. Balance the abridgment of the individual right against the proffered government interest.** Be as specific as possible when articulating the right abridged and the specific government interest underlying the law.

## C. LEVELS OF SCRUTINY UNDER SUBSTANTIVE DUE PROCESS. [§ 470]

### RATIONAL BASIS REVIEW

| NATURE OF RIGHT ABRIDGED | ENDS | MEANS | BURDEN OF PROOF |
|---|---|---|---|
| Low–Level Liberty Interest | Legitimate Government Interest (within an enumerated power of Congress or 10th Amendment Police Power of a state) | Rationally Related (arguably advances the goal sought) | Stays with plaintiff |

# CHAPTER XIV

## STRICT SCRUTINY

| NATURE OF RIGHT ABRIDGED | ENDS | MEANS | BURDEN OF PROOF |
|---|---|---|---|
| Fundamental Right | Compelling Government Interest (very important government goal) | Narrowly Tailored (directly and narrowly addresses the problem—not overbroad) | Shifts to the government after the plaintiff has shown an abridgement of the fundamental right |

## D. SUBSTANTIVE DUE PROCESS REVIEW OF ECONOMIC LEGISLATION. [§ 471]

From 1897 to 1934, the Court used the doctrine of substantive due process to strike down state laws which abridged the liberty to contract. **From 1934 to the present, the Court has upheld virtually all state laws which regulate economic matters. For substantive due process purposes, the right to contract and the right to pursue employment are low-level liberty interests, the abridgment of which receives only rationality review (the Court asks whether a legitimate government interest is being advanced by the law, and whether the means chosen can rationally be said to advance that interest).**

1. **Early Substantive Due Process Cases Dealing With Economic Interests. [§ 472]**

   Until 1934, the Court considered the right to contract to be an important aspect of liberty.

   *Allegeyer v. Louisiana*, 165 U.S. 578 (1897). [§ 473]

   The Court invalidated, on substantive due process grounds, a Louisiana law which precluded unapproved insurance companies from issuing policies on property located within the state. The Court relied on the liberty interests of pursuing an occupation and freely entering into contracts.

   *Lochner v. New York*, 198 U.S. 45 (1905). [§ 474]

   The Court invalidated a New York law that limited the number of hours a person could work in a bakery to no more than 60 per week or 10 per

# SUBSTANTIVE DUE PROCESS AND FUNDAMENTAL RIGHTS

day. The liberty provision of the due process clause of the Fourteenth Amendment protects the ability to contract and to purchase or sell labor. The Court rejected the state's health argument that the law was needed to protect the health of bakery employees. The Court's ruling obviously promoted a laissez faire theory of employment, at the expense of the state's power to regulate for the common good.

2. **The Modern Hands–Off Approach to Cases Dealing with Economic Interests. [§ 475]**

Beginning in 1934, the Court began to reject the right to contract as a limitation on government power.

*Nebbia v. New York*, 291 U.S. 502 (1934). [§ 476]

The Court upheld a New York law that regulated milk prices. Contract rights, while part of the liberty protected by the due process clause, are not absolute, and may be abridged when the state regulates in the common interest. Such a law will be upheld if it is not arbitrary or capricious, and has a reasonable relation to a proper legislative purpose.

*West Coast Hotel Co. v. Parrish*, 300 U.S. 379 (1937). [§ 477]

The Court upheld a Washington state law setting a minimum wage for women. The Court accepted the state's police power argument of protecting female workers, and rejected the plaintiff's argument that the law unduly abridged the liberty interest in freely entering into a contract.

*U.S. v. Carolene Products Co.*, 304 U.S. 144 (1938). [§ 478]

The Court upheld a federal law that prohibited the shipment of "filled milk" in interstate commerce ("filled milk" refers to milk or cream to which fat or oil has been added). The Court said it should uphold the law if any state of facts existed, or could have been presumed to exist, which would support the law. Any arguably rational basis for the law would be enough to uphold it.

*Day-Brite Lighting v. Missouri*, 342 U.S. 421 (1952). [§ 479]

The Court upheld a law that required employers to give employees paid time off to vote. The Court refused to sit as a "super-legislature" that would second-guess the state; debatable economic or social issues should be left to state legislatures.

*Williamson v. Lee Optical*, 348 U.S. 483 (1955). [§ 480]

# CHAPTER XIV

The Court upheld an Oklahoma law which prohibited optometrists from fitting eyeglass lenses without a prescription from an ophthalmologist. The Court said it would uphold a law if the legislature thought an evil existed and the law was a rational way to correct it.

*Ferguson v. Skrupa*, 372 U.S. 726 (1963). [§ 481]

The Court upheld a Kansas law prohibiting anyone but lawyers from engaging in the business of debt adjusting ("debt adjusting" was defined by the statute as the practice of a debtor hiring a debt adjuster who, for a fee, would distribute among certain specified creditors money that was paid periodically by the debtor). The Court said that courts should not substitute their social and economic beliefs for those of a state legislature.

*Duke Power Co. v. Carolina Environmental Study Group, Inc.*, 438 U.S. 59 (1978). [§ 482]

The Court upheld a federal law setting a cap on monetary damages recoverable in nuclear power plant accidents. The Court said it would defer to the congressional judgment unless it was arbitrary or irrational. It also said that in economic cases, laws come to the Court with a presumption of constitutionality, and the burden is on the one attacking the law to prove that the legislature acted irrationally.

## E. SUBSTANTIVE DUE PROCESS REVIEW OF SOCIAL LEGISLATION. [§ 483]

**Not all liberty interests are fundamental; some may be abridged upon a showing of rationality by the state. The Court uses low-level rationality review when a law is challenged as violating some non-fundamental social interest.** The following are cases in which the Court determined the right at issue to be merely a low-level liberty interest.

1. **Choice of Hairstyle.**

   **A police officer's right to choose his or her hairstyle is a low-level liberty interest.**

   *Kelley v. Johnson*, 425 U.S. 238 (1976). The Court upheld a police department regulation regulating the length and style of hair of police officers. The Court said that even if a liberty interest were implicated by the regulation, there is no fundamental or basic right of police officers to wear their hair any way they want. The plaintiffs were not able to show that the regulation was without a rational basis.

# SUBSTANTIVE DUE PROCESS AND FUNDAMENTAL RIGHTS

2. **Registration of Prescription Drug Users.**

    **Prescription drug users do not have a right to prevent their names from being placed on a state computer list.** This is another low-level liberty interest.

    *Whalen v. Roe*, 429 U.S. 589 (1977). The Court upheld a New York law that required the names of prescription-drug users to be sent to a central computer for record-keeping purposes. The Court found no fundamental privacy interest implicated here, so rationality review applied. The legislature could rationally have concluded that the law would aid in deterring and catching people who were abusing prescription drugs.

3. **Attorney's Right to Practice Law.**

    **A prosecutor does not violate an attorney's Fourteenth Amendment right to practice law by executing a search warrant on the attorney while his client is testifying before a grand jury.**

    *Conn v. Gabbert*, 526 U.S. 286 (1999). The Court ruled that an attorney was not deprived of a liberty interest in practicing law when the attorney was searched, pursuant to a valid warrant, when his client was testifying before a grand jury. This brief interruption of a lawyer's duties, as a result of legal process, distinguishes this case from those in which an attorney was totally prohibited from practicing law.

## F. SUBSTANTIVE DUE PROCESS REVIEW OF FUNDAMENTAL RIGHTS. [§ 484]

**Whenever a government regulation abridges a fundamental right, the Court will use strict scrutiny to review the law; the state will have to show a compelling interest and narrowly tailored means to justify the law.** The fundamental right may be enumerated (such as certain provisions of the Bill of Rights which have been applied to the states), or unenumerated (such as the right to privacy). A right will be deemed fundamental if it is "essential to an Anglo–American system of jurisprudence," or "implicit in the concept of ordered liberty."

1. **Two Types of Fundamental Rights—Enumerated or Unenumerated. [§ 485]**

    Fundamental rights may be enumerated or unenumerated. **Enumerated fundamental rights are those provisions of the Bill of Rights which are so important that they are applied against the states as well as against the federal government.** The Court has selectively incorporated certain

Bill of Rights provisions by declaring them to be aspects of liberty under the Due Process Clause of the Fourteenth Amendment. Unenumerated fundamental rights are rights which are not listed in the Constitution, but have been deemed by the Court to be so important as to be protected by the Constitution against government intrusion (such as the right to privacy).

> **a. The Bill of Rights provisions that have been incorporated are:**
>
> > (1) All First Amendment rights: Speech, both religion clauses, press, to peaceably assemble, and to petition the government for the redress of grievances;
> >
> > (2) The Fourth Amendment prohibition against unreasonable searches and seizures;
> >
> > (3) All provisions of the Fifth Amendment, except the requirement that all criminal prosecutions be started only on a grand jury indictment;
> >
> > (4) All Sixth Amendment rights;
> >
> > (5) All Eighth Amendment rights.
>
> **b. Unenumerated fundamental rights are:**
>
> > (1) The right to privacy;
> >
> > (2) The right to interstate travel;
> >
> > (3) The right to vote; and
> >
> > (4) The right of political association.

**2. Alternative to Substantive Due Process: Fundamental Rights Strand of Equal Protection. [§ 486]**

When a legislature passes a law that abridges a fundamental right, a court may apply one of two methods of analysis: substantive due process, or the fundamental rights strand of equal protection. In both, the level of judicial scrutiny rises from rationality review to strict scrutiny because a fundamental right is abridged. **A substantive due process analysis is called for when a legislature passes a mandatory law (a requirement or a prohibition)**

# SUBSTANTIVE DUE PROCESS AND FUNDAMENTAL RIGHTS

which affects all persons within the relevant population (such as a state law prohibiting abortions to all women). **A fundamental rights strand of equal protection analysis is called for when the legislature sets up a classification system which deprives only a certain group of persons of a fundamental right (a poll tax classifies along wealth lines, and deprives poor people of the right to vote).** Usually, there is nothing about the classification itself that raises the level of scrutiny (there is no suspect class being disadvantaged), but the fact that the classification system operates to deprive a class of persons of a fundamental right raises the scrutiny. Courts are not always clear about which analysis they are using, but one thing is certain—whichever label is applied to the analysis, the Court applies strict scrutiny because a fundamental right is being abridged.

As you go through the following cases, be aware of whether the state law applies to all persons who possess the trait the government is trying to regulate. If the law affects all persons within the relevant population, then substantive due process analysis will apply. For example, if a state wanted to cleanse the gene pool by sterilizing all felons who committed crimes involving moral turpitude, that law would be analyzed under substantive due process. If the law affects only a certain group of persons within the relevant population, then the fundamental rights strand of equal protection analysis is called for. If the state sterilized only some morally corrupt felons, but not others, that law would be analyzed under the fundamental rights strand of equal protection (equal protection principles are applied because the government has set up classifications within a category of persons, all of whom have a trait relevant to the purpose of the law).

3. **Specific Fundamental Rights. [§ 487]**

   **The following cases illustrate the development of fundamental rights in the areas of procreational and family autonomy, interstate travel, voting, and political association.**

   a. **Right to Make Decisions Concerning the Care, Custody, and Control of Children. [§ 488]**

   **The Court has said that there is a fundamental right of parents to rear their children, including the right to decide where and how to educate them.**

   (1) **Choice of School. [§ 489]**

   **Parents Have a Right to Determine Which Schools Their Children Will Attend.**

   *Meyer v. Nebraska*, **262 U.S. 390 (1923).** The Court invalidated a state law which prohibited the teaching of any foreign language (other than the "dead" ones) in any elementary school. The Court relied on the unenumerated rights to marry, establish a home, and bring up children.

***Pierce v. Society of Sisters*, 268 U.S. 510 (1925).** The Court invalidated a state law which required all students to attend public, rather than private or religious, schools. The Court referred to the right of parents and guardians to direct the upbringing and education of children under their control.

**(2) Grandparent Visitation Rights. [§ 490]**

**A state may not grant broad-based non-parental visitation rights only upon a showing that the visitation would be in the best interest of the child.**

*Troxel v. Granville*, 530 U.S. 57 (2000). The Court invalidated a Washington statute that permits any person to petition for visitation rights at any time and authorizes a state court to grant visitation if it decides it would be in the child's best interest. Writing for a plurality, Justice O'Connor reaffirmed that parents have a fundamental right to make decisions concerning the care, custody, and control of their children. The statute could be used even if there were no finding of unfitness on the part of the parents, and the parents' decision regarding the best interest of the child received no weight from the Court. The plurality however, did not employ any particular level of judicial scrutiny. Justice Thomas, concurring, agreed that there is a fundamental right of parents to rear their children and argued that any abridgement of that right should receive strict scrutiny

**(3) No Right to a Public School Education. [§ 491]**

**There is no right to a public school education. State methods of funding public education receive rational basis review.** As long as every student in the state receives a minimally adequate education, the Court will uphold the funding scheme. It does not make the funding system unconstitutional for some school districts to be funded at higher levels than others.

***San Antonio Independent School District v. Rodriguez*, 411 U.S. 1 (1973).** The Court upheld a Texas system of financing public schools under which per-pupil funding varied from $356 to $594 per student. The Court applied rationality review, asserting that there is no fundamental right to a public school

# SUBSTANTIVE DUE PROCESS AND FUNDAMENTAL RIGHTS

education, and that a state's funding scheme is constitutional if it provides an adequate minimum educational offering in every school in the state.

***Plyler v. Doe*, 457 U.S. 202 (1982).** The Court invalidated, under equal protection analysis, a Texas statute that denied free public education to the children of illegal aliens. Applying heightened scrutiny (but not strict), the Court appeared to treat public school education as more important than a mere government benefit. The critical factor was that a state, by law, completely excluded a class of children from its public schools.

***Kadrmas v. Dickinson Public Schools*, 487 U.S. 450 (1988).** The Court upheld, under rationality review, state and local laws which resulted in some school districts charging a fee for bus transportation to public schools. The Court restricted *Plyler* (previous case) to its facts, and emphasized that since there is no fundamental right to a public school education, rationality review is appropriate. Even though poor students could not afford the bus ride to school, the Court found the fee requirement rationally related to the legitimate government interest of saving money for other school district operations.

b. **Right to Privacy. [§ 492]**

There is no right to privacy enumerated in the Constitution. **The Court has offered different doctrinal bases for the existence of such a right (see, *Griswold v. Connecticut*, § 496), but today it is accepted that the right to privacy is an aspect of liberty protected by the due process clauses.**

(1) **Abortion and Reproductive Freedom. [§ 493]**

The Court has extended constitutional protection to such activities as marriage, contraception, and abortion. In each of these areas, the Court has ruled that there is a constitutional right of privacy which presumptively protects the ability of a person or persons to engage in certain activity. A state must have a compelling reason to restrict or prohibit the exercise of one of these rights. The following cases trace the Court's development of the right of privacy in the areas of marriage and procreational autonomy.

(a) **Right to Marriage and Procreation. [§ 494]**

The Court has recognized marriage and procreation as fundamental rights that are protected by the Due Process Clauses of the Constitution.

# CHAPTER XIV

*Skinner v. Oklahoma*, 316 U.S. 535 (1942). The Court invalidated, under equal protection, an Oklahoma law that authorized the sterilization of repeat felons whose crimes involved moral turpitude. The law was designed to cleanse the gene pool of the offspring of recidivist felons. Under the law, however, white-collar crooks were exempted from the sterilization requirement. The Court used strict scrutiny because the law deprived certain persons of the fundamental rights of marriage and procreation. This case involves a non-suspect classification (one set of recidivist felons versus another) that in turn abridged fundamental rights. If the legislature had said that all recidivist morally turpitudinous felons were to be sterilized, this would be a substantive due process case.

**(b) Right to Marry. [§ 495]**

The Court has held that the right to marry is an aspect of liberty protected by the Due Process Clauses of the Constitution.

*Zablocki v. Redhail*, 434 U.S. 374 (1978). The Court invalidated, under equal protection, a Wisconsin law that refused to grant a marriage license to anyone who had minor children whom he or she was obligated to support, unless there was proof of payment of the child-support obligations. The classification effected by the law significantly interfered with the exercise of the fundamental right to marry.

**(c) Right of Married Couples to Receive Information About Contraceptives. [§ 496]**

The Court has recognized the right of privacy as encompassing the right of married couples to receive information about contraceptives.

*Griswold v. Connecticut*, 381 U.S. 479 (1965). The Court invalidated a state law which made it a crime to give advice or information about contraceptives to married couples. The Court said that the law violated a fundamental right to marital privacy. Justice Douglas said the right to marital privacy came from penumbras, formed by emanations from the First, Third, Fourth, Fifth, and Ninth Amendments (enumerated rights have certain corollary rights which flow

# SUBSTANTIVE DUE PROCESS AND FUNDAMENTAL RIGHTS

from them). Justice Douglas did not place the right to marital privacy in the liberty provision of the due process clause, but that is where the Court places it today.

(d) **Right of Unmarried Persons to Receive Contraceptives. [§ 497]**

The Court has held that unmarried persons, as well as married couples, have a constitutional right to access to contraceptives.

*Eisenstadt v. Baird*, 405 U.S. 438 (1972). The Court invalidated, under equal protection, a Massachusetts law criminalizing the distribution of contraceptives to unmarried persons. This law violated the rights of single persons, under the Equal Protection Clause, to be treated the same as married persons in terms of access to contraceptives. In effect, the Court recognized a fundamental right of unmarried adults to have access to contraceptives.

(e) **Right of Minors to Purchase Non–Prescription Contraceptives. [§ 498]**

The Court has held that minors have a privacy right to obtain non-prescription contraceptives.

*Carey v. Population Services International*, 431 U.S. 678 (1977). The Court invalidated a New York law which, in part, prohibited the sale of non-prescription contraceptives to persons under the age of 16. A plurality said that a state law inhibiting the privacy rights of minors would be valid only if it advanced some significant (not compelling) state interest. A ban on contraceptives to minors would not serve the state interest of deterring underage sex.

(f) **Abortion Rights. [§ 499]**

The Court has held that a woman has a fundamental right to decide whether or not to terminate her pregnancy.

*Roe v. Wade*, 410 U.S. 113 (1973). The Court invalidated state laws criminalizing abortion, except in a case where the woman's life was in danger. The Court, 7–2, ruled that a pregnant woman has a fundamental right to decide whether or not to terminate her pregnancy. The Court

# CHAPTER XIV

recognized two state interests, each of which becomes compelling at a different point during pregnancy. A state's interest in maternal health or life becomes compelling at the end of the first trimester, providing a basis for regulation during the second and third trimester. A state's interest in potential human life becomes compelling at viability (24–28 weeks) and provides a basis for a state restricting or prohibiting abortion during the third trimester. The Court also held that a fetus is not a person entitled to protection under the Fourteenth Amendment.

### (i) Spousal Consent Laws Invalid. [§ 500]

The Court has held that states may not require a woman to obtain the consent of her spouse before she may have an abortion.

*Planned Parenthood v. Danforth*, 428 U.S. 52 (1976). The Court invalidated a state law requiring spousal consent for an abortion, and requiring parental consent for an unmarried woman under the age of 18 to get an abortion. A husband cannot be given a veto power over his wife's decision to terminate a pregnancy; as between spouses, the woman's interest always prevails.

### (ii) Judicial Bypass Procedure When a Minor Wants an Abortion. [§ 501]

The Court has held that parental consent laws are invalid unless accompanied by a judicial bypass procedure.

*Bellotti v. Baird*, 443 U.S. 622 (1979). The Court invalidated a Massachusetts law which required the consent of both parents before a minor could have an abortion. A plurality set forth rules for a judicial bypass to allow a minor to get an abortion without her parents' notice or consent. If a state requires parental consent (one or both), it must also provide a confidential alternative procedure (usually a court hearing, but not necessarily) at which a judge makes one of two decisions. If the minor is competent to make the abortion decision, she decides. If she is not competent, due to age or mental status, the judge decides what is in her best interest.

*Ayotte v. Planned Parenthood of Northern New England*, 546 U.S. 320 (2006). Justice O'Connor, in her last

# SUBSTANTIVE DUE PROCESS AND FUNDAMENTAL RIGHTS

opinion on the Court, ruled that a state parental notification law must explicitly permit a doctor to perform an abortion in a medical emergency even without parental notification. New Hampshire's Parental Notification Prior to Abortion Act prohibits a doctor from performing an abortion on a pregnant minor until 48 hours after written notice of the minor's intent to abort is delivered to her parent or guardian. The Act does not require notice for an abortion necessary to prevent the minor's death if there is not enough time to notify the parents. However, the Act does not permit a doctor to perform an abortion in a medical emergency without parental notification. In a narrow ruling, the Court remanded the case to the Court of Appeals which had prohibited enforcement of the law in its entirety, even when the medical emergency exception was not an issue. The Court said that narrower injunctive relief, if available under the statute's severability clause, might save the statute by prohibiting its unconstitutional application to that small class of cases in which a minor needs an immediate abortion to avoid serious harm to her heath.

### (iii) Government Funding of Abortion. [§ 502]

The Court has held that a woman's right to decide whether or not to terminate her pregnancy is not violated by a state law which refuses to fund welfare abortions.

*Maher v. Roe*, 432 U.S. 464 (1977) and *Harris v. McRae*, 448 U.S. 297 (1980). The Court held that neither a state nor the federal government has a duty to pay for abortions for indigent women, even if the government pays the expenses of childbirth for indigent women. The Court said that the government, through its refusal to subsidize welfare abortions, was placing no obstacle in the path of an indigent woman who wanted an abortion—her poverty was the obstacle. These cases are not true substantive due process cases because there was no government action mandatorily prohibiting abortions by indigent women. In other words, she still had a choice to exercise her right to terminate her pregnancy. The plaintiffs in these cases

# CHAPTER XIV

argued that non-funding of welfare abortions effectively prohibited women from exercising their right to terminate their pregnancies.

### (iv) Use of Public Facilities or Employees to Perform Abortions. [§ 503]

The Court has held that states may prohibit the use of public facilities or employees to perform abortions.

*Webster v. Reproductive Health Services*, 492 U.S. 490 (1989). The Court ruled on a number of provisions of a Missouri law regulating abortion. The Court refused to rule on the preamble of the law which declared that human life begins at conception. It said that no one had been injured by the language of the preamble, so it created no ripe case or controversy. The Court upheld provisions of the law prohibiting the use of public employees or public facilities to perform an abortion unless necessary to save the life of the mother. Use of public employees or facilities was considered a form of subsidy which the state had no duty to provide. The Court also upheld a provision of the law which required physicians to perform certain tests on a fetus of any woman who wants an abortion, and is at twenty or more weeks of pregnancy (the earliest point of viability was at twenty-four weeks). The Court upheld this second-trimester law designed to protect the state's interest in potential human life because of a possible four-week margin of error in estimating gestational age.

### (v) Two–Parent Notification; 48–Hour Wait for a Minor Seeking an Abortion. [§ 504]

The Court has upheld state laws requiring a minor to notify both parents as long as an appropriate judicial bypass was available. Also, states may require a minor to wait 48 hours after notifying one parent before she can have an abortion.

*Hodgson v. Minnesota*, 497 U.S. 417 (1990). The Court invalidated a state law which required two-parent notification (not consent) coupled with a 48-hour wait before a minor could get an abortion. The two-parent notification requirement, without any bypass

# SUBSTANTIVE DUE PROCESS AND FUNDAMENTAL RIGHTS

provided, was held to be counterproductive to the state's goal of promoting family harmony when there was a non-communicative, dysfunctional family, and superfluous when there was a well-functioning family. The Court upheld the two-parent notification requirement with bypass, and upheld a 48–hour wait for a minor after she notified one parent of her intent to have an abortion.

### (vi) Federally–Funded Family Planning Clinics; Conditions on Receipt of Federal Money. [§ 505]

The Court has held that Congress may properly withhold federal funds from family planning clinics that mention abortion as a method of family planning.

*Rust v. Sullivan*, 500 U.S. 173 (1991). The Court upheld a federal law which prohibited federally-funded family planning clinics from mentioning abortion as a method of family planning. The Court treated this as a subsidy case, and reasoned that the clinics had a choice—they could refuse the federal money and discuss abortion as a method of family planning, or accept the federal money and comply with the conditions on the receipt of the money. Since this was a federal (not state) law, the liberty interest asserted was based in the Fifth Amendment Due Process Clause.

### (vii) "Undue Burden" Analysis in Abortion Cases. [§ 506]

Justice O'Connor has adopted an "undue burden" analysis in abortion cases. Post-viability, a state may restrict or prohibit abortion. Pre-viability, a state may not pass a law which, by purpose or effect, imposes an undue burden on a woman's decision to terminate her pregnancy.

*Planned Parenthood of Southeastern Pennsylvania v. Casey*, 505 U.S. 833 (1992). In *Casey*, the Court reviewed five provisions of a Pennsylvania law regulating abortion. The Court upheld an informed consent requirement for adult women, a requirement that an adult woman wait twenty-four hours after receiving certain information before she can have an abortion, a

# CHAPTER XIV

requirement that a minor get the informed consent of one of her parents before she has an abortion (a judicial bypass was provided if the minor does not want to or cannot get the consent of a parent), and certain reporting requirements. The Court struck down a spousal notification requirement.

Although the Court retained the central holding of *Roe*, that a woman has a fundamental right to decide whether to terminate her pregnancy, seven Justices rejected the trimester framework of *Roe*. Four Justices (Rehnquist, White, Scalia, and Thomas) voted to overrule *Roe* completely. Two Justices (Blackmun and Stevens) voted to retain all of *Roe*. Three Justices (O'Connor, Kennedy, and Souter) voted to throw out the trimester framework, but retain the central right to decide. Justice O'Connor, writing the operative opinion in *Casey*, split pregnancy into two parts: pre-viability and post-viability. Post-viability, a state may seriously restrict, even prohibit, abortion. Pre-viability, a state may impose relatively nonintrusive requirements, but may not place an "undue burden" on the woman's decision to abort. An undue burden exists when a state law has the purpose or effect of placing a substantial obstacle in the path of a woman who wants to abort a non-viable fetus. Criminalizing abortion would be an undue burden as would spousal consent, or the spousal notice law struck down in *Casey*. Some informed consent laws, and a twenty-four hour waiting period for an adult woman would not be undue burdens. Many of the restrictions received by the Court in pre-*Casey* cases will have to be revisited to see how they fare under the undue burden standard of *Casey*.

**(viii) State Statute Banning "Partial Birth Abortions" Violates the Constitution. [§ 507]**

The Court invalidated a state law banning an abortion procedure know as dilation and extraction (commonly referred to as "partial birth abortion").

*Stenberg v. Carhart*, 530 U.S. 914 (2000). The Court, in a 5–4 decision written by Justice Breyer, struck down a Nebraska statute which prohibited the performance of an abortion by a method known as dilation and extraction. Reaffirming the principles of

# SUBSTANTIVE DUE PROCESS AND FUNDAMENTAL RIGHTS

*Casey* (previous case), the Court invalidated the law on two separate grounds. First, the law did not have any exception for the life or health of the mother, as required by *Roe* and *Casey*. Second, the Court said the statute was worded so broadly that even though it was primarily aimed at preventing the dilation and extraction method of abortion, it could be applied to another more commonly used method, called dilation and evacuation. That application would impose an undue burden on a woman's decision to terminate her pregnancy, thus running afoul of *Casey*.

The court upheld the Partial–Birth Abortion Act of 2003, a federal statute, that prohibited the intact D & E method of abortion (also known as a partial-birth abortion).

*Gonzales v. Carhart,* 550 U.S. 124 (2007). The Court, in a 5–4 opinion written by Justice Kennedy, held that the Act was not unconstitutionally vague, did not impose an undue burden on a woman's right to choose abortion, and the omission of a health exception did not require the facial invalidation of the statute. As to vagueness, the court held that the Act provides physicians of ordinary intelligence with notice of what procedure is criminal under the Act. The Act provides that a living fetus be delivered vaginally to one of two anatomical landmarks (thereby providing objective standards for a doctor to follow), requires performance of an overt act that kills the fetus, and has a scienter requirement. The Court ruled that since the Act applies only to a certain method of abortion, there was no undue burden on the woman's right to choose an abortion because the abortion could be performed by another method. The Court held that the absence of a health exception does not unduly burden the abortion right because there is documented medical disagreement about whether the Act's prohibition would ever impose serious health risks on women. Medical uncertainty provides a sufficient basis to conclude the absence of a health exception could be raised in a proper as-applied challenge in a discrete case.

# CHAPTER XIV

(2) **State Prohibition of Adult Consensual Homosexual Activity Violates the Due Process Clause. [§ 508]**

**The Court held that a state statute making it a crime for two persons of the same sex to engage in certain intimate sexual conduct is an abridgment of liberty protected under the Due Process Clause.**

*Lawrence v. Texas*, 539 U.S. 558 (2003). The Court, with five justices relying on a substantive due process rationale, invalidated the application of a Texas anti-sodomy statute to adult males who had engaged in a consensual sexual act in the privacy of a home. In reaching its result, the Court overruled *Bowers v. Hardwick*, 478 U.S. 186 (1986), in which the Court upheld the application of a Georgia criminal sodomy statute to consenting adults who engaged in homosexual activity. In *Bowers*, the Court rejected the argument that the constitutional right of privacy was broad enough to protect this activity, and also rejected the claim that this activity was protected because it took place in the home. In *Lawrence*, the majority said that the liberty protected by the Constitution allows homosexuals the right to choose to enter relationships in the confines of their homes and their private lives and retain their dignity as free persons. The majority does not say that there is a fundamental right to engage in homosexual activity, nor does it apply the traditional strict scrutiny standard. Rather, it concludes that Texas has no legitimate state interest underlying its law (rejecting the morality argument), and thus the Texas statute fails rational basis scrutiny. Justice O'Connor agrees that the Texas statute is unconstitutional, but relies on the Equal Protection Clause to reach her conclusion. Refusing to join in the majority's overruling of *Bowers*, she instead says that a law branding one class of persons as criminal based solely on a state's moral disapproved of that class violates the Equal Protection Clause.

(3) **Liberty Interest in Refusing Unwanted Medical Treatment. [§ 509]**

**A majority of the Court has recognized a low-level liberty interest in refusing medical treatment; so far, this has not been deemed to be a fundamental right.**

*Cruzan v. Director, Missouri Department of Health*, 497 U.S. 261 (1990). The Court upheld a Missouri statute that required proof by clear and convincing evidence that an incompetent

# SUBSTANTIVE DUE PROCESS AND FUNDAMENTAL RIGHTS

person would have wanted to discontinue lifesaving food and water from being artificially administered. Nancy Cruzan had been in a persistent vegetative state for seven years when her parents sued to have the tubes removed. A majority of the Court found that there was a liberty interest in refusing unwanted medical treatment, but only four Justices deemed the interest fundamental.

(4) **No Fundamental Right to Physician–Assisted Suicide. [§ 510]**

**The Due Process Clause of the Fourteenth Amendment does not create or protect a fundamental liberty interest in assisted suicide.**

*Washington v. Glucksberg,* 521 U.S. 702 (1997). The Court unanimously upheld a State of Washington law which criminalizes assisting a person to commit suicide. The plaintiffs (including three seriously ill patients and four doctors) asserted a Due Process Clause liberty interest of a mentally competent, terminally ill adult to commit physician-assisted suicide. Relying heavily on history and legal tradition (mainly Anglo–American common law), the Court concluded that there exists no fundamental liberty interest in committing physician-assisted suicide. As part of its substantive due process analysis, the Court required a "careful description" of the asserted liberty interest. Rejecting broader characterizations of the asserted liberty interest (i.e., the "right to die," or the "liberty to shape death") the Court concluded that the proper tradition to consult was that concerning physician-assisted suicide. After concluding that no such fundamental liberty interest existed, the Court found that Washington's asserted state interests, including preserving human life and avoiding a possible slide toward voluntary and involuntary euthanasia, easily met the rational-basis test of being legitimate government interests.

(5) **No Equal Protection Violation When a State Allows a Patient to Refuse Lifesaving Medical Treatment but Prohibits Physician–Assisted Suicide. [§ 511]**

**Under the Equal Protection Clause, there is a rational distinction between a patient refusing unwanted lifesaving medical treatment, and a patient receiving assistance in committing suicide.**

*Vacco v. Quill,* 521 U.S. 793 (1997). The Court unanimously ruled that New York does not violate the Equal Protection

# CHAPTER XIV

Clause by allowing competent adults to refuse unwanted lifesaving medical treatment, but prohibiting assisted suicide. The Court said that since a prohibition on assisted suicide does not abridge any fundamental right (See *Glucksberg*, prior case), or discriminate against any suspect or quasi-suspect class, rational basis scrutiny is called for under equal protection analysis. Disagreeing with the Second Circuit Court of Appeals, the Court saw a clear distinction between refusing unwanted medical treatment (thus letting nature take its course), and taking affirmative steps to bring about death (by allowing a doctor to prescribe life-ending medication). The Court recognized a number of state interests that justified its ban on assisted suicide, among them preserving life, avoiding a possible slide towards euthanasia, and maintaining the physician's role as healer.

### (6) Family Living Arrangements. [§ 512]

**Family living arrangements are protected as an aspect of liberty, but the Court has not clearly elevated this activity to fundamental right status.**

*Belle Terre v. Boraas*, 416 U.S. 1 (1974). The Court upheld, under rationality review, a village zoning ordinance which limited land use to one-family dwellings. Plaintiffs were six unrelated college students who were prohibited from living together. The Court treated this as a law which affected only low-level social interests, and was therefore valid under rational basis review.

*Moore v. East Cleveland*, 431 U.S. 494 (1977). The Court invalidated a zoning ordinance which prohibited Grandma from living with her two grandsons, who were cousins, but would have allowed the living arrangement if the grandsons were brothers. While not crystal clear on the level of scrutiny it used, the Court said it would "examine carefully" any zoning law which affected freedom of personal choice in matters of family life.

### c. Right to Interstate Travel. [§ 513]

**The Court has recognized a fundamental right to interstate travel, protecting different aspects of the right under different provisions of the Constitution.**

# SUBSTANTIVE DUE PROCESS AND FUNDAMENTAL RIGHTS

**(1) Shapiro v. Thompson, 394 U.S. 618 (1969).**

The Court invalidated, under equal protection, state statutes which denied welfare payments to indigents who had lived in the state less than a year. The classification system set up by these statutes unduly deterred or punished the fundamental right to interstate travel, and was thus invalid as not being narrowly tailored to achieve any compelling government interest.

**(2) Saenz v. Roe, 526 U.S. 489 (1999).**

The Court invalidated a California statute which limited maximum welfare benefits available to a family that lived in the state for less than a year to the amount payable by the state of the family's prior residences. The Court also ruled that Congress could not authorize such discrimination by statute.

The Court identified three components of the right to interstate travel, and the constitutional bases for each of these rights:

   a. The right of a citizen of one state to enter and leave a state. This right was not implicated in the case, so the Court had no need to identify a constitutional basis for it.

   b. The right to be treated as a welcome visitor rather than an unfriendly alien when temporarily present in a state. the Court based this right in the Privilege and Immunities Clause of Article 4, § 2, which removes from the citizens of each State the disabilities of alienage in the other States.

   c. The right of the newly arrived citizen to be treated like other residents of the state. This Right is protected by the Privileges or Immunities Clause of the Fourteenth Amendment; a ruling which breathed new life into that clause, which had been dormant since the *Slaughter-House Cases*, 83 U.S. 36 (1873).

**(3) Starns v. Malkerson, 401 U.S. 985 (1971).**

The Court summarily affirmed the decision of the District Court, which held that a one-year waiting period to establish resident status for in-state tuition purposes at a state university did not violate equal protection. Since higher education, although valuable, is not a basic necessity of life, and the waiting period did not have the purpose of deterring people from moving into the state, the District Court held that the waiting period did not infringe on the exercise of the right to interstate travel. Without the infringement of a fundamental right, the classification received only rational basis scrutiny, and was upheld.

**(4) Memorial Hospital v. Maricopa County, 415 U.S. 250 (1974).**

The Court struck down, under equal protection, an Arizona statute that required a one-year residency as a condition to an indigent receiving nonemergency medical care at the county's expense. Although wealth is a nonsuspect class, the Court held that strict scrutiny applied because the classification operated to deter or penalize the exercise of the fundamental right to interstate travel. The Court stated that not all waiting periods or residency requirements would be held to violate the right to interstate travel, and suggested that the determinative inquiry is whether the benefit being withheld constitutes a "basic necessity of life." Thus, waiting periods that operate to withhold welfare benefits or medical care will be subject to strict scrutiny, but the Court has declined to strike down ones that only affect whether a person receives lower, in-state tuition (prior case).

d. **Right to Vote. [§ 514]**

**While the right to vote is not enumerated in the Constitution, the Court considers it a fundamental right. Notice how the following cases use the Equal Protection Clause to invalidate restrictions on voting.**

(1) **Unequal Numbers of People in Voting Districts. [§ 515]**

The Court has held that if electoral districts within a state have greatly varying numbers of voters in them, the right to vote of persons in the more populous districts will be diluted.

*Reynolds v. Sims*, 377 U.S. 533 (1964). The Court invalidated, under equal protection, a number of state laws which set up electoral districts with greatly varying numbers of people in them. The disparity in numbers among districts meant that some persons' votes were worth more than others. The Court said that the right to vote is a fundamental matter in a democratic society, and is preservative of other basic civil and political rights.

(2) **Statewide Manual Recount of Votes in a Presidential Election [§ 516]**

**A statewide manual recount of votes in a presidential election must be done under uniform rules that apply in each county of the state.**

# SUBSTANTIVE DUE PROCESS AND FUNDAMENTAL RIGHTS

*Bush v. Gore*, 531 U.S. 98 (2000). The Court, under equal protection, reversed an order of the Florida Supreme Court requiring a statewide manual recount of presidential ballots on which voting machines failed to detect a vote for president. Emphasizing that a state must ensure that each person's vote must count as much as another's, the Court ruled that a state must formulate uniform standards by which to conduct a manual recount, and those standards must be applied equally in each county in the state. Applying the one person one vote rule of *Reynolds v. Sims* (previous case), the Court said there must be uniform statewide standards to guide the ballot examiners in deciding whether the intent of the voters can be discerned from the recounted ballots. If no statewide standards are provided, there is too great a danger of some votes not being counted, while identical ballots in other counties would be counted.

### (3) Poll Tax. [§ 517]

The Court has held that a state-imposed poll tax as a prerequisite to voting is unconstitutional.

*Harper v. Virginia State Board of Elections*, 383 U.S. 663 (1966). The Court invalidated, under equal protection, a poll tax imposed as a prerequisite to voting. While the wealth classification by itself did nothing to raise the level of scrutiny, the Court based its analysis on the fundamental right to vote, which is preservative of all other rights.

### (4) Voting Limited to Certain Parties. [§ 518]

The Court has held that states may not pass laws that limit the right to vote in school district elections to property owners or parents with children in the local public schools.

*Kramer v. Union Free School District*, 395 U.S. 621 (1969). The Court invalidated, under equal protection, a state law that restricted voting in school district elections to property owners or parents who had children in the local public schools. The Court used strict scrutiny to invalidate the law.

However, the Court has upheld, against a facial challenge, a state-imposed photo identification requirement to vote.

*Crawford v. Marion County Election Board,* 128 S.Ct. 1610 (2008). The Court voted 6–3, to uphold an Indiana voter

# CHAPTER XIV

identification law requiring voters to present government issued photo identification in order to be able to vote. Rejecting a facial attack on the statute, the Court voted that even-handed restrictions protecting the integrity and reliability of the electoral process meet constitutional standards. The Court balanced the burden on individual voters against relevant and legitimate state interests to conclude that the requirement was valid. The Court said that the photo-ID requirements did not substantially burden eligible voters, and was supported by Indiana's interests in deterring and detecting voter fraud and protecting public confidence in elections.

### (5) Durational Residency Requirements for Voting. [§ 519]

The Court has held that certain durational residency requirements for voting violate equal protection.

*Dunn v. Blumstein*, 405 U.S. 330 (1972). The Court invalidated, under equal protection, a state requirement that a person have resided in the state for one year and in the county for three months before being eligible to vote. The Tennessee law curtailed the fundamental interest in voting.

### (6) Race-based Voting Requirements Violate the Fifteenth Amendment. [§ 520]

The Court has held that restricting the right to vote in statewide elections based on race violates the Fifteenth Amendment.

*Rice v. Cayetano*, 528 U.S. 495 (2000). The Court invalidated a provision of the Hawaii Constitution that limits the right to vote in statewide elections for trustees of the Office of Hawaiian Affairs to "Hawaiians," a term which is statutorily defined on the basis of ancestry. Ruling that ancestry was really a proxy for race, and that neither Congress nor the states may deny the right to vote on the basis of race, the Court said that Hawaii's ancestry requirement to vote violates the Fifteenth Amendment.

e.  **Right to Political Association. [§ 521]**

**While the Constitution does not enumerate such a right, the Court has deemed it fundamental because it is essential to our system of government.** If a state law imposes a severe burden on the right of political association, the state must show that the law is narrowly tailored to achieve a compelling state interest. If the state law does not impose a severe burden on the right of political

# SUBSTANTIVE DUE PROCESS AND FUNDAMENTAL RIGHTS

association, the state must show that its regulatory interests are sufficiently weighty to justify the abridgement of the right.

**(1) Restricting Access to the Ballot. [§ 522]**

The Court has held that states may not preclude access to the ballot without a showing of a compelling government interest and means that are narrowly tailored.

*Williams v. Rhodes*, 393 U.S. 23 (1968). The Court invalidated, under equal protection, a number of Ohio laws which made it virtually impossible for a new political party to be placed on the ballot. The laws violated the right to vote, and the right of political association, and were not narrowly tailored to achieve any compelling governmental interest.

*New York State Board of Elections v. Lopez Torres,* 552 U.S. 196 (2008). The Court upheld, against a First Amendment challenge, New York's system of choosing nominees for the State Supreme Court (which is the trial court in New York). Under New York laws, political parties select their nominees for Supreme Court Justice at a convention of delegates chosen by party members in a primary election. The convention nominees appear automatically on the general-election ballot, along with any independent candidates who meet certain statutory requirements. This system was challenged as violating the First Amendment rights of challengers running against candidate favored by party leaders. The Court said that the real complaint was that the convention process following the delegate election did not give challengers a realistic chance to win their party's nomination because party leaders controlled the delegate election and effectively determined the nominees. The Court rejected this argument, saying that the New York system simply reflects the fact that the party leadership has more support than a candidate not supported by the leadership.

**(2) Filing Fee to Become a Candidate. [§ 523]**

**The Court has invalidated, as an abridgement of the right of political association, filing fees that unduly burdened a minority party's or an indigent candidate's right to get on the ballot.**

*Lubin v. Parish*, 415 U.S. 709 (1974). The Court invalidated, under equal protection, a California law requiring payment of a

# CHAPTER XIV

filing fee of 2% of the salary of the office sought. The filing fee kept indigents off the ballot in some cases. A filing fee to become a candidate cannot unduly burden a minority party's or an indigent candidate's right of political association.

(3) **Banning a Person From Being the Candidate of More Than One Party. [§ 524]**

**State laws that prohibit candidates from being nominated for the same office by more than one party do not unconstitutionally abridge the right to political association of a party unable to nominate another party's candidate.**

*Timmons v. Twin Cities Area New Party*, 520 U.S. 351 (1997). The Court upheld Minnesota "anti-fusion" statutes which prohibit a person from appearing on the ballot as the candidate of more than one party. Reaffirming the existence of a fundamental right of political association, the Court adopted a sliding-scale analysis to analyze the infringement of the right. State laws imposing severe burdens on the right of political association must be narrowly tailored to achieve a compelling state interest. Lesser burdens receive a lower level of review, and a state's important regulatory interests will usually justify reasonable, non-discriminatory restrictions. The Minnesota laws in *Timmons* were justified by the state's interest in ballot integrity and political stability.

(4) **Blanket Primary Infringes Political Parties' Freedom of Association. [§ 525]**

**A "blanket" primary election scheme that allows voters to vote for any candidate, regardless of party affiliation, infringes political parties' right of association if the primary system chooses the general-election nominee of the party.**

*California Democratic Party v. Jones*, 530 U.S. 567 (2000). The Court held that California may not, consistent with the First Amendment, use a "blanket" primary to determine a political party's nominee for the general election. Under the blanket primary system, each primary ballot lists every candidate regardless of party affiliation and allows voters to choose freely among them. The candidate of each party who wins the greatest number of votes becomes that party's nominee in the ensuing general election. The Court reasoned that by forcing the party to associate with nonmembers (and thereby having nonmembers

# SUBSTANTIVE DUE PROCESS AND FUNDAMENTAL RIGHTS

influence the choice of its nominees), the blanket primary system violates the parties' right of association. The Court then found that the blanket primary system was not narrowly tailored to achieve any alleged compelling interest on the part of the state.

*Washington State Grange v. Washington State Republican Party*, 128 S.Ct 1184 (2008). The Court distinguished *California Democratic Party v. Jones* (prior case), and upheld a modified blanket primary system passed by the initiative process in the State of Washington. In 2004, Washington voters passed an initiative providing that candidates must be identified on the primary ballot by their self-designated party preference, that voters may vote for any candidate, and that the two top vote getters, regardless of party preference, advance to the general election. Political parties asserted that the law, on its face, violates a party's associational rights by usurping its power to nominate its own candidates, and by forcing it to associate with candidates it does not endorse. The Court distinguished *Jones* by asserting that the Washington primary system does not, by its terms, choose the parties' nominees. Under the initiative, the choice of an official party representative does not occur. Parties may nominate their own candidate outside the state-run primary. Because the Washington initiative does not severely burden these political parties' associational rights, the Court saw no need to apply the strict scrutiny compelling interest standard.

**(5) Restricting Primaries to Voters Registered With a Party. [§ 526]**

**A state may limit participation in a primary election to persons registered with a party or registered as Independent voters.**

*Clingman v. Beaver*, 543 U.S. 1041 (2005). The Libertarian Party of Oklahoma challenged the constitutionality of a state statute that prohibited it from opening its primary to anyone not registered with its party except registered Independent voters. The Libertarian party argued that the Court should apply strict scrutiny because the statute burdened its right to political association in violation of the First Amendment. The Court held that the Libertarian party's right to political association was not severely burdened because the party only needed to persuade voters to change their registration to that of an Independent to vote in its primary. Voters who could not be persuaded to change their party affiliation obviously were not very concerned with exercising their right to politically associate with the Libertarian party, and applying strict scrutiny to strike down the statute would severely hamper the state's ability to run elections fairly and efficiently.

f. **Right of Access to Courts. [§ 527]**

Be aware of how the importance of the right sought to be protected in court determines whether the Court is willing to protect access to the courts. For example, the Court has ruled that a state court must waive court costs for an indigent who wants to file a divorce action, but a federal court does not have to waive court fees for an indigent who wants to file for bankruptcy. The inference is that the right to dissolve a marriage is more important than the right to go bankrupt.

(1) **Trial Transcripts. [§ 528]**

The Court has held that an indigent defendant who wants to appeal his or her conviction is entitled to a free trial transcript.

*Griffin v. Illinois*, 351 U.S. 12 (1956). The Court ruled that a state must give a free trial transcript (or its equivalent) to an indigent criminal defendant who wants to appeal his or her conviction. Both equal protection and due process principles dictate that protecting an appellant's fundamental rights to a fair trial cannot depend on the amount of money the appellant has.

(2) **Trial Transcript for Appeal of an Order Terminating Parental Rights. [§ 529]**

**An indigent person who wants to appeal a court order terminating his or her parental rights is entitled to a free trial transcript.**

In *M.L.B. v. S.L.J.*, 519 U.S. 102 (1997), the Court held that a mother whose parental rights were terminated by a court order may not be denied an appeal simply on the basis that she cannot afford the record preparation fees. Although fee requirements normally receive rational basis scrutiny, the Court held that since this case involved state intrusions into fundamental family relationships, both equal protection and due process principles required a closer scrutiny. This case is similar to a fundamental rights strand of equal protection analysis, but the Court is careful to not explicitly analyze the case in that manner. Those cases typically involve a law that, through a nonsuspect clas-

# SUBSTANTIVE DUE PROCESS AND FUNDAMENTAL RIGHTS

sification, interferes with the exercise of a fundamental right, but here the fee requirements interfere with the exercise of the right to appeal, which is not a fundamental right in civil cases. But because of the relationship between the right to appeal and the protection of the underlying right of a parent to rear her child, the Court employed heightened scrutiny. The Court declared that since termination orders are "unique" in their severity of state intrusion, this holding does not extend to appeals by indigent persons from other civil cases, including those involving other domestic relations matters.

**(3) Appointed Counsel for First Appeal of a Conviction. [§ 530]**

The Court has held that a state must appoint counsel for an indigent defendant pursuing his or her first appeal of a conviction.

*Douglas v. California*, 368 U.S. 815 (1961). The Court ruled that a state must appoint counsel for an indigent pursuing his or her first appeal, as of right. Again, principles of equal protection and due process dictated this result.

**(4) Waiver of Court Fees to Get a Divorce. [§ 531]**

The Court has held that a state must waive court fees for an indigent seeking a divorce.

*Boddie v. Connecticut*, 401 U.S. 371 (1971). The Court invalidated the application of a state's court fees and costs to an indigent seeking to go to court to get a divorce. Since this was the only forum in which a divorce could be obtained, a state could not use a system which excluded poor people from that forum. Does *Boddie* mean that there is a fundamental right to divorce?

**(5) No Waiver of Court Fees to Declare Bankruptcy. [§ 532]**

The Court has held that a federal bankruptcy court does not have to waive the filing fee for an indigent who wants to declare bankruptcy.

*U.S. v. Kras*, 409 U.S. 434 (1973). The Court ruled that federal fees imposed as a condition of filing for bankruptcy did not violate the due process or equal protection principles of the Fifth Amendment. Going bankrupt is not a fundamental right, but only a low-level economic interest which may be abridged by a showing of rationality.

# CHAPTER XIV

## REVIEW PROBLEMS—SUBSTANTIVE DUE PROCESS AND FUNDAMENTAL RIGHTS

**PROBLEM 1.** The State of Oz passed a law which requires that all abortions be performed in full-service hospitals with neo-natal intensive care units (a neo-natal intensive care unit provides specialized care for newborn infants). Jane Roe has just found out she is pregnant, and wants an abortion. She is in her seventh week of pregnancy. Is this law constitutional?

**Answer:** No. This law would be an undue burden on a woman's right to an abortion prior to viability. At seven weeks of pregnancy, there is no chance that the fetus will survive, so the requirement of a neo-natal intensive care unit is irrational, and would clearly impose an undue burden on a woman who wants a pre-viability abortion. See § 506 for further review.

**PROBLEM 2.** The State of Oz passed a law prohibiting home schooling; all children must attend state-approved public, private, or religious schools. Tina and Tom want to educate their children at home. What constitutional argument might they make to challenge this law?

**Answer:** Tina and Tom would want to argue that there is an unenumerated right of parents to direct the educational upbringing of their children. The Court has, in the past, struck down state laws which imposed too great a burden on this right. For example, remember that in *Pierce v. Society of Sisters*, 268 U.S. 510 (1925), the Court invalidated a state law which required all students to attend public, rather than private or religious, schools. See §§ 489, 490 for further review.

**PROBLEM 3.** The City of Id School District has a regulation prohibiting the possession of condoms on school property. The school authorities claim that students having condoms in school contributes to sexual activity among the students. Stan Studly, a senior at Id High School, files a lawsuit challenging this policy. Does he have an argument?

**Answer:** Yes, the Court has said that minors do have a privacy interest in acquiring and possessing non-prescription contraceptives. However, this right may be abridged if the government has a significant (not compelling) reason for its action. Unfortunately, the Court has never indicated what sort of government interest would indeed be significant enough to justify such an abridgment. The argument that it would deter sexual activity by minors has been expressly rejected. See § 498 for further review.

**PROBLEM 4.** The State of Oz is having troubles with school financing. Millage requests are consistently rejected by the voters (millages are special

# SUBSTANTIVE DUE PROCESS AND FUNDAMENTAL RIGHTS

property-based taxes commonly used to fund public schools). Part of the problem is that Oz has a very large retirement community, and many of the older folks do not want to spend money on educating someone else's kids. As a result, Oz passes a law that restricts voting in school district elections to property owners or parents who have children in Oz public schools. Is this law constitutional?

**Answer:** No. The Court has ruled that there is a fundamental right to vote, and that this sort of classification violates the voting rights of the excluded classes of people. See § 518 for further review.

# CHAPTER XV

# EQUAL PROTECTION

## A. INTRODUCTION. [§ 533]

**Under equal protection analysis, the Court reviews legislation to see if a government is intentionally discriminating against a class of people entitled to special constitutional protection.** Remember that there is only one Equal Protection Clause: it is in the Fourteenth Amendment, and only pertains to states and political subdivisions of states. If the federal government discriminates, the plaintiff's argument is based in the Due Process Clause of the Fifth Amendment; this is because the Court has said that there is an equal protection component of the Due Process Clause of the Fifth Amendment (See *Bolling v. Sharpe*, 347 U.S. 497 (1954)). Under equal protection analysis, individuals who are similarly situated must be treated substantially the same under the law. Under equal protection analysis, it is the classification that is the focus of scrutiny, whereas under substantive due process, the focus is on the individual right being abridged.

When doing an equal protection analysis, see if the government is classifying retrospectively or prospectively; is it trying to punish, or is it trying to prevent? If a government is trying to punish someone for acts already done, it may base the classification system on relevant facts (all drunk drivers who committed accidents will be thrown in jail—this is a very tight classification because it is based on proven facts). If a government is trying to prevent undesirable future conduct, it must guess who is going to engage in the conduct. For instance, if a state wants to prevent drunk driving, it may decide to set its drinking age at 21, based on the assumption that people over 21 years old are generally more responsible than those under 21. This classification is underinclusive (does not reach enough people) because there are irresponsible people over the age of 21. It is overinclusive (reaches too many people) because there are people under 21 who are responsible. Under equal protection analysis, when a government is trying to prevent certain conduct from happening in the future, the Court will scrutinize how well the government guessed at which people will engage in the undesirable conduct.

Under equal protection analysis, the Court determines which class of persons has been disadvantaged by a law (for instance, a law may disadvantage women by excluding them from certain employment opportunities). The Court then decides whether the disadvantaged class is "suspect" (race, ethnicity, or sometimes alienage), "quasi-suspect" (gender or illegitimacy), or "non-suspect" (age, wealth, mental status, sexual orientation, socio-economic, or sometimes alienage).

**If a government intentionally disadvantages a "suspect" class, strict scrutiny applies; if a government intentionally disadvantages a "quasi-suspect" class, intermediate scrutiny applies; and if a government intentionally disadvantages a "non-suspect" class, rational basis review applies.**

Historically, the reason for the Court applying strict scrutiny to laws that classified on the basis of race or ethnicity was that members of racial minority groups were politically powerless in the sense that they could not vote and, hence, could not protect themselves by participating in the democratic process. To compensate for this inability of certain groups to protect themselves through the ballot box, the Court looked very carefully at (applied strict scrutiny to) laws which discriminated on the basis of race.

| **Suspect Classes** | **Quasi–Suspect Classes** | **Non–Suspect Classes** |
|---|---|---|
| Race | Gender | Age |
| Ethnicity | Illegitimacy | Wealth |
| Alienage |  | Mental Status |
| (sometimes) |  | Sexual Orientation |
|  |  | Socio–Economic |
|  |  | Alienage |
|  |  | (sometimes) |

**To make a prima facie equal protection argument, a plaintiff must show disparate impact and intent.** To demonstrate, "disparate impact," the plaintiff must prove that the law disproportionately burdens a particular group. (In attacking a state law that gives veterans a lifetime preference on civil service exams, a female plaintiff showed that women were disproportionately burdened by the law because 98% of the beneficiaries of the veterans' preference law were men.) "Intent" means that the government intended to discriminate against a class **because of** a specific trait such as race or gender. The plaintiff may prove intent by demonstrating that a statute facially discriminates against a group of people, or that enough circumstances exist so that a reasonable inference of intent exists. For instance, a plaintiff may show governmental intent to discriminate by looking at legislative history, departure from normal procedures in enacting a law, or the degree or foreseeability of the disparate impact of the law. A law may be facially discriminatory (the classification is obvious from the language of the law), or discriminatory as

# EQUAL PROTECTION

applied (the law is facially neutral, but is applied so as to intentionally disadvantage a certain class of persons).

1. **Class of One. [§ 534]**

    **The Equal Protection Clause may give rise to a cause if action on behalf of a class of one, even when the plaintiff does not allege membership in a class or group.**

    *Willowbrook v. Olech*, 528 U.S. 562 (2000). Grace Olech alleged that the Village of Willowbrook, demanded a 33-foot easement from her (and her late husband) as a condition of connecting her property to the municipal water supply. The Olechs alleged that the city only required a 15 foot easement from other property owners seeking such access. The Court ruled that the suit could be brought under The Equal Protection Clause, even though Grace Olech was a class of one, if she alleged that she has been intentionally treated differently from others similarly situated and that there is no rational basis for the difference in treatment.

    *Engquist v. Oregon Department of Agriculture,* 128 S.Ct. 2146 (2008). The court held that the class-of-one theory of equal protection does not apply in the public employment context. Engquist was a state employee who sued her agency and her supervisor, asserting under the class-of-one theory, that she was fired for arbitrary reasons. The Court distinguished this case from *Village of Willowbrook v. Olech* (previous case) on the basis that there is a critical difference between the government acting as a lawmaker and the government acting as an employer. The Court said that in the public employment context, government has significantly greater leeway in its dealings with citizen employees than in bringing its sovereign power to bear on citizens at large.

## B. LEVELS OF SCRUTINY. [§ 535]

Under equal protection analysis, how suspect the class is determines the level of scrutiny (and who has the burden of proof).

1. **Rational Basis Review. [§ 536]**

    **If a government is intentionally discriminating against a non-suspect class, rational basis review is used by a court.** At rationality review, the plaintiff has the burden of proof all the way through the case: the plaintiff must show that there is no legitimate reason for the law, or that the means (the classification system) are not rationally related to the goal sought.

# CHAPTER XV

| SUSPECTNESS OF CLASS DISADVANTAGED | ENDS | MEANS | BURDEN OF PROOF |
|---|---|---|---|
| Non–Suspect | Legitimate Government Interest (within an enumerated power of Congress or 10th Amendment Police Power of a state) | Rationally Related (may be very under- or over-inclusive) | Stays with plaintiff |

2. Intermediate Scrutiny. [§ 537]

If a government is intentionally discriminating against a quasi-suspect class, intermediate scrutiny is used by a court. At intermediate scrutiny, the burden of proof shifts to the government once the plaintiff shows that a quasi-suspect class has been disadvantaged.

| SUSPECTNESS OF CLASS DISADVANTAGED | ENDS | MEANS | BURDEN OF PROOF |
|---|---|---|---|
| Quasi–Suspect | Significant or Important | Substantially Related (not very under- or over-inclusive) | Shifts to the government after plaintiff has shown an intentional discrimination against one of the appropriate classes |

3. Strict Scrutiny. [§ 538]

If a government is intentionally discriminating against a suspect class, strict scrutiny is used by a court. At strict scrutiny, the burden of proof shifts to the government once the plaintiff shows that a suspect class has been disadvantaged.

| SUSPECTNESS OF CLASS DISADVANTAGED | ENDS | MEANS | BURDEN OF PROOF |
|---|---|---|---|
| Suspect | Compelling government interest (very important government goal) | Narrowly Tailored (very little under- or over-inclusiveness) | Shifts to the government after plaintiff has shown an intentional discrimination against an appropriate class |

# EQUAL PROTECTION

## C. INTENT REQUIRED TO MAKE AN EQUAL PROTECTION ARGUMENT. [§ 539]

The Constitution prohibits only intentional discrimination (See *Washington v. Davis*, 426 U.S. 229 (1976)). To make out a prima facie equal protection argument, a plaintiff must show both disparate impact and intent. Intent to discriminate may be evident in the language of the statute (facial discrimination), or it may be inferred from the circumstances surrounding the passage or application of a facially neutral statute (as applied discrimination).

1. **Examples of Cases Dealing With the Intent Requirement. [§ 540]**

    a. **Unequal Application. [§ 541]**

    **The Court has held that intent may be shown by the manner in which a facially neutral law is applied.**

    *Yick Wo v. Hopkins*, 118 U.S. 356 (1886). The Court invalidated a San Francisco ordinance prohibiting laundries from operating in wooden buildings unless a board of supervisors granted an exemption. All non-Chinese applicants got exemptions, and no Chinese applicants got them. Even though the ordinance was neutral on its face, it was applied "with an evil eye and an unequal hand," and was based solely on hostility toward Yick Wo's race and nationality.

    b. **Statistical Evidence. [§ 542]**

    **Statistical evidence alone is not enough to show intent.**

    *Washington v. Davis*, 426 U.S. 229 (1976). The Court upheld the validity of a test used to screen applicants for jobs as police officers in the District of Columbia, even though the test had a racially disproportionate impact. The statistical evidence alone was not enough to make out a prima facie case of an equal protection argument; intent was also needed, and could not be inferred from language of the test itself, or from its application.

    c. **Factors. [§ 543]**

    **The Court has identified several factors to consider when trying to prove intent.** Each factor is applied to determine whether there is a constitutionally neutral reason for a law (other than mere racial or sexual discrimination, for instance). The factors include the statistical impact of the law on a particular group, the legislative history of the law, departure from normal procedures in passing the law, and any other evidence that would indicate a purely racial or sexual purpose underlying the law.

*Arlington Heights v. Metropolitan Housing Development Corp.*, 429 U.S. 252 (1977). The Court rejected an equal protection challenge to a village zoning ordinance which had the effect of prohibiting racially integrated low-income housing. No racially discriminatory intent was shown. The Court said that a plaintiff need not show that racial animus was the sole motivation behind a law, just that a discriminatory purpose was **a** motivating factor behind the government action. **There are a number of things to consider when trying to prove intent: the statistical impact of the law on a particular group; a pattern or effect of the law unexplainable on grounds other than race; the legislative or actual history of the government action; or a departure from normal procedural sequence.** While none of these alone may be dispositive of intent, a court will consider the totality of circumstances in deciding the intent question.

d. **Degree and Foreseeability of Disparate Impact. [§ 544]**

**The Court has held that the degree of the disparate impact, along with its foreseeability, are relevant to proving intent; that is, if the disparate impact is unusually severe and was easily foreseen by the legislators who passed the law, a court may consider those factors when determining whether intentional discrimination exists.**

*Personnel Administrator v. Feeney*, 442 U.S. 256 (1979). The Court upheld a Massachusetts law giving a lifetime preference on civil service exams to veterans, even though 98% of the beneficiaries of the law were men. While rejecting the gender-based equal protection challenge, the Court said that degree of disparate impact, as well as its foreseeability are relevant factors in determining intent.

2. **Intent in Jury Selection Cases. [§ 545]**

In jury selection cases involving both grand and petit juries, the Court has almost gotten to the point of accepting a racially discriminatory effect alone as establishing a prima facie case of an equal protection violation. **The rule in jury selection cases is that once a litigant shows substantial underrepresentation of a certain racial (or gender) group, he or she has made a prima facie case of showing discriminatory purpose, and the burden of proof shifts to the government.**

# EQUAL PROTECTION

a. **Disproportionate Representation. [§ 546]**

**Disproportionate representation of racial or ethnic groups on juries is sufficient to make a prima facie case of discriminatory purpose.**

*Castaneda v. Partida*, 430 U.S. 482 (1977). The Court held that a defendant had made out a prima facie case of discrimination against Mexican–Americans in the composition of the grand jury that indicted him. The equal protection argument was based on the disparity between the numbers of Spanish-surnamed persons in the county and those on the grand jury. Once the defendant shows such a disparity, the burden shifts to the government to justify it on some neutral basis.

b. **Peremptory Challenges. [§ 547]**

**A defendant in a criminal case may make a prima facie case of discriminatory purpose by showing the use of peremptory challenges to exclude racial or ethnic groups from the jury.**

i) In ***Batson v. Kentucky*, 476 U.S. 79 (1986)**, the Court held that a defendant in a criminal case may make out a prima facie equal protection case by showing that a prosecutor used peremptory challenges to exclude jurors because of their race. The defendant must show that he or she is a member of a cognizable racial group, and that the prosecutor has used peremptory challenges to exclude members of the defendant's race. The exclusion of members of a certain racial group, coupled with any other relevant circumstances (such as the prosecutor's questions during voir dire), may create an inference of intent to discriminate based on race. (The Court has extended this analysis to civil cases, and to the use of peremptory challenges based on gender. *Edmonson v. Leesville Concrete Co.*, 500 U.S. 614 (1991); *J.E.B v. Alabama ex rel T.B.*, 511 U.S. 127 (1994)).

ii) In ***Powers v. Ohio*, 499 U.S. 400 (1991)**, the Court held that a white defendant had standing to challenge racial discrimination against black persons in the use of peremptory challenges. The Court said that the racially discriminatory use of peremptory challenges by the prosecution endangers the fairness of a criminal trial and thus causes a cognizable injury to the defendant. The Court also found that the excluded juror and the defendant have a common interest in excluding racial discrimina-

# CHAPTER XV

tion from the courtroom, thus satisfying the "relationship" requirement for third-party standing. Finally, the Court said that, as a practical matter, the excluded jurors face serious barriers (primarily economic) to bringing suit on their own behalf, thus meeting the "genuine obstacle" requirement.

iii) In *Campbell v. Louisiana,* **523 U.S. 392 (1998)**, the Court extended *Powers* (previous case) to hold that a white defendant has third-party standing to raise equal protection and due process objections to alleged racial discrimination against black persons in the selection of grand jurors. The Court ruled that a white defendant in such a case meets the three requirements for third-party standing for much the same reasons articulated by the Court in *Powers.*

3. **Intent in Racial Gerrymandering Cases. [§ 548]**

   **The shape and size of voting districts may be relevant to showing intent.** For example, an oddly-shaped voting district that contains predominantly white voters may indicate intentional discrimination.

   a. **Shape of Voting Districts. [§ 549]**

   **A plaintiff may prove intent by showing a drastic change in the geographical shape of a voting district.**

   *Gomillion v. Lightfoot*, 364 U.S. 339 (1960). The Court found intent to discriminate and allowed a cause of action based on an alleged violation of the Fifteenth Amendment (prohibiting racial discrimination in relation to voting). An Alabama law changed the shape of Tuskegee from a square to a 28–sided figure, allegedly removing from the city all but four or five black voters, and leaving all the white voters in the city. This bizarre redistricting seemed to reflect nothing but racial discrimination.

   b. **Strangely Shaped Voting Districts. [§ 550]**

   **The strange shape of a particular district is relevant to proving intentional discrimination.**

   *Shaw v. Reno*, 509 U.S. 630 (1993). The Court concluded that the plaintiffs had stated a claim on which relief could be granted under the Equal Protection Clause. The case involved an alleged racial gerrymander, in which a North Carolina congressional district snaked 160 miles through ten counties, and was, for much of its length, not

# EQUAL PROTECTION

much wider than the interstate highway it followed. The purpose of the districting plan was to increase black voting strength and create a majority-black district. A plaintiff challenging such a plan may make an equal protection claim by alleging that the law, though facially race-neutral, rationally cannot be understood as anything but an attempt to segregate voters based on race. The Court remanded the case to district court for consideration of whether the North Carolina redistricting plan violated the Equal Protection Clause.

*Shaw v. Hunt,* 517 U.S. 899 (1996). This case is a continuation of *Shaw v. Reno* (previous case). In *Reno,* the Court remanded the case to district court for further consideration of whether the North Carolina redistricting plan classified voters by race and whether that classification survived strict scrutiny. The district court held that the plan was constitution al, but the Supreme Court ruled that the plan violated the Equal Protection Clause because it was not narrowly tailored to achieve the state's proffered compelling interests of ameliorating past racial discrimination or complying with provisions of the federal Voting Rights Act.

c. **Race as the Predominant Factor in Drawing District Lines. [§ 551]**

**There is no threshold requirement of showing a bizarre district shape to make an equal protection argument.** All the plaintiff must show is that race was the predominant factor underlying the drawing of the district lines.

*Miller v. Johnson,* 515 U.S. 900 (1995). The Court held that a party challenging a state's legislative redistricting plan is not confined in his or her proof to evidence regarding a district's shape, nor must the plaintiff make a threshold showing that the challenged district has a bizarre shape (See *Shaw v. Reno,* § 550). **The primary element of an equal protection challenge to a state redistricting plan is that race was the predominant factor underlying the state's drawing the voting district lines.** The Court invalidated a Georgia congressional redistricting plan because it found that race was the predominant factor underlying the state's drawing the voting district lines. Specifically, the Court found that Georgia drew the district lines according to race in order to create a third majority-black district to comply with preclearance demands of the Justice Department. The Court found that the majority-black population centers were all at the periphery of the district which covered over 6,700 square miles and split eight counties and five municipalities while extending from Atlanta to the Atlantic.

*Bush v. Vera*, 517 U.S. 952 (1996). The Court ruled that three bizarrely shaped Texas congressional districts failed strict scrutiny analysis under the Equal Protection Clause because the state reapportionment plan was not narrowly tailored to achieving the state's proffered compelling interests of remedying past racial discrimination or complying with provisions of the federal Voting Rights Act. Justice O'Connor, writing for herself, Chief Justice Rehnquist, and Justice Kennedy, asserted that strict scrutiny of congressional redistricting plans is required when a plaintiff shows that race was the predominant factor motivating the legislative and redistricting decision. Justice Thomas, writing for himself and Justice Scalia, asserted that strict scrutiny is required when a plaintiff shows that race was a factor in the creation of a majority-minority voting district.

### d. Politics as the Predominant Factor in Drawing District Lines. [§ 552]

Even though district lines were deliberately drawn to create a largely African-American district, it is permissible because the predominant reason for doing so was political and not racial.

*Easley v. Cromartie*, 532 U.S. 234 (2001). The Court held that even though the Congressional district had snake-like boundaries, split cities and towns, and had an unusually large proportion of African-American voters, race was not the predominant factor in drawing the district's lines. The predominant factor was to ensure a Democratic "safe district", as African-Americans predominantly vote Democratic. Thus the primary reason for the boundary manipulation was political, rather than racial, and it comported with the requirements of equal protection.

## D. REVIEW OF LAWS THAT DISCRIMINATE ON THE BASIS OF RACE OR ETHNICITY. [§ 553]

**Any racial classification will receive strict scrutiny from a reviewing court.** State or federal laws that invidiously discriminate on the basis of race (those that reinforce race-based stereotypes) receive strict scrutiny. State or federal race-based affirmative action laws also receive strict scrutiny. Affirmative action laws are those that discriminate against a particular racial or ethnic group to compensate for a prior discrimination against another racial or ethnic group.

*Johnson v. California*, 543 U.S. 499 (2005). An African-American inmate sued the California Department of Corrections (CDC) for temporarily segregating

# EQUAL PROTECTION

new and transferred prisoners by race for up to 60 days in violation of the equal-protection clause of the Fourteenth Amendment. The CDC argued that the temporary segregation period was necessary to reduce race-based gang violence and that the Supreme Court should give deference to the judgment of the CDC and apply rational basis scrutiny to the policy instead of strict scrutiny. The Supreme Court held that strict scrutiny was the appropriate standard of review because the policy expressly classified inmates by race and there was almost no chance that a new or transferred inmate would be placed in a cell with someone of a different race. Although the Court held that the CDC had a compelling interest in maintaining security and discipline in its prisons, the Court remanded the case to allow a lower court to determine whether the policy withstood strict scrutiny analysis.

1. **Separate but Equal. [§ 554]**

    **From 1896 to 1954, the Court upheld the "separate but equal" doctrine, under which a law separating the races was constitutional if it provided equal facilities or benefits for each race.** The Court simply ignored the blatant racial discrimination intrinsic in the very act of separation.

    **STUDY QUESTION:** Is there a constitutional difference between imposed segregation and requested segregation? It would clearly violate equal protection if a state university prohibited black and white students from living in the same dormitory. Is it any different if black students, for reasons of racial pride and cultural integrity, request and receive separate living quarters (or a student union)? Does the reason for the segregation change its constitutional status?

    a. **"Separate But Equal" Constitutional. [§ 555]**

    **The Court, in 1896, upheld a state law requiring separate railroad accommodations for blacks and whites.**

    *Plessy v. Ferguson*, 163 U.S. 537 (1896). The Court upheld a Louisiana law requiring that railway companies provide "equal but separate accommodations for the white and colored races." Plessy, who asserted that he was seven-eighths Caucasian and one-eighth African blood, was arrested for refusing to leave a whites-only passenger car. The Court rejected the argument that the law imposed a badge of inferiority on blacks, asserting that if any feelings of inferiority flowed from the application of the law, it was "solely because the colored race chooses to put that construction upon it."

# CHAPTER XV

b. **"Separate But Equal" Unconstitutional. [§ 556]**

**The Court, in 1954, ruled that separate educational facilities are inherently unequal and therefore unconstitutional.**

*Brown v. Board of Education I*, 347 U.S. 483 (1954). The Court ruled that separate educational facilities for children in public schools are inherently unequal. The Court said that such segregation violates the equal protection clause even if the physical facilities and other tangible benefits may be equal. While public school education is not a fundamental right, it is preservative of other basic interests such as the right to participate in the processes of government. Enforced separation of the races not only reinforces a sense of inferiority on the part of black school children, but severely affects their motivation to learn.

c. **Integration of Segregated Schools. [§ 557]**

**The Court has held that segregated schools must be integrated "with all deliberate speed."**

*Brown v. Board of Education II*, 349 U.S. 294 (1955). The Court remanded the cases it decided in *Brown I*, with directions for the lower courts to take such actions as necessary to integrate the public schools with all deliberate speed.

d. **Equal Protection as Applied to the Federal Government. [§ 558]**

**The Court has held that equal protection guarantees bind the federal government through the Due Process Clause of the Fifth Amendment.**

*Bolling v. Sharpe*, 347 U.S. 497 (1954). On the same day as *Brown I*, the Court ruled unconstitutional public school segregation in the District of Columbia schools. Since Congress (not a state) passes laws for the District of Columbia (Article 1, section 8, clause 17), the Fourteenth Amendment was not applicable to the case. The Court ruled that separate-but-equal schools violated the Due Process Clause of the Fifth Amendment, which has an implicit equal protection guarantee within it.

2. **Post–*Brown* Remedies for School Segregation. [§ 559]**

After the *Brown* cases, school desegregation became a widespread and controversial topic across the country. **When deliberate (intentional) segregation of schools was found, courts would order remedial steps**

# EQUAL PROTECTION

**to be taken.** Intentional segregation would be found if a school district was operating a dual school system (primarily one-race schools), and was under a statutory mandate to segregate at the time of *Brown I*. If there was no statutory mandate as of 1954, a plaintiff would have to make the normal showing of intent under equal protection analysis. **Once a school district is found to have intentionally created a dual school system, the remedial powers of district courts are very broad, including ordering busing, reassignment of teachers and students, and altering of attendance zones.**

STUDY TIP: Whenever you see a school desegregation question, determine whether there was a law or policy on the books in 1954 that required segregated schools. If so, the Court will impute segregative intent to a school district presently operating a system of one-race schools (a dual school system). If no statute or policy required segregation in 1954, a plaintiff will have to prove intent by looking at the actions of the school board.

a. **Post-*Brown* Cases Involving School Desegregation. [§ 560]**

The Court dealt with strong resistance by some school districts to the mandate of *Brown*. In those cases, the Court made it clear that state officials could not use the fear of public hostility or violence as an excuse to maintain segregated schools. In other cases, the Court had to evaluate school districts' attempts to comply with *Brown*, along with the power of federal courts to require local school districts to comply with the mandate to desegregate local schools.

(1) **Attempted Nullification of Brown by State Officials. [§ 561]**

**The Court rejected an attempt by state officials to nullify *Brown* by preventing black students from attending public high schools.**

*Cooper v. Aaron*, 358 U.S. 1 (1958). The Court unanimously reaffirmed *Brown* in the face of massive resistance from the Governor and legislature of Arkansas. After school authorities set up a desegregation plan, Governor Faubus sent troops to stop black students from entering previously all-white Central High School. Faubus was enjoined from further interference by a federal district court, and federal troops were sent to Arkansas to protect the rights of the black high school students. The Court refused to delay the integration of Little Rock schools, despite the argument that the intense publicity and hostility engendered

# CHAPTER XV

by the desegregation plan would detract from the educational process. The Court said that *Brown* could not be nullified, directly or indirectly, by the actions of state officials.

### (2) County–Run Private White Schools. [§ 562]

**A county may not operate private white schools in an attempt to avoid integration.**

*Griffin v. County School Board*, 375 U.S. 391 (1964). The Court, saying that the time for deliberate speed had run out, invalidated the action of a county closing its public schools to avoid complying with a desegregation order. Private white schools were set up and supported by state and local grants. A state may not allow one county to close its public schools for the sole purpose of racial discrimination, and then subsidize allegedly "private" schools for whites.

### (3) Freedom-of-Choice Plans. [§ 563]

**States may not enact so-called "freedom of choice" plans in an attempt to avoid integration.** "Freedom of choice" plans purport to allow students to choose where they will attend school. The problem with such a plan as an integrative remedy is that virtually none of the white students chose to attend schools with high minority enrollment.

*Green v. County School Board*, 391 U.S. 430 (1968). The Court invalidated a "freedom-of-choice" plan which did virtually nothing to integrate public schools which had been segregated by law as of *Brown I*. The Court said that school boards operating state-compelled dual school systems as of 1954 had an affirmative duty to integrate their schools. In effect, the Court said that the law requiring segregated schools in 1954 created the intent necessary for an equal protection argument. Once that is present, all that need be shown is disparate impact, in the form of a dual school system.

### (4) Presuming Intent Throughout a School District. [§ 564]

**Where a court finds segregative intent on the part of a school board in relation to a large part of a school district, a court will presume that the intent to discriminate exists throughout the entire district.**

*Keyes v. School District*, 413 U.S. 189 (1973). The Court, for the first time, dealt with an equal protection challenge to school

# EQUAL PROTECTION

board action when there had never been a law requiring segregated schools. The Court held that a finding of segregative intent by the school board in relation to a meaningful portion of a school district (an attendance zone within the district) creates a presumption that the intentionally segregative actions of the school board were responsible for segregated schools in the rest of the district. The school board would then have the burden of showing that segregation in the other schools was not a result of its actions.

### (5) Dual School System. [§ 565]

**The failure of a school board to eliminate its dual school system has been found to support an Equal Protection claim.**

*Columbus Board of Education v. Penick*, 443 U.S. 449 (1979). The Court upheld a system-wide desegregation remedy. Even though there was no state law mandating segregation, the lower court found that the Columbus schools were officially segregated by race in 1954. This, plus the fact that the board knowingly continued to fail to take steps to eliminate its dual school system, allowed the plaintiffs to show both dual school system and intent, thereby making out a prima facie equal protection argument.

### b. Post-*Brown* Cases Dealing With the Remedial Power of Federal Courts. [§ 566]

**Federal courts have extremely broad equitable powers to remedy unconstitutional school segregation by ordering busing, redrawing district lines, or assigning teachers or students based on race.** An interesting question is when should a court end its supervision of a local school board's activities? For the answer, see the *Dowell* 570 and *Freeman* 571 cases, later in this subsection.

### (1) Remedial Powers. [§ 567]

**Federal courts have broad remedial powers to remedy segregation.**

*Swann v. Charlotte–Mecklenburg Board of Education*, 402 U.S. 1 (1971). The Court set guidelines for the exercise of equitable jurisdiction by lower courts in desegregation cases. Once a right and a violation have been shown, the scope of a district court's power to remedy past wrongs is broad. The Court listed the following guidelines: a court may consider the racial composition of the students in a school district as a starting point for crafting an equitable remedy (there is, however, no constitutional right to any certain degree of racial balance within the school system); a small number of one-race schools does not necessarily mean that the school district is segregated by law; alteration of the boundaries of school districts or attendance zones is permissible, even if administratively awkward or inconvenient; and busing may be used to desegregate, as long as it does not detract from the educational process by requiring inordinately long bus rides.

(2) **Cross–District Busing. [§ 568]**

**Cross-district busing may be an appropriate remedy where segregation in one school district produces a segregative effect in another.**

*Milliken v. Bradley*, 418 U.S. 717 (1974). The district court in *Milliken* ordered cross-district busing between Detroit and 53 suburban school districts. While the Court invalidated this particular busing order, it said that cross-district busing would be a permissible remedy if there had been a constitutional violation in one district that produces a significant segregative effect in another. The general principle is that the scope of the remedy must be proportionate to the scope of the proven constitutional violation; whichever school districts are proven to be co-discriminators may be included within a busing order.

(3) **Termination of Federal Court Supervision. [§ 569]**

**A desegregation decree should be dissolved if the school board has complied with the decree in good faith and the vestiges of past discrimination have been eliminated to the extent practicable.**

*Oklahoma City Board of Education v. Dowell*, 498 U.S. 237 (1991). The Court dealt with the question of when a remedial court order should be dissolved. The Oklahoma City Board of Education had been under a court order to integrate its schools, which it did, in part through a busing plan. The Board wanted to adopt what was basically a neighborhood school system, but the result was that about half the schools became one-race schools because of housing patterns. The Court said that the desegregation decree should be dissolved if the school board has complied in good faith, and the vestiges of past discrimination have been

# EQUAL PROTECTION

eliminated to the extent practicable. Justice Marshall, in dissent, said that a court order imposing a desegregation plan should not end so long as conditions likely to inflict the stigmatic injury persist, and there are feasible methods of eliminating such conditions (there always are—just leave the desegregation decree in effect).

**(4) School Board Compliance With Discrete Requirements of a Court Decree. [§ 570]**

**Federal courts need not retain control over every aspect of school administration where the school board has shown it has complied with some specific requirements of the court decree.**

*Freeman v. Pitts*, 503 U.S. 467 (1992). The Court said that when a court is deciding whether to end a court-ordered desegregation plan, it may withdraw judicial supervision of discrete categories of activity in which the school district has achieved compliance; it need not retain control over every aspect of school administration until full compliance is achieved. Three factors to consider when deciding to terminate a desegregation plan are: whether there has been full compliance with the decree; whether retention of judicial control is necessary or practicable to achieve compliance with the decree; and whether the school district has demonstrated a good-faith commitment to complying with the decree.

**(5) Court–Ordered Salary Increases and Funding of Remedial Education Programs. [§ 571]**

**Federal courts may not fashion interdistrict remedies that exceed the scope of an intradistrict violation.**

*Missouri v. Jenkins*, 515 U.S. 70 (1995). The Court, reaffirming the three-part test of *Freeman v. Pitts* (previous case), ruled that a federal district court exceeded its remedial authority when it required Missouri to fund salary increases for virtually all instructional and noninstructional staff within the Kansas City School District, and to continue to fund remedial "quality education" programs. The district court has found an intradistrict violation in that student achievement levels in the Kansas City School District were still at or below national norms at many grade levels. The order requiring salary increases, which was designed to improve the "desegregative attractiveness" of

# CHAPTER XV

the Kansas City schools (to attract white suburban students to the Kansas City School District), was an interdistrict remedy beyond the scope of the intradistrict violation in the case. Furthermore, the order requiring continued funding of "quality education" programs was based on an erroneous assumption by the district court; whether or not Kansas City students are at or below national norms of student achievement is not the test for determining whether a previously segregated school district has achieved unitary status—the three-part test of *Freeman v. Pitts* is the appropriate standard. Under *Freeman*, a court should ask the following: whether the school district has fully complied with the desegregation decree; whether continued judicial control is necessary or practicable to achieve compliance with the decree; and whether the school district has demonstrated a good-faith commitment to complying with the decree.

(6) **Termination of Federal Court Supervision. [§ 572]**

**A state has not met its burden of proving that the prior segregative system has been dismantled if it perpetuates policies that continue to have segregative effects.**

*U.S. v. Fordice*, 505 U.S. 717 (1992). The Court dealt with the question of whether Mississippi had taken appropriate steps to dismantle a public university system in which some schools were almost exclusively white and some were almost exclusively black. The Court remanded for review in light of the following standard: If the State perpetuates policies and practices traceable to its prior system that continue to have segregative effects, and such policies are without sound educational justification and can be practicably eliminated, the State has not met its burden of proving that it has dismantled its prior system.

3. **Affirmative Action. [§ 573]**

**An affirmative action program is a governmental program which gives a preference to members of specified racial or ethnic groups. These programs are most common in the areas of education and employment. Race-based affirmative action programs, whether they are imposed by a state or the federal government, receive strict scrutiny by a reviewing court: the government has the burden of showing that the affirmative action program is narrowly tailored to achieve a compelling government interest.**

In the area of employment, affirmative action programs are compensatory; they are designed to make up for past discrimination against members of racial or ethnic groups favored by the affirmative action program. For an affirmative action program to be constitutional, it must be a remedy for a past violation. Also, the scope of the affirmative action plan must be proportionate to the scope of the violation. Past discrimination by society as a whole (engaged in by both governmental and private actors) does not count as a violation which will justify a state or federal affirmative action program based on race. At least in the employment context, there must be some basis in evidence indicating that the government (or some specific agency of government) contributed in some discernible way to a prior system or scheme of racial discrimination. For instance, if a state (or the federal government) wanted to implement a voluntary affirmative action program based on race, the state must show that it contributed (at least as a passive participant) to a previous racially discriminatory system or scheme. The Court does not force a state to admit an intentional act or pattern of past racial discrimination (that would subject the state to civil rights lawsuits), it simply requires the state to assert that it had been a passive, negligent, or inadvertent contributor to past racial discrimination. This kind of admission qualifies as a past wrong which will justify a remedial race-based affirmative action program.

Race-based affirmative action cases in education adopt a different theory. The Court does not require that a university or law school justify its affirmative action admissions programs by pointing to some prior discrimination. Rather than a remedial theory, the Court simply asks whether the affirmative action admissions program meets strict scrutiny. The Court has held that diversity in the classroom is a compelling government interest, and that an admissions program that is narrowly tailored to achieve that goal is constitutionally permissible.

a. **State Race–Based Affirmative Action Plans. [§ 574]**

**State race-based affirmative action programs receive strict scrutiny: The government must show a compelling reason for the program, and the means must be narrowly tailored to achieve that goal.** Societal discrimination does not count as a violation that would justify a state race-based affirmative action plan. To have a voluntary affirmative action plan based on race, a state must show at least that it was a passive participant in some prior discrimination against a racial group. For instance, a state spending millions of dollars in the construction industry contributed to the systematic discrimination against racial groups in the industry.

# CHAPTER XV

**(1) Race–Based Exclusions. [§ 575]**

**The Court has held that exclusion from a program based solely on race is illegal, even if the purpose of the exclusion is to increase the number of racial minority members who participate in the program.**

*Regents of the University of California v. Bakke*, 438 U.S. 265 (1978). The Court, in a divided vote, issued two rulings: The University of California at Davis Medical School violated the federal statutory rights of Allan Bakke, a white applicant to medical school who was denied access to 16 (out of 100) spots set aside for minority applicants; and race may be considered as one of many factors in a university admissions program. In addition to his claim that his Fourteenth Amendment rights were violated by the set-aside program, Bakke also alleged that the Davis program violated his rights under Title VI of the Civil Rights Act of 1964, which prohibits racial discrimination in any program receiving federal funds. Justice Powell, along with Chief Justice Burger and Justices Stewart, Stevens, and Rehnquist ruled in favor of Bakke's Title VI claim. Justice Powell also said (alone) that Bakke's Fourteenth Amendment rights were violated. Justice Powell, joined by Justices Brennan, White, Marshall, and Blackmun, ruled that race may be considered as one factor in an admissions program. Justice Powell made the following constitutional points: strict scrutiny is the appropriate level of review in race-based affirmative action cases; societal discrimination does not count as a violation justifying an affirmative action plan; and, while attainment of a diverse student body may be a compelling government interest, exclusion of applicants from a certain number of spots, based on their race alone, is not a narrowly-tailored means because it is not related to any prior discrimination by the medical school (in fact, the medical school was found to have a clean record in terms of past racial discrimination). Justice Brennan argued that past societal discrimination does count as a violation that would justify an affirmative action program, that intermediate scrutiny is the appropriate level of review, and that whites, as a group, do not suffer the same kind of stigma as blacks when their respective groups are discriminated against. Justice Stevens, relying solely on Bakke's statutory argument, concluded that Title VI prohibited the exclusion of any individual from a federally funded program based on race.

# EQUAL PROTECTION

(2) **Non–Remedial Justification for a University Race–Based Affirmative Action Plan. [§ 576]**

**The Court ruled that a university may assert a compelling interest in assembling a racially and ethnically diverse student body, but that a point system which operated to guarantee admission to minority applicants was not narrowly tailored to achieve that goal.**

*Gratz v. Bollinger*, 539 U.S. 244 (2003). The Court, by a 6–3 vote, struck down a race-based admissions program used by the University of Michigan's College of Literature, Science, and the Arts (LSA). Under the program, a member of an underrepresented minority group (African–Americans, Hispanics, and Native Americans) would be automatically awarded 20 points out of 100 points needed for admission to LSA. Plaintiffs challenged this program as violative of the Equal Protection Clause. Relying on Justice Powell's opinion in *Bakke* (§ 576), the Court rejected the argument that diversity cannot qualify as a compelling state interest, but held that the awarding of 20 points (out of 100 needed for admission) was not narrowly tailored to achieving the University's goal of educational diversity. The Court focused on the importance of considering each applicant as an individual, and said that the LSA policy did not provide the individualized consideration contemplated by Justice Powell in *Bakke*. The main reason why the point system was found to fail the "narrowly-tailored" requirement was that the 20–point distribution to each member of an underrepresented minority group made the factor of race decisive (not just a "plus") for virtually every minimally qualified underrepresented minority applicant.

(3) **Individualized Law School Admissions Process Is Narrowly Tailored to Achieving Compelling Interest in a Diverse Student Body. [§ 577]**

**The Court upheld a law school's use of race in its admissions process as a narrowly-tailored means to achieve a compelling interest in diversity in the classroom.**

*Grutter v. Bollinger*, 539 U.S. 306 (2003). The Court, by a 5–4 vote, upheld the admissions policy of the University of Michigan Law School which considered race or ethnicity as a "plus" factor in an applicant's file, rather than making it the decisive factor in the admissions decision (See *Gratz*, § 577.1). The

# CHAPTER XV

Court, applying strict scrutiny, held that diversity in the classroom is a compelling government interest, and that the Law School's use of race was narrowly tailored to achieving that goal. The Court accepted the Law School's argument that it needed a "critical mass" of minority students to assure that the diversity goals of cross-racial understanding and the breaking down of racial stereotypes would be met. Justice O'Connor, for the majority, focused on the highly individualized, holistic review of an applicant's file, distinguishing this approach from the mechanistic use of a point system in *Gratz* (§ 576).

**(4) Race–Based Student Assignments Violate the Constitution. [§ 578] The Court struck down voluntary plans adopted by public school districts that assigned pupils to schools on the basis of their race.**

*Parents Involved in Community Schools v. Seattle School District No. 1*, 551 U.S. 701 (2007).

The courts struck down voluntarily adopted student assignment plans that relied on race to determine which public schools certain children may attend. The Court used strict scrutiny to review the school districts' plans, and held that they did not remedy the effects of past discrimination, nor did they advance the compelling interest in diversity in higher education recognized in *Grutter* (§ 577). Chief Justice Roberts, for the Court, said that race was not considered by the school districts as part of a broader effort to achieve exposure to diverse people, ideas, cultures and viewpoints, but was, for some students, the sole determinative factor in pupil assignment. The Seattle, Washington school district, which has never operated legally segregated schools or been a subject to court-ordered desegregation, classified students as white or non-white, and used those classifications as a tiebreaker to assign certain students to certain high schools. The Jefferson County, Kentucky school district was subject to a desegregation decree until 2000, when it was dissolved by a district judge. In 2001, the district adopted a plan under which students were classified as black or "other" in order to make some student assignments. Justice Breyer, dissenting for four justices, argued that strict scrutiny should not be the standard of review when racial discrimination is inclusionary rather than exclusionary.

# EQUAL PROTECTION

(5) **Proportional Representation by Race in the Work Force. [§ 579]**

**Layoffs are an impermissible means to achieve equal representation in the work force.**

*Wygant v. Jackson Board of Education*, 476 U.S. 267 (1986). The Court invalidated a plan of the Jackson, Michigan school board under which white teachers with more seniority would be laid off before minority teachers who were retained to keep a certain percentage of minority teachers in the classroom. There was no majority opinion of the Court, but five Justices agreed that layoffs of innocent white teachers was an unconstitutional means to achieve even permissible goals. Five Justices also rejected societal discrimination as the violation which would justify an affirmative action plan, and rejected the school board's "role model" argument, under which a certain percentage of minority teachers must be maintained as role models for minority students.

(6) **Standard of Review. [§ 580]**

**When reviewing a state-based affirmative action program, courts will apply strict scrutiny. In addition, states may not use societal discrimination as a basis for enacting an affirmative action program.**

*Richmond v. J.A. Croson Co.*, 488 U.S. 469 (1989). The Court invalidated a Richmond, Virginia set-aside program under which 30% of city construction money was earmarked for Minority Business Enterprises. A majority of the Court agreed that a state race-based affirmative action program should receive strict scrutiny, and that societal discrimination would not justify such a program. If a state or city wants to setup a voluntary affirmative action program, it must show that it was at least a "passive participant" in a system of racial discrimination. The idea is to have the state or city admit to some complicity in past racial discrimination so that there is something more specific than societal discrimination to justify the voluntary affirmative action plan.

b. **Federal Race–Based Affirmative Action Plans. [§ 581]**

**Federal race-based affirmative action programs receive strict scrutiny: The government must show a compelling reason for the program, and the means must be narrowly tailored to achieve**

# CHAPTER XV

that goal. After *Adarand v. Pena* (see § 585), the rules for federal affirmative action programs based on race are the same as the rules for state affirmative action programs based on race.

**(1) Pre-Adarand Federal Race–Based Affirmative Action Cases. [§ 582]**

Prior to the *Adarand* case (see, § 585), federal race-based affirmative action programs received intermediate scrutiny from the courts.

**(a) Federal Minority Business Set–Asides. [§ 583]**

Pre-*Adarand*, the Court upheld a federal set-aside for minority business enterprises.

*Fullilove v. Klutznick*, 448 U.S. 448 (1980). The Court upheld a federal set-aside of public works money for Minority Business Enterprises. There was no majority opinion of the Court, but Chief Justice Burger, writing for three Justices, did say that in a remedial context, Congress must have some leeway in crafting the means to achieve its goals. Justice Marshall, for three Justices, clearly advocated an intermediate level of scrutiny. Justice Stewart, for two Justices, said that race should never be the criterion used to allocate government benefits.

**(b) Broadcast Licenses. [§ 584]**

Pre-*Adarand*, the Court upheld the use of racial preferences in granting broadcast licenses.

*Metro Broadcasting v. FCC*, 497 U.S. 547 (1990). The Court upheld an FCC policy which granted a racial preference to applicants for broadcast licenses, and for the sale and transfer of certain licenses. A majority of the Court, through Justice Brennan, said that intermediate scrutiny is the appropriate standard of review for a congressional race-based affirmative action program. The Court also said that Congress may enact such programs even if they are not "remedial" in the sense of compensating victims of past governmental or societal discrimination. In other words, Congress may set up an affirmative action plan even without any assertion of past societal discrimination. In this sense *Metro Broadcasting* is clearly the most liberal of the Court's affirmative action rulings in the race area.

# EQUAL PROTECTION

### (2) Federal Race–Based Affirmative Action Programs Receive Strict Scrutiny. [§ 585]

**After the *Adarand* decision, federal race-based affirmative action programs receive strict scrutiny—the same standard the Court uses when reviewing state race-based affirmative action programs.**

*Adarand Construction Inc. v. Pena*, 515 U.S. 200 (1995). In *Adarand*, the Court reviewed a clause in a federal highway construction contract which provided bonuses for subcontracting with small businesses owned by socially and economically disadvantaged individuals. Under the federal law, certain racial and ethnic minorities are presumed to be socially and economically disadvantaged. The Court held that strict scrutiny applies to all race-based affirmative action programs, state or federal. To the extent that *Fullilove* (see § 583) and *Metro Broadcasting* (see § 584) are inconsistent with this holding, they are overruled. The Court ruled that societal discrimination will not justify a federal race-based affirmative action program, and that Congress (like a state under *Croson* (see § 580)) must make a specific showing of some participation in past racial discrimination if it wants to implement a race-based affirmative action program. The Court remanded the case for consideration under the strict scrutiny standard.

## 4. Interracial Sexual Relations. [§ 586]

A number of states, at one time or another, have had laws prohibiting sexual relations between blacks and whites (Alabama, in 1972, was the last state to repeal its anti-miscegenation law). These anti-miscegenation laws have consistently been struck down by the Court. In these cases, the state usually argued that there was not an equal protection problem because black people and white people were treated the same—neither could associate with the other. Be aware of the "separate but equal" aspect of this argument.

### a. Interracial Sexual Relations. [§ 587]

**The Court upheld an 1883 state law that prohibited interracial sexual relations.**

*Pace v. Alabama*, 106 U.S. 583 (1883). The Court upheld an Alabama statute that prohibited adultery or fornication between a black person and a white person, and that imposed greater penalties on those persons than on sexual partners of the same race. The Court

# CHAPTER XV

said that equal protection guarantees were not violated as long as the black and white participants in the offense were equally punished.

b. **Overnight Visits. [§ 588]**

**A state may not pass a law that prohibits a biracial couple from staying together overnight.**

*McLaughlin v. Florida*, 379 U.S. 184 (1964). The Court overruled *Pace v. Alabama* (previous case), and invalidated a Florida statute which made it a crime for a white person and a black person of opposite sexes, not married to each other, to habitually occupy the same room in the nighttime. The Court did not consider the racial classification in the law to be a rational means of achieving any legitimate state goal.

c. **Interracial Marriage. [§ 589]**

**A state may not pass a law that prohibits interracial marriage.**

*Loving v. Virginia*, 388 U.S. 1 (1967). The Court invalidated a Virginia law which criminalized marriage between a white and any non-white person. Any non-white racial classes could intermarry with no criminal sanctions. The Court thoroughly rejected the argument that equal protection guarantees were not violated because whites and blacks were treated equally—neither could marry the other. It recognized this law for what it was—a blatant attempt by the state to reinforce invidious stereotypes of racial inferiority (one of the asserted state interests underlying the law was to prevent "a mongrel breed of citizens"). Be aware that the law also abridged the fundamental right to marry.

d. **Child Custody. [§ 590]**

**Child custody decisions may not be based solely on race.**

*Palmore v. Sidoti*, 466 U.S. 429 (1984). The Court held violative of equal protection a state's denial of child custody to a white mother for the sole reason that her new husband was black. While race may not be the sole determining factor in a child custody decision, it may be considered along with other factors to determine who gets custody of a child.

## E. REVIEW OF LAWS THAT DISCRIMINATE ON THE BASIS OF ALIENAGE. [§ 591]

An alien is a person who is not a citizen of the United States. Aliens are protected by the Equal Protection Clause of the Fourteenth Amendment, as

# EQUAL PROTECTION

well as the equal protection component of the Due Process Clause of the Fifth Amendment. Be careful about which government (federal or state) is discriminating against aliens. **A federal law discriminating against aliens will receive only rational basis review; the plaintiff must show that the law is not rationally related to a legitimate federal interest. When a state discriminates against aliens, strict scrutiny will apply, unless the state is excluding aliens from politically sensitive positions—then rational basis review will apply.** This "political function" exception applies when a state (or city) excludes aliens from elected positions, important non-elected positions (involving the formulation or implementation of public policy), or employment as public school teachers, police officers, or probation or parole officers. Being a notary public is not within the political function exception, so a state exclusion of aliens from that position is subject to strict scrutiny.

1. **Federal Laws That Discriminate Against Aliens. [§ 592]**

    **Because of Congress' power to regulate immigration and naturalization, the Court is extremely deferential to federal laws regulating aliens: rationality review is the appropriate level of scrutiny.**

    a. **Welfare Benefits. [§ 593]**

        **Congress may impose restrictions on an alien's eligibility for welfare benefits.**

        *Mathews v. Diaz*, 426 U.S. 67 (1976). The Court upheld a federal law imposing restrictions on an alien's eligibility for Medicare benefits. The Court said that because alienage issues touch on our country's relations with foreign countries, the Court should be extremely deferential to any decision of Congress or the President dealing with aliens. The Court likened the Court's role in federal alienage cases to its role in political question cases.

    b. **Government Employment. [§ 594]**

        **Congress may not bar resident aliens from civil service employment without a showing that the restrictions were based on a legitimate national interest.**

        *Hampton v. Wong*, 426 U.S. 88 (1976). The Court invalidated a federal regulation barring resident aliens from civil service employment. The Court said that when the federal government asserts a legitimate national interest as the basis for a law, the Court will apply only rational basis review. In this case, it was unclear whether the federal government acted to advance a national interest having to do with aliens or foreign relations, or whether it was simply regulating to enhance workplace efficiency.

# CHAPTER XV

2. **State Laws That Discriminate Against Aliens. [§ 595]**

   **When a state discriminates against aliens, strict scrutiny applies unless the alien is being excluded from a politically sensitive position; then rationality review applies.**

   a. **Government Employment in General. [§ 596]**

   **A state cannot exclude aliens from all government employment.**

   *Sugarman v. Dougall*, 413 U.S. 634 (1973). The Court invalidated a New York law that excluded aliens from all employment subject to competitive tests. The Court applied the strict scrutiny standard, and said that New York's law was not narrowly drawn to achieve any compelling interest such as protecting the political process.

   b. **Practice of Law. [§ 597]**

   **A state cannot exclude aliens from the practice of law.**

   *In re Griffiths*, 413 U.S. 717 (1973). The Court invalidated, under strict scrutiny, Connecticut's exclusion of resident aliens from the practice of law. The Court said that the practice of law was not so close to the core of the political process as to place lawyers within the political function exception.

   c. **Police Officers. [§ 598]**

   **A state can exclude aliens from being police officers.**

   *Foley v. Connelie*, 435 U.S. 291 (1978). The Court upheld, under rational basis review, New York's exclusion of aliens from its police force. The Court reasoned that police perform discretionary functions which are essential to the carrying out of public policy and the laws of the state.

   d. **Public School Teachers. [§ 599]**

   **A state can exclude aliens from positions as public school teachers.**

   *Ambach v. Norwick*, 441 U.S. 68 (1979). The Court upheld, under rational basis review, New York's exclusion of aliens from positions as public elementary or secondary teachers. The Court said that teachers are within the public function exception because they inculcate national ideals, and prepare students for the obligations of citizenship.

# EQUAL PROTECTION

e. **Probation Officers. [§ 600]**

**A state can exclude aliens from positions as probation officers.**

*Cabell v. Chavez–Salido*, 454 U.S. 432 (1982). The Court upheld, under rational basis review, California's exclusion of aliens from positions as state probation officers. Probation officers, like police officers in general, perform functions that are central to the political functioning of the state—applying the criminal laws and public policy of California.

f. **Notary Public. [§ 601]**

**A state cannot exclude an alien from a position as a notary public.**

*Bernal v. Fainter*, 467 U.S. 216 (1984). The Court invalidated, under strict scrutiny, a Texas law that excluded aliens from positions as notaries public. Since this job was mainly clerical, and did not involve functions going to the heart of representative government, the political function exception did not apply, and strict scrutiny was called for.

**STUDY TIP:** If you get an alienage question in which a state is discriminating against aliens, there is a good chance that the professor is asking about the political function exception. Be aware of the specific positions the Court has ruled on (teachers, police or probation officers, notaries public, and lawyers), as well as the principle that a state is usually free to exclude aliens from positions that go to the heart of representative government.

3. **Interplay Between Preemption and Alienage Analysis. [§ 602]**

**When a state law discriminating against aliens imposes requirements on aliens over and above those mandated by Congress, there may be a preemption problem in that the state law may be frustrating the purpose of the federal law.** Be aware of this issue if you get a question that specifically mentions both a federal and a state law regulating aliens.

a. **Instate Tuition. [§ 603]**

**A state cannot deny instate tuition to aliens domiciled in the state.**

*Toll v. Moreno*, 441 U.S. 458 (1979). The Court invalidated, on supremacy grounds, a University of Maryland rule denying instate

# CHAPTER XV

tuition to certain aliens, despite the fact that Congress had allowed these aliens to establish domicile in the state. This ancillary burden violated the Supremacy Clause because it imposed burdens on aliens over and above those imposed by Congress, thereby interfering with federal regulation of immigration.

    **b. Welfare Benefits. [§ 604]**

    **A state cannot deny welfare benefits to resident aliens.**

    *Graham v. Richardson*, 403 U.S. 365 (1971). The Court invalidated, on supremacy grounds, state statutes which denied welfare benefits to resident aliens. The Court said that such laws conflict with overriding national policies in an area (the regulation of immigration) constitutionally entrusted to Congress.

## F. REVIEW OF LAWS THAT DISCRIMINATE ON THE BASIS OF GENDER. [§ 605]

**Federal or state laws that discriminate on the basis of gender receive intermediate scrutiny by the Court; government must show a significant or important reason for the classification, and means that are substantially related.** The rules are the same whether females or males are disadvantaged. Under equal protection analysis, a government must treat equally those persons who are similarly situated in terms of the purpose of the law. In some cases, the Court has said that there are constitutionally relevant differences between women and men. For instance, if the purpose of the draft is to fill all positions in the military, men and women are similarly situated because both can hold military positions. However, if the purpose of the draft is to fill only combat positions, men and women are not similarly situated because (by federal law) only men can fill combat positions.

    **1. Tracing the Development of Gender Analysis Under Equal Protection. [§ 606]**

    The Court has gone from affording women virtually no constitutional protection (*Bradwell*, § 607 below), to almost making gender a suspect classification (*Frontiero*, § 609 below), to holding that gender is a quasi-suspect class, entitled to intermediate scrutiny review.

        **a. Women as Lawyers. [§ 607]**

        **The Court upheld an early state law prohibiting women from being lawyers.**

        *Bradwell v. Illinois*, 83 U.S. 130 (1873). The Court upheld the power of the Illinois Supreme Court to deny women the opportunity to be

# EQUAL PROTECTION

lawyers. A concurring opinion said that the " . . . paramount destiny and mission of woman are to fulfill the noble and benign offices of wife and mother. This is the law of the Creator." While *Bradwell* has not been specifically overruled, such a law would clearly be unconstitutional today as lacking any legitimate reason for its existence.

b. **Women as Estate Administrators. [§ 608]**

**A state cannot give an automatic preference to men as estate administrators.**

*Reed v. Reed*, 404 U.S. 71 (1971). For the first time, the Court invalidated, on equal protection grounds, a state law discriminating on the basis of gender in the choice of estate administrators. The Court, not using any form of heightened scrutiny, said that the automatic preference for men over women was so arbitrary as to violate the Equal Protection Clause.

c. **Spousal Dependency Allowances. [§ 609]**

**Federal law may not treat male and female members of the armed forces differently in relation to dependency allowances for spouses.**

*Frontiero v. Richardson*, 411 U.S. 677 (1973). This case was the closest the Court has ever come to establishing gender as a suspect class. Justice Brennan, for four Justices, used strict scrutiny to invalidate a federal law which treated male and female members of the armed forces differently in terms of establishing dependency allowances for their spouses. A male soldier could automatically claim his wife as a dependent, even if she were rich. A female soldier, however, had to prove that her husband was dependent on her before she got the benefits. A majority of the Court agreed that this scheme violated the equal protection component of the Due Process Clause of the Fifth Amendment.

d. **Drinking Age. [§ 610]**

**A state may not have different drinking ages for men and women.**

*Craig v. Boren*, 429 U.S. 190 (1976). The Court, adopting the intermediate level of scrutiny, invalidated a law which discriminated against males by requiring them to be 21 years old to buy beer, when females could buy it at age 18. The idea underlying this prospective law (prospective because it attempted to prevent future misconduct rather than punish past misdeeds) was that 18–20 year-old males were likely to drink, drive, and cause accidents. However, only about 2% of that group actually engaged in the undesired behavior, making the law about 98% overinclusive—too much for intermediate scrutiny. At intermediate scrutiny, the means chosen by the government must be substantially related to achieving the goal of the law. The Court will not tolerate a high degree of overinclusiveness in cases of gender discrimination.

e. **Peremptory Challenges. [§ 611]**

**Peremptory challenges based on gender may not be used to exclude potential jurors.**

*J.E.B. v. Alabama*, 511 U.S. 127 (1994). The State of Alabama used nine of its ten peremptory challenges to remove male jurors in a paternity and support trial against a putative father. The Court held that the Equal Protection Clause prohibits discrimination in jury selection on the basis of gender.

f. **Nursing School. [§ 612]**

**Men cannot be prohibited from attending a state nursing school.**

*Mississippi University for Women v. Hogan*, 458 U.S. 718 (1982). The Court invalidated a Mississippi statute which prohibited males from attending the Mississippi University for Women School of Nursing. The Court reaffirmed the intermediate level of review for gender cases, and said it made no difference that the plaintiff was male rather than female.

g. **Military School. [§ 613]**

**Women cannot be prohibited from attending a state military school.**

*U.S. v. Virginia*, 518 U.S. 515 (1996). The Court ruled that the Equal Protection Clause was violated by Virginia Military Institute (VMI), a state military college, excluding women from attending the school. The Court said that VMI would have to demonstrate an "exceedingly persuasive justification" for its male-only admissions policy, showing at least that the categorical exclusion of women from the student body was substantially related to an important governmental objective. The Court rejected Virginia's proposed remedy of creating a separate, all-female military training school in the state.

# EQUAL PROTECTION

2. **Discrimination Based on Pregnancy Is Not Gender Discrimination Under the Equal Protection Clause. [§ 614]**

   **The Court has held that, under the Constitution, it is not gender discrimination for a state to discriminate on the basis of pregnancy.** Pregnant persons are all female, but non-pregnant persons are both male and female. Therefore, the classification does not discriminate against all women, only pregnant women.

   *Geduldig v. Aiello*, 417 U.S. 484 (1974). The Court upheld, against an equal protection gender-discrimination claim, California's exclusion of pregnancy and childbirth coverage from its disability insurance system. The Court said that, even though only women get pregnant, the law does not exclude anyone because of gender. The classes created by the law are pregnant persons versus non-pregnant persons. The first class is all female, but the second class is made up of both men and women, so there is no "clean" discrimination against women as a class. Since this case, Congress passed the Pregnancy Discrimination Act, which includes discrimination based on pregnancy within the definition of gender discrimination under Title VII.

3. **Remedial Discrimination in Favor of Women. [§ 615]**

   **Even under the intermediate level of scrutiny, the Court usually upholds laws which compensate women for past economic discrimination against them as a class.** The Court is willing to accept societal discrimination against women as the justification for these "economic affirmative action plans."

   a. **State Property Tax Exemption for Widows. [§ 616]**

      **The Court upheld a state law that provided property tax exemptions for widows but not widowers.**

      *Kahn v. Shevin*, 416 U.S. 351 (1974). The Court upheld a Florida property tax exemption for widows, but not widowers. Economically, women are in a worse position than men, and the tax exemption for widows simply recognizes and attempts to remedy that disparity. The Court said that "[w]hether from overt discrimination or from the socialization process of a male-dominated culture, the job market is inhospitable to the woman seeking any but the lowest paying jobs."

   b. **Higher Old–Age Benefits for Female Wage–Earners. [§ 617]**

      **The Court upheld a federal law that provided higher old-age benefits to female wage-earners.**

# CHAPTER XV

*Califano v. Webster*, 430 U.S. 313 (1977). The Court upheld a federal Social Security law which resulted in female wage-earners receiving higher monthly old-age benefits than male wage-earners. This law is valid as a means of redressing society's longstanding disparate treatment of women.

   c.   **Alimony. [§ 618]**
   **Females may not be exempted from paying alimony.**

   *Orr v. Orr*, 440 U.S. 268 (1979). The Court invalidated an Alabama law requiring husbands, but not wives, to pay alimony. The Court held that, on the facts, Alabama could not use gender as a substitute for need in determining who may receive alimony payments. Individualized hearings had already been provided for, and it would impose only minimally more of a burden on the state to make specific findings regarding the financial needs of particular spouses. Case-by-case determinations of who should receive alimony would be a more narrowly tailored means to achieve the state's goal of ensuring fairness in the payment and receipt of alimony.

4. **In Some Cases, Women and Men Are Not Similarly Situated in Relation to the Purpose of a Law. [§ 619]**

   **There may be constitutionally relevant differences between women and men in relation to the purpose of a law.** The Court has held in a few cases that biological differences between the sexes may be the basis for a government treating men and women differently, as long as the government is not simply reinforcing gender stereotypes. These differences may make it permissible for a government to treat men and women differently.

   a.   **Women as Prison Guards. [§ 620]**

   The Court upheld a state law that excluded women from **positions as guards in all-male prisons.**

   *Dothard v. Rawlinson*, 433 U.S. 321 (1977). The Court upheld the exclusion of women from positions as guards in a male, maximum-security, unclassified prison. The Court said that a female guard's ability to maintain order could be adversely affected by the fact that she is a woman, irrespective of other physical traits such as height, weight, or strength. The Court found that women and men are not similarly situated in relation to the purpose of the law, which was to ensure safety and control in the prison.

   b.   **Different Treatment of Males and Females Under a Statutory Rape Law. [§ 621]**
   **Statutory rape laws that punish males for having sex with underage females, but do not punish the underage female, are permissible.**

# EQUAL PROTECTION

*Michael M. v. Superior Court*, 450 U.S. 464 (1981). The Court upheld a California statutory rape law which punished males for having sex with underage females, but did not punish the underage female. Justice Rehnquist, for four Justices, said that the sexes were not similarly situated in relation to the purpose of this criminal law, which was deterrence. Justice Rehnquist said that only females can get pregnant, so only females have the natural deterrent of fear of pregnancy to keep them from engaging in underage consensual sex. Since males do not have this biological deterrent, the state may impose criminal penalties "to roughly 'equalize' the deterrents on the sexes."

c. **Male–Only Registration for the Draft. [§ 622]**

**The federal government may require males only to register for the draft.**

*Rostker v. Goldberg*, 453 U.S. 57 (1981). The Court upheld, against an equal protection gender challenge, the male-only registration for the military draft. Justice Rehnquist, for the Court, said that the gender discrimination was permissible because men and women are not similarly situated in relation to the purpose of the registration and the draft. According to Justice Rehnquist, men and women are not similarly situated because the purpose of the registration (and any potential draft) would be to fill combat positions, from which women were excluded by a pre-existing law. Justice Marshall, in dissent, said that the purpose of any potential draft would be to fill both combat and non-combat positions, so men and women are similarly situated, and the all-male registration violates the equal protection component of the Due Process Clause of the Fifth Amendment.

d. **Citizen Mothers versus Citizen Fathers of Illegitimate Children Born Outside the United States. [§ 623]**

**The federal government may confer citizenship at birth on an illegitimate child born outside the United States to an alien father and an American mother, while conditioning citizenship to an illegitimate child born outside the country to an alien mother and an American father on the confirmation of the father-child relationship.**

*Nguyen v. Immigration and Naturalization Services*, 533 U.S. 53 (2001). The Court upheld a federal statute which set forth the rules for acquisition of citizenship by illegitimate children born outside the United States. Under the law, the citizenship of such a child born to an alien father and a citizen mother is established at birth. However, if such a child is born to an alien mother and a citizen father, citizenship is not established until the father or the child takes steps to confirm their relationship. The Court relied on the fact that mothers and fathers of illegitimate, foreign-born children are not similarly situated in terms of obviousness of blood relationship and, in many cases, custody of the child. The Court held that the statute was consistent with the equal protection guarantee of the Fifth Amendment Due Process Clause and, under the prevailing equal protection standard, was substantially related to achieving the significant government interest of assuring that a biological parent-child interest exists.

## G. REVIEW OF LAWS THAT DISCRIMINATE ON THE BASIS OF ILLEGITIMACY. [§ 624]

**Whenever a government discriminates against illegitimate children, intermediate scrutiny applies—the government must show a significant or important reason for the law, and the means must be substantially related to achieving that goal.** It is not a legitimate purpose for the government to try to punish illegitimate children for the actions of their parents, so do not accept any justification for a law that strikes you as punitive. From 1968 to 1988, the Court traveled an uneven path in illegitimacy cases, using some form of heightened scrutiny, but never articulating a clear standard. In 1988, in *Clark v. Jeter*, 486 U.S. 456 the Court unanimously adopted intermediate scrutiny as the standard in illegitimacy cases.

1. **An Illegitimate Child Suing for His or Her Mother's Wrongful Death. [§ 625]**

    **An illegitimate child cannot be prohibited from suing for his or her mother's wrongful death if a state allows a legitimate child to bring such an action.**

    *Levy v. Louisiana*, 391 U.S. 68 (1968). The Court invalidated a Louisiana wrongful death statute which precluded an illegitimate child, but not a legitimate child, from suing for the wrongful death of the mother. Birth status was irrelevant to any harm to the mother, and the law only advanced the illegitimate goal of punishing children for the actions of their parents. This law failed even rational basis review.

2. **The Mother of an Illegitimate Child Suing for Her Child's Death. [§ 626]**

    **A state cannot preclude the mother of an illegitimate child from suing for her child's death.**

# EQUAL PROTECTION

*Glona v. American Guarantee & Liability Insurance Co.*, 391 U.S. 73 (1968). The Court invalidated a Louisiana law which precluded the mother of an illegitimate child from suing for her child's death. Finding no rati onal basis for the law, the Court rejected the argument that a woman would have a child out of wedlock just so she could be compensated for the child's death.

3. **Intestacy. [§ 627]**

   **A state may impose some restrictions on an illegitimate child's ability to inherit under intestacy laws.**

   *Labine v. Vincent*, 401 U.S. 532 (1971). The Court upheld a Louisiana law which precluded an illegitimate child from taking a father's property through intestate succession unless the father had legitimated the child. This case is something of an aberration in the development of the Court's illegitimacy cases.

4. **Worker's Compensation Recovery. [§ 628]**

   **A state may not preclude an illegitimate child from recovering under the state's Workers' Compensation laws.**

   *Weber v. Aetna Casualty & Surety Co.*, 406 U.S. 164 (1972). The Court invalidated a Louisiana workers' compensation law which precluded recovery by dependent, unacknowledged illegitimate children, but allowed recovery by legitimate children and by acknowledged illegitimate children. While *Weber* did not overrule *Labine* (see previous case), it seriously undermined any precedential value it might have had.

5. **Denial of Welfare Benefits. [§ 629]**

   **Welfare benefits may not be denied to families with illegitimate children.**

   *New Jersey Welfare Rights Organization v. Cahill*, 411 U.S. 619 (1973). The Court invalidated a New Jersey law which disbursed benefits to poor families only if those families were composed of two married adults and one or more legitimate children. Married adults who had illegitimate children did not qualify for benefits. The Court reasoned that punishing the illegitimate child is an ineffectual way to deter adults from engaging in irresponsible sexual relationships.

6. **Denying Illegitimate Children a Presumption of Dependency for Inheritance Purposes. [§ 630]**

   **The federal government may deny illegitimate children a presumption of dependency for inheritance purposes.**

# CHAPTER XV

*Mathews v. Lucas*, 427 U.S. 495 (1976). The Court upheld a federal law, challenged under the equal protection component of the Due Process Clause of the Fifth Amendment, which afforded a presumption of dependency to legitimate children and a certain class of illegitimate children (those whose parents had acknowledged paternity in writing) in terms of their ability to inherit from a deceased parent, while denying that presumption to all other classes of illegitimate children. The Court relied to a large extent on the fact that the statute allowed the class of excluded illegitimate children to prove their dependency and qualify for benefits.

7. **Restrictions on Inheritance From an Intestate Father. [§ 631]**

   **A state is limited in its ability to impose restrictions on an illegitimate child's ability to inherit from an intestate father.**

   *Trimble v. Gordon*, 430 U.S. 762 (1977). The Court invalidated an Illinois law that allowed children born out of wedlock to inherent by intestate succession only from their mothers, whereas children born in wedlock may inherit by intestate succession from both their mothers and fathers. The Court ruled that the statute went too far by requiring not only an acknowledgement by the father, but also the marriage of the parents, thereby excluding many illegitimate children whose rights could be protected by some less intrusive means that would still protect the state's interests.

8. **Permissible Limitations on Inheritance From an Intestate Father. [§ 632]**

   **A state may impose narrowly drawn restrictions on the ability of illegitimate children to inherit from intestate fathers.**

   *Lalli v. Lalli*, 439 U.S. 259 (1978). The Court upheld a New York law which precluded illegitimate children from inheriting from their fathers through intestate succession unless there was a court order during the father's life which established paternity. The plurality distinguished this case from *Trimble* (previous case) on the basis that the New York law did not require the marriage of the child's mother and father as a prerequisite to intestate inheritance.

9. **Right to Veto an Illegitimate Child's Adoption. [§ 633]**

   **It is impermissible for a state to give the mother, but not the father, of an illegitimate child the right to veto the child's adoption.**

   *Caban v. Mohamed*, 441 U.S. 380 (1979). The Court invalidated a New York law which gave the mother of an illegitimate child, but not the father, the right to veto the child's adoption. While this gender-based distinction makes sense when the child is an infant or when the father has never had any substantial relationship with the child, it is unconstitutional when the father has acknowledged paternity and established a substantial relationship with the child.

10. **Father's Inability to Sue for the Wrongful Death of An Illegitimate Child. [§ 634]**

    **A state may prohibit the father of an illegitimate child from suing for the child's wrongful death unless the father had legitimated the child.**

    *Parham v. Hughes*, 441 U.S. 347 (1979). The Court upheld a Georgia law which allowed the mother of an illegitimate child to sue for the child's wrongful death, but denied the father the right to sue unless he had legitimated the child. A plurality of the Court said that this law reflected the fact that mothers and fathers of illegitimate children are not similarly situated—everyone knows who the mother is, but it is not always clear who the father is.

11. **Time Limit to Sue for Parental Support. [§ 635]**

    **A state may not impose a one-year statute of limitations for an illegitimate child to sue for parental support.**

    *Mills v. Habluetzel*, 456 U.S. 91 (1982). The Court unanimously invalidated a Texas law requiring an illegitimate child to sue for parental support within the first year of the child's life, or be precluded from ever bringing a support action. There was no similar limitation placed on the ability of a legitimate child to sue for support.

12. **Time Limit to Establish Paternity. [§ 636]**

    **A state may not impose a two-year statute of limitations for an illegitimate child to establish paternity and receive support.**

    *Pickett v. Brown*, 462 U.S. 1 (1983). The Court unanimously invalidated a Tennessee law which set a two-year limit on an illegitimate child's right to sue to establish paternity and receive support. The Court ruled that the two-year limitation was not substantially related to the legitimate state interest of preventing fraudulent claims.

13. **Different Statutes of Limitation for Legitimate and Illegitimate Children. [§ 637]**

    **A state may not impose different statutes of limitations for legitimate and illegitimate children.**

# CHAPTER XV

*Clark v. Jeter*, 486 U.S. 456 (1988). The Court unanimously invalidated a Pennsylvania law which allowed legitimate children to sue for parental support at any time, but required illegitimate children to bring support actions within six years of birth. Justice O'Connor, for the Court, said that both gender and illegitimacy classifications receive intermediate scrutiny, under which a statutory classification must be substantially related to an important government objective.

14. **Citizenship Requirements for Illegitimate Children Born Outside the United States. [§ 638]**

    **The federal government may confer citizenship at birth on an illegitimate child born outside the United States to an alien father and an American mother, while conditioning citizenship to an illegitimate child born outside the country to an alien mother and an American father on the confirmation of the father-child relationship.**

    *Nguyen v. Immigration and Naturalization Services*, 533 U.S. 53 (2001). The Court upheld a federal statute which set forth the rules for acquisition of citizenship by illegitimate children born outside the United States. Under the law, the citizenship of such a child born to an alien father and a citizen mother is established at birth. However, if such a child is born to an alien mother and a citizen father, citizenship is not established until the father or the child takes steps to confirm their relationship. The Court relied on the fact that mothers and fathers of illegitimate, foreign-born children are not similarly situated in terms of obviousness of blood relationship and, in many cases, custody of the child. The Court held that the statue was consistent with the equal protection guarantee of the Fifth Amendment Due Process Clause and, under the prevailing equal protection standard, was substantially related to achieving the significant government interest of assuring that a biological parent-child interest exists.

## H. REVIEW OF LAWS THAT DISCRIMINATE ON THE BASIS OF AGE. [§ 639]

Laws that discriminate based on age receive rational basis scrutiny—the plaintiff must show that there is no legitimate reason for the law, or that the means are not rationally related to the asserted government interest.

1. **Mandatory Retirement Age. [§ 640]**

    States may impose a mandatory retirement age for police officers.

    a. *Massachusetts Board of Retirement v. Murgia*, 427 U.S. 307 (1976).

        The Court upheld, under rational basis review, a state law requiring uniformed police officers to retire at age 50. It does not matter that

# EQUAL PROTECTION

some very healthy, fit police officers may be forced to retire by this bright-line rule. At rationality review, the law may be very overinclusive so long as it is not irrational.

**b.** *Gregory v. Ashcroft*, **501 U.S. 452 (1991).**

The Court, using rational basis review, upheld a Missouri law which required judges to retire at age 70. Since no fundamental right was affected, there was nothing to raise the scrutiny from rationality review.

**2. Different Retirement Ages for Different Workers. [§ 641]**

**Federal law may impose different mandatory retirement ages for different government jobs.**

*Vance v. Bradley*, 440 U.S. 93 (1979). The Court upheld a federal law which required Foreign Service officers to retire at age 60, when most civil service employees were allowed to work until the age of 70. Congress implemented the lower retirement age for Foreign Service officers to ensure that those officers would be capable of facing the rigors of overseas duty. The Court applied rational basis scrutiny in upholding the law against the Fifth Amendment challenge.

**STUDY TIP:** Age is a non-suspect class, and discrimination on that basis alone will do nothing to raise the level of judicial scrutiny. However, if an age classification is used to abridge a fundamental right, the scrutiny may go up because of the impact of the classification system on the right. For example, in *Carey v. Population Services International*, 431 U.S. 678 (1977), the Court used heightened scrutiny to invalidate a law prohibiting the sale of non-prescription contraceptives to minors under the age of 16. It was the right of privacy, not the age classification, which caused the Court to raise the level of review and invalidate the law.

## I. REVIEW OF LAWS THAT DISCRIMINATE ON THE BASIS OF MENTAL STATUS. [§ 642]

**Laws that discriminate against the mentally retarded or the mentally ill receive rational basis review—the plaintiff has the burden of showing that there is no legitimate reason for the law, or that the means are not rationally related to the asserted government interest.**

# CHAPTER XV

1. **Group Homes for the Mentally Retarded. [§ 643]**

    **Laws that restrict the location of group homes for the mentally retarded may not be based on antipathy toward the mentally retarded.**

    *City of Cleburne v. Cleburne Living Center, Inc.*, 473 U.S. 432 (1985). The Court invalidated, under rational basis review, a city's denial of a special use permit for the operation of a group home for the mentally retarded. The Court refused to afford the mentally retarded the status of a quasi-suspect or suspect class. The Court said that the mentally retarded are a very diverse class of people, and the lack of homogeneity within the class (mildly retarded to profoundly retarded) made this the kind of group of people best dealt with by a legislature. The Court was also unwilling to begin adding to the list of quasi—suspect or suspect classes. If the mentally retarded were given special protection by the Court, why not the mentally ill, the infirm, or the disabled? On the facts, the Court invalidated the law because its only real basis appeared to be antipathy toward the mentally retarded.

2. **Different Treatment of the Mentally Ill and the Mentally Retarded. [§ 644]**

    **State laws that distinguish between mentally ill and mentally retarded persons are permissible.**

    *Heller v. Doe*, 509 U.S. 312 (1993). The Court, using rational basis review, upheld a Kentucky law which set different standards of proof for commitment of the mentally ill and the mentally retarded, and allowed guardians and family members to participate as parties in commitment proceedings for the mentally retarded, but not for the mentally ill. To commit a mentally ill person, the state had to show beyond a reasonable doubt that statutory criteria were met. To commit a mentally retarded person, the state only had to show by clear and convincing evidence that statutory criteria were met. The court said it was rational for Kentucky to distinguish between the two groups because mental retardation is a life-long condition that is easily diagnosed, whereas mental illness may not manifest itself consistently over time, and is more difficult to diagnose in many cases.

## J. REVIEW OF LAWS THAT DISCRIMINATE ON THE BASIS OF SEXUAL ORIENTATION. [§ 645]

**Laws that discriminate on the basis of sexual orientation receive rational basis review—the plaintiff must show that there is no legitimate reason for**

**the law, or that the means are not rationally related to the asserted government interest.** A voter-initiated state constitutional amendment prohibiting state or local governments from passing laws to protect persons of homosexual, lesbian, or bisexual orientation fails rational basis scrutiny under the Equal Protection Clause. *Romer v. Evans*, 517 U.S. 620 (1996). The Court invalidated a Colorado state constitutional amendment, passed by statewide referendum, which prohibited any unit of state or local government from taking any action which prohibited discrimination against or granted special protection to persons based on their homosexual, lesbian, or bisexual orientation or conduct. This amendment effectively repealed a number of municipal ordinances banning discrimination based on sexual orientation in housing, employment, education, public accommodations, and health and welfare services. The Court ruled that this amendment violated the Equal Protection Clause because it prohibited only a specific group of persons from using state and local electoral processes (short of a state constitutional amendment) to protect themselves from discrimination in a wide range of public and private transactions. The Court ruled that the amendment failed rational basis scrutiny because it identified persons by a single trait (sexual orientation), and then denied them the possibility of protection solely because they possessed that trait.

## K. REVIEW OF LAWS THAT DISCRIMINATE ON THE BASIS OF SOCIAL OR ECONOMIC INTERESTS. [§ 646]

**Laws that discriminate on the basis of social or economic interests receive rational basis review—the plaintiff must show that there is no legitimate reason for the law, or that the means are not rationally related to the asserted government interest.** For instance, laws which discriminate between classes of people in relation to pursuing an occupation, receiving unemployment benefits, or receiving welfare payments will receive only rational basis review.

1. Selective Restrictions on Advertising. [§ 647]

   **The Court upheld an early state law that placed selective restrictions on advertising.**

   *Railway Express Agency v. New York*, 336 U.S. 106 (1949). The Court upheld, under rational basis review, a New York City traffic regulation which prohibited advertising for hire on vehicles on New York streets, but allowed the owner of a vehicle to advertise his or her own business on the vehicle. The Court accepted the city's argument that it was trying to enhance the safety of the streets, and set forth the rule that, at rationality review, a government may deal with a problem a bit at a time. The government may have concluded that truck owners who advertise their own goods pose less of a safety problem than those who advertise for hire. This case came down well before the Court gave First Amendment protection to commercial speech.

2. **Selective Ban on Push–Cart Vendors. [§ 648]**

**The Court upheld a local ordinance that banned most, but not all, push-cart vendors.**

*New Orleans v. Dukes*, 427 U.S. 297 (1976). The Court upheld, under rational basis review, a New Orleans ordinance banning push-cart vendors from the French Quarter, except those vendors who had worked there for eight or more years. Since there was no fundamental right abridged or suspect class disadvantaged, the Court upheld the law, saying that it is the job of the legislature, not the courts, to judge the wisdom of economic legislation.

3. **Exclusion of Methadone Users From Government Employment. [§ 649]**

**Methadone users may be excluded from safety-sensitive as well as non-safety-sensitive government jobs.**

*New York City Transit Authority v. Beazer*, 440 U.S. 568 (1979). The Court upheld, under rational basis review, a Transit Authority rule which excluded methadone users from any employment with the Authority. This ban included non-safety—sensitive jobs, and was upheld in the face of the statistical fact that 75% of those who have been on methadone for at least a year are free from illicit drug use. At rationality review, a law does not have to be narrowly tailored (or even substantially related to achieving the law's goal), and may be over-inclusive in that it disadvantages too many people.

4. **Federal Retirement Law. [§ 650]**

**The Court upheld a federal retirement law that prevented certain employees from receiving "double-dip" retirement benefits.**

*United States Railroad Retirement Board v. Fritz*, 449 U.S. 166 (1980). The Court upheld, under rational basis review, a federal law which prevented certain workers from receiving "double-dip" retirement benefits. Under the law, a person qualified for the windfall benefits only if he or she was active in the railroad business as of 1974. As a result, a person with

# EQUAL PROTECTION

24 years of experience would not qualify for the windfall unless he or she worked for the railroad in 1974, whereas a person with 11 years of experience would qualify for the windfall if he or she worked with the railroad in 1974. The workers with more experience challenged the law under the equal protection component of the Due Process Clause of the Fifth Amendment. The Court found that Congress had not acted arbitrarily or irrationally, and said that it would uphold a law if there were any plausible reason for it, even though Congress may not have relied on the reason when passing the law.

## L. IRREBUTTABLE PRESUMPTIONS USED TO DEPRIVE A PERSON OF A GOVERNMENTAL BENEFIT OR THE EXERCISE OF A RIGHT. [§ 651]

**Under the irrebuttable presumption doctrine, a government sets up a conclusive presumption (no hearing provided) of disability or unfitness to perform a function or exercise a right. These bright-line rules disadvantage all persons within a class, and do not provide any mechanism for proving fitness or ability.** The theoretical basis for the doctrine is not clear, but most commentators agree that it shares aspects of procedural due process and equal protection analyses. The cases present the procedural due process problem of not providing a hearing for those who are disadvantaged; they present the equal protection problem of classifying too broadly—too many people are disadvantaged by the classification effected by the law. This doctrine had its heyday in the mid–1970's, and is not used much by courts today.

1. **Presumption That Unmarried Fathers Are Unfit Parents. [§ 652]**

    **States may not conclusively presume that all unmarried fathers are unfit parents.**

    *Stanley v. Illinois*, 405 U.S. 645 (1972). The Court invalidated an Illinois statute which conclusively presumed that all unmarried fathers are unfit parents. Upon the mother's death, the State, rather than the unmarried father, would get custody of a child. The Court said this classification was clearly overbroad in that it disadvantaged too many unmarried fathers (those who would be fit parents), and that the state must provide individualized hearings on the question of fitness.

2. **Presumption That Certain College Students Are Not State Residents. [§ 653]**

    **States may not conclusively presume that certain classes of college students are not state residents.**

# CHAPTER XV

*Vlandis v. Kline*, 412 U.S. 441 (1973). The Court invalidated a Connecticut statute under which certain students were conclusively presumed to be out-of-staters, and thereby subject to a higher tuition regardless of their having established residency in the state. The Due Process Clause of the Fourteenth Amendment prohibited such an irrebuttable presumption, and required the state to give the student some sort of individualized opportunity to prove his or her residence.

3. **Presumption of Ineligibility for Food Stamps. [§ 654]**

   **Federal laws may not conclusively presume ineligibility for food stamps.**

   *U.S. Department of Agriculture v. Murry*, 413 U.S. 508 (1973). The Court invalidated a provision of the federal Food Stamp Act which provided that a household would not be eligible for food stamps if it included a person over 18 years of age who had been claimed as a tax dependent during the previous year by someone who was not a member of the household. The Court rejected this irrebuttable presumption, and said that the government must provide some kind of opportunity to show need.

4. **Presumption That Pregnant Teachers Cannot Teach Beyond a Certain Time. [§ 655]**

   **A state may not conclusively presume that a pregnant teacher is unable to teach beyond a certain time in her pregnancy.**

   *Cleveland Board of Education v. LaFleur*, 414 U.S. 632 (1974). The Court invalidated school board rules which required all pregnant teachers to take leave without pay for four or five months (depending on the school board) before the expected date of birth. The Court objected to the irrebuttable presumption of physical incompetency even when medical evidence would indicate that the pregnant teacher was fully able to continue teaching.

5. **Presumption That Spouses of Stepchildren Do Not Qualify for Death Benefits. [§ 656]**

   **A state may presume that spouses of stepchildren do not qualify for death benefits.**

   *Weinberger v. Salfi*, 422 U.S. 749 (1975). The Court upheld, against an irrebuttable presumption challenge, provisions of the Social Security Act which required a spouse or stepchild of a wage earner to have had their relationships to the wage earner for at least nine months before qualifying

# EQUAL PROTECTION

for death benefits. The Court distinguished the earlier irrebuttable presumption cases, saying that this one involved merely a noncontractual claim to receive funds from the public treasury, something which deserved no constitutional protection.

6. **Presumption That Certain Workers Are Disabled. [§ 657]**

   **The Court upheld a federal law that provided for a presumption of total disability for coal miners with black-lung disease.**

   *Usery v. Turner Elkhorn Mining Co.*, 428 U.S. 1 (1976). The Court upheld, against an irrebuttable presumption challenge, a provision of the Federal Coal Mine Health and Safety Act which said that if a coal miner can show by medical evidence that he or she has an advanced case of black-lung disease, the miner is irrebuttably presumed to be totally disabled. If the miner dies, it is irrebuttably presumed that the black-lung disease was the cause of death. The Court used rational basis review to uphold Congress' method of compensating coal miners who suffered from the disease.

7. **Presumption That a Child Born to a Married Woman Is a Child of Her Marriage. [§ 658]**

   **A state may presume that a child born to a married woman is a child of her marriage.**

   *Michael H. v. Gerald D.*, 491 U.S. 110 (1989). The Court upheld a California law which conclusively presumed that a child born to a married woman is a child of the marriage. Michael was, in all probability, the natural father of a child to whom he asserted parental rights. However, Gerald, not Michael, was the husband of the child's mother. Under California law, Gerald was conclusively presumed to be the child's father. In a plurality opinion, Justice Scalia rejected Michael's argument that the law created an unconstitutional irrebuttable presumption. Justice Scalia reasoned that since Michael had no fundamental parental interest simply because of genetic parenthood, the state's interest in protecting marital relationships was sufficient to override Michael's low-level liberty interest in seeing his child. Justice Brennan dissented, arguing that such a conclusive presumption has the fatal procedural flaw of not providing a hearing in which the adulterous father can offer proof of paternity.

## REVIEW PROBLEMS—EQUAL PROTECTION

**PROBLEM 1.** Bob Green applied for a position as a state police officer with the State of Oz. He was rejected, following an interview with the personnel director.

# CHAPTER XV

Bob is convinced that he was turned down because of his race. He files suit, claiming a violation of his equal protection rights under the Fourteenth Amendment. What does Bob need to prove to make out a prima facie case of an equal protection violation? Who has the burden of proof in this case?

**Answer:** To make out a prima facie case of an equal protection violation, a plaintiff must show disparate impact and intent. Bob must show that members of his racial group have been disproportionately excluded from positions as state troopers. He must then show that the disparate treatment was intentional—the government was excluding people because of their race. Once Bob has shown disparate impact and intent, the burden shifts to the government to show a compelling reason for the discrimination, and narrowly tailored means. Remember that at rationality review, the burden of proof stays with the plaintiff, but at intermediate or strict scrutiny, it shifts to the government. See §§ 533, 538 for further review.

**PROBLEM 2.** The State of Oz has established an affirmative action program for its State Police Department (SPD). Concerned that racial minorities are not adequately represented in the ranks of command officers, the legislature has required that for every white officer promoted to a command position, an officer belonging to one of a listed number of racial or ethnic minorities also be promoted to a command position. Under this program, there are two promotion lists; one white and one non-white. Todd White, a white officer, was up for promotion to a command position, but was turned down. He claims that he was rejected because of his race. Todd's performance evaluations and test scores were higher than the non-white officer who received a promotion. Todd sues. Does he have a case?

**Answer:** Yes. This is a state race-based affirmative action program, so strict scrutiny applies. The state must show a compelling interest and narrowly tailored means. With a state race-based affirmative action plan, societal discrimination does not count as the justification for the program. The State of Oz would have to show, at least, that it was a passive participant in some system or pattern of racial discrimination in the past. There is nothing in the facts to indicate that the State was implicated in any prior racial discrimination. If that is true, Todd cannot be excluded solely because of his race. See §§ 574, 580 for further review.

**PROBLEM 3.** The governor of the State of Oz has issued an order excluding aliens from serving on the governing boards of state colleges or universities. These are all appointed positions, and the governor has refused to consider applications or nominations from non-citizens of the United States. Harriet Howe was an alien, but applied for a position on the board of State University. Through a clerical mistake,

# EQUAL PROTECTION

her file was put in with those of citizens of the United States, and she got an interview with the governor. Upon learning of Harriet's alien status, the governor told her that she was not eligible for any such position. Harriet sues. Discuss her equal protection arguments.

**Answer:** If a state discriminates against aliens, strict scrutiny applies, unless the alien is excluded from a position that deals with the formulation or implementation of public policy. If that is true, rational basis review applies. To answer this kind of question, you must make a judgment call about the nature of the position from which aliens are excluded. If the governing boards of colleges and universities are engaged in important public policy decisions, then this position is within the political function exception and rationality review applies. If these positions are not all that important to the functioning of representative government, then strict scrutiny applies. See §§ 595–601 for further review.

**PROBLEM 4.** The City of Id owns and operates a very fancy country club, whose clientele is primarily male. To provide a pleasant atmosphere for its male members, the country club employs only females as servers in its dining room. Tom Penn applies for a job as a waiter and is rejected. He sues. Does Tom have a case?

**Answer:** Yes. Gender discrimination receives intermediate scrutiny. Tom will be able to show that he was intentionally discriminated against because he is a male. The city would then have to show a significant reason for the discrimination, and substantially related means. There is no significant reason for the gender discrimination here, so Tom would win. See § 605 for further review.

# Chapter XVI

# FREEDOM OF SPEECH

## A. OVERVIEW OF FREE SPEECH ANALYSIS. [§ 659]

**The First Amendment says that Congress shall make no law abridging the freedom of speech. Freedom of speech is a fundamental right which applies to the states by way of the liberty provision of the Due Process Clause of the Fourteenth Amendment. For purposes of the First Amendment, speech includes oral, written, and symbolic communication.** The first thing you must do in a free speech analysis is make sure that a court is willing to characterize certain activity as speech. While this is usually not a problem with oral or written communication (because words are used), it is an issue with symbolic speech (communication by conduct alone, without words). For instance, is flag burning speech? Nude dancing? Draft card burning? Cross burning? Blowing up a building to protest a war? Obviously, in some cases a court will not be willing to attach the label of "speech" (and thereby apply constitutional protections), even though on some level, something is communicated. (Yes, I took a gun and blew away that person, but it was simply an expression of my pent-up anger.) Remember that the First Amendment does not provide absolute protection for all speech. Speech may be regulated, or in some cases prohibited, if the government is able to show that a regulable, non-speech evil (such as a breach of the peace, or overthrow of the government) occurs at the same time as the speech activity or as a result of it. In general terms, free speech analysis is an inquiry about how convincingly the government has established a connection between the speech it is attempting to regulate and the evil which allegedly goes along with the speech. A court must resolve the question of whether the incidental restriction on speech is justified by the government's interest in preventing the non-speech evil.

1. **Procedural Issues. [§ 660]**

    **Once you are satisfied that speech is being regulated, check for certain procedural problems.** The two procedural problems that arise most often are vagueness and overbreadth.

    a. **Vagueness. [§ 661]**

        **A vague law provides no or insufficient standards for its enforcement.** Two problems are presented by such a law: no notice to the person to whom the law may be applied; and too much discretion on the part of the government official applying the law.

### b. Overbreadth. [§ 662]

**A law is overbroad to the extent that it is capable of punishing protected speech.** Remember that freedom of speech is a fundamental right, so the means of regulation must be narrowly tailored. An excellent example of an overbroad law occurred in *Board of Airport Commissioners v. Jews for Jesus, Inc.*, 482 U.S. 569 (1987), where the Court invalidated an airport authority regulation which prohibited all First Amendment activity in the airport terminal.

### c. Licensing Systems for Movies or Books. [§ 663]

The Court has set forth rules for licensing systems for movies or books. Basically, the Court requires that if the government intends to deny a permit, it has the burden of going to court for a prompt judicial decision of the merits, and the government has the burden of justifying its refusal to grant the permit, (see § 685).

## 2. Is the Government Prohibiting Speech or Merely Channeling It? [§ 664]

See if the government is trying to prohibit the speech entirely, or just move it around (change the time, place, or manner of the speech). If the government is trying to prohibit the speech entirely, you will probably use one of the specific tests or analyses, such as clear and present danger, fighting words, obscenity, commercial speech, or defamation. If the government is just trying to move the speech around, you apply the rules for what are called "time, place, or manner restrictions." **To be valid, a time, place, or manner restriction must be: a) content-neutral (can't be regulating because the government disapproves of the speech); b) narrowly tailored to achieving a significant government interest; and c) leave open ample alternative channels of communication.**

## B. DUE PROCESS CONCERNS THAT ARISE WITH LAWS THAT REGULATE SPEECH. [§ 665]

### 1. Vagueness. [§ 666]

**Vagueness problems arise when a statute or regulation has no standards, or insufficient ones, to guide the government official applying the law.** The absence of specific standards requires a person to guess whether he or she may be prosecuted under a certain statute, or will be granted a permit from a licensing board. The absence of notice to the

# FREEDOM OF SPEECH

person is compounded by the excessive discretion vested in the government. Without specific standards being provided, the police officer or the permit-giver gets to make up standards as he or she goes along.

a. **Display of Red Flag. [§ 667]**

**It is unconstitutionally vague for a state to prohibit the public display of a red flag as a symbol of opposition to government.**

*Stromberg v. California*, 283 U.S. 359 (1931). The Court invalidated, on vagueness grounds, a California statute which prohibited public use or display of a red flag "as a sign, symbol or emblem of opposition to organized government" (the legislature said that the use of red flags, especially by members of the Communist party, indicated opposition to organized government). While the opinion was phrased in terms of vagueness, the Court pointed out that this law was also potentially overbroad in that it could be used to punish constitutionally protected use of a red flag. The case is an early example of symbolic speech, where the communication happens without words, simply by some readily understandable conduct.

b. **Attempts to Incite Insurrection. [§ 668]**

**It is unconstitutionally vague for a state to criminalize speech under a statute prohibiting attempts to incite insurrection when the statute does not include the occurrence or imminence of violence as an element of the offense.**

*Herndon v. Lowry*, 301 U.S. 242 (1937). The Court invalidated, on vagueness grounds, an Alabama statute that made it a crime to attempt to incite insurrection, including persuading others to join in a combined resistance to the lawful authority of any state. The Court held that this statute did not provide a sufficiently ascertainable standard of guilt, and, as a result, could result in the punishment of much protected speech.

c. **Treating a U.S. Flag Contemptuously. [§ 669]**

**It is unconstitutionally vague for a state to impose criminal penalties for treating contemptuously a United States flag.**

*Smith v. Goguen*, 415 U.S. 566 (1974). The Court invalidated, on vagueness grounds, a statute which made it a crime to "treat contemptuously" a United States flag. The Court said that the statute provided no warning or notice to persons to whom it might be applied, and gave police, judges, and juries too much discretion to impose their personal preferences when applying the statute.

    d.  **Being Required to Produce "Credible and Reliable" Identification. [§ 670]**

**It is unconstitutionally vague for a state to require a person to produce "credible and reliable" identification when requested to do so by a police officer.**

*Kolender v. Lawson*, 461 U.S. 352 (1983). The Court invalidated, on vagueness grounds, a state law requiring persons on the street to present "credible and reliable" identification when asked by a police officer. The Court said this law, in its vagueness, gave too much discretion to the police for arbitrary and selective enforcement.

    e.  **Police Officer Ordering Apparent Gang Members to Disperse. [§ 671]**

**It is unconstitutionally vague for an ordinance to require a police officer to order a person whom he reasonably believes to be a gang member to leave the area.**

***Chicago v. Morales*,** 527 U.S. 41 (1999). The Court invalidated, on vagueness grounds, a Chicago Gang Congregation Ordinance which prohibited criminal street gang members from loitering in public places. If a police officer observed a person whom he reasonably thought to be a gang member loitering in a public place with one or more persons, he shall order them to disperse. The law violated procedural due process in that it failed to give adequate notice to people to whom it might be applied and it might have authorized arbitrary and discriminatory enforcement.

2.  **Overbreadth. [§ 672]**

**A statute is overbroad to the extent that it may be used to punish or restrict protected speech (speech that the government may not restrict under any of the First Amendment analyses).** The Court has said that for a litigant to make a facial overbreadth challenge to a statute, he or she must show that the overbreadth of the statute is substantial in relation to the plainly legitimate applications of the law (in other words a facial challenge will be available only if the statute is capable of punishing a great deal of protected speech). While the vagueness and overbreadth analyses are separate and distinct inquiries, the two concepts frequently arise together. For instance, a vague statute (for example, anyone who wilfully annoys another person is guilty of a misdemeanor) is capable of

# FREEDOM OF SPEECH

being applied to protected speech because of the discretion it gives to the government official applying the law. As you read the following cases, be aware of the interplay between the vagueness and overbreadth doctrines.

a. **Civil Service Employees Participating in Political Activities. [§ 673]**

   **It is permissible for a state to restrict political activity by certain state employees.**

   *Broadrick v. Oklahoma*, 413 U.S. 601 (1973). The Court upheld, against a facial overbreadth challenge, an Oklahoma law restricting political activity by certain government civil service employees. The law prohibited them from taking part in political activity or campaigns. As part of their facial attack, plaintiffs challenged this law on the basis that it might be applied to speech activity which they had not engaged in (wearing buttons or displaying bumper stickers). The Court rejected their overbreadth challenge, saying that, especially when conduct and not merely speech is involved, the Court will entertain an overbreadth challenge only when the overbreadth is real and substantial in relation to the plainly legitimate sweep of the statute.

b. **Use of the Word "Lust" to Define Obscenity. [§ 674]**

   **It violates principles of overbreadth for a state to use the word "lust" in defining obscenity.**

   *Brockett v. Spokane Arcades, Inc.*, 472 U.S. 491 (1985). The Court invalidated part of a state obscenity statute because it was overbroad in that it used the word "lust" in defining obscenity, a definition which would have allowed the punishment of constitutionally protected material. The Court said that the general rule on invalidation of a statute on overbreadth grounds is that a Court should, if possible, strike only the specific part of the statute that may have overbroad application, and leave the rest of the statute to be applied in a normal manner.

c. **Congregating in Such a Manner as to Annoy Passersby. [§ 675]**

   **It violates principles of vagueness and overbreadth for a city to criminalize merely congregating on a sidewalk in a manner annoying to passersby.**

   *Coates v. Cincinnati*, 402 U.S. 611 (1971). The Court invalidated, on vagueness and overbreadth grounds, an ordinance that made it a crime for three or more persons to assemble on a sidewalk and conduct themselves in a manner annoying to passersby. The Court said this statute was constitutionally defective because it provided no ascertainable standard of prohibited conduct, and because it could be used to punish protected exercises of the right to assembly.

d. **Prohibiting Judicial Candidates From Announcing Their Views on Disputed Legal or Political Issues. [§ 676]**

**It is an unconstitutional content-based restriction on political speech for a state judicial conduct rule to prohibit candidates for judicial office from announcing their views on disputed legal or political issues.**

*Republican Party of Minnesota v. White*, 536 U.S. 765 (2002). The Minnesota Supreme Court adopted a canon of judicial conduct that prohibits a candidate for judicial office from announcing his views on disputed legal or political issues. As justification for the rule, the state asserted interests in preserving the impartiality of the state's judiciary, and preserving the appearance of impartiality of the judiciary. The Court held that this was a content-based restriction of speech and, as such, strict scrutiny is the appropriate standard to apply. The canon was not narrowly tailored because it does not restrict speech for or against particular parties (who may obviously hold a certain position on an issue), but only speech for or against particular issues. The Court also discussed the fact that Minnesota has a system of electing judges, and it is somewhat anomolous to ask people to vote for judicial candidates who are forbidden to discuss their positions on issues relevant to the election.

e. **Criminalizing The Commercial Creation, Sale, or Possession of Depictions of Animal Cruelty. [§ 676.1]**

**It violated the substantial overbreadth doctrine for Congress to criminalize the commercial creation, sale, or possession of certain depictions of animal cruelty**

*U.S. v. Stevens*, 130 S.Ct. 1577 (2010). Congress passed a law which prohibited certain depictions of animal cruelty. The law applied to any visual or auditory depiction in which a living animal is intentionally mutilated, tortured, wounded or killed, if that conduct violates state or federal law where this creation or possession takes place. The statute exempted depictions with "serious religious, political scientific, educational, journalistic, historical or artistic value." The Court, 8–1, ruled that the statute was substantially overbroad, and that Stevens could not be constitutionally punished for selling dog-fighting videos. The Court said that depictions of animal cruelty are not categorically unprotected by the First Amendment, and that the law in question was content-based and therefore presumptively invalid under the First Amendment. The Court pointed out that the statute could be applied to clearly protected activities, such as hunting magazines and videos, and that the statute was also flawed because depictions of entirely lawful conduct may be found criminal if those depictions later find their way into states where the same conduct is prohibited. For instance, the statute could be applied to criminalize a magazine or video depicting lawful hunting that is sold in the Nation's Capitol, where hunting is illegal.

## C. PRIOR RESTRAINTS. [§ 677]

**A prior restraint is any government action that stops speech before it can be communicated.** A prior restraint is especially suspect because the government is prohibiting the speech based purely on speculation that it will cause some evil or societal harm that the government has a right to prevent. Constitutional law courses usually treat two kinds of prior restraints: 1) those imposed by an injunctive order of a court, and 2) those imposed by the application of a licensing system. Both kinds of prior restraints must be justified by an extremely important government interest. Other kinds of prior restraints that you should be aware of are informal prior restraints (government action short of passing a statute that prevents speech from being communicated), and contractually agreed on prior restraints.

1. **Injunctive Orders Imposing Prior Restraints. [§ 678]**

   **Court orders imposing prior restraints are presumed unconstitutional, and the government has a heavy burden of justifying such a restriction on speech.** It would be possible to justify such an injunction if the government asserted some compelling reason of national security, military secrets, or the like.

   a. **Perpetual Injunction Against a Newspaper. [§ 679]**

   **A court may not perpetually enjoin the publication in a newspaper of any malicious, scandalous, or defamatory material.**

   *Near v. Minnesota*, 283 U.S. 697 (1931). The Court invalidated, as a prior restraint, the application of an ordinance that authorized a court to perpetually enjoin the publication in a newspaper of any malicious, scandalous, or defamatory material. The Court said that prior restraints may be justified only in exceptional cases, such as to

# CHAPTER XVI

prevent obstruction of the nation's recruiting service, or to prevent the publication of the location of troops during wartime.

b. **Publication of the Pentagon Papers. [§ 680]**

**The Court refused to enjoin the publication of the Pentagon Papers (pertaining to the Vietnam war) absent a compelling reason for the injunction.**

*New York Times Co. v. U.S.*, 403 U.S. 713 (1971) (The Pentagon Papers Case). The Court refused to enjoin newspapers from publishing a classified study of the history of U.S. decisionmaking in Vietnam. In a per curiam opinion, the Court said that any system of prior restraints comes to the Court with a heavy presumption against its constitutional validity, and that the government has a heavy burden of justifying the judicial enforcement of such a prior restraint.

c. **Publication of Contents of an Illegally Made Wiretap. [§ 681]**

**The Court held that there is a First Amendment right to publish, for both the media and an innocent recipient, an illegal interception of a phone conversation.**

*Bartnicki v. Vopper*, 532 U.S. 514 (2001). The Court held that 18 U.S.C. § 251l(1)(c) was an unlawful prior restraint on speech. A radio commentator received and then played on the air a tape of a conversation between the Teacher's Union president and the chief union negotiator, which included threats against School Board members' homes. While the interception was illegal, the commentator's receipt of it was not. The Court held that the media have a right to publish information of public concern even if they knew that it had been originally stolen or illegally obtained.

d. **Criminal Contempt Citation as a Prior Restraint. [§ 682]**

**The Court upheld criminal contempt citations of demonstrators who marched in violation of a court order.**

*Walker v. Birmingham*, 388 U.S. 307 (1967). The Court upheld criminal contempt citations of demonstrators who had marched in violation of an injunctive order issued by an Alabama court. The order enjoined the demonstrators from marching without a permit issued pursuant to the local parade ordinance. The Court held that although the ordinance and the resulting order may have been unconstitutional prior restraints on speech, the demonstrators were not free simply to disregard the court order. They could have challenged the validity of the court order, but chose not to. In a later case, *Shuttlesworth v. Birmingham*, 373 U.S. 262 (1973), the Court reversed the convictions of another group of demonstrators who had been convicted of violating the ordinance that was the basis of the injunction in *Walker*. In that case, the Court was dealing with a violation of the ordinance itself, rather than a violation of an injunctive order. The Court found that the ordinance amounted to a prior restraint because it gave too much discretion to the permit-giver. The moral of the story is that the Court will not permit individuals to violate an injunctive order restricting speech, even though that order later turns out to be unconstitutional.

2. **Licensing Systems as Prior Restraints: Cases Involving Review of Films Before Exhibition. [§ 683]**

    If properly drafted, a permit system for movies is constitutional. **For a movie-licensing system to pass constitutional muster, the government must have the burden of proving the work is obscene, must promptly go to court or issue the permit or license, and must ensure that there is a prompt, final judicial decision regarding the alleged obscenity of the work.**

    a. **Movie–Licensing Systems May Be Constitutional. [§ 684]**

        **A film-licensing system may be constitutional if it meets specific constitutional standards.**

        *Times Film Corp. v. Chicago*, 365 U.S. 43 (1961). The Court rejected a facial challenge to the City of Chicago's film-licensing system under which a film must be submitted to the commissioner of police who must apply statutory standards to determine whether to grant or deny a permit. The applicant had a right to appeal a denial to the Mayor, whose decision was final. The Court upheld, in principle, the constitutionality of an appropriately drafted licensing system, and rejected the argument that the only way a government may fight obscenity is through a criminal prosecution after it has been disseminated.

    b. **Movie–Licensing Systems. [§ 685]**

        **A licensing scheme for adult businesses will be constitutional if the government carries the burden of proving to a court that the work in question is obscene.**

        *Freedman v. Maryland*, 380 U.S. 51 (1965). The Court set forth the procedure that must be followed for a local censorship board to revoke the license of a book or film distributor who is disseminating obscene material, or to impose a prior restraint on the dissemination of such material. The Court ruled that any system which requires the prior submission of a film or book to a censor must meet the following requirements: The government must meet the burden of proving that the work is obscene; the censor must issue the license promptly or go to court to enjoin the showing of the film or sale of the book; and there must be a prompt, final judicial decision, following an adversary hearing, to minimize the deterrent effect of a possibly erroneous denial of a license. In *Littleton, Colo. v. Z.J. Gifts D–4 LLC*, 541 U.S. 774 (2004), the Court rejected a facial challenge to a city ordinance which requires a bookstore, novelty store, or video store selling sexually oriented material to have an adult business license. Clarifying the *Freedman* standards, the Court ruled that a licensing scheme for adult businesses must provide for a prompt judicial determination of any challenge to the denial of a license, not just prompt access to judicial review. The Court also ruled that the First Amendment does not require any special procedures for ensuring prompt judicial review, but that ordinary judicial review procedures will suffice.

c. **Permit Systems for Fundraisers. [§ 686]**

**A state may not impose a licensing scheme on professional fundraisers unless the scheme requires the state to issue the license or get a court order authorizing the denial of a license.**

*Riley v. National Federation of the Blind of North Carolina, Inc.*, 487 U.S. 781 (1988). The Court, using the *Freedman* standards (see previous case), invalidated a North Carolina law which required professional fundraisers to be licensed if they were going to solicit for charitable organizations. If the solicitor were a volunteer, or employed by the charity, he or she could solicit immediately upon submitting an application. This scheme violated *Freedman* because it did not require the government to promptly issue the license or go to court to get an order authorizing the denial of the license.

3. **"Informal" Prior Restraints. [§ 687]**

Informal government action, short of passing a statute, may operate as a prior restraint. A state may not use its power to informally influence what books may be sold. For example, **it is unconstitutional for a state commission to threaten obscenity prosecutions against booksellers who sell books from a state compiled list of objectionable books.**

*Bantam Books v. Sullivan*, 372 U.S. 58 (1963). The Court held unconstitutional the actions of the Rhode Island Commission to Encourage Morality in

# FREEDOM OF SPEECH

Youth, which included compiling a list of "objectionable" books and notifying distributors that the list would be given to local police departments. The Commission also informed the distributors that it had a duty, when appropriate, to urge the Attorney General's office to begin obscenity prosecutions against what it considered to be offending parties. The Court treated this scheme as an informal prior restraint, the purpose of which was to intimidate booksellers to stop selling the books on the list.

4. **Contractually Agreed Upon Prior Restraints. [§ 688]**

   **It is permissible for the CIA to require that its employees get agency approval before publishing a book about activities that occurred during their employment with the CIA.**

   *Snepp v. U.S.*, 444 U.S. 507 (1980). The Court upheld the validity of an agreement between the Central Intelligence Agency and one of its employees under which he agreed not to publish any information he obtained during his employment with the CIA, unless he had the prior approval of the agency. Snepp published a book, without agency approval, about certain CIA activities in South Vietnam. The Court ruled that the government was entitled to a constructive trust on all profits Snepp might earn from the book. The Court said that the CIA, even without an agreement, could have imposed reasonable restrictions on the speech activity of employees to advance the government's compelling interests in the secrecy of information needed for national security, and in the appearance of confidentiality necessary for the functioning of an intelligence agency.

## D. TIME, PLACE, OR MANNER RESTRICTIONS. [§ 689]

**If the government is not completely prohibiting speech, but is just restricting its time, place, or manner, the Court uses the following four-part analysis:**

1) Is the restriction **content-neutral**?

2) Is it directed at achieving a **significant government interest**?

3) Is it **narrowly tailored** to achieve that interest?

4) Does it leave open ample **alternative channels of communication**?

The rationale for restricting the speech is that the medium or method of communication creates certain secondary effects which the government has the

# CHAPTER XVI

power to regulate. For example, the government might want to regulate the location of adult movie theaters because of the effect they have on surrounding property values. **Remember that a government may never regulate speech just because it dislikes or disapproves of the speech; such a regulation would be content based, and would be invalid under a strict scrutiny analysis.** (It is not a compelling, or even legitimate, reason for a government to suppress speech because it does not approve of it.)

1. **Requirements for a Valid Time, Place or Manner Restriction. [§ 690]**

    **For a time, place, or manner restriction to be constitutional, it must meet the following requirements.** These analyses are discussed below.

    a. **The Restriction Must Be Content-Neutral. [§ 691]**

    **A government may not restrict speech because of antipathy toward that speech.** The Court casts this rule in terms of the requirement that a law be content-neutral if it is to be upheld as a valid time, place, or manner restriction. **The Court has treated laws as content-neutral under either of two analyses: the government does not even look at the content of the speech when it regulates; or the government looks at content, not to approve or disapprove of it, but to see if the content causes some "secondary effect" which the government has the power to regulate.**

    (1) **When the Government Does Not Even Consider Content. [§ 692]**

    An example of the first kind of content-neutrality, where the government does not even look at the content of the regulated speech, is *Ward v. Rock Against Racism*, 491 U.S. 781 (1989), in which the Court upheld a regulation of the City of New York requiring the use of sound systems provided by the city for concerts in Central Park. The regulation did not concern itself with the content of the music, just with its noise level. The City did not care whether it was Mozart or Metallica; it wanted to protect the peace and quiet of those who lived around Central Park.

    (2) **When the Government Considers Content to See if It Causes a Regulable "Secondary Effect." [§ 693]**

    The second kind of content-neutrality is illustrated by *Renton v. Playtime Theatres, Inc.*, 475 U.S. 41 (1986), in which the Court upheld a zoning ordinance which dispersed "adult movie theaters" throughout the city. Even though the government did look at the content of the movies to determine whether they fit the category of "adult entertainment," the Renton ordinance was directed at the secondary effects (crime rising and property values dropping) caused by a concentration of adult movie theaters in one section of the city. The Court treated this ordinance as content-neutral, and upheld it is a valid time, place, or manner restriction. The same kind of ordinance was upheld by the Court in *Young v. American Mini Theatres, Inc.*, 427 U.S. 50 (1976).

However the continued validity of this second kind of content-neutrality was thrown in doubt by *Los Angeles v. Alameda Books Inc.*, 535 U.S. 425 (2002), in which the Court reversed a lower court decision granting a summary judgment against the City of Los Angeles on the basis that its zoning ordinance violated the First Amendment. The ordinance prohibited more than one adult entertainment business in the same building. The plaintiffs argued that the City had not shown that multiple-use adult establishments produced the secondary effects needed to justify the ordinance. The Court ruled that the City could survive a summary judgment challenge by relying on a previous study to demonstrate that its ban on multiple-use adult establishments served its interest in reducing crime. Four Justices questioned the accuracy of an ordinance like that in *Renton* being described as content-neutral. Justice Kennedy, concurring, described such ordinances a content-based, and Justice Souter, for three Justices, rejected the content-based/content-neutral distinction and said that such a zoning ordinance should be given a First Amendment label of its own (content-correlated).

b. **The Restriction Must Be Narrowly Tailored. [§ 694]**

The regulation does not have to be the least drastic means of achieving the government's goal. **The Court has said that a regulation will be valid so long as the means are not substantially broader than necessary to achieve the government's goal; a court will not invalidate a law simply because it is able to conclude that the government could have chosen some alternative means that might have been less restrictive of speech.**

c. **The Restriction Must Advance a Significant Government Interest. [§ 695]**

The government does not need a compelling interest to support a time, place, or manner restriction. **A significant or important** interest will suffice because the object of the law is not to suppress speech, but to deal with the non-speech secondary effect which the government has a right to prevent or restrict.

d. **The Restriction Must Leave Open Ample Alternative Channels of Communication. [§ 696]**

Since the object of a time, place, or manner restriction is to move speech around, not to prohibit it, the government must leave available other ways for the speaker to communicate. If there are no ample alternative channels of communication, the regulation is tantamount to a prior restraint, and strict scrutiny applies.

2. **Time, Place, or Manner Restrictions in a Public Forum. [§ 697]**

The time, place, manner rules developed in the public forum area. Public forum doctrine is treated more fully later in the book (see § 810, below), but **the main idea is that certain public places (streets, sidewalks, parks, public amphitheaters) have been used for speech purposes for so long that the public has a right of access to them for speech purposes. Since there is a guaranteed right of access to these places, the government may not prohibit persons from speaking; it may only impose time, place, or manner restrictions.** In these public forum cases, remember that the government owns the property, and the place is used for some non-speech purpose (such as a post-office, a military base, state government buildings, parks, or even streets). **Time, place, or manner analysis in public forum cases is used to strike a balance between the speaker's right of access, and the government's ability to maintain the use of the place for its intended purpose.**

a. **Prohibition of Loud Noise. [§ 698]**

A city may prohibit sound trucks from operating above a certain decibel level.

*Kovacs v. Cooper*, 336 U.S. 77 (1949). The Court upheld a Trenton, New Jersey ordinance which prohibited any sound truck or loudspeaker which emitted loud and raucous noises. Justice Reed, for a plurality, said that the ordinance, as interpreted by state courts, permitted the use of electronic amplification devices, and was only directed at the loud and raucous manner of the broadcast.

b. **Prohibition of Picketing Based on Its Content. [§ 699]**

A city cannot selectively prohibit picketing based on the message on the picket signs.

# FREEDOM OF SPEECH

*Police Department of Chicago v. Mosley*, 408 U.S. 92 (1972). The Court invalidated a Chicago ordinance prohibiting picketing within 150 feet of a school, with the exception of peaceful picketing of any school involved in a labor dispute. The Court said this ordinance was not content neutral, and therefore was not to be analyzed under time, place or manner rules.

c. **Prohibition of Loud Noise Near a School. [§ 700]**

   **A state can prohibit loud noise near a school building while the school is in session.**

   *Grayned v. Rockford*, 408 U.S. 104 (1972). The Court upheld an anti-noise ordinance which prohibited any person on property adjacent to a school building from making any noise which would disrupt the functioning of the school. Unlike *Mosley* (previous case), there were no exceptions for any specific kinds of speech. The Court treated this ordinance as simply a restriction on the manner of speech, irrespective of the content.

d. **Prohibition of the Broadcast of Offensive Language During Daytime. [§ 701]**

   **The federal government can prohibit an indecent radio broadcast during the daytime when children are likely to be in the audience.**

   *FCC v. Pacifica Foundation*, 438 U.S. 726 (1978). The Court upheld an action by the Federal Communications Commission to channel an indecent radio broadcast to times when children probably would not be in the audience. The FCC basically told the station not to play George Carlin's "Seven Dirty Words" monologue when children are likely to be listening to the radio. This is a permissible time regulation because the government was trying to prevent offending the sensibilities of children (which is a significant government interest), the means were narrowly tailored, and the monologue could still be disseminated to the public.

e. **Picketing Outside the Supreme Court Building. [§ 702]**

   **The federal government cannot prohibit picketing or demonstrating on public sidewalks outside the Supreme Court Building.**

   *U.S. v. Grace*, 461 U.S. 171 (1983). The Court invalidated a federal law which prohibited picketing or the carrying of flags or banners on the public sidewalks outside the Supreme Court building. The Court rejected the time, place, or manner argument, saying that this law operated as a total prohibition of a specific kind of speech.

f. **Sleeping Overnight in a National Park. [§ 703]**

**The National Park Service can prohibit sleeping overnight in a national park, even if the sleeping constitutes symbolic speech.**

*Clark v. Community for Creative Non–Violence*, 468 U.S. 288 (1984). The Court upheld the action of the National Park Service which refused permission for demonstrators to sleep overnight in a national park near the White House. The protesters wanted to dramatize the plight of the homeless. Assuming that symbolic speech was involved, the Court used time, place, manner analysis to uphold the restriction.

g. **Focused Picketing Outside a Residence. [§ 704]**

**A town can prohibit focused picketing outside someone's house as long as the picketers are free to walk up and down the block to demonstrate.**

*Frisby v. Schultz*, 487 U.S. 474 (1988). The Court upheld a town ordinance forbidding focused picketing in front of a person's residence. (Focused picketing is picketing in one place—here, outside someone's residence.) The Court said that this law met time, place, or manner requirements because it was passed to protect the privacy interests of residents, and left open the ability to walk up and down the street with picket signs as a means of protest.

h. **Permit Required to Conduct Large Scale Event in a Public Park. [§ 705]**

**A municipal ordinance that requires a permit to conduct a large-scale event in a public park is merely a content-neutral time, place, and manner restriction on the use of a public forum.**

*Thomas v. Chicago Park District*, 534 U.S. 316 (2002). The Court unanimously upheld a Chicago Park District ordinance requiring individuals to obtain a permit before conducting large-scale events in public parks. The ordinance, which was upheld as a content-neutral time, place, manner restriction on the use of a public forum, provided that the District may deny a permit on any one of thirteen grounds, must process applications within 28 days, and must explain its reason for a denial. An appeal was provided to the District's general superintendent, and then to state court. The ordinance was held to be content-neutral, and designed to coordinate multiple uses of the parks, assure preservation of the park facilities, and prevent dangerous or unlawful uses. As a content-neutral regulation of a public forum, the Court said the ordinance did not have to meet the more stringent requirements of *Freedman v. Maryland* (§ 604).

i. **Prohibition of Signs That Cast Foreign Embassies Into Public Disrepute. [§ 706]**

**The District of Columbia cannot prohibit signs near embassies just because the signs might denigrate the foreign countries which operate the embassies.**

*Boos v. Barry*, 485 U.S. 312 (1988). The Court invalidated a District of Columbia ordinance banning the display of any sign within 500 feet of a foreign embassy if the sign would tend to bring the foreign government into "public odium" or "public disrepute." The Court rejected the argument that the law was content neutral; it was directed at the emotive impact of the speech, something which is not a "secondary effect" for purposes of content neutrality.

j. **Prohibition of Political Activity Near a Polling Place. [§ 707]**

**A state can prohibit political activity near a polling place on election day.**

*Burson v. Freeman*, 504 U.S. 191 (1992). With no majority supporting a particular rationale, the Court upheld a Tennessee law prohibiting the display or distribution of campaign material or the soliciting of votes within 100 feet of the entrance to a polling place. The Court did not apply time, place, or manner analysis because the restriction was found to be content-based. Four Justices said the law passed strict scrutiny analysis, and Justice Scalia upheld it on the basis that a polling place is not a traditional public forum, so reasonable restrictions are acceptable.

k. **Prohibition of Residential Signs. [§ 708]**

**A city cannot prohibit all (or most) residential signs; such a ban forecloses an entire medium of communication.**

*Ladue v. Gilleo*, 512 U.S. 43 (1994). The Court invalidated a city ordinance which barred all residential signs, except those falling within one of ten exemptions. The city's asserted interest was to reduce visual blight. Gilleo had displayed on her front lawn a sign protesting the Persian Gulf war. Assuming that the law was content-neutral, the Court ruled that the ordinance was not a valid time, or place, or manner restriction because it did not leave open adequate alternative channels of communication. The ordinance virtually foreclosed an important medium of communication of political or religious messages.

l.  **Prohibition of the Distribution of Anonymous Literature. [§ 709]**

    **A government cannot prohibit the distribution of anonymous literature. However, a state can generally force disclosure of referenda petitions with names and addresses.**

    (1) *Talley v. California*, 362 U.S. 60 (1960).

    The Court invalidated a Los Angeles ordinance which prohibited the distribution of unsigned literature. In *Talley*, the ordinance was applied to the distribution of anonymous handbills urging people to boycott certain Los Angeles merchants who allegedly engaged in discriminatory employment practices. The Court rejected the argument that the ordinance was a sufficiently tailored means to identify those engaged in fraud, false advertising and libel.

    (2) *Mcintyre v. Ohio Elections Commission*, 514 U.S. 334 (1995).

    The Court invalidated an Ohio statute prohibiting the distribution of anonymous campaign literature designed to promote election or defeat of candidates, to promote adoption or defeat of any issue, or to influence voters in elections. The Court treated the Ohio statute as a content-based restriction on core political speech, and concluded that it was not justified by Ohio's asserted interests in preventing fraudulent and libelous statements and in providing the electorate with relevant information about political campaigns.

    (3) *Doe v. Reed*, 130 S.Ct. 2811 (2010).

    An eight-justice majority ruled that the compelled disclosure of signatory information on referendum petitions is subject to review under the First Amendment, but does not as a general matter violate the First Amendment. In 2009, the governor of Washington signed into law a measure that expanded the rights and responsibilities of state-registered domestic partners, including same-sex domestic partners. A group called Protect Marriage Washington collected enough signatures on a petition to place a referendum on the ballot opposing the state law. Proponents of the state law invoked the Washington Public Records Act (PRA) to get copies of the petition, which contained the signers' names and addresses. The petition sponsors sued to enjoin public release of the petition, making both a facial and an as-applied challenge to the application of the PRA. The Court, ruling only on the facial challenge, said that the state's interest in preserving the integrity of the electoral process is sufficient to defeat a facial challenge to such a disclosure requirement. Specifically, the Court relied on the state's interests in rooting out fraud and promoting transparency and accountability in the electoral process. The Court remanded for resolution of the question of whether, as applied, fulfilling the PRA disclosure request would subject the signers of the petition to a significant enough threat of harassment to overcome the state interests.

m. **Limitations on Charitable Solicitation in Federal Offices. [§ 710]**

The President may, by executive order, limit access to federal offices for purposes of soliciting funds for charity.

*Cornelius v. NAACP Legal Defense and Educational Fund, Inc.*, 473 U.S 788 (1985). The Court upheld an executive order limiting participation in a charitable solicitation drive in federal places of employment to non-profit charitable groups which provided certain health or welfare services. The Court reasoned that the charitable solicitation project was a non-public forum, and that restricting access to federal offices for purposes of charitable solicitation was a reasonable means of ensuring the efficient functioning of the workplace.

n. **Permit Requirement for Door-to-Door Solicitors. [§ 711]**

**A municipal ordinance that make it illegal for uninvited canvassers to go on private residential property to promote any cause, without first obtaining a permit, violates the First Amendment.**

*Watchtower Bible & Tract Society of New York Inc. v. Stratton, Ohio*, 536 U.S. 150 (2002). The village of Stratton, Ohio passed an ordinance which prohibited canvassers from going door-to-door to promote any "cause" without getting a permit from the mayor's office by completing and signing a registration form. The ordinance was challenged by a group of Jehovah's Witnesses who challenged the ordinance as violating their rights to free exercise of religion, free speech, and free press. The Court struck down the ordinance as it applies to religious proselytizing, anonymous political speech, and the distribution of handbills. The Court did not apply any specific standard of review because the amount of speech affected by the ordinance and the nature of the regulation resulted in its unconstitutionality. Had the ordinance been applied only to commercial activities and the solicitation of funds, it might have withstood constitutional scrutiny as an acceptable means to achieve the city's interests in protecting residents' privacy and preventing fraud. However, the ordinance applied to a variety of causes, including religious and political speech. The requirement of signing the registration form also compromised the anonymity to which speakers are entitled under *McIntyre v. Ohio Elections Commission* (§ 709).

3. **Time, Place, or Manner Restrictions Imposed Through an Injunction, Rather Than a Generally Applicable Ordinance. [§ 712]**

**The Court has said that a time, place, or manner restriction imposed by an injunctive order is to be subject to more stringent review than one effected by a general ordinance.** Because the injunction is directed at an actual or threatened violation of a legislative or judicial decree (as opposed to an ordinance, which is directed at an entire class of potential violators), it carries greater risks of censorship and discrimination. **The test for a content-neutral injunction is whether it burdens no more speech than is necessary to serve a significant government interest.**

   a. **Injunctive Orders Prohibiting Demonstrations for a Certain Period of Time. [§ 713]**

   **The Court invalidated an ex parte order restraining a white supremacist group from holding any rally for ten days in the county, if the rally would disturb or endanger the citizens of the county.**

   *Carroll v. President and Commissioners of Princess Anne*, 393 U.S. 175 (1968). The Court invalidated an ex parte order, granted with no notice to or communication with a white supremacist group, prohibiting the group from holding any demonstration or rally within the county for ten days if the rally would disturb or endanger the citizens of the county. The Court said that any such order must be precisely tailored to the facts of the case, and must be couched in the narrowest terms that will accomplish the pin-pointed objective permitted by the essential needs of public order.

# FREEDOM OF SPEECH

b. **Restrictions on Expressive Activity Around Abortion Clinics and Residences of Clinic Staff. [§ 714]**

   **The Court has upheld certain restrictions on expressive activity near abortion clinics, but has invalidated others as burdening more speech than necessary to achieve the government's interests.**

   (1) *Madsen v. Women's Health Center, Inc.*, 512 U.S. 753 (1994). The Court reviewed an injunction issued by a Florida state court which prohibited anti-abortion protesters from demonstrating in certain places and in various ways outside a health clinic that performs abortions. **The Court said that the injunction must burden no more speech than is necessary to serve the significant government interests of protecting a pregnant woman's freedom to seek lawful medical or counseling services, ensuring public safety, and protecting property and privacy rights.** The Court upheld a 36-foot buffer zone around the clinic entrances and driveway. It also upheld noise restrictions which were in effect during surgery and recovery periods at the clinic.

   The Court struck down, as overinclusive, the following restrictions in the injunction: a 36-foot buffer zone around private property to the north and west of the clinic; a 300-foot "no-approach zone" around the clinic, in which anti-abortion protesters were barred from approaching clinic patients; and a 300-foot buffer zone around the residences of clinic staff, in which there can be no picketing or demonstrating. The Court also invalidated a blanket ban on images that were observable to patients inside the clinic (such as posters with pictures of aborted fetuses).

   (2) *Schenck v. Pro–Choice Network of Western New York*, 519 U.S. 357 (1997). The Court reviewed an injunction issued by a New York state court that imposed "fixed" and "floating" buffer zones around abortion clinics and women who wanted to enter the clinics. The Court reaffirmed *Madsen* (prior case), saying that a time, place and manner restriction imposed by injunctive order (rather than by statute) must burden no more speech than necessary to serve a significant government interest. Applying that test, the Court upheld 15-foot "fixed" buffer zones which prohibited demonstrating around abortion clinic doorways, parking lot entrances and driveways. The Court also upheld an order that allowed two "sidewalk counselors" inside the "fixed" buffer zone (to try to dissuade a woman from having an abortion), but required the counselors to "cease and desist" their

counseling if requested to do so by the woman to whom they were talking. The Court struck down that part of the injunctive order that created 15–foot "floating" buffer zones around persons or vehicles entering or leaving the abortion clinics. These buffer zones prevented speakers from talking to someone from a normal conversational distance or from leafletting on a public street. In its analysis, the Court used the same government interests it relied on in *Madsen:* ensuring public safety and order, promoting the free flow of traffic on streets and sidewalks, protecting property rights, and protecting a woman's right to seek pregnancy-related medical services.

**(3)** *Hill v. Colorado*, **530 U.S. 703 (2000).** The Court upheld a Colorado statute that regulates speech-related conduct within 100 feet of the entrance to any health care facility. The statute makes it unlawful within the regulated areas for any person to "knowingly approach" within eight feet of another person, without that person's consent for the purpose of leafletting, displaying a sign, or speaking with that person. The statute was challenged facially by a group of anti-abortion protesters who wished to confront women outside abortion clinics. The Court upheld the statute as a content-neutral time, place, or manner restriction. The Court distinguished *Schenck* (previous case) in two ways. First, *Schenck* involved a judicial decree, not a statute, and therefore posed greater risks of censorship and discriminatory application. Second, unlike the floating buffer zone in *Schenck*, which required a protester either to stop talking or to get off the sidewalk whenever a patient came within 15 feet, the Colorado statute allows a protester to stand still while a person moving towards or away from a health care facility walks past her.

## E. CONTENT–BASED RESTRICTIONS ON SPEECH. [§ 715]

There are certain times when the government looks at the content of speech to determine whether and how to regulate the speech. Be aware of the evil that the government is trying to prevent or punish. Identification of the evil will take you into the appropriate analysis, and will answer the question of which test to use to answer an exam question.

**STUDY TIP:** **When you get a free speech question, and are trying to figure out which test to use, focus on the evil the government is trying to prevent. Once you identify the evil, it will**

# FREEDOM OF SPEECH

**take you directly into the appropriate analysis.** For instance, if the government is concerned about consumers being defrauded by certain types of advertising, it's a commercial speech case; if the government is trying to prohibit sexually-oriented speech because it lowers the moral tone in the community, or causes anti-social sexual behavior, it's an obscenity case. Be aware of this issue as we go through the different sections and cases.

1. **Clear and Present Danger Analysis. [§ 716]**

   **Under clear and present danger analysis, the government tries to punish a speaker for inciting a listener to engage in illegal activity.** This is a case-by-case determination which looks at all the circumstances surrounding the speech (intent of the speaker, nature of the speech, identity of the speaker, composition of the audience, political or military climate) to see if there is a high enough probability that the speaker would have incited or did incite a listener or listeners to break the law. **The modern test, from the *Brandenburg* case (see § 726), asks whether the speaker's advocacy of illegal action is directed to inciting or producing imminent lawless action and is likely to incite or produce such action by the audience.**

   a. **In General. [§ 717]**

   **The purpose of the clear and present danger test is to determine when the government may punish a speaker for causing his or her audience to engage in illegal acts.** In some cases, a legislature may be able to establish that some regulable evil always happens when certain speech is engaged in (burning one's draft card always impairs the functioning of the Selective Service system). When a legislature cannot categorically establish that a regulable evil always happens when certain speech occurs, the clear and present danger is used to connect the regulable evil and the speech, thus enabling the government to restrict speech as a by-product of regulating the non-speech evil.

   b. **Development of the Clear and Present Danger Doctrine. [§ 718]**

   The clear and present danger test began as a tool of statutory construction in 1919. The Court used the test to allow the punishment of speech under a federal Espionage Act. **By 1969, in *Brandenburg v. Ohio* (see § 726), the test had become constitutionalized in the sense that the First Amendment now prohibits the punishment of speech unless it creates a clear and present danger of some evil that the government has a right to prevent.**

# CHAPTER XVI

(1) **Genesis of the Clear and Present Danger Doctrine. [§ 719]**

**The clear and present danger doctrine began in 1919 when the Court used it to affirm convictions under the 1917 Espionage Act.**

*Schenck v. U.S.*, 249 U.S. 47 (1919). The Court affirmed convictions for violations of the 1917 Espionage Act, which made it a crime to attempt to cause insubordination in the armed forces or obstruct recruiting. The defendants mailed literature to men eligible for the draft, arguing that the draft violated the Thirteenth Amendment prohibition of slavery. Justice Holmes said that the question is whether words are used in such circumstances and are of such a nature as to create a clear and present danger of an evil that Congress has the power to prevent.

(2) **"Bad Tendency" Test. [§ 720]**

**In a dissenting opinion, Justice Holmes argued that the government may punish speech only if it creates an imminent danger of some evil that the government has a right to prevent.**

*Abrams v. U.S.*, 250 U.S. 616 (1919). (Justice Holmes' dissent). The Court in *Abrams* affirmed convictions under amendments to the Espionage Act of 1917. The defendants had distributed leaflets criticizing President Wilson for sending troops to fight in Russia. The majority used a "bad tendency test," under which speech could be punished if it would tend to bring about some substantive evil. Justice Holmes, in dissent, said that only the present danger of immediate evil or an intent to bring it about warrants congressional punishment of speech.

(3) **Specific Statutory Prohibition of Certain Speech. [§ 721]**

**The Court, in the 1920's, refused to apply the clear and present danger test, affirming the conviction of a speaker solely because he engaged in speech that was specifically prohibited by statute.**

*Gitlow v. New York*, 268 U.S. 652 (1925). The Court, in applying the First Amendment against the states, affirmed a conviction under New York's Criminal Anarchy Law, which prohibited advocacy of the violent overthrow of the government. Gitlow was convicted for distributing 16,000 copies of a radical manifesto which urged strikes and other actions as methods of establishing socialism. The Court said that since the statute specifically prohibited certain language, the clear and present danger test was irrelevant, and the speech could be punished if its natural tendency and probable effect was to bring about a substantive evil. Justice Holmes dissented, saying Gitlow's speech was protected under clear and present danger principles.

(4) **Specific Statutory Prohibition of Certain Speech. [§ 722]**

**The Court, in the 1920's, refused to apply the clear and present danger test, affirming the conviction of a speaker who engaged in allegedly subversive speech. The Court refused to review the jury finding that the speaker engaged in illegal speech activity.**

*Whitney v. California*, 274 U.S. 357 (1927). The Court affirmed a conviction under California's Criminal Syndicalism Act, which prohibited advocating or teaching any doctrine which espouses crime, sabotage, or unlawful acts of force or violence as a means of bringing about economic or political change. The Act also criminalized organizing or belonging to any organization that advocates or teaches criminal syndicalism. Charlotte Whitney was convicted of joining and organizing the Communist Labor Party of California. The Court refused to review the finding of the jury that Ms. Whitney had engaged in activity contrary to the Act. Justice Brandeis, in a concurring opinion, argued that the clear and present danger test is required, even in a case like *Whitney*, when the statute specifically proscribes speech. Under the Brandeis approach, the Court has a serious role in reviewing these kinds of convictions, unlike the majority view, which basically rubber stamps the factfinding decision of the jury.

(5) **"Gravity of the Evil" Version of the Clear and Present Danger Test. [§ 723]**

**In 1951, the Court applied a version of the clear and present danger test which asked whether the gravity of the evil, discounted by its improbability (the unlikelihood of its occurrence), justifies such invasion of free speech as is necessary to avoid the danger the government is trying to prevent.**

*Dennis v. U.S.*, 341 U.S. 494 (1951). The Court affirmed convictions under the Smith Act, a federal law which prohibited acting or conspiring to act to teach or advocate the duty or propriety of overthrowing the government by force or violence. The defendants were convicted of conspiring to organize the Communist Party of the United States, a group whose goals included the forceful overthrow of the United States government. Chief Justice Vinson, for a plurality, adopted a new version of the clear and present danger test: Whether the gravity of the evil, discounted by its improbability, justifies such invasion of free speech as is necessary to avoid the danger the government is trying to prevent. Compare this to the approach the Court used in *Schenck v. U.S.*, where the focus was on whether words are used in such circumstances and are of such a nature as to create a clear and present danger of an evil that Congress has the power to prevent.

**(6) Present Advocacy of Future Violent Action May Be Punishable. [§ 724]**

**The government may punish the present advocacy of future violent action if the speech plus its surrounding circumstances make it highly likely that the evil will occur at some specific time in the future.**

*Yates v. U.S.*, 354 U.S. 298 (1957). The Court reversed convictions under the Smith Act for organizing the Communist Party and conspiring to bring about the forcible overthrow of the government. The Court, in an attempt to clarify *Dennis* (previous case), said that it would be constitutional for a government to punish the present advocacy of future violent action if a conspiracy is involved, the group is of sufficient size and cohesiveness, and is sufficiently oriented toward action, and other circumstances are such as to create a high probability that evil will occur. Advocacy of ideas is always protected; incitement of action may not be.

**(7) Punishing Membership in the Communist Party. [§ 725]**

**The Government may not criminalize all membership in the Communist Party; active members may be punished if they intend to bring about illegal goals of the organization and they take some action to effectuate these goals.**

*Scales v. U.S.*, 367 U.S. 203 (1961). The Court affirmed convictions under the membership clause of the Smith Act which made it a crime to be a knowing member of any group which advocates the forcible overthrow of the government. The Court distinguished "active" from "passive" members, saying that not all membership in the Communist Party can be made a crime. Scales was Chairman of the North and South Carolina Districts of the Community Party and, as such, had knowledge of the party's illegal goals, and a specific intent to bring them about.

**(8) Criminalizing the Act of Providing Material Support to a Foreign Terrorist Organization. [§ 725.1]**

**Congress may prohibit Americans from giving material support to terrorist groups, even if that support is intended to advance the political and humanitarian activities of the terrorist group.**

*Holder v. Humanitarian Law Project*, 130 S.Ct. 2705 (2010). The Court rejected vagueness and First Amendment challenges to a federal law which made it a crime to knowingly provide material support or resources to a foreign terrorist organization. Individuals and groups claimed they wanted to support the nonviolent activities of Turkish and Sri Lankan separatist groups which had been designated "foreign terrorist organizations" by the Secretary of State. The Court, 6–3, first rejected a Fifth Amendment Due Process Clause vagueness challenge to the statute. The Court said that the statute was clear in its application to the plaintiffs' proposed conduct, and that the prescribed activity only covered advocacy performed in coordination with, or at the direction of a foreign terrorist organization. The Court made it clear that advocacy engaged in entirely independent of the terrorist organization is permitted under the statute; only acting in concert with the terrorist organization is prohibited.

The Court also rejected plaintiffs' argument that the statute violated the First Amendment because it banned pure political speech. The Court emphasized that the statute does not prohibit independent advocacy or even membership in the terrorist groups. The Court gave deference to Congressional and Executive findings that all contributions to foreign terrorist organizations, even allegedly benign ones, further the terrorist goals of such organizations. The Court said that there was no First Amendment violation in relation to the specific speech activities identified by the plaintiffs.

# CHAPTER XVI

**(9) Speech That Incites Imminent Lawless Action and Is Likely to Produce It. [§ 726]**

**The government may punish speech if it is directed to inciting imminent lawless action and is likely to cause such action.**

*Brandenburg v. Ohio*, 395 U.S. 444 (1969). The Court reversed the conviction of a Ku Klux Klan leader under the Ohio Criminal Syndicalism statute which prohibited assembling with others to advocate the duty or propriety of violent overthrow of the government. Brandenburg made some hateful but inconsequential statements at a Klan rally, and was arrested. The Court gives us the modern version of the clear and present danger test, which is that a state cannot proscribe advocacy of the use of force or of the violation of the law unless the advocacy is directed to inciting or producing imminent lawless action and is likely to incite or produce such action. The test is needed to ensure that the law only punishes incitement to illegal action, as opposed to advocacy of abstract ideas.

**(9) Speech Must Be Directed to a Specific Person or Group. [§ 727]**

**The Court has ruled that if speech is not directed to a specific person or group, it is not punishable under the clear and present danger doctrine because it is not likely to produce any imminent lawless action.**

*Hess v. Indiana*, 414 U.S. 105 (1973). The Court reversed a conviction of an antiwar demonstrator who, after police had cleared a street during a rally on campus, said loudly, "We'll take the fucking street later (or again)." Hess was convicted under a disorderly conduct statute. The Court applied *Brandenburg*, and concluded that Hess' speech was not directed to any specific person or group, so it was not intended to advocate any imminent lawless action, nor was it likely to produce any.

2. **Fighting Words, Offensive Speech, Hate Speech. [§ 728]**

**These three kinds of speech have one common thread: each involves nasty, scurrilous language that is intended or likely to offend some people or inflict psychic trauma on the members of the audience.** The constitutional question is when does this kind of speech cross the line and become regulable by the government. Remember that preventing hurt feelings, or psychic trauma, is not a legitimate government interest. There must be more, such as preventing a breach of the peace.

# FREEDOM OF SPEECH

a. **Definition of Fighting Words. [§ 729]**

**Fighting words are scurrilous epithets, delivered in person to the listener, which are likely to cause an average addressee to retaliate against the speaker.** The theory is that fighting words are not essential to the expression of an idea, and are of such little social value that they may be prohibited, usually under breach-of-the-peace statutes. **Statutes which attempt to proscribe fighting words are very susceptible to attacks based on vagueness and overbreadth.**

(1) **Probability of Violence. [§ 730]**

**A breach-of-the-peace conviction will not be upheld unless the speech creates a probability of violence.**

*Cantwell v. Connecticut*, 310 U.S. 296 (1940). The Court reversed a breach-of-the-peace conviction of a Jehovah's Witness who stopped two men on the street and played for them an anti-Catholic phonograph record. One of the men told Cantwell to go away, and he did. The Court found that there was no assault, bodily threat, or personal abuse in Cantwell's message. Given the absence of any clear and present danger of a breach of the peace, the Court considered Cantwell's communication to be protected speech.

(2) **Fighting Words as Unprotected Speech. [§ 731]**

**Fighting words are not protected by the First Amendment.**

*Chaplinsky v. New Hampshire*, 315 U.S. 568 (1942). The Court unanimously affirmed the conviction of a Jehovah's Witness who called a city marshal a "God damned racketeer," and a "damned Fascist." The statute prohibited anyone from addressing any offensive, derisive, or annoying word to anyone lawfully in a public place, or calling anyone by any offensive or derisive name. The Court said there were certain categories of speech that were outside the concern of the First Amendment, including fighting words—words which by their very utterance inflict injury or tend to incite an immediate breach of the peace. **The first part of the test, words which by their very utterance inflict injury, is not used as an independent basis for regulating speech; the reason is that preventing psychological trauma or hurt feelings is not an evil the government has a right to prevent. The second test of *Chaplinsky*, words which tend to incite an immediate breach of the peace, is theoretically still a valid method of regulation.** The fighting

# CHAPTER XVI

words doctrine requires a personally abusive epithet to be directed to the listener in such a manner as to provoke an average addressee to violence.

### (3) Speech That Invites Dispute. [§ 732]

**Speech cannot be punished merely because it invites dispute.**

*Terminiello v. Chicago*, 337 U.S. 1 (1949). The Court reversed the breach-of-the-peace conviction of a speaker who made scurrilous comments about various political and racial groups. The statute prohibited speech which "stirs the public to anger, invites dispute, brings about a condition of unrest, or creates a disturbance." The statute was fatally overbroad in that the speaker could have been convicted for speech that "invited dispute," something the First Amendment clearly protects.

### b. Offensive Speech. [§ 733]

**Offensive speech is speech that is usually sexually oriented (but not obscene) and is offensive to mainstream sensibilities. The general rule in this category of cases is that government cannot regulate this speech just because it doesn't like it, or because it offends the sensibilities of adults.** This speech may be regulated to protect children, or if it falls within one of the other proscribable categories (such as clear and present danger, or fighting words).

### (1) Punishing Speech Because of Its Offensiveness. [§ 734]

**Speech cannot be prohibited merely because it is offensive.**

*Cohen v. California*, 403 U.S. 15 (1971). The Court reversed a breach-of-the-peace conviction for wearing into a public courthouse a jacket that said "Fuck the Draft." The speech was not obscene because it was not sexually oriented; it was not fighting words because it was not a personally abusive epithet directed to a specific listener; and it did not unduly invade the privacy interests of anyone in that public place. The Court recognized the emotive value of speech, saying that "one man's vulgarity is another's lyric."

### (2) Restrictions on Offensive Speech. [§ 735]

**The government may channel offensive speech away from children.**

*FCC v. Pacifica Foundation*, 438 U.S. 726 (1978). The Court upheld the power of the FCC to order a radio station to play

# FREEDOM OF SPEECH

George Carlin's monologue, "Filthy Words," only later at night when children were not likely to be in the audience. The monologue was not obscene, but used explicit sexual and excretory language. Protecting the sensibilities of children was the significant government interest that justified this restriction on speech.

(3) **Government Ban on Indecent Telephone Messages. [§ 736]**

**The government may not totally ban non-obscene sexually oriented speech.**

*Sable Communications v. Federal Communications Commission*, 492 U.S. 115 (1989). The Court invalidated a provision of the Federal Communications Act which totally banned "indecent" interstate commercial telephone messages. The speech here was not obscene under prevailing federal standards, and this law, (unlike the one in *Pacifica*) (prior case), totally prohibited the speech, rather than just channeling it to certain hours.

(4) **Government Ban on Indecent Messages on the Internet. [§ 737]**

**The government may not criminalize transmission on the Internet of material that is indecent as to minors or that describes sexual or excretory activities in terms that are potentially offensive as to minors.**

*Reno v. American Civil Liberties Union*, 521 U.S. 844 (1997). The Court invalidated two provisions of the Communications Decency Act of 1996 (CDA) which were designed to protect minors from harmful materials on the Internet. One provision prohibited the knowing transmission on the Internet of obscene or indecent messages to anyone under eighteen years of age. The other prohibited the transmission on the Internet to minors of patently offensive materials (as judged by contemporary community standards) that depict sexual or excretory activities or organs. The Court invalidated these provisions as content-based restrictions that swept within their scope a great deal of speech that adults have a constitutional right to send and receive on the Internet. The overbreadth of the CDA provisions meant that the law was not narrowly tailored to the government's interest in protecting minors from receiving harmful material on the Internet.

*Ashcroft v. American Civil Liberties Union*, 535 U.S. 564 (2002). After the Court's holding in *Reno v. ACLU* (above),

# CHAPTER XVI

Congress attempted to address the problem of pornography and indecency on the internet by passing the Child Online Protection Act (COPA). COPA makes it a crime to display on the internet, for commercial purposes, any material that is harmful to minors. The definition of "harmful to minors" tracks the three-part obscenity test of *Miller v. California* (§ 745), and thus requires jurors to apply "contemporary community standards" in assessing material. This case involved a facial challenge to COPA, arguing that the law violated adults' First Amendment rights because of its overbreadth. In a narrow ruling, the Court said that COPA's reliance on "community standards" to determine what material is harmful to minors does not make the statute substantially overbroad for purposes of the First Amendment. Because COPA incorporated the other prongs of *Miller*, the Court indicated that there was less of a likelihood that the statute would violate free speech rights. The Court remanded the case for a determination of whether COPA suffers from substantial overbreadth for reasons other than its use of community standards, whether the statute is unconstitutionally vague, or whether it may fail strict scrutiny.

*Ashcroft v. American Civil Liberties Union*, 542 U.S. 656 (2004), On remand (see previous case), the Third Circuit again affirmed the granting of the preliminary injunction by the District Court. The Third Circuit ruled that the Child Online Act (COPA) was not the least restrictive means available for the Government to try to achieve its goal of preventing minors from using the Internet to gain access to harmful materials. The Court ruled that COPA was a content-based restriction on speech, and that the government has the burden of proving that proposed alternatives will not be as effective as the restrictions in COPA. The Court accepted the argument that blocking and filtering software is a less restrictive means to achieve the goals of COPA. The Court emphasized that filters impose selective restrictions on speech at the receiving end, not universal restrictions at the source of the transmissions, and that promoting filter use does not criminalize any category of speech, thus reducing or eliminating any chilling effect on the targeted speech.

*U.S. v. American Library Association, Inc.*, 539 U.S. 194 (2003). The Court rejected a facial challenge to the Children's Internet Protection Act (CIPA), which conditions public libraries' receipt of federal funds on the installation of software to block obscene or pornographic images and to prevent minors from accessing material harmful to them. Chief Justice Rehnquist, writing for four Justices, asserted that CIPA was a valid exercise of Congress' Spending Power because the use of Internet filters does not violate the First Amendment rights of library patrons, so requiring their use is a valid condition on the receipt of federal funding. Chief Justice Rehnquist opined that public forum analysis and heightened judicial scrutiny were inappropriate analyses because they are incompatible with the broad discretion that public libraries must have to consider content in making collection decisions. Justices Kennedy and Breyer concurred in the result, focusing on the provisions of the law which requires a librarian to unblock filtered material or disable the filter on an adult user's request.

(5) **Restrictions on Sexually Offensive Speech on Cable Television. [§ 738]**

**Congress may impose some restrictions on the ability of a cable television system operator to prohibit or channel non-obscene sexually offensive programming.**

*Denver Area Educational Telecommunications Consortium, Inc. v. FCC*, 518 U.S. 727 (1996). The Court reviewed three provisions of a 1992 federal law which regulated the ability of cable television system operators to prohibit or channel sexually offensive programming. The Court upheld the provision of the law which permits cable television system operators to prohibit programming containing "patently offensive" sex-related material from being shown on "leased access channels" (these are channels reserved under federal law for commercial lease by parties unaffiliated with the cable television system operator). The Court invalidated the provision of the law which applied to leased access channels and which required cable television system operators who decided to carry "patently offensive" programming to segregate such programming on a single channel and to block access to that channel unless a subscriber consented in writing to receive the channel. The Court invalidated the provision of the law which allowed cable television system operators to prohibit the showing of sexually offensive programming on public, educational, or governmental use channels (these are channels required by local governments to be dedicated for these purposes).

*U.S. v. Playboy Entertainment Group, Inc.*, 529 U.S. 803 (2000). The Court reviewed a provision of the Telecommunications Act of 1996, which required that cable television operators providing channels dedicated to sexually-oriented programming to either fully scramble or fully block those channels or to limit their transmission to hours when children are unlikely to be viewing, between 10 p.m. and 6 a.m. The purpose of the provision was to prevent children from hearing or seeing images resulting from "signal bleeds." A majority of the cable operators, with no other practical choice, opted for the second approach and limited the time these types of programs were transmitted to all households, whether these households wanted to view this type of programming or not. The Court held that this provision was unnecessarily restrictive content-based legislation violative of the First Amendment. The statute failed to satisfy strict scrutiny because the interest of protecting and shielding children from indecent speech can be accomplished by a less restrictive alternative. That alternative was found in another provision of the statute which required a cable operator, upon request by a subscriber to fully scramble or fully block any channel the subscriber does not wish to receive. The Court stated that when a plausible, less restrictive alternative is offered to a content-based speech restriction, it is the Government's obligation to prove that the alternative will be ineffective to achieve its goals.

c. **Hate Speech. [§ 739]**

**Hate speech is offensive speech that is derogatory toward racial or ethnic groups. This speech is punishable under other established tests (clear and present danger, fighting words), but is not independently punishable based on the emotional injury it inflicts on the targeted group.** However, the Court has held that a state may increase the sentence for an assaultive crime (a pre-existing, predicate offense) if the criminal chose his or her victim based on race or ethnicity.

(1) **Content–Based Restrictions on Hate Speech. [§ 740]**

**The government cannot selectively ban certain categories of fighting words based on their content. In other words, the government cannot prohibit only those fighting words which it dislikes.**

*R.A.V. v. St. Paul*, 505 U.S. 377 (1992). The Court invalidated a "hate-speech" ordinance which made it a crime to place on public or private property any symbol or object, including a burning cross or Nazi swastika, which will cause anger, alarm, or resentment on the basis of race, color, creed, religion, or gender. R.A.V. and others burned a cross inside the fenced backyard of a black family. The Court, through Justice Scalia, invalidated this ordinance because it was a content-based restriction which failed strict scrutiny review because there were content-neutral alternatives that the city could have chosen to meet its compelling interest of eradicating racial hostility. The problem with the ordinance is that it reaches within the category of fighting words, and prohibits only those content-specific fighting words which the government dislikes.

(2) **Threats. [§ 741]**

**A state may, consistent with the First Amendment, ban "true threats," which include cross burning carried out with the intent to intimidate.**

*Virginia v. Black*, 538 U.S. 343 (2003). The Court upheld a Virginia statute which banned cross burning with intent to intimidate. Relying on *Watts v. United States*, 394 U.S. 705 (1969), in which the Court upheld a federal statute which made it a felony to knowingly and willfully threaten the President, the Court said that true threats comprise a category of speech unprotected by the First Amendment. A proscribable threat is a statement in which the speaker means to communicate a serious expression of an intent to commit an act of unlawful violence to a particular person or group of persons. The Court added that the speaker need not actually intend to carry out the threat. The Court ruled that the Virginia statute was consistent with *R.A.V.* (§ 740) because it does not single out for punishment only that speech directed at one of a list of specified disfavored topics. Rather, burning a cross with intent to intimidate is punishable regardless of whether it is done because of the victim's race, gender, religion, political affiliation, sexual preference, or any other reason.

The Virginia statute also had a provision which said that any burning of a cross shall be prima facie evidence of intent to intimidate. The Court ruled that the prima facie evidence provision is invalid because it chills constitutionally protected speech. Under the provision, it is possible that the government will prosecute and convict someone who engages only in lawful political speech at the core of the First Amendment. The provision could be used to bring within the statute expression which is distasteful, but only doubtfully threatening.

# CHAPTER XVI

(3) **Hateful Beliefs. [§ 742]**

**A person cannot be punished for abstract beliefs, no matter how reprehensible or anti-social.**

*Dawson v. Delaware*, 503 U.S. 159 (1992). The Court excluded as irrelevant to the capital sentencing phase of a murder case evidence that Dawson was a member of the Ayran Brotherhood, a white racist prison gang. The victim in Dawson's case was white. The Court found that admission of the evidence might tend to punish Dawson for his abstract beliefs, which, while reprehensible and anti-social, had not been shown to be related to the murder of which Dawson was convicted.

(4) **Sentence Enhancement. [§ 743]**

**A criminal defendant's sentence may be enhanced if the defendant chose his or her victim on the basis of race.**

*Wisconsin v. Mitchell*, 508 U.S. 476 (1993). The Court unanimously ruled that there was no First Amendment problem with a Wisconsin statute that increased the sentence for aggravated battery when the defendant selected the victim based on the victim's race. The Court characterized the law as punishing the conduct of selecting a victim, rather than punishing any abstract racist beliefs.

(5) **Sentence Enhancement as Jury Question. [§ 744]**

**Any fact that increases the punishment for a crime beyond its statutory maximum must be submitted to a jury and proved beyond a reasonable doubt.**

*Apprendi v. New Jersey*, 530 U.S. 466 (2000). The Court invalidated a New Jersey "hate crime" statute that allows a sentencing court to increase the sentence if it finds, by a preponderance of the evidence, that the defendant's purpose was to intimidate the victim because of race, color, gender, handicap, religion, sexual orientation, or ethnicity. The Court ruled that the Sixth Amendment right to a jury trial and the Fourteenth Amendment right to due process require that any fact that increases the punishment for a crime above the statutory maximum (other than the fact of a prior conviction) must be submitted to the jury and proven beyond a reasonable doubt.

3. **Obscenity. [§ 745]**

**Obscenity is sexually oriented speech that fails the test of *Miller v. California*, (below): 1) whether the average person, applying contemporary**

community standards, would find that the book or movie appeals to prurient interest; 2) whether the work depicts, in a patently offensive way, sexual conduct that is specifically defined by state law; and 3) using a reasonable person standard (not contemporary community standards), whether the work, taken as a whole, lacks serious literary, artistic, political, or scientific value. A state may not criminalize the private possession of obscenity by an adult, but may criminalize the private possession of child pornography by an adult. For a state to be able to criminalize the private possession of child pornography, the pornographic material must be defined as a videotape or film of children in explicit sex scenes. The state's interest in preventing child pornography is to stop sexual exploitation of children, an interest not present in the typical obscenity case. (Written descriptions of children engaged in sex do not fall within this analysis because no child is being forced to engage in any sexual activity, so the government interest in preventing sexual exploitation of children is not present.)

a. **Development of the Obscenity Doctrine. [§ 746]**

The Court has had an extremely difficult time figuring out obscenity law. That obviously says something about the nature of the speech being regulated, and the government's proffered reasons for its restrictions. **Think about why obscenity is unprotected. Does it lower the moral tone of the community? Does it degrade women? Does it contribute to or cause rape, sexual assault, child sexual abuse, or discrimination against women in private and public aspects of life?** How explicit must the sex be to be unprotected by the First Amendment? Consider these issues as we go through the obscenity cases.

(1) **First Test for Obscenity Adopted by the Court. [§ 747]**

**The first test for obscenity adopted by the court was whether, to the average person applying contemporary community standards, the dominant theme of the material, taken as a whole, appeals to the prurient interest.**

*Roth v. U.S.*, 354 U.S. 476 (1957). The Court, in upholding the facial validity of two state statutes regulating obscenity, held that obscenity is not within the protection of the First Amendment. It said that all ideas having even the slightest redeeming social importance get the full protection of the Constitution, and that the test for judging obscenity is whether to the average person, applying contemporary community standards, the dominant theme of the material, taken as a whole, appeals to the prurient interest.

# CHAPTER XVI

(2) **The Court Clarifies the Obscenity Rules. [§ 748]**

**The Court ruled that, for a work to be obscene, it must be utterly without redeeming social value.**

*Memoirs v. Massachusetts*, 383 U.S. 413 (1966). The Court reversed a state obscenity conviction, with Justice Brennan writing a plurality opinion for himself and two other Justices. According to Justice Brennan, a work could be deemed obscene only if the state could prove each of the following elements: 1) the dominant theme of the material, taken as a whole, appeals to prurient interest; 2) the work is patently offensive because if affronts contemporary community standards; and 3) the work is utterly without redeeming social value. This last prong created the biggest problem because, to secure a criminal conviction, the prosecutor had to show, beyond a reasonable doubt, that something did not exist.

(3) **Modern Obscenity Test. [§ 749]**

**Today, for a work to be obscene, it must lack serious literary, artistic, political, or scientific value.**

*Miller v. California*, 413 U.S. 15 (1973). A majority in *Miller* articulated a new obscenity standard: 1) whether the average person, applying contemporary community standards, would find that the work, taken as a whole, appeals to prurient interest; 2) whether the work depicts, in a patently offensive way, sexual conduct that is specifically defined by state law; and 3) whether the work, taken as a whole, lacks serious literary, artistic, political, or scientific value (SLAPS test). **Note that as we go from *Roth/Memoirs* to *Miller*, we go from the work having to be "utterly without redeeming social value," to the work "lacking serious literary, artistic, political, or scientific value." Theoretically, this new standard should be easier for prosecutors to meet.**

(4) **Third Prong of Miller Judged by a Reasonable Person Standard. [§ 750]**

**The question of whether a work lacks serious literary, artistic, political, or scientific value is to be judged by a reasonable person (as opposed to contemporary community standards) test.**

*Pope v. Illinois*, 481 U.S. 497 (1987). The Court emphasized that the third prong of *Miller* (SLAPS test) is to be judged by a reasonable person standard, rather than by contemporary community standards. The idea is to provide a more uniform standard throughout the country, thereby reducing regional differences in First Amendment interpretation.

b. **Right to Possess Obscenity and Right to Receive Information. [§ 751]**

   **A person has a constitutionally protected right to possess adult obscenity (no children as actors) in the privacy of his or her home.**

   However, there is no constitutionally protected right to watch obscene movies in a theater, even if the theater very carefully restricts its clientele to consenting adults.

   (1) **Private Possession of Obscenity. [§ 752]**

      **The government may not criminalize the private possession of obscenity in the home.**

      *Stanley v. Georgia*, 394 U.S. 557 (1969). The Court reversed a conviction for possession of obscenity in the privacy of the home. Stanley had three reels of obscene films in his home, but the Court, through Justice Marshall, said that the First Amendment protects the right to be let alone in one's home, at least so far as the books a person may read, or the films he may watch. The government may criminalize the importation, exportation, transportation, or sale of obscenity, but not its simple possession in the home.

   (2) **Commercial Exhibition of Obscenity to Consenting Adults. [§ 753]**

      **The government may prohibit the showing of obscene films in a movie theater restricted to consenting adults.**

      *Paris Adult Theatre I v. Slaton*, 413 U.S. 49 (1973). The Court upheld a state court's injunction against the showing of obscene films in a movie theater restricted to consenting adults. The Court distinguished *Stanley* (previous case), saying that the privacy of the home that was controlling in *Stanley* was not present in the commercial exhibition of obscene movies in a theater.

c. **Child Pornography—No Right to Sell or Privately Possess Child Pornography. [§ 754]**

   **The Court has ruled that a state's interest in preventing the sexual exploitation of children is so great that it overrides a**

# CHAPTER XVI

**person's interest in the possession of child pornography.** Note that in these cases, the states have defined child pornography as the use of children in explicit sex scenes. A written depiction of child sexual activity would have to be subjected to the *Miller* obscenity analysis.

**(1) Sale of Child Pornography. [§ 755]**

**The government may prohibit the sale of child pornography, regardless of whether it is obscene under *Miller*.**

*New York v. Ferber*, 458 U.S. 747 (1982). The Court upheld the state conviction of a seller of films showing young boys masturbating. The Court said that preventing the commercial sexual exploitation of children was a sufficiently compelling state interest to uphold the law. It is irrelevant whether these films meet the *Miller* obscenity standards; the state is regulating for an entirely different reason, and even non-obscene films could be subject to prosecution under the child pornography law.

**(2) Private Possession of Child Pornography. [§ 756]**

**The government may prohibit all possession of child pornography, even in the privacy of the home.**

*Osborne v. Ohio*, 495 U.S. 103 (1990). The Court upheld an Ohio statute that criminalized the private possession of child pornography. Osborne possessed photographs of a nude boy in a number of sexually explicit poses. *Stanley v. Georgia* (a state cannot criminalize the private possession of obscenity) was distinguished on the basis of the state interest advanced in each case. In *Stanley*, the state was trying to prevent obscenity from poisoning the minds of viewers; in *Osborne*, the state was trying to prevent sexual abuse and exploitation of children.

**(3) Virtual Child Pornography. [§ 757]**

**The government may not prohibit computer-generated child pornography because there is no actual sexual abuse of children involved in the making of the images.**

*Ashcroft v. Free Speech Coalition*, 535 U.S. 234 (2002). The Court invalidated two provisions of the federal Child Pornography Prevention Act of 1996 (CPPA). The Act prohibited the knowing reproduction, distribution, sale, reception or possession of any computer-generated image or picture that is or appears to be of a minor engaging in sexually explicit conduct. The Court, relying on *Broadrick v. Oklahoma* (§ 673), invoked the overbreadth doctrine and ruled that the CPPA was unconstitutional because it could be used to restrict a substantial amount of protected speech. It also distinguished this case from *Ferber* (§ 755) and *Osborne* (§ 756) on the basis that the laws in those cases addressed the evil of sexual abuse of children, something that is not present in the case of computer-generated child pornography. Contributing to the overbreadth of the statute was the fact that it extends to images that are not obscene under the *Miller* test (§ 749). Because of the excessive overbreadth of the statute, the Court did not address the void-for-vagueness challenge to the CPPA.

*United States v. Williams*, 128 S.Ct. 1830 (2008). The Court upheld, against overbreadth and vagueness challenges, a federal statute that criminalized the pandering or solicitation of child pornography. The Court distinguished the law at issue in this case from the one in *Ashcroft v. Free Speech Coalition* (previous case). In *Free Speech Coalition*, the statute criminalized the possession and distribution of material that had been pandered as child pornography, regardless of whether it actually was that. Thus, a person could face prosecution for possessing constitutionally protected material that someone else had pandered. Positing that offers (commercial or non-commercial) to engage in illegal transactions are categorically excluded from First Amendment protection, the Court said that the federal law in question only prohibits offers to provide and requests to obtain child pornography. The statute did not target the underlying material, but rather the collateral speech introducing such material into the child-pornography distribution network. The Court said that the statute was sufficiently focused to withstand both overbreadth and vagueness challenges.

d. **Factoring Children into the Obscenity Equation. [§ 758]**

**A state may not generally prohibit the sale of sexually-oriented material that is not suitable for consumption by children. The result would be that the adult population would have its reading or viewing choices reduced to a level appropriate for children.** The Court also said that a state may prohibit the sale of material to minors if it is obscene *as to minors*, irrespective of whether it is obscene as to adults.

# CHAPTER XVI

(1) **Books That Are Unsuitable for Children. [§ 759]**

**The state cannot prohibit books merely because they are unfit for children.**

*Butler v. Michigan*, 352 U.S. 380 (1957). The Court invalidated a Michigan law prohibiting the sale of books likely to have "a potentially deleterious influence on youth." Such a law would reduce the adult population to reading only what is fit for children.

(2) **Defining the "Average Person." [§ 760]**

**Children may not be considered in determining the "average person."**

*Pinkus v. U.S.*, 436 U.S. 293 (1978). The Court ruled that when allegedly obscene works are distributed only to adults, children may not be considered when a jury is applying the standard of "the average person applying contemporary community standards." Including children in the mix would lower the average too greatly.

(3) **Variable Definitions of Obscenity. [§ 761]**

**States may define obscenity differently for minors than for adults.**

*Ginsberg v. New York*, 390 U.S. 629 (1968). The Court, using a doctrine of "variable" obscenity, held that a state could define obscenity differently as to minors (as compared to adults), and prohibit the sale to minors of works that would be non-obscene and therefore acceptable to adults.

e. **Pornography as Sex Discrimination: The Feminist Perspective. [§ 762]**

**The government may not prohibit pornography merely because it depicts women in a certain way.** In recent years, feminist scholars have tried to change the terms of the debate about pornography. **Rather than asking whether a given work, as a whole, violates the** *Miller* **standards for obscenity, Professor Catherine MacKinnon and author Andrea Dworkin have drafted a statute which is based on the premise that pornography** *is* **sex discrimination (it does not matter whether the work passes** *Miller***).** Pornography is defined as the graphic, sexually **explicit subordination of women**

332

**through pictures or words that depict women in a subordinated, degrading, or humiliating fashion.** The problems with this kind of ordinance are that it is view point based, and does not fit into any traditional method of First Amendment analysis.

*American Booksellers Association v. Hudnut*, 771 F.2d 323 (7th Cir. 1985), affirmed 475 U.S. 1001 (1986). The Supreme Court summarily affirmed a decision of the Seventh Circuit Court of Appeals invalidating an Indianapolis anti-pornography statute. The ordinance asserted that pornography causes rape, battery, child sexual abuse, prostitution, and discrimination against women in education, jobs, and other important aspects of public and private life. Anyone injured by a person who has seen or read pornography has a cause of action against the maker or seller. Judge Easterbrook, for the court, ruled that the ordinance was viewpoint based because the city preferred certain kinds of depictions of women, but prohibited others. In addition, Judge Easterbrook was troubled by the slippery slope argument; if this ordinance is constitutional, what about ones that prohibit certain speech about racial, ethnic, or religious groups, or about homosexuals? The court also said that the evils described in the ordinance all took place after some sort of "mental intermediation" by the consumer of the pornography. This intervening mental step (between reading pornography and engaging in the evil act) breaks the chain of causation and injects some uncertainty regarding whether the evil will actually occur.

4. Commercial Speech. [§ 763]

   **Commercial speech is speech that advertises a product or service, usually for profit. To determine whether a restriction on commercial speech is permissible, first ask whether the commercial speech concerns a lawful activity, and whether it is misleading to consumers. If the commercial speech is not misleading, and is an advertisement for a lawful product or service, apply the following three-part test:**

   **a) Does the government have a substantial (not compelling) reason for the regulation?;**

   **b) Does the restriction directly advance the government interest?; and**

   **c) Is the restriction narrowly tailored to achieve the government interest?**

Remember that the main reason commercial speech is constitutionally protected is to benefit and protect consumers.

# CHAPTER XVI

a. **Development of Commercial Speech Doctrine. [§ 764]**

Up until the mid–1970's, commercial speech was not protected under the First Amendment, but was simply a kind of economic transaction which a government could regulate for any rational reason. Today, commercial speech is protected under the First Amendment, but receives only an intermediate level of protection.

(1) **Consumer's Right to Receive Information. [§ 765]**

**Commercial speech protects the consumer's right to receive information.**

*Virginia State Board of Pharmacy v. Virginia Citizens Consumer Council*, 425 U.S. 748 (1976). The Court invalidated a Virginia statute which prohibited the advertising of prescription drug prices by pharmacists. The law was challenged by consumers who asserted a right to receive information about prescription drug prices. **Speech does not lose First Amendment protection because money is spent to disseminate it, or because the advertiser has an economic interest in the advertisement.** The consumer also has a strong interest in the free flow of commercial information. The Court said that certain restrictions, such as time, place, or manner regulations would be permissible, but it did not articulate any specific test by which to analyze commercial speech.

(2) **Prevailing Test in Commercial Speech Cases. [§ 766]**

**The Court has adopted a four-part test to use in determining whether commercial speech is entitled to constitutional protection.**

*Central Hudson Gas & Electric Corporation v. Public Service Commission*, 447 U.S. 557 (1980). The Court invalidated a regulation of the New York Public Service Commission which completely banned promotional advertising by an electrical utility company. The Court adopted what is the prevailing analysis in commercial speech cases. First, for commercial speech to be protected by the First Amendment, it must be for a lawful activity, and not be misleading. If the speech meets both those requirements, a court will ask whether the government has a substantial (not compelling) reason for the regulation, whether the regulation directly advances the asserted government interest, and whether the law is narrowly tailored to achieve the government interest. This is a form of intermediate

# FREEDOM OF SPEECH

scrutiny which is similar to the rules for time, place, or manner restrictions (See § 688, above).

(3) **Government Power to Channel Advertising. [§ 767]**

**If the government has the power to prohibit an activity, it has the power to channel its advertising.**

*Posadas de Puerto Rico Associates v. Tourism Company of Puerto Rico*, 478 U.S. 328 (1986). The Court upheld regulations of the Tourism Company of Puerto Rico which prohibited advertising of casino gambling to Puerto Rican residents, but allowed it if aimed at non-Puerto Rican residents. The purpose of the regulations was basically to save the locals from themselves. The Court applied the *Central Hudson* analysis (previous case) to uphold the regulations. In dicta, Justice Rehnquist said that because the government could have totally banned the activity of casino gambling, it must, as a less intrusive matter, have the power to restrict advertising for the activity. This doctrine has been disavowed or discredited by a majority of the Court in *44 Liquormart, Inc. v. Rhode Island* (See § 766).

(4) **Distinctions Between Commercial and Noncommercial Speech. [§ 768]**

**Restrictions that distinguish between commercial and noncommercial speech must be narrowly tailored to further the government's asserted interests.**

*City of Cincinnati v. Discovery Network, Inc.*, 507 U.S. 410 (1993). The Court invalidated a Cincinnati ordinance that required the removal from city streets of 62 newsracks containing commercial publications, but allowed to remain on the streets 1,500 to 2,000 newsracks which sold newspapers which were devoted primarily to covering current events. Applying the *Central Hudson* analysis (see § 766), the Court said that the city's distinction between commercial and noncommercial speech was not at all related to the asserted government interests (aesthetics and safety), and thus fails the "narrowly tailored means" requirement of *Central Hudson*.

(5) **Restrictions on Lottery Advertising. [§ 769]**

(a) **The federal government may place restrictions on lottery advertising by broadcasters who are licensed by a state that does not have a lottery.**

# CHAPTER XVI

*U.S. v. Edge Broadcasting Co.*, 509 U.S. 418 (1993). The Court upheld a federal law which prohibits the broadcast of lottery advertising by a broadcaster who is licensed by a state that does not have a lottery. Edge Broadcasting was licensed by North Carolina, a state that does not have a lottery. Edge operated near the border of Virginia (a state which has a lottery), and had over 90% of its listening audience in Virginia. The Court applied the *Central Hudson* test (see § 766) to uphold the law. Discussing the means analysis from *Central Hudson*, Justice White, for a majority, said that commercial speech doctrine requires a fit that is not necessarily perfect, but reasonable. Does this lower the standard for the last prong of *Central Hudson?*

**(b) The federal government may not prohibit the broadcasting of lottery information by radio and television stations located in a state where casino gambling is legal.**

*Greater New Orleans Broadcasting Association, Inc. v. U.S.*, 527 U.S. 173 (1999). The Court invalidated a federal law and an implementing Federal Communications Commission Regulation which prohibited radio and television broadcasters from carrying advertising about privately operated casino gambling regardless of the station's or casino's location. Again applying the **Central Hudson** test (see § 766), the Court held that federal law may not prohibit advertising of lawful, private casino gambling by stations located in a state where casino gambling is legal. The law failed the third and fourth prongs of **Central Hudson** (the means analysis) because it contained exemptions for state-run casinos, tribal casinos, and even some commercial casino gambling. The fact that the law distinguished among different types of owners of casinos had no relationship to the government's asserted interest of alleviating the social costs of casino gambling.

**(6) Advertising of Alcohol Content. [§ 770]**

**Congress cannot prohibit beer labels from displaying alcohol content.**

*Rubin v. Coors Brewing Co.*, 514 U.S. 476 (1995). The Court invalidated a provision of the Federal Alcohol Administration Act (FAAA) which prohibited beer labels from displaying

# FREEDOM OF SPEECH

alcohol content. Coors Brewery sued when its application for approval of a proposed beer label was turned down by the Bureau of Alcohol, Tobacco, and Firearms. Applying the test of *Central Hudson* (see § 766), the Court found that Congress did have a substantial interest underlying FAAA: protecting the interests of citizens by curbing "strength wars"—competition by brewers on the basis of the alcohol strength of their beers. The Court found that the provision of the FAAA at issue did not directly advance the asserted governmental interest because other provisions of federal law allowed statements of alcohol contents in certain beer advertisements, as well as required statements of alcohol content on the labels of wines and spirits.

(7) **Advertising Liquor Prices. [§ 771]**

**A State cannot pass a law which prohibits the advertisement of retail liquor prices except at the place of sale.** Such a law is not saved by the Twenty–First Amendment which repealed Prohibition and gave states extensive power to regulate the sale or use of alcoholic beverages.

44 Liquormart, Inc. v. Rhode Island, 517 U.S. 484 (1996). The Court invalidated a Rhode Island statute which prohibited the advertising of retail liquor prices, except at the place of sale. A majority of the Court, in a fractionated set of opinions, applied the commercial speech analysis of *Central Hudson* (See § 766) and found that Rhode Island could not completely ban advertisements that provide consumers with truthful, accurate information about retail liquor prices. The Court also ruled that the Twenty–First Amendment, which repealed Prohibition and gave states great power to regulate the sale and use of alcohol, does not qualify or diminish the First Amendment protections given to commercial speech. a majority of the court also disavowed or discredited the doctrine from the *Posadas* case (See § 767) that if a government has the power to prohibit an activity, it automatically has the power to channel the advertising for that activity.

(8) **Regulation of Tobacco Advertising to Minors. [§ 772]**

**A State cannot restrict cigarette advertising because this subject has been preempted by federal law. State laws that prohibit advertising of tobacco products to minors must be narrowly tailored to achieving the state's interest in preventing minors from having access to tobacco products.**

# CHAPTER XVI

*Lorillard Tobacco Company v. Reilly*, 533 U.S. 525 (2001). The Court invalidated Massachusetts regulations that prohibited advertising of cigarettes within 1000 feet of a public playground, park, or school, or at the point of sale below five feet from the floor of the place where cigarettes are sold. The Court said that the state regulations pertaining to cigarettes were expressly preempted by the Federal Cigarette Labeling and Advertising Act. With respect to smokeless tobacco products and cigars, the Court said the regulations failed the fourth prong of the *Central Hudson* test (See § 766) because they were not narrowly tailored to achieving the state's interest in preventing minors' access to tobacco products. The Court upheld a regulation requiring that tobacco products be placed behind the counter and sold to customers only by a salesperson. This regulation was narrowly tailored to preventing minors from getting access to tobacco products.

**(9) Prohibition of Advertising of Compounded Drugs. [§ 773]**

**Congress cannot prohibit drug providers from advertising compounded drugs in return for their exemption from standard drug approval requirements imposed by the Food and Drug Administration (FDA).**

*Thompson v. Western States Medical Center*, 535 US. 357 (2002). The Court invalidated provisions of the federal Food and Drug Administration Modernization Act (FDAMA) which exempted "compounded drugs" from FDA standard drug approval requirements so long as doctors and pharmacists do not advertise or promote the compounding of any drug. Drug compounding is a process by which a pharmacist or doctor mixes or alters ingredients to create a medication suited to the needs of a particular patient. Congress was trying to balance the effectiveness of the FDA's drug approval policy with preserving the availability of compounded drugs for patients who cannot use commercially available drugs. Using the test from *Central Hudson* (§ 761), the Court ruled that Congress failed to show that the speech restrictions were not more extensive than necessary to serve the asserted interests. The Court suggested a number of less drastic means which would advance the statute's goals just as effectively as those chosen by Congress. Among them were a ban on the use of commercial-scale manufacturing equipment in compounding drugs, and a prohibition on pharmacists compounding drugs in anticipation of receiving prescriptions.

# FREEDOM OF SPEECH

b. **Advertising by Lawyers and Certified Public Accountants. [§ 774]**

The nature of the legal profession justifies greater restrictions on lawyer advertising than on that of other professions. How dangerous are we?

(1) **In–Person Solicitation for Money by a Lawyer. [§ 775]**

**States may ban in-person solicitation for money by lawyers.**

*Ohralik v. Ohio State Bar Association*, 436 U.S. 447 (1978). The Court upheld a state bar association's suspension of a lawyer for violating a ban on in-person solicitation of clients for money. Ohralik solicited one client when she was in traction in a hospital room following an accident. He used a hidden tape recorder while soliciting another accident victim on the day she got home from the hospital. The Court said that in-person solicitation by lawyers for economic gain created too great a risk of overreaching or overriding the will of the potential client. Compare *Ohralik* with the next case.

(2) **In–Person Solicitation for Money by a Certified Public Accountant. [§ 776]**

**States may not ban in-person solicitation for money by Certified Public Accountants.**

*Edenfield v. Fane*, 507 U.S. 761 (1993). The Court held that, unlike lawyers, Certified Public Accountants could not be prohibited from engaging in in-person solicitation of clients for pecuniary gain. The Court said that a CPA, unlike a lawyer, is not trained in the art of persuasion, and is therefore not as dangerous when soliciting potential clients.

(3) **Board of Accountancy Cannot Censure Truthful Advertising. [§ 777]**

**States cannot censure truthful advertising by lawyers concerning their qualifications as Certified Public Accountants.**

*Ibanez v. Florida Department of Business and Professional Regulation, Board of Accountancy*, 512 U.S. 136 (1994). The Court ruled that the Florida Board of Accountancy (Board) could not, consistent with the First Amendment, censure the truthful advertising by a lawyer of the fact that she was also a

# CHAPTER XVI

Certified Public Accountant (CPA) and a Certified Financial Planner (CFP). Ibanez, in her advertising as an attorney, indicated that she was a CPA and a CFP, both of which were true. The Board censured her for "false, deceptive, and misleading" advertising. The Court ruled that this was protected commercial speech, rejecting the assertions of the Board regarding the nature of Ibanez's speech.

(4) **Solicitation by Mail. [§ 778]**

**States may not prohibit a lawyer from soliciting clients by mail to join a lawsuit to vindicate personal rights.**

*In re Primus*, 436 U.S. 412 (1978). The Court ruled that South Carolina could not discipline an ACLU lawyer who solicited female clients by mail to ask if they would like to join a class-action suit which claimed that women had been illegally sterilized as a condition of continued receipt of welfare money. There was no in-person solicitation here, and the lawyer was not soliciting for economic gain. The Court said that because political expression and association are implicated in this kind of case, the government would have a tougher time justifying this regulation than one directed at a proposed commercial transaction.

(5) **Restrictions on Solicitation by Mail. [§ 779]**

**A state bar association can impose a thirty-day waiting period before a lawyer can send targeted direct mail solicitation to accident victims.**

*Florida Bar v. Went For It*, 515 U.S. 618 (1995). The Court upheld Florida Bar rules prohibiting lawyers from sending targeted direct-mail solicitations to victims and their relatives for thirty days following an accident or disaster. Applying *Central Hudson* (see § 766), the Court ruled that the Florida Bar had two substantial reasons for its rules: protecting the privacy of injury victims and their families, and preventing the erosion of confidence in the legal profession resulting from such solicitation. The Florida Bar rule was also narrowly tailored to achieve its objective, being limited to a fairly brief thirty-day prohibition of solicitation.

(6) **Use of Illustrations in Lawyer Advertising. [§ 780]**

**A state bar may not prohibit the use of accurate and nondeceptive illustrations in newspaper ads to solicit clients.**

*Zauderer v. Office of Disciplinary Counsel*, 471 U.S. 626 (1985). The Court held that a state bar association may not discipline a lawyer who uses accurate and nondeceptive illustrations in newspaper ads to solicit clients. Zauderer placed ads soliciting clients who might have been injured by the use of the Dalkon Shield Intrauterine Device. The Court held that Zauderer could mention in the ads the fact that he had represented other women in similar litigation. The Court also ruled that a bar association could require a lawyer who advertises contingent-fee arrangements to disclose that a client may have to pay court costs, even though no actual "fee" may be owed to the lawyer.

(7) **Targeted Mailing by Lawyers for Pecuniary Gain. [§ 781]**

**A state bar may not prohibit solicitation by mail for pecuniary gain to persons who might face specific legal problems.**

*Shapero v. Kentucky Bar Association*, 486 U.S. 466 (1988). The Court invalidated a bar association rule that prohibited lawyers from engaging in targeted mailing for pecuniary gain. A lawyer was protected in mailing truthful letters to specific persons who might face specific legal problems. The Court found that this kind of targeted mailing created no greater danger to consumers than did the newspaper ads upheld in other cases.

## F. SYMBOLIC SPEECH. [§ 782]

**Symbolic speech is communication effected through conduct; there are no words involved.** Examples are draft card burning, flag burning, cross burning, nude dancing, and what happens when you cut in front of another driver on the highway. Symbolic speech always involves both a communicative element and a conduct element. **The argument is that the government has the power to regulate the conduct component of symbolic speech, and thereby impose some incidental burden on the communicative aspect of that conduct.** As with any other speech question, look to see whether the government is totally prohibiting the symbolic speech (usually by a criminal statute), or just moving it around (imposing a time, place or manner restriction). Be aware of the strong similarity between the analysis for prohibition of symbolic speech and the time, place, manner rules.

1. **Prohibition of Symbolic Speech. [§ 783]**

   **If a government is prohibiting symbolic speech, use the four-part test from *U.S. v. O'Brien* (see § 786) to determine the law's constitutional-**

**ity:** 1) Is the law within a constitutional power of the government?; 2) Does the law further an important or substantial government interest?; 3) Is the government interest unrelated to the suppression of free expression? (Is it content-neutral?); and 4) Is the incidental restriction on speech no greater than essential to furthering the government interest? (Are the means narrowly tailored?)

2. **Time, Place, or Manner Restrictions on Symbolic Speech. [§ 784]**

    **If a government is simply trying to channel the symbolic speech in some way, use the four-part test for evaluating time, place, or manner restrictions** (see *Renton v. Playtime Theatres, Inc.*, § 693 above): 1) Is the law content-neutral? (The government cannot regulate the speech just because it does not like it); 2) Does the government have a significant or important reason for the law?; 3) Are the means narrowly tailored to achieve the asserted interest; and 4) Are there ample alternative channels of communication available?

    > STUDY TIP: The only difference between the *O'Brien* and the time, place, manner analyses is that the latter has the requirement of "ample alternative channels." The existence of ample alternative channels of communication is relevant only when the government is simply moving speech around, but is irrelevant when the government is totally prohibiting the speech. This is because when the government decides to totally prohibit symbolic speech, it does not want there to be any alternative channels of communication. For example, if the government prohibits draft card burning, it does not want anyone to engage in that activity anywhere, anytime.

3. **Application of Symbolic Speech Analysis. [§ 785]**

    a. **Draft–Card Burning. [§ 786]**

    **The federal government may prohibit draft-card burning.**

    *U.S. v. O'Brien*, 391 U.S. 367 (1968). The Court upheld a conviction for burning a draft card in violation of a federal law which made it a crime to knowingly destroy or mutilate a draft card. O'Brien burned his draft card on the steps of the South Boston Courthouse to protest the Vietnam war. The Court ruled that when the government criminalizes symbolic speech (communication having both speech and non-speech elements), the law will be upheld if: 1) it is within the constitutional power of the government; 2) it furthers an important or substantial government interest; 3) the government interest is unrelated to the suppression of free expression; and 4) the incidental burden on speech is no greater than essential to the furtherance of the government interest. (Today, this prong is phrased in terms of whether the means are narrowly tailored to achieve the government goal.).

b. **Flag Burning. [§ 787]**

   **The government may not prohibit flag desecration merely because it is done in a manner that offends onlookers.**

   (1) *Texas v. Johnson*, 491 U.S. 397 (1989).

   The Court invalidated Gregory Johnson's conviction for violating a Texas statute making it a crime to desecrate an American flag. Under the statute, a person could not desecrate a flag in such a way that he or she knows will seriously offend one or more persons likely to discover the act of desecration. Under prevailing federal law, the respectful burning of an American flag is an accepted method of disposing of a worn or tattered flag. Johnson's actions were symbolic speech, but the Court refused to use the *O'Brien* test (previous case) because the Texas law was content based (respectful burning is permissible, disrespectful burning is not). Content-based restrictions receive strict scrutiny, and the Texas law failed that standard because criminalizing flag burning was not narrowly tailored to achieve the State's interest of preserving the flag as an unalloyed symbol of our country.

   (2) *U.S. v. Eichman*, 496 U.S. 310 (1990).

   The Court invalidated the federal Flag Protection Act which prohibited the desecration of the American flag. The federal law was invalid for the same reason as the state law in *Texas v.* **Johnson** (previous case): it was content based because federal law provides that it is appropriate to dispose of a flag by burning it respectfully.

c. **Nude Dancing. [§ 788]**

   **A generally applicable public nudity statute may be applied to prohibit nude dancing.**

   *Barnes v. Glen Theatre, Inc.*, 501 U.S. 560 (1991). The Court upheld an Indiana statute prohibiting public nudity as applied to nude

# CHAPTER XVI

dancing, which a majority of Justices considered entitled to at least some First Amendment protection. Chief Justice Rehnquist, for himself and Justices O'Connor and Kennedy, used the *O'Brien* test (see § 786) to uphold the law. The state's prohibition on public nudity in general is not related to suppression of speech, and is narrowly tailored to achieve the significant government interests of order and morality. Justice Souter also used the *O'Brien* analysis to uphold the law. Justice Scalia asserted that no First Amendment scrutiny was called for because this was simply a generally applicable law directed at conduct, not speech. (For an interesting comparison, see the discussion of Justice Scalia's opinion for the Court in a leading Free Exercise Clause case, *Employment Division v. Smith*, 494 U.S. 872 (1990) (§ 961, below.)

*City of Erie v. Pap's A.M.*, 529 U.S. 277 (2000). The Court upheld a municipal ordinance making it a crime to knowingly or intentionally appear in public in a state of nudity. The ordinance was applied to Kandyland, an Erie establishment featuring totally nude erotic dancing by women. Justice O'Connor, for herself, Chief Justice Rehnquist, and Justices Kennedy and Breyer, again applied the *O'Brien* test (see § 786) and found that the ordinance was a constitutional attempt by the city to combat crime and other negative secondary effects caused by the presence of adult entertainment establishments. Justice Scalia, joined by Justice Thomas, upheld the statute not because it met some lower level of First Amendment scrutiny (*O'Brien*), but because, as a general law regulating conduct, it was not subject to First Amendment scrutiny at all.

d. **Signs on Public Property. [§ 789]**

   **A city may prohibit the placing of all signs on public property.**

   *Los Angeles City Council v. Taxpayers for Vincent*, 466 U.S. 789 (1984). The Court used the *O'Brien* analysis (earlier in this section) to uphold a Los Angeles ordinance which prohibited placing signs on public property, including political campaign signs. The ordinance was content-neutral because it applied to all signs, and was narrowly tailored to protect the city's interest in aesthetics.

e. **Overnight Sleeping in National Parks. [§ 790]**

   **The federal government may prohibit persons from sleeping overnight in national parks.**

   *Clark v. Community for Creative Non–Violence (CCNV)*, 468 U.S. 288 (1984). The Court upheld a National Park Service regulation which prohibited overnight sleeping in national parks. CCNV wanted to erect a tent city and sleep overnight in Lafayette Park to protest the plight of the homeless. Conceding that symbolic speech was involved, the Court applied time, place, manner analysis, and concluded that the ban on overnight sleeping was narrowly tailored to advancing the content-neutral government interest in maintaining national parks in an intact and attractive condition.

## G. SPEECH IN PUBLIC SCHOOLS. [§ 791]

**Whenever you see a speech question in a public school setting asking you to analyze the constitutionality of a restriction on student speech, be very careful of the role the school authorities play in the communicative process.** Are the school officials simply allowing students to come onto school grounds and express themselves, with no hint of the school authorizing or sponsoring the speech? Are the school authorities officially providing (paying for and sponsoring) the medium of communication (such as a school newspaper or assembly)? Are the school officials taking affirmative steps to decide which books shall be removed from (or placed in) the school library?

1. **Non–School–Sponsored Speech. [§ 792]**

    If the school officials are simply allowing students to come in from the outside and speak, without school sponsorship of the speech, the test is whether the student's speech materially and substantially interferes with the functioning of the school or disrupts the discipline of the school.

    *Tinker v. Des Moines School District*, 393 U.S. 503 (1969). The Court overturned the suspensions of high school students for wearing black armbands to school to protest the Vietnam war. The ban on armbands was enacted by the school specifically in response to the anticipation of such a protest. Other symbols, such as the Iron Cross, a symbol of Nazism, were allowed, making the armband ban content based. The Court said that neither students nor teachers shed their constitutional rights to free speech at the schoolhouse gate, and that the school could not punish these students based on an undifferentiated fear or apprehension of disturbance. Requiring a case-by-case analysis, the Court said that this kind of prohibition cannot be upheld unless there is some specific factual showing that the speech would materially and substantially interfere with the functioning of the school, or disrupt the discipline of the school.

2. **School–Sponsored Speech. [§ 793]**

    **If the school sponsors the student speech, such as a newspaper, yearbook, or assembly, content-neutral restrictions may be imposed if**

# CHAPTER XVI

**they are reasonably related to a legitimate educational or pedagogical interest,** such as teaching students journalistic ethics, or the ability to engage in civil discourse in public.

a. *Bethel School District v. Fraser*, 478 U.S. 675 (1986).

**The Court upheld the ability of a school board to discipline a student for delivering a lewd, suggestive speech at an officially sponsored school assembly. The Court did not rely on the *Tinker* test of whether the speech materially or substantially disrupted the functioning or discipline of the school. Rather, it upheld the suspension as a reasonable method of advancing the legitimate educational goal of teaching students to speak in a civil manner in public gatherings.**

b. *Hazelwood School District v. Kuhlmeier*, 484 U.S. 260 (1988).

The Court upheld the ability of a high school principal to remove from the officially sponsored high school newspaper two articles, one dealing with the experiences of pregnant students at the school, the other with the impact of divorce on students at the school. The principal thought that some of the abortion article's references to sexual activity and birth control were inappropriate for some students, and that the identities of the students involved were not adequately protected. The principal also was concerned about the identities of the divorced parents being divulged, and that the parents had no chance to respond to the allegations in the article. **The Court ruled that educators may censor or edit school-sponsored expressive activities as long as their actions are reasonably related to legitimate pedagogical concerns.** Here, the concerns were with journalistic ethics (protecting identities), and ensuring grade and age appropriateness in the school newspaper's articles.

c. *Morse v. Frederick*, 551 U.S. 393 (2007).

The court upheld the suspension of a high school student for displaying a banner that read "BONG HiTS 4 JESUS." The banner was displayed at a school-sponsored event, and school authorities viewed it ass promoting illegal drug use. In January 2002, the Olympic Torch Relay was passing through Juneau, Alaska on its way to Salt Lake City, Utah. Principal Morse of Juneau–Douglas High School permitted the high school students to leave the school to watch the Relay. Frederick, a senior at the high school, arrived late for school and joined his friends outside the school. They unfurled a 14–foot banner with the "BONG HiTS" message. Morse confiscated the banner and imposed a 10–day suspension on Frederick. Chief

# FREEDOM OF SPEECH

Justice Roberts, eschewing both the Tinker analysis (no disruption here), and the Hazelwood analysis (no school imprimatur), said that deterring drug use by schoolchildren is a compelling interest, and that school administrators may prohibit speech that encourages that activity.

3. **Removal of Books From a School Library. [§ 794]**

   **If a school board removes books from a school library, its decisions will be upheld if content-neutral, and reasonably related to a legitimate educational or pedagogical goal** such as ensuring that vulgar or grade-inappropriate books are not available to students.

   *Board of Education v. Pico*, 457 U.S. 853 (1982). The Court dealt with the narrow question of whether and how the First Amendment limits the ability of a school board to remove books from (not acquire books for) junior high and high school libraries. Students brought a civil rights action to challenge a school board's decision to remove certain books from school libraries on the basis that the books were "anti-American, anti-Christian, anti-Semitic, and just plain filthy." Justice Brennan wrote a plurality opinion in which he said that it would violate the First Amendment for the school board to remove the books because they disagreed with the ideas expressed. However, if the school board removed the books because they were vulgar or not suitable for students of certain ages or maturity levels, the removal would be constitutionally permissible. Judge Brennan's main point is that a school board is not free to impose a political or religious orthodoxy on students, but it may act to protect the rights and sensibilities of students. This is obviously a very fine line to draw, especially because it focuses on the motivation of the school board members in removing the books.

## H. PUBLIC FORUM ANALYSIS. [§ 795]

**Public forum analysis is called for whenever a person is speaking on or by means of public property.** It may be a street, park, sidewalk, public amphitheater, school mailbox system, or any other governmentally owned and operated property. **The goal of public forum analysis is to balance a person's right to use public property for speech purposes against the government's right to maintain the property for its intended use.** There are three ways that public forums may come into existence: 1) by tradition, some public places have become forums for speech purposes (streets, parks, sidewalks); 2) the government may designate publicly owned property to be a forum; and 3) speakers, usually protestors or demonstrators, may commandeer publicly owned property for use as a forum. The Court has set forth the following guidelines for each of these types of public forum.

# CHAPTER XVI

1. **Traditional Public Forum. [§ 796]**

   **A traditional public forum is government property which has historically been used for speech purposes.** Public streets, sidewalks, parks, and public amphitheaters are examples of traditional public forums. In a traditional public forum, the government may not prohibit all communicative activity. In other words, **speakers have a presumptive right of access to traditional public forums for speech purposes. Given this presumptive right of access, what a government usually does is channel the speech in certain ways by employing a time, place, or manner restriction. (See §§ 689–696 above).** To be valid, a time, place or manner restriction must be content neutral, narrowly tailored to achieve a significant or important government interest, and leave open ample alternative channels of communication. If a government applies a content-based restriction, the law must be narrowly tailored to achieve a compelling government interest.

2. **Designated Public Forum. [§ 797]**

   A state may designate property to be a public forum. Once having done so, it may un-designate it as a public forum, returning the property to its prior, non-speech use.

   a. **Designated Open Forum. [§ 798]**

      If the government designates the property as an open, or unlimited public forum, the same rules apply as in the traditional public forum: guaranteed access exists during the duration of the designation as an open forum; content-based restrictions get strict scrutiny; and properly drawn time, place, or manner restrictions are permissible.

   b. **Designated Limited Forum. [§ 799]**

      If the government designates the property as a limited or non-public forum, the following rules apply: properly drawn time, place, or manner restrictions are permissible; content-based restrictions get strict scrutiny; and total or selective restrictions (including exclusion) of speakers are permissible if they are rationally related to the legitimate government interest in maintaining the normal, non-speech use of the public property. Remember that these total or selective restrictions on speakers may not be based on government dislike of the speech; they must be justified by some content-neutral reason pertaining to the normal operation of the public place.

# FREEDOM OF SPEECH

*Greer v. Spock*, 424 U.S. 828 (1976). The Court upheld regulations at Fort Dix which prohibited speeches and demonstrations of a partisan political nature, but allowed other civilian speakers and entertainers onto the base. Fort Dix is not a traditional public forum, so there is no presumptive right of access to the base for speech purposes. The regulation forbidding political speech was rationally related to the legitimate military objective of keeping military activities free from partisan politics. **If the base authorities had allowed Republican speakers in and kept Democratic speakers out (or vice-versa), that action would be viewpoint-based (preferring one kind of speech over another within a category of speakers), subject to strict scrutiny, and in all probability invalid.**

3. Commandeered Public Forum. [§ 800]

**A speaker may go onto public property to speak even though the property is not a traditional public forum, and the government has not designated the property to be a forum for speech purposes.** By definition, these speakers are trying to commandeer public property for speech purposes, regardless of the normal, non-speech function of the place. **In these cases, the Court has in the past (it is doubtful that a majority of the Court would do so today) looked to see if the manner of expression is basically incompatible with the normal activity of the government property at the time the speech is engaged in. If they are compatible, the government property will be considered a public forum; if not, the property will not be treated as a public forum, and reasonable restrictions on speech will be upheld.** The idea here is that the government should not have complete power to exclude speakers from public property by designating the property closed to speakers entirely, or open to only a small number of speakers whose speech the government deems compatible with the normal use of the place. **If the Court does not recognize the creation of new forums through the "commandeering" process, a government may designate all public property, other than traditional forums, to be off limits to speakers.**

*Brown v. Louisiana*, 447 U.S. 323 (1966). The Court reversed breach-of-the peace convictions of five black men who sat, in "silent and reproachful presence," in the reading room of a public library to protest the racial segregation of library facilities in the town of Clinton, Louisiana. Justice Fortas, writing for himself and two other Justices, said that this symbolic speech was protected by the First Amendment because there was no evidence that use of the library by others was disrupted by this silent protest. In other words, these protesters "commandeered" the public library for communicative purposes, and their speech was protected because of its compatibility with the normal use of the place.

# CHAPTER XVI

> **STUDY TIP:** If you get a question where the speech has taken place on or by means of government property, determine which kind of forum the facts describe, then apply the applicable rules. To a large extent, the label controls the analysis.

4. **Application of Public Forum Analysis. [§ 801]**

   a. **Government Power to Regulate Public Places. [§ 802]**

   **The government does not have the same power to exclude speakers from public property that owners of private property enjoy.**

   *Hague v. C.I.O.*, 307 U.S. 496 (1939). **The Court rejected the argument that a government's ownership of property confers on it the same power to exclude speakers as that enjoyed by the owner of private property.** Justice Roberts, in a plurality opinion, said: "Wherever the title of streets and parks may rest, they have immemorially been held in trust for the use of the public and, time out of mind, have been used for purposes of assembly, communicating thoughts between citizens, and discussing public questions Such use of the streets and public places has, from ancient times, been a part of the privileges, immunities, rights, and liberties of citizens."

   b. **Handbilling on Public Streets. [§ 803]**

   **A city may not totally prohibit handbilling on public streets.**

   *Schneider v. Irvington*, 306 U.S. 628 (1939). The Court reversed convictions for violating city ordinances prohibiting the distribution of handbills in the streets or other public places. The Court said that a government may regulate the conduct of those using the streets, so long as their right to speak or distribute literature is not abridged. The city's interest in preventing litter was not sufficiently important to justify a total ban on distributing handbills; less drastic means, such as punishing litterers, were available.

   c. **Protesting on Jail Grounds. [§ 804]**

   **A state may prohibit protesting on jail grounds.**

   *Adderley v. Florida*, 385 U.S. 39 (1966). The Court affirmed trespass convictions of students who protested on the grounds of a county jail that were reserved for jail uses. The Court said that, at least in this context, the state has the same right as the owner of private property to preserve its property for its intended use. The dissenting justices considered the jailhouse grounds to be every bit as much a seat of government, and therefore a public forum, as a statehouse, courthouse, or legislative chamber.

d. **Picketing Near Schools. [§ 805]**

**A city may not selectively prohibit picketing near a school.**

*Police Department of Chicago v. Mosley*, 408 U.S. 92 (1972). The Court invalidated an ordinance which prohibited all picketing on a public side walk within 150 feet of a school building, from 30 minutes before school starts until 30 minutes after it ends, except for peaceful labor picketing, which was allowed during the school day. This was a content-based distinction, based on the message on a picket sign. The Court emphasized that selective exclusions from a public forum may not be based on content alone, nor may they be justified by reference to content alone.

e. **Noise Near Schools. [§ 806]**

**A state may impose a generally applicable ban on noise near schools.**

*Grayned v. Rockford*, 408 U.S. 104 (1972). The Court upheld convictions under an anti-noise ordinance which prohibited anyone on public or private property adjacent to a school from making any noise which disrupts the functioning of the school. About 200 persons were 100 feet away from a high school, protesting the administration's failure to act on complaints of black students at the school. In assessing the reasonableness of the ordinance, the Court said that the crucial question is whether the manner of expression is basically incompatible with the normal activity of a particular place at a particular time.

f. **Access to School Mailbox Systems. [§ 807]**

**A school board may grant selective access to a school mailbox system.**

*Perry Educational Association v. Perry Local Educators' Association*, 460 U.S. 37 (1983). The Court rejected Equal Protection and First Amendment challenges to an agreement between a school board and the union that represented the teachers in the district. Under the contract, the union had access to the school mailbox system (a designated limited forum), but another union, which lost the election to represent the teachers, did not have access. The Court said that the school district had not created an open public forum, so reasonable, content-neutral restrictions are permissible. The Court found that the loser union was not excluded because of any message it might convey, but because of its status, which was not being a member of the official school community. The Court upheld the ability of the school district to allow some outside groups (such as the Cub Scouts, YMCAs, and parochial schools) to use the mailbox system, because those decisions were based on the status or nature of the groups, not the content of their speech.

g. **Signs Near Embassies. [§ 808]**

**The District of Columbia may not prohibit signs near embassies merely because the messages on the signs may be offensive to persons in the embassies.**

*Boos v. Barry*, 485 U.S. 312 (1988). The Court invalidated a District of Columbia ordinance prohibiting the display of any sign within 500 feet of a foreign embassy if the sign tends to bring that foreign government into public odium or public disrepute. The Court considered this a content-based restriction on political speech in a public forum; the ordinance was directed only at the emotive impact of the speech on the listener—something that is not a "secondary effect" for purposes of free speech analysis. The Court upheld another part of the ordinance which, as narrowed by the Court of Appeals, prohibited congregating within 500 feet of an embassy when the police reasonably believe that the congregation of people poses a threat to the security or peace of the embassy. This regulation merely restricted the place and manner of speech in a public forum, and was related to achieving the significant government interest of preventing security threats to embassies.

h. **Picketing in Front of a Residence. [§ 809]**

**A city can prohibit focused picketing in front of a residence.**

*Frisby v. Schultz*, 487 U.S. 474 (1988). The Court upheld an ordinance which prohibited "focused picketing," which is picketing that takes place solely in front of and is directed at a particular residence. The ordinance was directed at anti-abortion protesters who picketed outside a doctor's home for an hour and a half. This ordinance was upheld as a valid place or manner restriction, advancing the significant government interest in protecting the privacy rights of residents, and leaving the picketers free to march up and down the street with their picket signs.

i. **Fees for Use of Public Property. [§ 810]**

   **A city cannot require payment of a fee to use public property.**

   *Forsyth County v. The Nationalist Movement*, 505 U.S. 123 (1992). The Court invalidated an ordinance that required an applicant for a permit to use public property for a parade, assembly, or any other use to pay a fee up to $1,000 per day, with the county administrator setting the amount to cover the cost of maintaining public order. In effect, the amount of the fee was determined by the content of the speech; the more controversial the speech, the more it would cost to police the area. The ordinance also gave the administrator too much discretion in deciding whether to charge any fee at all, or to determine its amount.

j. **Airport Terminals. [§ 811]**

   **Government-owned airport terminals are not public forums for speech purposes; therefore, the government may prohibit activities that are inconsistent with the use of the terminals.**

   *International Society for Krishna Consciousness v. Lee*, 505 U.S. 672 (1992). **The Court held that a government-owned airport terminal is not a public forum.** The Court upheld as reasonable a Port Authority regulation forbidding the repetitive solicitation of money within the terminals. It invalidated a regulation forbidding the distribution of literature in the airport terminals. Chief Justice Rehnquist said that publicly-owned airport terminals are not traditional public forums, nor did the Port Authority designate them as public forums. As a result, restrictions on speech will be analyzed to see if they are reasonably related to maintaining the normal use of the place. The ban on repetitive solicitation of money was rationally related to keeping the airport functioning; the ban on distribution of literature was not. The Court reasoned that repetitive solicitation of money is considerably more disruptive of pedestrian traffic within the terminals than is the simple distribution of literature.

5. **Designated Forums and Religious Speakers. [§ 812]**

   **If a government entity, such as a university or a school district, opens its facilities to speakers, it may not exclude religious speakers from using the forum. It does not establish religion, in contravention of the First Amendment, to allow religious speech along with other kinds of speech.**

# CHAPTER XVI

a. **Religious Student Groups at Universities. [§ 813]**

   **A university may not exclude religious student groups from using its facilities when other student groups have been granted access to university buildings for speech purposes.**

   *Widmar v. Vincent*, 454 U.S. 263 (1981). The Court ruled that a state university could not exclude religious groups from using its facilities once the university opened its rooms to registered student groups for speech purposes. The Court rejected the argument that this content-based exclusion was justified by the state's interest in avoiding the establishment of religion that would result from allowing the religious group to speak. Simply permitting the religious groups to speak, along with numerous other student groups, does not equal endorsement or establishment of religion.

b. **Religious Student Groups in High School. [§ 814]**

   **Public schools may not exclude religious student groups from using school facilities when other high school groups have been granted access to school facilities for speech purposes.**

   *Board of Education v. Mergens*, 496 U.S. 226 (1990). The Court upheld the federal Equal Access Act, which prohibits public schools receiving federal funds from making content-based exclusions of students from school facilities which have been opened for speech purposes. The school allowed a number of non-curricular groups to use the facilities, but refused to allow the Christian Club to use a room. Following *Widmar* (previous case), the Court said that there is no establishment of religion effected by including the Christian Club with other student organizations.

c. **Members of the Public Who Engage in Religious Speech. [§ 815]**

   **A school may not exclude members of the public who engage in religious speech from using school facilities when other public groups have been granted access to school facilities for speech purposes.**

   (1) *Lamb's Chapel v. Center Moriches Union Free School District*, 508 U.S. 384 (1993). The Court ruled that a school which opened its facilities to the general public for speech purposes could not deny a church group access to the school property. The school had designated its property as a limited forum, but had denied access to the religious group because of the content of its speech. As in *Widmar*, the Court rejected the

argument that the school would establish religion by allowing the religious group to use the facilities. Inclusion of religious speakers along with numerous others does not violate the Establishment Clause.

(2) *Good News Club v. Milford Central School*, 533 U.S. 98 (2001). The Court ruled that a school violated the free speech rights of a private Christian organization for children ages 6 to 12 by excluding it from meeting after hours in the school building. The school had a policy authorizing district residents to use its building for a number of different speech purposes. The Good News Club was refused permission to meet at the school to sing songs, hear Bible lessons, memorize scripture, and pray. The school claimed that these activities were the equivalent of worship and, as such, were prohibited under their policy. The Court, following *Widmar* and *Lamb's Chapel*, ruled that this was unconstitutional viewpoint discrimination in a limited public forum, and thus violated the free speech rights of the Good New Club. The Court also opined that permitting the Club to meet on school premises after hours would not establish religion, and so the school had no compelling reason to justify excluding the Club from its designated limited forum.

d. **Religious Student Publications. [§ 816]**

**A school may not deny funding to a religious student publication if it funds other student journals.**

*Rosenberger v. Rector and Visitors of the University of Virginia*, 515 U.S. 819 (1995). The Court ruled that the University of Virginia could not deny funding for the publication of a recognized student group's journal on the basis that the journal was religious in content. The university set up a program under which payments are made from a Student Activities Fund for the publication of student journals and magazines. When a religious student group, otherwise eligible for funding, applied for funding of its newspaper, Wide Awake: A Christian Perspective at the University of Virginia, the university turned it down, asserting that to fund a religious student publication would violate the Establishment Clause. The Court, relying on *Widmar* (see § 813) and *Lamb's Chapel* (see § 815), said that a university does not establish religion by granting access to its facilities to a wide spectrum of student groups, even if some of them are religious. The Court saw no difference between a university granting access to its facilities (*Widmar*) and a university funding the

# CHAPTER XVI

publication of student journals; both cases involved the university creating a limited forum for the purpose of enhancing diversity of student expression.

## I. THE FIRST AMENDMENT AND THE ELECTORAL PROCESS: REGULATION OF BALLOT ACCESS, AND LIMITATIONS ON CONTRIBUTIONS AND EXPENDITURES. [§ 817]

**Participation in the electoral process, by voting, becoming a candidate, or spending money to influence an election, involves the fundamental rights of free speech and freedom of political association.** The government interests in regulating these activities are to enhance equality of access to the electoral system and to prevent corruption or the appearance of corruption in the electoral process.

1. Restrictions on Voting and Becoming a Candidate. [§ 818]

   The Court scrutinizes very carefully any state or local law which interferes with a person's right to become a candidate, or a political party's right to set the qualifications to participate in party primaries.

   a. **Filing Deadlines.**

   A state cannot have different filing deadlines for independent candidates and major-party candidates.

   *Anderson v. Celebrezze*, 460 U.S. 780 (1983). The Court invalidated an Ohio statute which required independent candidates for President to file their nominating petitions in March to be able to appear on the general ballot in November. The March filing deadline preceded by a number of months the time when major parties chose their candidates for the general election ballot. **This requirement violated the First Amendment right of political association, and did not adequately advance the state's interest in political stability or voter awareness.**

   b. **Requirements to Vote in a Party Primary.**

   State law cannot require party membership to vote in a party primary.

   *Tashjian v. Republican Party of Connecticut*, 479 U.S. 208 (1986). **The Court invalidated a Connecticut law which required voters in a party primary to be members of the party.** The law was challenged by the state Republican Party which had a rule allowing independent voters to vote in Republican primary elections for state and federal offices. **The Court ruled that the state law violated the First Amendment rights of political association of members of the Republican Party of Connecticut.** The Court rejected the state's asserted interests of avoiding administrative burdens, minimizing voter confusion, and protecting the integrity of the two-party system.

c. **Political Parties Supporting Primary Candidates.**

**State law cannot prohibit political parties from supporting or opposing candidates in party primaries.**

*Eu v. San Francisco County Democratic Central Committee*, 489 U.S. 214 (1989). The Court invalidated a state law which prohibited political parties from supporting or opposing candidates in party primaries. Applying strict scrutiny, **the Court ruled that there was no compelling state interest that justified the abridgment of the fundamental right of political association.**

2. **Limitations on Campaign Contributions and Expenditures. [§ 819]**

**Be very careful to distinguish a direct monetary contribution to a candidate from an independent expenditure on the candidate's behalf. The rationale for the distinction is that even though you may spend your own money however you want to help someone get elected, the government has an important interest in avoiding the appearance of a contributor buying a candidate by contributing money to that candidate.** Hence, the Court allows greater limitations on contributions to candidates than it does on expenditures.

The Court also distinguishes between contributions to a candidate (restrictions allowed) and contributions to a political action committee (PAC) supporting a ballot referendum such as lowering property taxes (restrictions not allowed). The rationale for this distinction is that while you can (appear to) own a candidate, you cannot own an idea.

a. **Limits on Federal Campaign Contributions. [§ 820]**

**The federal government may place limits on contributions to candidates for federal office.**

*Buckley v. Valeo*, 424 U.S. 1 (1976). **The Court upheld provisions of the Federal Election Campaign Act which limited contribu-

**tions to a candidate for federal office; it invalidated provisions of the Act which limited independent expenditures on behalf of a candidate.** Using First Amendment analysis, the Court said that the $1,000 limitation on expenditures for a candidate substantially restrains the quality and diversity of political speech, whereas the same limit on contributions to a candidate involves little direct restraint on political expression, and is necessary to achieve the government interest in preventing corruption and the appearance of corruption.

*McConnell v. Federal Election Commission*, 540 U.S. 93 (2004) The Court upheld most of the campaign finance restrictions imposed by the 2002 federal Bipartisan Campaign Reform Act (BCRA). The Court rejected a challenge to BCRA's ban on the use of "soft" or unregulated money by national parties. Title I of BCRA bars national party committees from soliciting, receiving, directing, or spending any soft money that affects federal elections. Rejecting a strict scrutiny analysis, the Court said that Title I is closely drawn to serve the government's important interest in preventing actual and apparent corruption of federal candidates and officeholders resulting from political parties selling access to candidates and officeholders to large, soft money donors.

The Court also upheld most of the provisions of Title II of BCRA, prohibit corporations and labor unions from using general treasury funds for communications that would affect federal elections. This section of the law was challenged on the basis that it blurred the *Buckley* distinction between regulations of contributions and regulation of expenditures. The Court, in refusing to draw a bright line between express advocacy for the election or defeat of a candidate and issue advocacy, said this section was also justified by the important government interest in preventing corruption in the electoral process.

b. **Limits on State Campaign Contributions. [§ 821]**

**State governments may place limits on contributions to candidates for federal office.**

*Nixon v. Shrink Missouri Government PAC*, 528 U.S. 377 (2000). The Court upheld a Missouri statute that imposed limits on contributions to state political candidates. The Court held that *Buckley* (previous case) is authority for comparable state regulation, and such limitations on contributions need not be limited to *Buckley's* dollar amount of $1,000. A state's interest in preventing corruption and the appearance of corruption flowing from large political campaign contributions is sufficient to justify the burden placed on First Amendment rights of speech and political association.

c. **State Limit on Campaign Contributions and on Spending by Candidates. [§ 822]**

**A state may not, consistent with the First Amendment, impose limits on expenditures by candidates for state office, or impose overly stringent contribution limits on individuals, organizations, and political parties.**

*Randall v. Sorrell*, 548 U.S. 230 (2006). The Court ruled, 6–3, with no majority opinion, to strike down Vermont's campaign finance law which limited the amount that candidates could spend on their own campaigns, and placed the most stringent limits in the country on contributions to candidates from individuals and political parties. Justice Breyer, writing the controlling opinion, said that the expenditure limits violate the First Amendment's free speech guarantees under *Buckley* (§ 839). He explained that expenditure limits restrict the amount of money a person or group can spend on political communication, thus reducing the quantity of expression by restricting the number of issues discussed, the depth of their exploration, and the size of the audience reached. Justice Breyer opined that Vermont's contribution limits violated the First Amendment because they, in their specific details, burdened protected interests in a manner disproportionate to the public purposes they were enacted to advance. Finding that Vermont's contributions limits are substantially lower than the limits the Court has previously upheld, and lower than comparable limit in other states, Justice Breyer concluded that these limits worked more harm to protected First Amendment interests than their anticorruption objectives could justify. Justices Thomas and Scalia said that *Buckley* was wrong to distinguish between contribution and expenditure limits, and that both types of restrictions should be subjected to strict scrutiny.

d. **Ballot Referenda. [§ 823]**

**States cannot limit the ability of corporations to spend money to influence certain ballot referenda.**

*First National Bank v. Bellotti*, 435 U.S. 765 (1978). The Court invalidated a Massachusetts law that criminalized certain expenditures by banks or business corporations to influence the vote on any referendum submitted to the voters, other than one materially

# CHAPTER XVI

affecting the property, business, or assets of the corporation. Asserting that the political speech of corporations is at the heart of the First Amendment, the Court found the state law to be content-based, and not supported by any compelling government interest.

e. **Expenditure of Corporate or Union Funds for Political Purposes. [§ 824]**

**Federal law can require the use of segregated funds by corporations or unions for political purposes.**

*Federal Election Commission v. National Right To Work Committee*, 459 U.S. 197 (1982). The Court upheld a federal law which prohibits corporations or labor unions from making contributions or expenditures to candidates in federal elections. However, the entities can set up segregated funds to be used for political purposes, but a corporation without capital stock can only solicit contributions to such funds from its members. This ban on outside solicitations was upheld as necessary to prevent corruption (or the appearance of corruption) resulting from large financial contributions to candidates. This case is different from *Bellotti* (previous case) in that *Bellotti* dealt with corporate contributions to support a ballot referendum rather than a candidate.

f. **Campaign Expenditures by Political Action Committees. Federal law cannot limit expenditures by political action committees to support presidential candidates. [§ 825]**

*Federal Election Commission v. National Conservative Political Action Committee*, 470 U.S. 480 (1985). **The Court invalidated a federal law which placed a $1,000 limit on expenditures by political action committees to support a presidential candidate.** Relying on the *Buckley v. Valeo* distinction between contributions and expenditures, the Court found no compelling government interest to justify this restriction on the political association rights of PAC members.

g. **Campaign Expenditures by Ideological Corporations. [§ 826] Federal law cannot limit political expenditures by non-profit, ideological corporations.**

(1) *Federal Election Commission v. Massachusetts Citizens for Life*, 479 U.S. 238 (1986). **The Court invalidated a federal law which prohibited corporations from using general treasury funds to make expenditures in relation to any election for**

**public office.** Under the law, expenditures by corporations must be made from separate, segregated funds. Massachusetts Citizens for Life (MCFL) is a nonprofit corporation dedicated solely to advancing pro-life positions and candidates. It has no connection to any business corporation. MCFL used general treasury funds to distribute a newsletter urging people to support pro-life candidates in an upcoming election. The Court said that the government could not restrict this kind of speech by a nonprofit, ideological corporation. **Three factors are important in immunizing MCFL's speech from government intrusion: 1) The corporation was formed solely to promote political ideas, and cannot engage in business activities; 2) no shareholders have a claim on the assets of the corporation; and 3) MCFL was not established by a business corporation or labor union, and it will not accept contributions from these entities.**

(2) *Austin v. Michigan State Chamber of Commerce*, 494 U.S. 652 (1990). The Court rejected First and Fourteenth Amendment challenges to a Michigan law which prohibits corporations (with the exception of media corporations) from making contributions to candidates, or expenditures for or against candidates. Expenditures may be made from a segregated fund. The Michigan Chamber of Commerce (MCC), a corporation which served both political and business purposes, and whose membership is made up of primarily for-profit corporations, challenged the law. Using the three factors from *Massachusetts Citizens for Life* (MCFL) (previous case), the Court distinguished MCFL from the MCC, primarily on the basis that MCC serves business purposes and has business members. The government interest served by the law is to prevent huge corporate expenditures from skewing the political process, especially when the amount of money spent by a corporation is unrelated to the degree of political support that may exist among the members. The Court also rejected the argument that the exemption for media corporations violated the Equal Protection Clause. The Court reasoned that different treatment of media and non-media corporations is constitutional because they are not similarly situated. The state has a compelling reason to protect the news-gathering and editorial functions of media corporations, an interest not present with non-media corporations.

# CHAPTER XVI

h. **Campaign Expenditures by Corporation and Unions. [§ 826.1]**

**The First Amendment does not allow political speech restrictions based on a speaker's corporate identity. However, disclosure and disclaimer provisions may constitutionally be imposed to insure that voters are fully informed.**

*Citizens United v. Federal Election Commission*, 130 S.Ct. 876 (2010). Citizens United, a nonprofit corporation, released a film entitled *Hillary: The Movie*. The movie was critical of then–Senator Hilary Clinton, who was running in the Democratic Party's 2008 Presidential primary elections. A cable television company offered to put the movie on a video-on-demand channel for a fee of $1.2 million. To promote this broadcast, Citizens United produced two ads to run on cable and broadcast, television. Federal law (2 U.S.C. § 441b) prohibited corporations from using general treasury funds to make independent expenditures that expressly advocate the election or defeat of a candidate. § 203 of the Bipartisan Campaign Reform Act (BCRA) amended § 441(b) to prohibit any "electioneering communications," which is defined as any broadcast, cable, or satellite communication that refers to a clearly identified candidate for federal office.

Considering the facial validity of § 441(b), the Court ruled 5–4, that the First Amendment does not allow political speech restrictions based on a speaker's corporate identity. The Court applied strict scrutiny, and rejected each of the government's justifications for the law. The Court first rejected the argument that the law was aimed at the "distorting effects of immense aggregations of wealth." The Court said that the law was aimed at a vast array of corporations, both large and small, and that factions of speakers should be checked by allowing them all to speak, not by the government choosing which speakers may enter the marketplace of ideas. The Court also, found insufficient the government's arguments that the law was necessary to prevent corporate speech from causing corruption, and that the law compelled dissenting shareholders from being compelled to fund corporate political speech.

The Court also ruled, 8–1, that disclaimers and disclosure requirement of BCRA were constitutional as applied to the documentary and the ads. Disclaimer and disclosure requirements do not prohibit anyone from speaking and can be justified by an interest in providing the electorate with information about election-related spending sources.

# FREEDOM OF SPEECH

i. **Campaign Expenditures by Political Parties. [§ 827]**

**Federal law cannot limit the expenditures of a political party in connection with the general election campaign of a congressional candidate.**

*Colorado Republican Federal Campaign Committee v. Federal Election Commission*, 518 U.S. 604 (1996). The Court invalidated a provision of the Federal Election Campaign Act which imposed dollar limitations on political party expenditures made independently by the party to support the general election campaign of a congressional candidate. The Court ruled that the federal law could not be applied to limit the expenditures of a committee of the Colorado Republican Party which had bought radio advertisements attacking the likely candidate of the Democratic Party.

j. **Political Parties' Expenditures Coordinated With Congressional Candidates. [§ 828]**

**Expenditures by a Political Party That Are Made In Concert With a Congressional Candidate Are "Contributions" Under Federal Election Campaign Act.**

*Federal Election Commission v. Colorado Republican Federal Campaign Committee*, 533 U.S. 431 (2001). The Court upheld, against a facial challenge, a federal limitation on political campaign contributions as applied to expenditures by a political party made in cooperation with a congressional candidate. Upholding the distinction between limits on contributions and limits on expenditures announced in *Buckley v. Valeo* (§ 839) (Congress may limit contributions to a candidate, but not expenditures for a candidate), the Court ruled that expenditures coordinated with a candidate are really "contributions" under federal law. The Court ruled that truly independent expenditures cannot be limited, but that coordinated expenditures are merely disguised contributions which Congress could conclude might be linked to political corruption.

## J. RESTRICTIONS ON SPEECH OF GOVERNMENT EMPLOYEES. [§ 829]

**When a government restricts the speech of its employees, the Court must balance the free speech rights of the employee against the interest of the government as employer in maintaining the functioning of the workplace.** Problems arise because the government is wearing two hats: it is an employer, just as any other entity might be, but it is also the sovereign, bound by

# CHAPTER XVI

constitutional limitations that do not apply to private employers. The fear is that the government, wearing its employer hat, may silence speech solely because that speech is critical of government policies or officials. **In this area, it is also important to distinguish between speech on matters of public concern and speech that is purely private. Speech of government employees that is on a matter of public concern is more important than purely private speech; disciplining or firing government employees for speech on a matter of public concern carries the danger of censorship.**

1. Loyalty Oaths. [§ 830]

    **Loyalty oaths will be upheld as long as they simply require an affirmation by the employee to abide by the Constitution. They will be suspect if they are used to punish someone for membership in a subversive organization;** that kind of oath would infringe upon the employee's freedom of political association.

    a. **Loyalty Oath as Violative of the Freedom of Association.**

       **Loyalty oaths that punish a person solely for membership in a subversive organization violate the freedom of association.**

       *Elfbrandt v. Russell*, 384 U.S. 11 (1966). The Court invalidated an Arizona statute which required all state employees to take a loyalty oath, and which required the dismissal of any employee who took the oath and then remained or became a member of the Communist Party. **The statute violated an employee's freedom of association because it required the dismissal of any employee who was a member of a subversive group, even though the person had no specific intent to further the illegal goals of the organization.** A person cannot be punished for mere "passive" membership in a subversive organization.

    b. **Loyalty Oath to Uphold the Constitution.**

       **Loyalty oaths to uphold the Constitution are permissible.**

       *Cole v. Richardson*, 405 U.S. 676 (1972). The Court upheld a loyalty oath which Massachusetts required its employees to sign. The oath bound the employee to uphold the Constitution, and to oppose the overthrow of the government by violence or any illegal or unconstitutional method. Richardson was fired from a job at a state hospital for refusing to sign the oath. The Court said that the oath simply required employees to abide by constitutional processes, and did not punish anyone for any membership or association.

# FREEDOM OF SPEECH

2. **Political Activity and Political Patronage in Public Employment Situations. [§ 831]**

   Two issues run through the cases in this area: the ability of a government employer to make employment decisions based on the political affiliation of an employee; and the ability of a government employer to discipline employees for their speech. The Court tries to balance the rights of the employee to belong to the political party of his or her choice and to speak on the job, against the ability of the government to run the workplace. **A public employee's speech will be protected if it is on a matter of public concern, and does not disrupt the workplace. Speech on a matter of private concern will not be protected in the same manner; discipline or dismissal for private speech is simply an ordinary employment decision.**

   a. **Politicial Activity of Government Employees. [§ 832]**

   The Court has upheld some restrictions on the political activity of government employees on the theory that such limitations are needed to prevent corruption or the appearance of corruption in government.

   (1) **Speech on Matters of Public Concern. [§ 833]**

   **Government employees retain the right to speak on matters of public concern.**

   (a) *Pickering v. Board of Education*, 391 U.S. 563 (1968).

   The Court ruled that a government employee does not give up First Amendment rights to comment on public issues by virtue of public employment. The Court balances the speech rights of public employees against the government's interests in the functioning of the workplace. In *Pickering*, a teacher published a letter in a newspaper that criticized school board policies. **The Court ruled that since the comments were on matters of public concern, and did not disrupt the functioning of the workplace, the teacher could not be punished for the speech.**

   (b) *Connick v. Myers*, 461 U.S. 138 (1983).

   The Court upheld the firing of an assistant district attorney for circulating a questionnaire regarding office policy. The employee sued under 42 U.S.C. § 1983, claiming that she was fired for exercising her right to free speech. **The Court held that when an employee does not speak on** matters of public concern, but only on issues of personal interest, a federal court ordinarily should not intervene in the dispute. To whatever limited extent the speech touched on public concern, Meyers' firing was justified by her supervisor's fear that her speech would disrupt the functioning of the office.

(c) *Rankin v. McPherson*, 483 U.S. 378 (1987).

The Court overturned the firing of a clerical employee in a constable's office when she remarked, after an assassination attempt on President Reagan, "If they go for him again, I hope they get him." The Court held that **this was speech on a matter of public concern, and that under the appropriate balancing approach, there was insufficient evidence that her comment disrupted the functioning of the office.**

(d) *Waters v. Churchill*, 511 U.S. 661 (1993).

The Court upheld the firing of a nurse from a public hospital for comments she made to a co-worker criticizing her supervisor and hospital policies regarding the use of nursing personnel. There was some dispute about what was said, but the hospital investigated, thought the speech disruptive, and fired Churchill. The Court reiterated the *Connick* test that a public employee's speech is protected if it is on a matter of public concern, and does not unduly disrupt the functioning of the workplace. **The Court said that the *Connick* test should be applied to what the employer reasonably thought the employee said, rather then to what the trier-of-fact ultimately determines was said.**

(e) *Board of County Commissioners v. Umbehr*, 518 U.S. 668 (1996).

The Court ruled that **independent contractors may not have their government contracts terminated in retaliation for their speech on matters of public concern unless, under *Pickering* (see § 852), that speech disrupts the functioning of the workplace.** In *Umbehr*, a trash hauler who criticized the Board of County Commissioners had his at-will contract terminated, and alleged that the termination was in retaliation for his speech. The Court applied *Pickering*, but adjusted the balance to reflect the

# FREEDOM OF SPEECH

fact that the government's and the individual's interests may be less strong in an independent contractor case than in the case of a regular employment relationship.

**(f)** *Garcetti v. Ceballos*, 547 U.S. 410 (2006).

The Court held that when public employees make statements pursuant to their official duties, they are not speaking as citizens for First Amendment purposes, and the Constitution does not protect them from employer discipline for their speech. Ceballos, a deputy district attorney, was asked by a defense attorney to review an affidavit used to obtain a search warrant. Ceballos determined that the affidavit contained misrepresentations, and he wrote a memo to his supervisors explaining his concerns and recommending dismissal of the case. After heated debate in the office, the supervisor proceeded with the case, and Ceballos was called by the defense to testify about his observations regarding the affidavit. After those events, Ceballos alleged that he was subjected to retaliatory employment actions, such as transfer to another workplace and denial of a promotion. He then filed suit, claiming a violation of his First Amendment rights. The Court, relying on *Pickering* (§ 852) and *Connick* (§ 853) said the first inquiry must be whether the employee spoke **as a citizen** on a matter of public concerns. If the answer is no, the employee has no First Amendment cause of action based on the employer's reaction to this speech. If the answer is yes, then there is a possibility of a First Amendment claim, and the question then becomes whether the government employer had an adequate justification for treating the employee differently from any other citizen; specifically, did the employee's speech disrupt the workplace. However, the Court held that when public employees make statements **pursuant to their official duties** the employees are not speaking as citizens for First Amendment purposes and the Constitution does not insulate their speech from employer discipline.

**(2) Political Activity by Federal Employees. [§ 834]**

**Federal law can prohibit federal employees from engaging in political activity.**

*U.S. Civil Service Commission v. National Association of Letter Carriers*, 413 U.S. 548 (1973). **The Court upheld a federal** law which prohibited federal employees from taking an active part in political management or political campaigns. **The prohibition is content neutral, applying equally to all partisan activities and all racial, ethnic, and religious groups.** Congress had overriding interests in removing the appearance of graft and corruption from the governmental process, and in ensuring that the operation of government is unaffected by partisan pressures.

(3) **Honoraria for Speeches. [§ 835]**

**Congress cannot prohibit low-level federal employees from accepting honoraria for speeches that do not relate to their government employment.**

*U.S. v. National Treasury Employees Union*, 513 U.S. 454 (1995). The Court invalidated, as applied to low-level federal employees, a provision of the Ethics in Government Act which broadly prohibited federal employees from accepting any compensation for making speeches or writing articles. The speeches and articles to which the prohibition had been applied concerned matters totally unrelated to government employment or public concerns (religion, history, dance, the environment). The Court said that while there may be some evidence of actual or apparent impropriety by Senators, Representatives, and high-level executive officials, there was insufficient evidence to extend the honorarium-ban to low level federal employees (below the rank of GS–16) who had at best a negligible ability to misuse their power by conferring favors in return for being compensated for a speech or article.

b. **Political Patronage in Government Employment. [§ 836]**

**Employment decisions based on political affiliation will be upheld if the government can show that they are necessary to the effective performance of the job.**

(1) **Dismissal from Government Employment Because of Political Affiliation. [§ 837]**

**Low-level public employees may not be dismissed merely because of their party affiliation.**

(a) **Elrod v. Burns, 427 U.S. 347 (1976). [§ 838]**

The Court invalidated a system of political patronage under which a new sheriff (a Democrat) fired a number of employees because they were not Democrats. **These partisan dismissals violated the employee's First Amendment rights of free speech and political association.** Justice Brennan, in dicta, said that patronage dismissals from high-level policymaking positions may be permissible to advance the interest of political loyalty from high-level associates.

(b) **Branti v. Finkel, 445 U.S. 507 (1980). [§ 839]**

The Court ruled that two assistant public defenders could not be fired because they were of a different political party than the new Public Defender. **The Court conceded that party affiliation may be an acceptable requirement for some government positions, and said that the test is whether the hiring authority can show that party affiliation is an appropriate requirement for the effective performance of the public office involved.**

(c) **O'Hare Truck Service, Inc. v. Northlake, 518 U.S. 712 (1996). [§ 840]**

The Court extended the principles of *Elrod* and *Branti* (previous cases) to cover independent contractors (as opposed to regular employees). In this case, a city took a tow truck service off the list of companies hired by the city on a contract basis. The reason for the removal was that the company's owner refused to contribute to the mayor's reelection campaign, instead supporting the mayor's opponent. The Court reiterated the rule that **a government employee or contractor cannot be dismissed because of party affiliation unless the government can show that party affiliation is an appropriate requirement for the effective performance of the public office involved.**

(2) **Political Affiliation Affecting Employment Decisions Other Than Dismissal. [§ 841]**

**Party affiliation may not be considered in any employment decision involving low-level employees.**

*Rutan v. Republican Party of Illinois*, 497 U.S. 62 (1990). The Court held violative of the First Amendment a governor's executive order which imposed a political patronage system on promotion, transfer, recall, and hiring decisions of low-level government employees. **The Court extended the rule from the**

# CHAPTER XVI

dismissal practices of *Elrod* and *Branti* (see §§ 838, 839) to all employment practices regarding low-level public employees.

## K. THE RIGHT NOT TO SPEAK: FREEDOM FROM GOVERNMENT COERCION, SUBSIDIES, OR TAXES. [§ 842]

**There is no enumerated constitutional right not to speak. However, in a number of cases, the Court has said that there is a right to be free from government compelled speech, whether compelled by a regulation, a subsidy, or a tax.** One of the basic tenets of the First Amendment is that government cannot force anyone to speak, or to endorse any political, religious, or social orthodoxy. An essential part of the theory in these cases is that the First Amendment protects not only freedom of speech, but also freedom of belief and freedom of conscience. In the following cases, be aware of the methods a government may use to try to favor some speech over others.

1. **The Right to Be Free From Compelled Speech. [§ 843]**

    **The government may not force a person to speak, or to affirm any prescribed belief or idea.** The unenumerated right not to speak is based in the free speech protections of the First Amendment. Be aware that if a person has religious objections to expressing a prescribed idea, the religion clauses of the First Amendment are also relevant. Compelled government speech may establish religion (being forced to recite an obviously sectarian prayer), or may violate the free exercise rights of a person who has religious scruples against expressing a particular message

    a. **Pledge of Allegiance. [§ 844]**

        **A state cannot require students to recite the Pledge of Allegiance.**

        *West Virginia State Board of Education v. Barnette*, 319 U.S. 624 (1943). The Court invalidated a state law which required all students to salute and pledge allegiance to the flag of the United States. Failure to do so could result in expulsion from school. Asserting that the compulsory salute and pledge requires affirmation of a belief and an attitude of mind, the Court said that the Bill of Rights, which protects a person's right to speak his or her mind, cannot allow the government to compel a person to utter what is not on his or her mind.

    b. **State Motto on a License Plate. [§ 846]**

        **A state cannot force someone to display the state motto on a license plate.**

370

# FREEDOM OF SPEECH

*Wooley v. Maynard*, 430 U.S. 705 (1977). The Court invalidated a New Hampshire law which required passenger vehicles to have license plates carrying the state motto, "Live Free or Die." The Court, through Chief Justice Burger, said that the freedom of thought protected by the First Amendment encompasses both the right to speak freely and the right to refrain from speaking at all. Private vehicles cannot be commandeered as mobile billboards for a state's ideological message.

c. **Utility Companies. [§ 846]**

**A state cannot require a utility company to disseminate speech of a consumer group.**

*Pacific Gas & Electric Co. v. Public Utilities Commission*, 475 U.S. 1 (1986). The Court ruled that a state may not require a private utility company to include in its billing envelopes speech of a consumer-advocacy group with which the utility disagrees. For years the utility company had sent a newsletter out with its bills. The newsletter included political editorials and information about utility services. The state Public Utilities Commission, in the interest of "equal access," required that an advocacy group be able to use the billing envelope four times a year to disseminate their message. The Court said this order would force the company to associate with speech with which it might disagree—a violation of the company's First Amendment rights.

d. **Cable Television. [§ 847]**

**Federal law can require cable television systems to carry certain programming.**

*Turner Broadcasting System v. Federal Communications Commission I*, 512 U.S. 622 (1994). The Court reviewed the federal Cable Television Consumer Protection Act, under which Congress required cable television systems to devote a specified portion of their channels to the transmission of local commercial and public broadcast stations. The Court ruled that these "must-carry" provisions were content neutral, incidental burdens on speech, which should receive intermediate scrutiny. The Court refused to extend to cable television the less rigorous standard of review applicable to radio and over-the-air television broadcasting. The Court remanded the case to federal district court to allow the government to demonstrate that the must-carry provisions were necessary to protect the economic health of local broadcasting.

# CHAPTER XVI

*Turner Broadcasting System v. Federal Communications Commission II*, 520 U.S. 180 (1997). The Court affirmed the opinion of the District Court that there was substantial evidence supporting the judgment of Congress that the must-carry provisions further the following important governmental interests: 1) preserving the benefits of free, over-the-air local broadcast television, 2) promoting the dissemination of information from a multiplicity of sources, and 3) promoting fair competition in the television programming market. The Court also ruled that the must-carry provisions do not burden substantially more speech than is necessary to achieve the government's interests.

e. **Private Parades. [§ 848]**

**A state cannot apply its public accommodations law to force parade organizers to include a group they do not wish to include.**

*Hurley v. Irish–American Gay, Lesbian and Bisexual Group of Boston*, 515 U.S. 557 (1995). The Court invalidated the application of Massachusetts' public accommodations law, which prohibits discrimination on the basis of sexual orientation, to private parade organizers who wanted to exclude from their parade a group who wished to proclaim pride in their homosexual and bisexual identities. The South Boston Allied War Veterans Council, a private group, was authorized by the City of Boston to organize the annual St. Patrick's Day parade. The Council refused to allow the Irish–American Gay, Lesbian and Bisexual Group of Boston (GLIB) to march in the parade. A state court found that the Council's refusal to allow GLIB to march in the parade violated a state law which prohibited discrimination based on sexual orientation in places of public accommodation. The Court ruled that parades are a form of expression protected under the First Amendment, and that application of the public accommodations law to the Council violated the parade organizers' right to choose the content of their message, as well as their right to decide what not to say.

2. **Government Subsidies of Speech. [§ 849]**

**As a general matter, government subsidies (financial inducements) are constitutional if they are rationally related to a legitimate government interest. However, when a subsidy or condition on the receipt of money requires a person or entity to forego or waive a constitutional right to be eligible for the money, the Court will scrutinize those laws under appropriate First Amendment analysis.** The idea here is that the government may not use its virtually unlimited economic power to require or control speech.

# FREEDOM OF SPEECH

a. **Tax Exempt Organizations. [§ 850]**

**The federal government may allow for selective deductibility of contributions to tax-exempt organizations as long as the deductions are not based on the content of the speech of those organizations.**

*Regan v. Taxation With Representation of Washington*, 461 U.S. 540 (1983). The Court upheld a section of the Internal Revenue Code which made contributions to tax-exempt organizations deductible unless a substantial part of the organization's activities involve lobbying. Another section of the law made contributions to veterans' organizations deductible even if they engage in substantial lobbying. The Court said that this law was not directed at the content of speech of veterans' groups; it simply gave them a break because of the status of veterans in our country.

b. **Public Broadcasting Station. [§ 851]**

**Federal law cannot prohibit public broadcasting stations from engaging in editorializing.**

*FCC v. League of Women Voters*, 468 U.S. 364 (1984). The Court invalidated a federal law which prohibited any non-commercial educational station receiving a grant from the Corporation for Public Broadcasting from engaging in editorializing. The Court found this content-based restriction on the speech of publicly funded stations to be especially suspect because it was aimed at expression of public issues, speech which is at the core of the First Amendment.

c. **Family Planning Clinics. [§ 852]**

**Federal law can prohibit federally-funded family planning clinics from discussing abortion as a method of family planning.**

*Rust v. Sullivan*, 500 U.S. 173 (1991). The Court upheld a regulation of the Department of Health and Human Services which prohibited family planning clinics receiving federal money from discussing, within the confines of the federally-funded project, abortion as a method of family planning. The clinic could still advocate abortion through programs that are separate from those receiving federal funds. Medical personnel in the federally-funded clinics remain free to discuss abortion as family planning, as long as they do so on their own time.

d. **National Funding for the Arts. [§ 853]**

**Federal law can require the National Endowment for the Arts to consider general standards of decency in deciding how to allocate competitive grant funds.**

# CHAPTER XVI

*National Endowment for the Arts v. Finley*, 524 U.S. 569 (1998). The Court rejected a facial attack on a federal statute which requires the National Endowment for the Arts to take into consideration general standards of decency and respect for the diverse beliefs and values of the American public in deciding who will be the recipients of federal grants for the arts. The Court ruled that since the government was acting as a patron, not a sovereign, any ambiguity in the statute was constitutionally permissible. The Court emphasized that the statute did not preclude awards to projects that might be indecent, it simply added one consideration (decency) to the general funding criteria of artistic excellence and artistic merit.

e. **Political Debates on Public Television. [§ 854]**

**Public television broadcasters have the right to exclude minor-party candidates from political debates as long as the exclusion is reasonable and not based on the candidate's views.**

*Arkansas Educational Television Commission v. Forbes*, 523 U.S. 666 (1998). The Court ruled that a state-owned public television broadcaster may exclude an independent candidate with little popular support from a congressional debate as long as the exclusion was a reasonable, viewpoint-neutral exercise of journalistic discretion. The Court reasoned that a candidate debate on public television was a nonpublic forum (as distinguished from a traditional or designated forum), and that the candidate was excluded not because of his viewpoint, but because his candidacy had not generated significant public support. The public television station had a legitimate interest in maintaining a manageable number of participants in such a debate, and public support was a reasonable criterion to apply in achieving that goal.

f. **Congressional Restriction on the Speech of Legal Services Corporation Lawyers. [§ 855]**

**Congress violated the First Amendment by prohibiting Legal Services corporation lawyers from challenging welfare laws on behalf of poor clients.**

*Legal Services Corporation v. Velazquez*, 531 U.S. 533 (2001). The Court struck down funding restrictions imposed by the Legal Services Corporation on local grantees who provide free legal representation to indigent people. Congress prohibited funding to any organization that represented clients in suits attempting to amend or otherwise change existing welfare law. Distinguishing cases like *Rust*

# FREEDOM OF SPEECH

(See § 874), in which the government itself is the speaker, the Court reasoned that the Legal Services program was designed to facilitate private speech, and that the government may not design a subsidy which effects such a fundamental restriction on the advocacy of attorneys and the functioning of the judiciary.

3. **Tax Exemptions as De Facto Subsidies for Certain Kinds of Speech. [§ 856]**

   **A state may not grant a sales tax exemption to certain publications based on the content of their message.** Government attempts to tax the press will also be dealt with in Chapter XVIII, Freedom of the Press.

   *Arkansas Writers' Project, Inc. v. Ragland*, 481 U.S. 221 (1987).

   The Court invalidated a state sales tax that taxed general interest magazines, but exempted newspapers and religious, professional, trade, and sports journals. This selective tax was content based, and not narrowly tailored to achieve a compelling government interest. The exemptions operated as a subsidy for the publications relieved of the sales tax.

   *Texas Monthly, Inc. v. Bullock*, 489 U.S. 1 (1989).

   The Court invalidated, on Establishment Clause grounds, a state sales tax exemption for religious books and periodicals. Justice Brennan, for a plurality, referred to the selective tax exemption as a "subsidy . . . targeted at writings that *promulgate* the teachings of religious faiths."

## L. FREEDOM OF ASSOCIATION. [§ 857]

There is no right of association enumerated in the Constitution. However the Court has afforded constitutional protection to different kinds of associational rights. Be aware of the different theories that run through the following cases which deal with the right of association.

1. **Association for Business Purposes. [§ 858]**

   **If people associate for business or commercial purposes, no fundamental constitutional interest is being advanced, and a government regulation of such associations will be valid if rationally related to a legitimate government interest.** The Court deals with these cases the same way it treats economic substantive due process cases. (See § 471, above.)

2. **Association for Personal Reasons. [§ 859]**

   **If people associate for purely personal reasons, the Court may recognize a fundamental right of intimate association which protects**

# CHAPTER XVI

**the basic element of personal liberty relating to the ability of persons to enter into and maintain intimate human relationships.** Under this theory, the issue is whether the association is sufficiently intimate to bring it within constitutional protections. The Court looks at three factors to decide this issue: 1) is it a relatively small group?; 2) is there a high degree of selectivity in decisions to begin and maintain the affiliation?; and 3) is there seclusion from others in critical aspects of the relationship (such as decisionmaking)?

3. **Association for First Amendment Purposes. [§ 860]**

   **If people associate for First Amendment purposes (speech or assembly), the Court may recognize a fundamental freedom of expressive association.** This right is not absolute, and a government may abridge it to advance a compelling government interest.

4. **Right Not to Associate, or Be Associated With, Certain Ideas. [§ 861]**

   **The court has recognized a right not to be associated with certain ideas or speech.** A typical case of this kind involves a union (or bar association) which uses members' dues for political purposes. The member has a right to not be associated with political speech with which he or she disagrees. The members may be forced to pay dues to cover the union's costs of performing labor representation functions, but may not be forced to contribute to the dissemination of speech that is extraneous to the union's function, as a bargaining agent.

5. **Cases Involving the Right of Association, and the Right Not to Associate. [§ 862]**

   a. **Membership Lists. [§ 863]**

   **A state cannot compel the disclosure of the membership list of a political organization.**

   *NAACP v. Alabama*, 357 U.S. 449 (1958). The Court ruled that Alabama could not compel the NAACP to disclose the names of its members. The Court unanimously said that the freedom to engage in association for the advancement of beliefs and ideas is a protected liberty under the Due Process Clause. Compelled disclosure would violate the privacy interests of the members of the group.

   b. **Union Dues. [§ 864]**

   **Union dues may not be spent to pursue objectives not related to the collective bargaining agreement such as the advancement of political views opposed by a union member.**

*Locke v. Karass*, 129 S.Ct. 798 (2009). The Court upheld, against a First Amendment challenge, a collective bargaining agreement between Maine and a local union which requires nonmember employees represented by the union to pay the local a "service fee" equal to the portion of union dues related to ordinary representational activities, such as collective bargaining or contract administration activities. The union did not charge the nonmembers for political, public relations, or lobbying activities. The service fee includes a charge that represents an "affiliation fee" that the local pays to the national union. The part of the service fee that goes to the national union is used for litigation expenses that benefit other locals or the national union itself, rather than the specific local union involved in the case. The nonmember plaintiffs argued that the First Amendment prohibits them from being charged for any part of the service fee that is used to pay for national litigation that does not benefit the local union. The Court held that a local may charge a nonmember a share of its contribution to a national's litigation expense if the subject matter of the national litigation bears an appropriate relation to collective bargaining, and the arrangement is reciprocal in the sense that the local's payment to the national union is for services that may ultimately inure to the benefit of the members of the local union because of their membership in the parent organization.

*Ysursa v. Pocatello Education Association*, 129 S.Ct. 798 (2009). The Court upheld an Idaho law that prohibits state and local public employees from having a portion of their wages deducted by their employer and remitted to their union's political action committee. Under the law, the public employees may authorize payroll deductions for general union dues. A group of Idaho public employee unions challenged the ban as a violation of their Free Speech rights. The Court applied rational basis scrutiny to the ban, saying that the law is not a restriction on the unions' political speech, but simply a refusal by the State to subsidize the speech by allowing public employee checkoffs for political activities. The Court accepted Idaho's argument that its legitimate interest underlying the law is to avoid the reality on appearance of government favoritism or entanglement with partisan politics.

c. **Bar Association Dues. [§ 865]**

**Bar association dues may not be spent to advance political views opposed by a member of the bar.**

*Keller v. State Bar of California*, 496 U.S. 1 (1990). The Court held that a state bar association may use compulsory dues for the purpose of regulating the legal profession or improving the quality of legal services available to the people of the state, but may not use them for political causes that the bar association members oppose.

### d. Mandatory Student Activity Fees. [§ 866]

A state university may allocate mandatory student activity fees to political and ideological groups even if some students object to those subsidies.

*Board of Regents of the University of Wisconsin v. Southworth*, 529 U.S. 217 (2000). The Court upheld a practice of the University of Wisconsin under which mandatory student activity fees were allocated to various campus groups to support their speech. The program, which is viewpoint-neutral, was designed to increase the diversity of speech on campus. The Court distinguished *Keller* and *Abood* (previous cases) on the basis that the contributions in those cases could only be used to fund speech that was germane to the purpose of the organization and not to fund the organizations' own political expression. The "germane speech" standard was irrelevant in a public university setting where the university attempts to stimulate the entire universe of speech and ideas.

### e. Contributions to Generic Advertising for an Industry. [§ 867]

**Forced contributions to generic advertising for an entire industry do not violate the First Amendment if they are ancillary to a comprehensive regulatory program restricting marketing autonomy.**

(1) *Glickman v. Wileman Brothers & Elliott, Inc*, 521 U.S. 457 (1997). The Court, by a vote of 5–4 upheld marketing orders promulgated by the Secretary of Agriculture which required California tree fruit growers to contribute to the cost of generic advertising of the California tree fruit industry. The growers argued that such forced contributions violated their commercial speech rights under the *Central Hudson* test (see § 761). The Court rejected the free speech argument entirely, relying on the following aspects of the generic advertising scheme: 1) the marketing orders do not limit a grower's ability to communicate any message to anyone; 2) the orders do not compel any grower to engage in any speech; and 3) the orders do not compel any grower to endorse or finance any political or ideological speech. Since the First Amendment did not apply, the Court upheld the marketing orders under the lenient rational basis test used to review economic legislation. The Court emphasized that the compelled contributions for advertising were part of a far broader regulatory system that did not principally concern speech.

(2) *U.S. v. United Foods, Inc.*, 533 U.S. 405 (2001). The Court struck down mandatory assessments imposed on mushroom handlers by a federal law which funded generic advertising of mushrooms. Unlike *Glickman*, the Court said that the compelled contributions were not part of any broader regulatory scheme, and that it had never upheld compelled subsidies for speech in the context of a program where the principal object is speech itself. Relying on the cases of *Abood*, (see § 885) and *Keller* (see § 886), the Court reiterated the rule that government cannot compel individuals to pay subsidies for speech to which they object. Assuming that the advertising was private speech, not government speech, the Court relied on *Abood* and *Keller* to reiterate the rule that government cannot compel individuals to subsidize speech to which they object.

(3) *Johanns v. Livestock Marketing Association*, 544 U.S. 550 (2005). The Court upheld a federal program that finances generic advertising to promote the beef industry. The Court ruled that because the advertising in question is the Government's own speech, it is not susceptible to a First Amendment compelled-subsidy challenge. Congress passed the Beef Promotion and Research Act of 1985 (Beef Act), which established a federal policy of promoting and marketing beef products. The Secretary of Agriculture implemented the Act through an Order which creates a Cattleman's Beef Promotion and Research Board and an Operating Committee. The Order imposes an assessment on all sales and importation of cattle. The assessment funds beef promotional campaigns which are approved by the Operating Committee and the Secretary. The plaintiffs argued that the Beef Act and the Order forced them to subsidize speech with which they did not agree. The Court distinguished *United Foods* (§ 886.2), *Keller* (§ 886), and *Abood* (§ 885) on the basis that each of these cases involved the subsidizing of private speech. This case, on the other hand, involved subsidizing government speech, which is not even amenable to First Amendment challenge.

**f. Privately Owned Shopping Centers. [§ 868]**

**A state constitution may confer a right of access to privately-owned shopping centers for speech purposes.**

*Pruneyard Shopping Center v. Robins*, 447 U.S. 74 (1980). The Court upheld a California constitutional provision that gave speakers access to privately-owned shopping centers for speech purposes. The owner of the shopping center objected to being forced to provide the forum for speech that he might not agree with. The Court said that since there was little likelihood that the speech would be ascribed to the owner, no specific message was dictated by the State, and the owner could simply post signs disavowing the speech, the owner's right not to be associated with the speakers or their ideas was not violated.

g. **Consumer Boycotts. [§ 869]**

**Consumer boycotts are protected as an aspect of the associational rights of an organization.**

*NAACP v. Clairborne Hardware Co.*, 458 U.S. 886 (1982). The Court ruled that the NAACP and its members could not be held liable in tort for damages resulting from an organized consumer boycott which was intended to protest racial discrimination. The boycott was political speech, lying at the core of the First Amendment. The Court ruled that liability may be imposed only on a person whose unlawful conduct was the proximate cause of an injury. It is not permissible for a state to punish one member of an association simply because another member broke the law.

h. **Gender Discrimination by Private Associations. [§ 870]**

**A state may require private associations to accept women as members.**

*Roberts v. U.S. Jaycees*, 468 U.S. 609 (1984). The Court ruled that a state equal opportunity statute could be applied to force a state branch of the Jaycees to admit women as members, despite their policy of restricting membership to males between the ages of 18 and 35. The Court recognized two kinds of freedom of association: intimate and expressive.

— **Freedom of intimate association has to do with starting and maintaining close personal relationships. This kind of association is evidenced by relative smallness of the group, a high degree of selectivity in starting and maintaining the affiliation, and seclusion from others in important aspects of the association.** The local chapters of the Jaycees failed to meet these criteria, and thus were not able to assert a right to intimate association as a defense to the state action of forcing the Jaycees to accept women as members.

— **Freedom of expressive association has to do with associating for First Amendment purposes: speech, assembly, and petitioning for the redress of grievances.** Freedom to associate for expressive purposes presupposes a freedom not to associate. Forced membership abridges the choice not to associate with certain people.

# FREEDOM OF SPEECH

The right to expressive association, while fundamental, is not absolute, and may be abridged to advance the state's compelling interest in eradicating gender discrimination.

i. **Discrimination Based on Sexual Orientation. [§ 871]**

**A state law forcing the Boy Scouts to admit a homosexual as an assistant scoutmaster would violate the Boy Scouts' First Amendment right of expressive association.**

*Boy Scouts of America v. Dale*, 530 U.S. 640 (2000). The Court held that applying New Jersey's public accommodations law to require the Boy Scouts to admit a homosexual as an assistant scoutmaster violated the Boy Scouts' right to expressive association. The Court reasoned that such forced membership is unconstitutional if the person's presence significantly affects the group's ability to advocate public or private viewpoints. The Boy Scouts assert that homosexuality is inconsistent with the values embodied in the Scout Oath and Law. The presence of a homosexual scoutmaster would force the Scouts to propound a point of view contrary to its beliefs.

j. **Welfare Benefits. [§ 872]**

**The federal government can reduce the welfare benefits of family members of striking workers.**

*Lyng v. UAW*, 485 U.S. 360 (1988). The Court upheld a provision of the federal Food Stamp Act providing that no family may become eligible for food stamps while any member of the household is on strike, nor shall any family receive increased food stamp allotments because the in come of the striking family member had decreased. The Constitution's protection of associational rights included the right of workers to associate to better assert their lawful rights. However, the Court said that the law neither ordered nor prevented workers from associating. The government's decision not to subsidize the exercise of a right does not equal the government abridging that right.

k. **Social Associations With Older Persons. [§ 873]**

**A city may prohibit persons over the age of 18 from using certain dance halls frequented by minors.**

*Dallas v. Stanglin*, 490 U.S. 19 (1989). The Court upheld a city ordinance prohibiting persons over the age of 18 from using certain dance halls. The Court said there was no general right of social association that would protect the ability to go to a dance hall.

l. **Access of Military Recruiters to Students on Campus [§ 874]**

**Congress may condition the receipt of federal funds on a university providing military recruiters with the same access to students as it grants to other recruiters.**

*Rumsfeld v. Forum for Academic and Institutional Rights*, 547 U.S. 47 (2006). The Court upheld the Solomon Amendment, a federal law which provides that educational institutions which deny military recruiters access equal to that provided other recruiters will lose certain federal funds. The law was challenged by the Forum for Academic and Institutional Rights (FAIR), an association of law schools and law faculties whose members have policies opposing discrimination based on sexual orientation. FAIR objected to the military's policy on gays in the armed forces, and argued that the Solomon Amendment forced them to choose between receiving federal funds and adhering to their non-discrimination policies. FAIR asserted that the forced inclusion of military recruiters violated their First Amendment freedoms of speech and association. The Court first said that a funding condition cannot be unconstitutional if it could be imposed directed, and that the First Amendment would not prevent Congress from directly imposing the Solomon Amendment's access requirement. The Court then opined that, as a general matter, the Solomon Amendment regulates conduct, not speech, and that any compelled speech is clearly incidental to the statute's regulation of conduct. The Court ruled that when it has found compelled speech violations, it has been the complaining speaker's own message that was affected by the compelled speech. Here, the Court said the law schools are not speaking when they host recruiting interviews. Thus, there is nothing to suggest that the schools agree with any speech by recruiters, and nothing that restricts what they may say about military recruiters. Distinguishing *Boy Scouts v. Dale* (§ 889.1), The Court ruled that the Solomon Amendment does not violate the law schools' freedom of expressive association. The statute did not force law schools to accept military recruiters as member of the law school community; rather they are outsiders who come onto campus for the limited purpose of hiring students. Students and faculty are free to associate to voice their disapproval of the military's message.

# FREEDOM OF SPEECH

m. **Requirement That A Student Group Accept All Comers As a Condition of Official Recognition By a Law School. [§ 874.1]**

**A public law school may condition recognition of student groups on their acceptance as members of all who want to join, even if the new members hold beliefs that contradict those of the student group.**

*Christian Legal Society v. Martinez*, 130 S.Ct. 2971 (2010). Hastings College of Law, a public school in California, extends recognition to student groups on the condition that the groups comply with the school's Nondiscrimination policy, which tracks state law in banning discrimination based on, among other categories, religion and sexual orientation. Under the Hastings policy, a student group must accept all comers, regardless of their statute or beliefs. The Christian Legal Society (CLS) requires members to sign a "Statement of Faith," which espouses the tenet that sexual activity should not occur outside of marriage between a man and a woman. Christian Legal Society excludes from membership anyone who engages in "unrepentant homosexual conduct" or holds religious convictions that differ from those on the Statement of Faith. Hastings rejected CLS's application for recognized student group status because CLS excluded students based on religion and sexual orientation. The Court considered only the question of whether a public law school's conditioning access to a student-organization forum on compliance with an all-comers policy violates the Constitution. The Court, 5–4, ruled that the all-comers policy is a reasonable, viewpoint–neutral condition on access to the forum, and does not violate the First Amendment.

Treating CLS's free speech, and expressive association arguments together, the Court declined to use strict scrutiny, and characterized the case as being within the limited-public-forum category. The Court distinguished cases like Dale (See § 871) which involved laws which compelled a group to admit unwanted members, from the instant situation in which Hastings is "dangling the carrot of subsidy, not wielding the stick of prohibition." CLS was still free to exclude certain people from membership, it simply did so at the expense of the benefits of official recognition by Hastings. Hastings asserted that its policy assured that educational opportunities were available to all students, and that it encourages tolerance and cooperation among students. The Court emphasized that since the Hastings policy draws no distinction between groups based on their message, it is viewpoint neutral.

The dissent by Justice Alito characterized the Hastings policy as violating the principle of viewpoint neutrality, and declared that "it is

# CHAPTER XVI

fundamentally confused to apply a rule against religious discrimination to a religious association." His point is that Hastings should not be able to require tolerance of a religious group that is, for doctrinal reasons, intolerant.

## REVIEW PROBLEMS—FREEDOM OF SPEECH

**PROBLEM 1.** The City of Id has an ordinance which prohibits any "loud or boisterous" demonstrations or gatherings within 500 feet of any church, synagogue, temple, or any other house of worship while religious services are being held inside the building. Madeline O'Murray, a member of Atheists United, is arrested for violating this ordinance. Discuss her arguments against the ordinance. What is Id's best argument in support of the ordinance?

**Answer:** Madeline's best argument is that the ordinance is vague; who knows what "loud and boisterous" means? The vagueness of the ordinance gives her no notice of what behavior is punishable, and it gives the Id police too much discretion in enforcing the law. She would also argue that the ordinance violates her free speech rights because a 500–foot buffer zone is not narrowly tailored to achieving the city's interests. Id will argue that this ordinance is a valid time, place, manner restriction. It is content neutral, and advances the significant government interest of protecting the privacy rights of worshippers. Id will argue that it is narrowly tailored, and that demonstrators still have ample alternative channels of communication. See §§ 661, 666, 689 for further review.

**PROBLEM 2.** The State of Oz has a statute which provides that any sentence for an assaultive crime will be increased by a specified percentage if the victim was chosen based on his or her race or ethnicity. Mario Macho was convicted of aggravated assault for beating Zeb Smith. At trial, there was evidence that Mario chose Zeb as a victim because Zeb is of Mobanian descent. At sentencing, the judge increased Mario's sentence by one-third because his crime was motivated by hatred for Mobanians. Mario challenges Oz's enhanced-sentence statute on the basis that it violates his free speech rights. He claims that he received extra punishment because of what he believes and what he said about Mobanians. Will Mario win?

**Answer:** No. The Court has upheld a statute which increases the penalty for an assaultive crime when the defendant selected his victim based on race. The Court said that the enhanced sentence punished the conduct of selecting a victim, not the abstract beliefs or utterances of the defendant. As a result, there is no constitutional infringement on the free speech rights of the criminal. See § 743 for further review.

**PROBLEM 3.** Bob Barrister, an attorney licensed in the State of Oz, wrote letters to all persons with Mobanian surnames in the City of Id asking if they would like to join a class action lawsuit challenging allegedly discriminatory employment practices in the City of Id. The State Bar of Oz censures Bob for this solicitation. May the State Bar constitutionally discipline Bob?

**Answer:** No. Targeted solicitation by mail is protected commercial speech. Mailing truthful letters to specific persons who might have specific legal problems creates no great danger to consumers. Also, Bob has the argument that, since this is a civil rights lawsuit, rights of political speech and association are involved, making this speech even more protected. See § 778 for further review.

**PROBLEM 4.** The principal of Id High School, a public school in the State of Oz, was perusing the page proofs of the high school yearbook when she saw some disturbing pictures: members of certain athletic teams had made obscene gestures on the team pictures. The principal decided to remove from the yearbook the pages on which the pictures appeared. Student editors of the yearbook sued, claiming censorship. Is the principal justified in her action?

**Answer:** Yes. In a case involving school-sponsored speech, a school official may impose restrictions on speech, including complete removal of certain stories or pictures, if the restrictions are rationally related to a legitimate educational purpose. The principal's actions here are rationally related to ensuring good taste and civility in student publications paid for by the school. See § 793 for further review.

**PROBLEM 5.** The State of Oz owns and operates a large airport terminal. It has regulations which prohibit passing out leaflets inside the terminal, and in-person solicitation for money. Joan Camel, a member of Smokers Against Regulation (SAR), is arrested for passing out leaflets attacking government restrictions on smokers. She is also charged with violating the ban on soliciting money from people inside the terminal. Joan sues, alleging a violation of her free speech rights. Does she have a case?

**Answer:** Yes and No. A government-owned airport terminal is not a public forum, so the government may impose restrictions on speech that are reasonably related to keeping the terminal functioning for its intended purpose. The Court has upheld a ban on in-person solicitation within a terminal because of its disruptive effect on pedestrian traffic in the terminal. It has struck down a ban on leafletting, saying that no great disruption flows from simply passing out pieces of paper. See § 811 for further review.

# Chapter XVII

# FREEDOM OF THE PRESS

## A. INTRODUCTION. [§ 875]

**Under the First Amendment, neither Congress nor a state may pass a law abridging freedom of the press. The main purposes of a free press are to inform the public, and to serve as a check on government (obviously these overlap).** Two big issues surrounding the press are whether it has any special immunity from laws that bind the rest of us, such as a right not to testify before a grand jury, (no, it does not), and whether the institutional status of the press confers any special privileges on it, such as a special right to attend trials, (no, again). Be aware of the tension between the freedom of the press and other constitutional concerns, such as the rights of litigants in civil or criminal trials. These tensions have been considered on numerous occasions by the Supreme Court.

## B. FREEDOM OF THE PRESS AND THE RIGHT TO A FAIR TRIAL. [§ 876]

**A recurrent problem involves the potential tension, if not conflict, between the right of the print and electronic media to gather and report news, and the right of a defendant to a fair trial.** What steps may a judge take to ensure a fair trial, especially in a criminal case, while protecting the First Amendment interests of the press? Remember that prior restraints (See § 677, above) are presumed unconstitutional, and the government has a heavy burden of justification for any such restriction on the press.

1. Pretrial Publicity. [§ 877]

   The Court reversed a murder conviction because the "carnival atmosphere" in the courtroom violated the defendant's right to a fair trial.

   *Sheppard v. Maxwell*, 384 U.S. 333 (1966). The Court reversed a murder conviction on the basis of the extreme publicity surrounding the case, and the "carnival atmosphere" in the courtroom. The Court chastised the trial judge for not using available procedures to preserve the fairness and dignity of the trial. The judge can use voir dire to ensure that jurors have not been unduly influenced by pretrial publicity, can sequester the jurors as soon as they are chosen, or can grant a continuance or change of venue. The Court also indicated that a trial judge could have imposed gag orders on the attorneys and witnesses if necessary, although the press must be free to report events that happen in the courtroom.

2. **Prior Restraints to Ensure Fairness of Trials. [§ 878]**

   **Trial judges may not use prior restraints on the media to ensure the fairness of a trial if there are less drastic means available.**

   *Nebraska Press Association v. Stuart*, 427 U.S. 539 (1976). The Court struck down a state court pre-trial restraining order which prohibited the media from publishing any confessions made by the defendant (unless made to the press), and any other facts "strongly implicative" of the defendant's guilt. The state judge had also restrained the publication of any testimony or evidence given at the preliminary hearing. Using prior restraint analysis, the Court concluded that the trial judge had less drastic means available to preserve the defendant's right to a fair trial, such as a change of venue, postponing the trial, or sequestration of jurors.

## C. ACCESS OF THE PRESS TO PRISONERS AND COURTROOMS. [§ 879]

**Members of the media do not have any special right of access to courtrooms or jails. Their rights are the same as those of the general public.** Members of the public have a presumptive First Amendment right to attend trials which may be overridden only if a judge articulates a compelling reason for closing the courtroom. Members of the public have no right to interview or visit with prisoners unless the prison authorities grant such a right.

1. **Access to Prisons or Inmates. [§ 880]**

   **Reporters have no special right of access to prisons or inmates whom they wish to interview.**

   *Pell v. Procunier*, 417 U.S. 817 (1974). The Court upheld a California prison regulation which prohibited face-to-face interviews between reporters and inmates they requested to interview. **The Court said that members of the press have no constitutional right of access to prisons or inmates beyond that afforded the general public.**

2. **Access to Jails. [§ 881]**

   **Reporters have no special right of access to jails.**

# FREEDOM OF THE PRESS

*Houchins v. KQED*, 429 U.S. 1341 (1978). The Court, in a very fragmented set of opinions, reversed a lower court order requiring a sheriff to grant reporters access to a jail facility. The seven members of the Court participating all agreed that the media have no greater right of access to jails than does the general public.

3. **No Sixth Amendment Right of Access to a Criminal Trial. [§ 882]**

   **Neither the public nor the press has a Sixth Amendment right of access to criminal trials; the Sixth Amendment right to a public trial belongs to the defendant.**

   *Gannett Co., Inc. v. De Pasquale*, 443 U.S. 368 (1979). The Court held that the Sixth Amendment's guarantee of a public trial belonged to the defendant, and was not assertable by the press or public as a basis for gaining access to a pretrial hearing in a murder case.

4. **First Amendment Right of Access to Criminal Trials. [§ 883]**

   **There is a presumptive First Amendment right of the public and the press to attend criminal trials.**

   *Richmond Newspapers, Inc. v. Virginia*, 448 U.S. 555 (1980). **The Court ruled that the public and the press have a First Amendment right to attend criminal trials.** The right is not absolute, but to close a courtroom, a judge must state on the record some overriding reason justifying closure. The Court overturned the decision of a state trial judge, acting pursuant to a state statute, to close a murder trial.

5. **Closed Proceedings Involving Minors. [§ 884]**

   **A state may not close every proceeding involving testimony by a minor victim of a sexual assault.**

   *Globe Newspapers Co. v. Superior Court*, 457 U.S. 596 (1982). The Court invalidated a state statute requiring the exclusion of the press and public from a courtroom during the testimony of a minor victim of a sexual assault in a criminal case. The Court said that the press and public had a fundamental right to attend criminal trials, and that a judge could only close a trial if specific circumstances required it, and if the reasons for closure were placed in the record by the judge.

6. **First Amendment Right of Access to Voir Dire. [§ 885]**

   **There is a presumptive first amendment right of the public and the press to attend voir dire of potential jurors in a criminal case.**

# CHAPTER XVII

*Press Enterprise Co. v. Superior Court*, 464 U.S. 501 (1984). The Court held that the public and the press had a presumptive First Amendment right of access to the voir dire examination of potential jurors in a criminal trial. As with trials, closure of voir dire could only be justified by an overriding interest articulated on the record.

## D. NO REPORTER'S PRIVILEGE. [§ 886]

**The general rule is that members of the media are no different from the rest of us in terms of being subject to generally applicable rules of law. If you want to know if a reporter must do something (or is prohibited from doing it), ask whether you must do it (or are prohibited from doing it).** Whatever answer applies to you applies to reporters. Do you have to testify before a grand jury? Do you have to comply with a search warrant? If you do, so do reporters.

1. **Grand Jury Testimony. [§ 887]**

    **Reporters do not have any special privilege that exempts them from testifying before a grand jury.**

    *Branzburg v. Hayes*, 408 U.S. 665 (1972). The Court held that reporters do not have any First Amendment privilege that would immunize them from testifying before state or federal grand juries. In *Branzburg*, a reporter argued that a reporter's privilege was necessary because forcing reporters to testify before grand juries would result in confidential sources refusing to give information to reporters. In rejecting that argument, the Court said that the First Amendment does not guarantee the press a constitutional right of special access to information not available to the public generally.

2. **Search Warrants. [§ 888]**

    **Members of the media have no special protection from search warrants.** Acting pursuant to a valid search warrant, police officers may search the offices of a newspaper for evidence of a crime.

    *Zurcher v. Stanford Daily*, 436 U.S. 547 (1978). The Court rejected the argument that newspapers have any special protection against complying with validly authorized search warrants. It also rejected the argument that when a newsroom is to be searched, a subpoena duces tecum, rather than a search warrant, must be used (a subpoena duces tecum is less intrusive than a search warrant because it does not authorize a wholesale search of the newspaper premises). The Court allowed a search of the offices of the Stanford Daily, a student newspaper, for pictures involving assaults on police officers during a demonstration at the Stanford University Hospital.

The pictures were sought as a part of a police investigation of alleged crimes occurring at the demonstration.

3. **Deposition Testimony. [§ 889]**

   **Reporters do not have a special privilege that permits them to refuse to testify during a deposition.**

   *Herbert v. Lando*, 441 U.S. 153 (1979). The Court ruled that the producer of a television documentary has no privilege to refuse to answer questions during a deposition in a libel suit. A retired Army officer sued CBS, claiming that he was defamed during a documentary about the Vietnam war. During his deposition, the producer was asked questions about newsgathering and editorial conversations, the answers to which might have implicated the producer in the alleged defamation of the Army officer. It was necessary for the plaintiff officer, a public figure, to prove actual malice in the libel suit, making it imperative for him to inquire into the motivation of the producer. The Court reasoned that honoring legitimate discovery requests would not significantly discourage frank editorial discussions.

4. **Breach of Promise of Confidentiality. [§ 890]**

   **Members of the media have no special immunity from a civil suit against them for breach of a promise not to divulge the name of a source.**

   *Cohen v. Cowles Media, Co.*, 501 U.S. 663 (1991). The Court ruled that a newspaper, just like any other entity, may be liable for damages under state promissory estoppel law if the newspaper breaches a promise not to print the name of a confidential source of information. Cohen was a Republican who provided information about a Democratic candidate to a newspaper on the condition that his (Cohen's) name not be published. The paper published Cohen's name, and was sued on a promissory estoppel theory, based on Cohen's detrimental reliance on the reporter's promise not to publish his name. The Court said that generally applicable laws do not offend the First Amendment simply because their enforcement against the press has incidental effects on its ability to gather and report the news.

## E. ACCESS BY INDIVIDUALS TO THE MASS MEDIA. [§ 891]

A First Amendment issue arises as to when the government may require the media to disseminate certain messages. Be aware of the different treatment of print and electronic media. **With the broadcast media, there are only a finite**

# CHAPTER XVII

number of frequencies available to broadcast radio and television (spectrum scarcity), so some government regulation is permissible to enhance equality of access and fairness of the range of ideas expressed. A government may not, however, require newspapers to give free reply space to political candidates.

1. **Federally–Mandated Reply Time on Television or Radio. [§ 892]**

    **The federal government may require a radio or television station to give reply time to answer personal attacks or political editorials.** The "fairness doctrine" is designed to prevent powerful corporations or wealthy individuals from controlling access to a medium of communication.

    *Red Lion Broadcasting Co. v. FCC*, 395 U.S. 367 (1969). **The Court held that Congress and the FCC do not violate the First Amendment by requiring a radio or television station to give reply time to answer personal attacks or political editorials.** Focusing on the right of the public to receive information, the Court said that it is permissible for Congress and the FCC to try to ensure fairness in radio and television broadcasting because there were more persons who wanted to broadcast than there were frequencies available. Since the "marketplace" was limited, imposing fairness was constitutional.

2. **No Right to Reply in Newspapers. [§ 893]**

    **Unlike the broadcast media, a newspaper may not be forced to provide a "right to reply."**

    *Miami Herald Publishing Co. v. Tornillo*, 418 U.S. 241 (1974). Distinguishing the press from the broadcast media, the Court invalidated a Florida "right to reply" statute which required a newspaper to give free reply space to any candidate whose personal character or official record had been attacked by the newspaper. The Court cited the economic cost to the newspaper of having to provide free reply space, plus the intrusion into editorial decisions as reasons for its holding. **Electronic media are different from newspapers because they enjoy a government-granted monopoly through the granting of licenses by the Federal Communications Commission. Hence, a government-required right of reply is permissible for radio and television, but not for newspapers.**

3. **Paid Editorial Advertisements. [§ 894]**

    **Broadcasters may not be forced to accept paid editorial advertisements.**

    *CBS v. Democratic National Committee*, 412 U.S. 94 (1973). The Court held that neither federal statutes nor the First Amendment requires broadcasters to accept paid editorial advertisements. The Democratic National Committee and a group opposing the Vietnam war were turned down when they tried to buy time to broadcast their positions on issues that were clearly of public importance. The Court said that the public interest would best be served by leaving editorial decisions in the hands of the network editors, rather than at the mercy of the wealthiest applicants for broadcast time.

4. Help–Wanted Advertisements. [§ 895]

   **A city can prohibit gender-specific help-wanted advertisements.**

   *Pittsburgh Press Co. v. Pittsburgh Commission on Human Relations*, 413 U.S. 376 (1973). The Court upheld a city ordinance prohibiting newspapers from carrying "help-wanted" advertisements in gender-designated columns. The National Organization for Women, Inc., filed a complaint with the Pittsburgh Commission on Human Relations, alleging that the Pittsburgh Press Co. was violating a city ordinance by running help-wanted advertisements in columns designated "Jobs–Male Interest," "Jobs–Female Interest," and "Male–Female." Relying on commercial speech analysis, the Court said that gender discrimination in employment is illegal commercial activity, and therefore regulable under such an ordinance.

5. Cable Television Franchises. [§ 896]

   **A city's refusal to grant a cable television franchise implicates the First Amendment.**

   *Los Angeles v. Preferred Communications, Inc.*, 476 U.S. 488 (1986). The Court said that cable television partakes of some of the same aspects of speech and the communication of ideas as do newspapers and books. The Court remanded for an analysis of the First Amendment issues involved in a city's refusal to grant a franchise to a cable television company. The cable television company was refused the franchise because it failed to participate in an auction which would award the single cable franchise in the area. The company asserted that the auction process allowed the city to discriminate among applicants for the cable franchise, and that such discrimination violated the company's First Amendment rights.

## F. SPECIAL TAXES ON THE PRESS. [§ 897]

**Generally applicable laws, including taxes, may be imposed on the press. However, taxes which single out a certain segment of the press for discriminatory treatment will be invalidated.**

1. Discriminatory Taxes on the Press. [§ 898]

   **A state may not impose a tax which targets specific members of the press for taxation, but exempts all others.**

# CHAPTER XVII

*Minneapolis Star & Tribune Co. v. Minnesota Commissioner of Revenue*, 460 U.S. 575 (1983). The Court invalidated a Minnesota tax scheme which targeted a small number of newspapers within the state. Under the Minnesota law, periodic publications were exempt from sales and use taxes until 1971, when the state applied the use tax to the cost of paper and ink used in producing periodic publications. In 1974, the state exempted the first $100,000 of paper and ink used by a publication in any one year, leaving the full tax burden to be borne by larger publications. The effect of the law was to exempt smaller publications from any tax burden. The Court objected to the law singling out larger periodicals for discriminatory treatment through selective taxation.

2. Sales Tax. [§ 899]

**A state may impose a sales tax on the sale of cable television services while exempting receipts from newspaper sales and subscription magazine sales.**

*Leathers v. Medlock*, 499 U.S. 439 (1991). The Court upheld an Arkansas sales tax which applied to cable television services, but exempted receipts from the sale of magazines and newspapers. The Court upheld the tax against a First Amendment challenge because the tax was not intended to create, nor did it have the effect of creating, a danger of suppressing particular ideas, and it did not discriminate on the basis of the content of speech. The Court also pointed out that the tax was not directed at a small group of speakers, but affected about 100 suppliers of cable television services, as well as sales of all tangible personal property and a broad range of other services. The imposition of the tax to a broad range of activities led the Court to conclude that the tax does not single out the press for discriminatory treatment and thus does not jeopardize the media's role as a watchdog of government activity.

3. Crime Victim Compensation. [§ 900]

**The Court struck down a state law requiring that victims of crimes receive all proceeds from books written by the criminals who committed those crimes.**

*Simon & Schuster, Inc. v. New York State Crime Victims Board*, 502 U.S. 105 (1991). The Court invalidated New York's "Son of Sam" law which required that all money received by an accused or convicted criminal for the rights to the story depicting his or her crime be given to the victims of the crime. The law covered not only criminals who were convicted in court, but also those who voluntarily (in the story) admitted a crime for which there has been no prosecution. The Court found this law to be presumptively unconstitutional (because content-based), and therefore subject to strict scrutiny. The state had compelling interests in ensuring that victims of crime are compensated by those who harm them, and in ensuring that criminals do not profit from their crimes. The means were not narrowly tailored, however, because the law was overinclusive, reaching works like the Autobiography of Malcolm X, which describes crimes committed by the civil rights leader before he became a public figure.

## REVIEW PROBLEMS—FREEDOM OF THE PRESS

**PROBLEM 1.** Quenda Quinine is an investigative reporter for the Daily Bugle. Quenda has been writing a series of stories on drug trafficking in the City of Id. She has been subpoenaed to testify before a federal grand jury investigating the interstate drug trade. Quenda refuses to testify, citing the First Amendment. She claims that if she has to testify, her sources of information will dry up. Does Quenda have to testify?

**Answer:** Yes. There is no reporter's privilege which exempts a journalist from testifying before a grand jury. Members of the media have no greater rights or protections than the general public. See § 887 for further review.

**PROBLEM 2.** The State of Oz has a sales tax which is applied to the receipts from the sales of newspapers and magazines, but exempts receipts from the sale of cable television services. Is this tax constitutional?

**Answer:** Yes. This tax is not directed at the content of speech, simply at certain media of communication. As a result, this content-neutral tax is not designed to, nor will it suppress particular ideas. See § 899 for further review.

**PROBLEM 3.** Gregory Gridlock IV is a United States Senator from the State of Oz. Greg is running for re-election, and has been the target of some nasty, unflattering editorials in the Id Daily Bugle, a large metropolitan newspaper. Relying on a statute of the State of Oz which requires that newspapers give free reply space to targets of unfavorable editorials or articles, Greg demands space in the Daily Bugle to respond to the attacks on his character and record. Is the Oz statute constitutional?

**Answer:** No. While the Court has upheld required reply time on radio and television, it has struck down such a requirement as to newspapers. The main difference is that radio and television stations operate pursuant to a government monopoly, whereas newspapers are privately owned and operated. See §§ 892, 893 for further review.

# Chapter XVIII

# THE RELIGION CLAUSES OF THE FIRST AMENDMENT

## A. INTRODUCTION. [§ 901]

**The First Amendment says that, "Congress shall make no law respecting an establishment of religion, or prohibiting the free exercise thereof...." These guarantees also apply to the states.** While most books treat the religion clauses separately, remember that there is an unavoidable tension between them, and it may be necessary to consider and discuss both clauses when answering a question. For example, a tension between the clauses exists regarding prayer in public schools. On the one hand, it could be argued that allowing school prayer establishes religion. On the other hand, it could be argued that forbidding school prayer violates the free exercise rights of children who want to pray in school. When deciding a freedom of religion case, a court may be forced to choose between Establishment Clause and Free Exercise Clause principles.

## B. THE ESTABLISHMENT CLAUSE. [§ 902]

The First Amendment says that Congress may not pass any law respecting the establishment of religion. This provision has been incorporated to apply against the states. **The Establishment Clause certainly prohibits a government from setting up or recognizing an official state church. It also prohibits government from forcing people to go to church or refrain from going to church. After these two extreme cases, the question is how much and what kind of government aid to religion is constitutionally permissible.**

1. **Establishment Clause Tests. [§ 903]**

    The Court has set forth two tests to use in analyzing most Establishment Clause questions.

    a. **The *Lemon* Test. [§ 904]**

        The *Lemon* test (from *Lemon v. Kurtzman*, 403 U.S. 602 (1971)) is used when government acts to prefer or advance religion over non-religion. The *Lemon* test was modified in *Agostini v. Felton*, 521 U.S. 203 (1997) (§ 922).

The original *Lemon* test was composed of the following elements:

1. The law must have a secular legislative purpose;

2. Its principal or primary effect must be one that neither advance nor inhibits religion; and

3. It must not foster an excessive government entanglement with religion.

In *Agostini v. Felton*, the Court modified the *Lemon* test as follows:

1. The law must have a secular purpose; and

2. Its principal or primary effect must be one that neither advances nor inhibits religion (the entanglement inquiry is now just one criterion in determining a statute's effect).

The Court then set out three criteria for determining a statute's effect. Government aid has the effect of advancing religion if it:

(1) results in governmental indoctrination;

(2) defines its recipients by reference to religion; or

(3) creates an excessive entanglement between government and religion.

The Court also said that the same criteria should be reviewed to determine whether a government aid program constitutes an endorsement of religion. Under the endorsement test (first enunciated in *Lynch v. Donnelly*, 465 U.S. 668 (1984) (§ 941)), the question is whether a reasonable observer would perceive that the government is, by purpose or effect, endorsing religion.

b. **The *Larson* Test. [§ 905]**

**The *Larson* test (from *Larson v. Valente*, 456 U.S. 228 (1982)) is used when government prefers one religion over another. If that happens, the Court uses a compelling interest test to analyze the law.** Strict scrutiny is called for because preferring one religion over another goes to the heart of Establishment Clause concerns.

**STUDY TIP: THE "ADD OTHER STUFF" THEORY.** If a government does something that arguably advances religion, the way for the government to immunize its action from constitutional attack is to "add other stuff." (You will not see this terminology anywhere else—trust me.) The fancy way to say this is that **the government must secularize the program by making it apply to non-religious as well as religious beneficiaries, or it must include non-religious items or activities.** Want to have a constitutionally accepted Christmas display? Don't just set up a creche; add other stuff: Santa, presents, and lots of reindeer. Want to lend textbooks to parochial school students? Make sure public and non-sectarian private school students get them too. In other words, add other stuff. This is not a very elegant formulation, but it works in a great many cases.

2. **Religion and Schools. [§ 906]**

The Court has been sensitive to the fact that school children are very impressionable, and are a captive audience. As a result, they are very susceptible to religious indoctrination, so the Court has been careful to maintain a clear separation of church and state in public school cases.

a. **Financial Aid to Parochial School Students or Their Parents. [§ 907]**

**As a general matter, state financial aid to religious school students or parents will be upheld if the aid is also given to students or parents in non-religious schools.**

(1) **Transportation. [§ 908]**

**A state can reimburse parents for transportation to and from school.**

*Everson v. Board of Education*, 330 U.S. 1 (1947). The Court upheld a local ordinance which reimbursed parents for the cost of sending their children on buses to public, parochial, and non-religious private schools. The class of beneficiaries was made up of religious and non-religious school parents. The secular purpose of the law was to provide safe transportation to and from school.

(2) **Textbooks. [§ 909]**

**A state can loan textbooks to religious and private non-religious schools.**

# CHAPTER XVIII

*Board of Education v. Allen*, 392 U.S. 236 (1968). The Court upheld the State of New York's program of lending state-approved secular textbooks to all secondary school children, including those in religious schools. The class of beneficiaries included students in religious and non-religious schools.

### (3) Salaries. [§ 910]

**A state cannot supplement the salaries of religious school teachers.**

*Lemon v. Kurtzman*, 403 U.S. 602 (1971). The Court invalidated state statutes which supplemented salaries of teachers in parochial schools. Such supplements would result in excessive entanglement between government and religion because the religious school teachers would have to be monitored to make sure they did not sneak religion into the secular subjects that the government was paying them to teach. See § 921 for a statement of the original *Lemon* Tests.

### (4) Maintenance Grants, Tuition Reimbursement, and Tax Benefits. [§ 911]

**A State cannot grant money to nonpublic schools for maintenance and repair costs, cannot reimburse parents for tuition to nonpublic schools, and cannot grant tax benefits solely to parents who send their children to nonpublic schools.** Since most nonpublic schools are religious, all of these measures unconstitutionally advance religion.

In *Committee for Public Education and Religious Liberty v. Nyquist*, 413 U.S. 756 (1973), the Court struck down a New York law which provided financial assistance to nonpublic schools in the form of maintenance and repair grants, tuition reimbursement for parents, and tax benefits for parents. The Court held that, although the law was supported by legitimate secular purposes, all three measures failed to satisfy the second element of the *Lemon* test in that they had a primary effect of advancing religion. The maintenance and repair grants were a direct subsidy to nonpublic schools, with no mechanism by which to prevent the funds from being spent for the upkeep of facilities being used for religious purposes. The tuition reimbursement and tax benefit measures to parents operated to encourage and reward parents for sending children to nonpublic schools, most of which were religious.

# THE RELIGION CLAUSES OF THE FIRST AMENDMENT

(5) **Special School Districts for Religious Groups. [§ 912]**

**A state cannot create a special school district for a religious group.**

*Board of Education of Kiryas Joel Village School District v. Grumet*, 512 U.S. 687 (1994). The Court invalidated, as violative of the Establishment Clause, a New York statute which created a public school district whose boundaries coincided with those of a neighborhood occupied by a discrete religious group. The district was created to provide services to the handicapped children of the Satmar Hasidic sect (practitioners of a strict form of Judaism). These services had already been available in surrounding community schools, to which the Satmar Hasidic parents refused to send their children. The creation of a special school district for one religious group crossed the line from permissible accommodation to impermissible establishment. This law also created the problems of government preferring one sect over another and excessive entanglement between government and religion.

**STUDY TIP:** **Whenever the government gives financial aid that benefits religion, the grant or benefit will probably be constitutional if it goes to an individual who, in turn, makes the decision to direct the money or benefit to a religious institution.** The idea is that the person, not the government, is choosing to prefer religion. Also, the aid will probably be constitutional if both religious and non-religious entities are the ultimate beneficiaries.

(6) **Aid for Handicapped Students. [§ 913]**

**States may provide money grants for handicapped students for use at religious institutions.**

*Witters v. Washington Department of Services for the Blind*, 474 U.S. 481 (1986). The Court upheld a Washington state statute which provided funds for the education of blind students. Witters used his state grant to study at a Christian college to become a pastor, missionary, or youth director. The Court relied on the fact that this was a generally applicable aid program and any money that ultimately went to religious institutions did so as a result of the independent choices of private recipients.

# CHAPTER XVIII

(7) **Sign–Language Interpreter. [§ 914]**

**States may provide sign language interpreters for religious school students.**

*Zobrest v. Catalina Foothills School District*, 509 U.S. 1 (1993). The Court upheld the practice of a school district providing a sign-language interpreter to a profoundly deaf student who chose to attend a parochial school. The Court held that this was a neutral, generally applicable benefit, and that the choice to place Jamie Zobrest (and his interpreter) in a parochial school was made by the parents, not the state. Also, the program did not relieve the parochial school of any cost it would otherwise have borne in educating Jamie Zobrest.

(8) **Public School Voucher Program. [§ 915]**

**A state school voucher program that offers tuition aid to parents to send their children to secular or religious private schools passes Establishment Clause muster because it is neutral with respect to religion, and any aid flowing to religious institutions is the result of private, independent choices of parents of schoolchildren.**

*Zelman v. Simmons–Harris*, 536 U.S. 639 (2002). Ohio setup a voucher program for families in any Ohio school district that is under state control pursuant to a federal court order. Tuition aid is given to parents, who decide to spend the money at secular or religious private schools of their choice. The Court upheld the program against an Establishment Clause challenge on the basis that it had a valid secular purpose (providing educational aid to poor children in failing public school systems), and that it did not have the primary effect of advancing religion. A five-person majority of the Court focused on the fact that the program was neutral with respect to religion and that a broad class of citizens were its beneficiaries. The Court also emphasized that any aid that ultimately flowed to religious institutions was the result of truly private, independent choices made by the parents. Based on the factors of neutrality and indirection (giving the money to private parties who decide where to spend it), the Court concluded that no reasonable observer would think that such a program reflected government endorsement of religion.

# THE RELIGION CLAUSES OF THE FIRST AMENDMENT

b. **Released Time, Religious Instruction in Public Schools, and Enrichment Classes in Religious Schools. [§ 916]**

Religious instruction in public school buildings violates the Establishment Clause because it has the effect of endorsing religion, and it creates a symbolic union between church and state.

(1) **Religious Instruction in Public School Buildings. [§ 917]**
Religious teachers cannot hold classes in a public school building.

*McCollum v. Board of Education*, 333 U.S. 203 (1948). The Court invalidated a released-time program in which religious teachers held classes in the public school building. Students who were not excused for religious study remained in the classroom. The Court objected to the use of the public building for religious purposes, and to the public school providing a captive audience from which the religious instructors could draw their students.

(2) **Released–Time. [§ 918]**

Public school students can leave school to go to religious education programs conducted in religious centers.

*Zorach v. Clauson*, 343 U.S. 306 (1952). The Court upheld a New York City program which allowed public school students to leave the school building to go to religious centers for instruction or devotional exercises. The public schools incurred no costs, unlike *McCollum* (previous case).

(3) **Public School Teachers in Religious Schools. [§ 919]**

**Public school teachers cannot teach enrichment classes in religious schools.** Public school teachers can provide supplemental remedial instruction on the premises of religious schools if safeguards are in place to prevent the endorsement of religion.

In two earlier cases, the Court invalidated programs in which public employees taught and provided guidance services on the premises of religious schools.

(a) **Grand Rapids School District v. Ball, 473 U.S. 373 (1985). [§ 920]**

The Court invalidated a program in which enrichment classes and adult education classes were taught by public

# CHAPTER XVIII

school teachers in parochial school classrooms that were leased to the public school system. The parochial school classrooms were secularized by removing all religious symbols and posting a sign declaring the room to be a public school classroom. The Court said this arrangement violated the Establishment Clause because it had a primary effect of advancing religion, and it created a "symbolic union" between the school district and the religious schools.

(b) **Aguilar v. Felton, 473 U.S. 402 (1985). [§ 921]**

The Court invalidated a New York City program which used federal funds to pay the salaries of public employees who taught and provided guidance services in parochial schools. The program was designed to aid educationally deprived children from low-income families. The Court said this program violated the excessive entanglement prong of *Lemon*.

(c) **Agostini v. Felton, 521 U.S. 203 (1997). [§ 922]**

The court reopened the *Aguilar* case and overruled it and the part of *Ball* allowing enrichment classes in parochial schools. The Court in *Agostini* held that a federally funded program providing supplemental remedial instruction to disadvantaged students on a neutral basis does not violate the Establishment Clause, even when the instruction is given in religious schools by government employees. To be constitutional, such a program must be secular, neutral, and non-ideological, and must supplement (not supplant) services already provided by the religious schools.

In *Agostini*, the Court modified the *Lemon* test as follows:

    1. The law must have a secular purpose; and

    2. Its principal or primary effect must be one that neither advances nor inhibits religion (the entanglement inquiry is now just one criterion in determining a statute's effect).

The Court then set out three criteria for determining a statute's effect. Government aid has the effect of advancing religion if it:

    (1) results in governmental indoctrination;

(2) defines its recipients by reference to religion; or

(3) creates an excessive entanglement between government and religion.

The Court also said that the same criteria should be reviewed to determine whether a government aid program constitutes an endorsement of religion. Under the endorsement test (first enunciated in *Lynch v. Donnelly*, 465 U.S. 668 (1984) (§ 941)), the question is whether a reasonable observer would perceive that the government is, by purpose or effect, endorsing religion.

(4) **Mitchell v. Helms**, 530 U.S. 793 (2000) (§ 923). The Court upheld a federal school aid program under which the federal government distributes funds to state and local government agencies, which in turn lend educational materials and equipment to public and private (including religious) schools. Justice Thomas, writing for a plurality, applied the modified *Lemon* test of *Agostini* (previous cases) and found that there is no constitutional violation when aid is allocated on the basis of neutral, secular criteria that neither favor nor disfavor religion, and is made available to both religious and secular beneficiaries on a nondiscriminatory basis. Justice Thomas focused on the facts that the aid was offered to a broad range of groups or persons without regard to their religion, and that any aid to a religious institution results from the genuinely independent and private choices of individual parents. The statute required that any aid be "secular, neutral, and nonideological." Justice O'Connor, joined by Justice Breyer concurred in the judgment, also using the *Agostini* version of the *Lemon* test, but disagreeing with what Justice O'Connor considered to be the plurality's inordinate emphasis on the neutrality principle (arguing that the plurality's treatment of neutrality came close to assigning that factor singular importance in future Establishment Clause cases).

c. **Prohibiting the Teaching of Evolution and the Teaching of Creation Science. [§ 924]**

**A state may not prohibit the teaching of evolution in public schools, nor may it require the teaching of creation science.**

# CHAPTER XVIII

(1) **Teaching of Evolution. [§ 925]**

**State law cannot prohibit the teaching of evolution in public schools.**

*Epperson v. Arkansas*, 393 U.S. 97 (1968). The Court invalidated an Arkansas statute which prohibited teaching in public schools and universities the theory that "mankind ascended or descended from a lower order of animals." The Court said the law was purely motivated by the religious purpose of advancing fundamentalist Christian beliefs.

(2) **Teaching of Creation Science. [§ 926]**

**State law cannot require the teaching of creation science whenever evolution is taught.**

*Edwards v. Aguillard*, 482 U.S. 578 (1987). The Court invalidated a Louisiana statute which prohibited public schools from teaching the theory of evolution unless they also taught creation science. Ruling that the law had no secular purpose, the Court rejected the state's argument that it was trying to advance academic freedom by requiring a balanced treatment of the beginning of humankind.

d. **Posting the Ten Commandments in Public Schools. [§ 927]**

**A state may not require the posting of the Ten Commandments in public school classrooms.**

*Stone v. Graham*, 449 U.S. 39 (1980). The Court invalidated a Kentucky statute requiring the posting of the Ten Commandments in each public classroom in the state, even though the poster had to carry the disclaimer that the secular application of the Ten Commandments is seen in its adoption as the fundamental legal code of Western civilization and the Common Law of the United States. The Court said there was no secular purpose underlying the law.

e. **Ten Commandments Outside the School Context. [§ 928]**

**The Court has been inconsistent in ruling on Ten Commandments displays on government property other than schools.**

*Van Orden v. Perry*, 545 U.S. 677 (2005). The Court ruled that a display of a monument inscribed with the Ten Commandments on the grounds of the Texas State Capitol does not violate the Establishment

Clause. The six-foot high monument, which stands among twenty-one historical markers and seventeen monuments, has stood on the Capitol grounds since 1961, when it was presented to the State of Texas by the Fraternal Order of Eagles, a national social, civic, and patriotic organization. Chief Justice Rehnquist, writing for himself and three other Justices, rejects the *Lemon* test as not useful for dealing with this sort of passive monument on the Capitol grounds. Instead, he focuses on the monument's nature and the Nation's history. According to Chief Justice Rehnquist, Texas' display of the Ten Commandments is simply an example of an unbroken history in our country of official acknowledgment of religion's role in American life. While the Ten Commandments are undeniably religious, they also have a historical meaning. When considering all the monuments and markers together, what Texas has done is treated them as representing several strands in the state's political and legal history. The Chief Justice also says that Texas' placement of the Commandments on the Capitol grounds is a much more passive use of those texts than in *Stone v. Graham* (§ 940), where the Ten Commandments confronted elementary school students every school day. Justice Breyer concurs in the judgment, saying that none of the Court's various Establishment Clause test applies, but that this case calls for the exercise of legal judgment. Because of the fact-intensive nature of these cases, Justice Breyer inquires into the context and history of this particular use of the Ten Commandments. He concludes that the Commandments convey a secular moral message about proper standards of social conduct, and a message about the historic relationship between there standards and the law. According to Justice Breyer, the circumstances of this display result in the Commandments conveying a predominately secular message. Justice Breyer also emphasizes the fact that the monument went unchallenged for forty years, indicating that few, if any, people understood it as establishing religion.

*Pleasant Grove City v. Summum*, 129 S.Ct. 1125 (2009). The Court ruled that the Free Speech Clause of the first Amendment is not violated by a city's rejection of a request by a religious group to erect a monument in a city park which already contains a number of monuments, including the Ten Commandments. Pioneer Park is a public park located in Pleasant Grove, Utah. The park contains 15 displays, 11 of which were donated by private entities. These displays include a Ten Commandments monument donated by the Fraternal Order of Eagles in 1971. Summum is a religious organization, founded in 1975, which twice requested permission to erect a monument in the park which would contain the "Seven Aphorisms of

# CHAPTER XVIII

Summum." This proposed monument would be similar in size and nature to the Ten Commandments monument. The City denied the requests. The Court held that placement of a permanent monument in a public park is a form of government speech, and is not subject to scrutiny under the Free Speech Clause. The Court distinguished between government regulation of private speech (subject to Free Speech Clause analysis) and government speech (free from Free Speech Clause analysis). The Court saw no distinction between monuments that are government-commissioned and government-financed and monuments that are privately financed and donated. The Court opined that, in the area of government speech, a city is entitled to say what it wishes, and to select the views it wants to express.

*McCreary County v. ACLU*, 545 U.S. 844 (2005). The Court affirmed the upholding of a preliminary injunction against two Kentucky counties that posted large, readily visible copies of the Ten Commandments in their courthouses. In a 5–4 ruling, the Court reaffirmed the first prong of the *Lemon* test (§ 921), and held that when a government acts with the predominantpurpose of advancing religion, it violates the central Establishment Clause value of official religious neutrality. To determine whether a reasonable observer would conclude that the government had no secular purpose underlying its action, the Court focused on the history, context, and evolution of the displays. The counties went through three versions of the display, with the Court finding that a secular purpose was lacking in each of them. First, the counties posted just the Ten Commandments in each courthouse. After being sued by the ACLU under 42 U.S.C. § 1983, the counties adopted resolutions calling for more extensive exhibits. These resolutions referred to the State legislature's acknowledgement of Christ as the "Prince of Ethics." These second displays included eight smaller historical documents containing religious references as their sole common element (i.e., the Declaration of Independence's "endowed by their Creator" passage). After the District Court found that neither of these two displays had a secular purpose, the counties revised the display one more time. With no new resolutions, and without repealing the previous resolutions, the counties put up nine framed documents of equal size. The Ten Commandments display was expanded to include an explanation that they have profoundly influenced the formation of Western legal thought and this Nation. The Court found that the counties failed in their attempts to secularize the display, and also found that no reasonable observer would conclude that, given its history and evolution, the third version of the display reflected anything but a religious purpose.

f. School Prayer, Moments of Silence, and Invocations at Graduation. [§ 929]

**The Court has consistently invalidated any form of government sponsored or coerced prayer in public schools.**

(1) Official School Prayer. [§ 930]

**A state cannot require that an official school prayer be said in public school classrooms.**

*Engel v. Vitale*, 370 U.S. 421 (1962). The Court invalidated the practice of a school board requiring a non-denominational prayer to be said in public school classrooms each day. The fact that the prayer was written by the New York Board of Regents was tantamount to an establishment of an official state religion.

(2) Minute of Silence. [§ 931]

**States may not require a minute of silence in public schools for meditation or voluntary prayer if the sole purpose is to endorse religion.**

*Wallace v. Jaffree*, 472 U.S. 38 (1985). The Court invalidated an Alabama law which authorized a minute of silence in public schools for meditation or voluntary prayer. This law ran afoul of the purpose prong of *Lemon* because the state's sole purpose was to endorse religion.

(3) Graduation Ceremonies. [§ 932]

**Clergy cannot offer the invocation and benediction at graduation ceremonies for junior and senior high school.**

*Lee v. Weisman*, 505 U.S. 577 (1992). The Court invalidated the practice of public school principals inviting members of the clergy to offer invocation and benediction prayers at junior high and high school graduations. The principals also provided the clergy with a pamphlet containing guidelines on the content of the prayers to be given. The Court ruled that government involvement with religious activity was so pervasive as to create a state-sponsored and state-directed religious exercise in the public schools. The Court alluded to the subtle coercion that exists in such a setting, and said that a student attending graduation could not avoid the fact or appearance of participation in the religious exercise.

# CHAPTER XVIII

(4) **Legislative Sessions. [§ 933]**

**A chaplain can open a legislative session with a prayer.**

*Marsh v. Chambers*, 463 U.S. 783 (1983). The Court upheld the practice of a paid chaplain opening each session of the Nebraska legislature with a prayer. The Court did not rely on *Lemon*, but used a historical analysis, focusing on the fact that when Congress passed the First Amendment, a member of the clergy opened the session with a prayer. The difference between *Marsh* and *Weisman* (previous case) is that the legislators are adults who voted to have the chaplain, whereas the graduates are minors who had the prayer imposed on them by the school district.

(5) **Student–Initiated, Student–Led Prayer at Football Games. [§ 934]**

**It is unconstitutional for a public school district to allow student-initiated, student-led prayers at high school football games.**

*Sante Fe Independent School District v. Doe*, 530 U.S. 290 (2000). Applying the principles of *Lee v. Weisman* (above), the court struck down as violative of the Establishment Clause a public school district policy which authorized high school students to vote on whether to have a student deliver an invocation before the high school football games. The Court ruled that this was the speech of the school district (not private speech in a public forum) and as such constituted both perceived and actual endorsement of religion. The Court emphasized that the majoritarian process used by the district guarantees that speakers representing minority religions will never be chosen to deliver the invocation, and that their view will effectively be silenced. In accord with *Lee*, the Court reasoned that students at a high school football game are, in reality, coerced into a religious setting because of the social pressure to attend football games or because of participation in the football team, the band, or the cheerleading squad.

(6) **School District Policy Requiring Willing Students to Recite the Pledge of Allegiance Containing the Words "Under God." [§ 935]**

**A non-custodial parent does not have third-party standing to challenge the constitutionality of requiring public school students to recite the Pledge of Allegiance.**

# THE RELIGION CLAUSES OF THE FIRST AMENDMENT

*In Elk Grove Unified School District v. Newdow*, 542 U.S. 1 (2004), a case in which an atheist father challenged the constitutionality of the words "under God" in the Pledge of Allegiance, the Court ruled that the father did not have standing to assert the Establishment Clause rights of his daughter. The Court relied on the fact that California domestic relations law deprives Newdow of the right to sue as his daughter's next friend, and that a state family court gave sole legal custody to the girl's mother. Expressing a reluctance to intervene in state domestic relations law, the Court refused to grant third-party standing to the father to pursue a claim which was contrary to the wishes of the custodial parent and potentially injurious to the daughter.

Chief Justice Rehnquist, joined by Justice O'Connor, would have found standing, and ruled on the merits that requiring schoolchildren to recite the Pledge of Allegiance did not violate the Establishment Clause. Chief Justice Rehnquist said that phrase "under God" in the Pledge is in no sense a prayer, nor an endorsement of any religion, but simply a patriotic exercise designed to foster national unity. He compared the Pledge to the motto "In God We Trust" on coins, and to the words "God save the United States and this honorable Court" used to open sessions of the Supreme Court. Justice O'Connor referred to the works in the Pledge as "ceremonial deism," and said that "under God" would pass the *Lemon* analysis (§ 921), because no reasonable observer would perceive the words as an endorsement of any specific religion, or even of religion over non-religion.

g. **Government Aid to Colleges and Universities. [§ 936]**

Government financial aid to church-affiliated colleges and universities is analyzed under the *Lemon* standards. **The Court is usually willing to assume a secular purpose (educating as many students as possible), and there will not be a primary effect of advancing religion if there is a guarantee by the institution that the money will be used only for secular purposes.**

(1) Construction Grants. [§ 937]

**It is constitutional for the government to offer construction grants to church-related colleges or universities for facilities to be used for non-sectarian instruction.**

*Tilton v. Richardson*, 403 U.S. 672 (1971). The Court upheld federal construction grants to church-related colleges and universities for academic facilities that would be used only for nonsectarian instruction. The Court invalidated a provision of the law that would have allowed the buildings to be used for religious purposes after 20 years. In so holding, the Court noted that college students are far less impressionable than students in primary and secondary schools.

### (2) Issuance of Revenue Bonds. [§ 938]

**States may enact bond programs which will allow religious institutions to issue revenue bonds for the construction of college or university buildings.**

*Hunt v. McNair*, 413 U.S. 734 (1973). The Court upheld a South Carolina construction assistance program which allowed colleges and universities to issue revenue bonds for the construction of buildings. The Court said that the primary effect prong of *Lemon* would be violated if aid went to an institution where religion thoroughly permeated all aspects of the educational program, or if the aid were used to fund a specifically religious activity.

### (3) State Grants to Religious Colleges. [§ 939]

**State grants to religious colleges are constitutional if not used for religious purposes.**

*Roemer v. Board of Public Works*, 426 U.S. 736 (1976). The Court upheld a Maryland program which gave annual grants to religious colleges and universities, based on the number of full-time students enrolled each year. Under the grant system, the state would ensure that the institution was not pervasively religious, and that the money would not be used for religious purposes.

## 3. Religious Symbols During the Holiday Season. [§ 940]

When does government cross the line between merely recognizing Christmas as a traditional, historical holiday celebrated by a great many people, and endorsing Christmas as an official government holiday? Recognition of the "winter-holiday season" is constitutional, but endorsing a particular religious holy day is not. **Government-sponsored Christmas displays will be constitutional if they are sufficiently secular to avoid the appearance of the government endorsing religion.** These cases raise the burning constitutional question of "How many reindeer do you need to save the display from constitutional attack?"

# THE RELIGION CLAUSES OF THE FIRST AMENDMENT

    a. **Holiday Displays Including Non–Religious Symbols. [§ 941]**

    **A Christmas holiday display will be deemed constitutional if it is secularized by the inclusion of non-religious symbols.**

    *Lynch v. Donnelly*, 465 U.S. 668 (1984). The Court held that it did not violate the Establishment Clause for a city to erect a Christmas display during the Christmas holiday season. The display included a creche with Jesus, Mary, and Joseph, along with reindeer, Santa, a Christmas tree, a clown, a teddy bear, and other festive stuff. The Court said that the display was simply a recognition of the winter holiday season, and that the inclusion of the creche did not "taint" the rest of the exhibit with excessive religiosity. (Is this the "fruit of the religious tree" doctrine?).

    b. **Holiday Displays With Only Religious Symbols. [§ 942]**

    **A Christmas holiday display will be deemed unconstitutional if it is composed solely of religious symbols.**

    *County of Allegheny v. ACLU*, 492 U.S. 573 (1989). The Court dealt with two holiday displays. It said that the Establishment Clause was violated when a creche, along with animals, shepherds, wise men, and an angel with a banner proclaiming "Gloria in Excelsis Deo," were placed on the grand staircase of the Allegheny County Courthouse. There was nothing to detract from the religious message of the display (they didn't "add other stuff"), so the Court said this was government endorsement of religion.

    The Court upheld another display which included a 45–foot Christmas tree at the center of the display, and an 18–foot menorah at the side. The Court's premise was that a Christmas tree is not a religious symbol, so the relative sizes and placements of the two symbols made this a non-religious display. If it had been a 45–foot menorah and an 18–foot Christmas tree, the county would have been in trouble. (A U.S. Court of Appeals judge later said that this kind of analysis was better suited to an interior decorator than a judge.)

4. **Tax Exemptions and Deductions for Religious Organizations. [§ 943]**

**State tax exemptions and deductions will be constitutional if both religious and non-religious taxpayers are able to claim them.**

    a. **State Tax Exemptions. [§ 944]**

    **State tax exemptions for religious, charitable, and educational institutions do not violate the establishment clause.**

*Walz v. Tax Commission*, 397 U.S. 664 (1970). The Court upheld a state tax exemption for property used for religious, educational, or charitable purposes. The state merely included churches within a broad class of property owned by non-profit, quasi-public corporations. Any indirect financial benefit to churches was not enough to violate Establishment Clause standards.

b. **State Tax Deductions for Educational Expenses. [§ 945]**

**State tax deductions for expenses of educating children are constitutional.**

*Mueller v. Allen*, 463 U.S. 388 (1983). The Court upheld a state tax deduction for certain expenses incurred by taxpayers in educating their children. Applying *Lemon*, the Court found a secular purpose of educating all children in the state. There was no primary effect of advancing religion because taxpayers with children in non-sectarian private and public schools also benefited. Taking a deduction involved only minimal entanglement (no ongoing relationship).

5. **Delegation of Sovereign Power to a Church. [§ 946]**

**A state may not delegate a sovereign function to a church.** Specifically, a state may not give to a church the power to veto the granting of a liquor license.

*Larkin v. Grendel's Den*, 459 U.S. 116 (1982). The Court invalidated a Massachusetts law which gave churches and schools the power to veto the grant of a liquor license to any establishment within 500 feet of the church or school. The Court said that a government cannot delegate discretionary governmental powers to religious bodies.

6. **Resolving Church Disputes on the Basis of Church Doctrine. [§ 947]**

**Civil courts may not decide disputes on the basis of religious doctrine. A civil court may apply "neutral principles" of secular law to decide matters such as property or trust disputes, but it must not entangle itself with religious doctrine.** To do so would implicate both the Free Exercise and Establishment Clauses.

*Jones v. Wolf*, 443 U.S. 595 (1979). The Court vacated a judgment of the Georgia Supreme Court involving a property dispute between factions of a Presbyterian church. The Court was not sure whether the state court relied solely on "neutral principles" of secular law in deciding the case. The Court reaffirmed that the First Amendment prohibits civil courts from

# THE RELIGION CLAUSES OF THE FIRST AMENDMENT

resolving church property disputes on the basis of religious doctrine and practice, and that civil courts should defer to the resolution of issues of religious doctrine by the authoritative ecclesiastical body of the church. Given these limitations, a state may adopt any method of settling church property disputes, so long as it involves no consideration of doctrinal matters.

7. **Grants to Religious Social Welfare Agencies. [§ 948]**

    **Religious entities (such as religious social-welfare agencies) may be recipients of governmental aid if they are not pervasively religious, and are among a group of beneficiaries which includes non-religious institutions.**

    *Bowen v. Kendrick*, 487 U.S. 589 (1988). The Court upheld a federal grant program which provided funding for services relating to adolescent sexuality and pregnancy. Recipients of the funds included public and private social welfare agencies including religious ones. The Court found a clearly secular purpose (helping adolescents through troubled times), and that there was no primary effect of advancing religion because the religious social welfare agencies were not pervasively sectarian institutions.

8. **Establishment Clause Issues in a Designated Public Forum. [§ 949]**

    **If a government opens its property to a wide range of speakers, it does not violate the Establishment Clause to allow religious speakers to use the property.** As a result, a government may not exclude religious speakers from a public forum.

    > **STUDY TIP:** Be aware of how the Establishment Clause argument gets raised here. A government is excluding speakers from a forum based on the content of their speech. This requires strict scrutiny. The government says its compelling interest is to avoid the establishment of religion that would result from allowing the religious group to speak. The Court applies *Lemon* to see if inclusion of religious speakers would establish religion. It does not, so the government has no compelling interest in excluding the religious speakers.

    a. **Religious Student Groups in a University. [§ 950]**

        **A state university may not exclude a religious student group from a designated public forum.**

        *Widmar v. Vincent*, 454 U.S. 263 (1981). The Court ruled that a state university could not exclude religious groups from using its facilities once the university opened its rooms to registered student groups for speech purposes. The Court rejected the argument that this content-based exclusion was justified by the state's interest in avoiding the establishment of religion that would result from allowing the religious group to speak. Simply permitting the religious groups to speak, along with numerous other student groups, does not equal endorsement or establishment of religion.

b. **Religious Student Groups in High School. [§ 951]**

**Public schools may not exclude a religious student group from a designated public forum.**

*Board of Education v. Mergens*, 496 U.S. 226 (1990). The Court upheld the federal Equal Access Act, which prohibits public schools receiving federal funds from making content-based exclusions of students from school facilities which have been opened for speech purposes. The school allowed a number of non-curricular groups to use the facilities, but refused to allow the Christian Club to use a room. Following *Widmar* (previous case), the Court said that there is no establishment of religion effected by including the Christian Club along with other student organizations.

c. **Religious Speakers. [§ 952]**

**A school may not exclude religious speakers from a designated public forum open to the public.**

*Lamb's Chapel v. Center Moriches Union Free School District*, 508 U.S. 384 (1993). The Court ruled that a school which opened its facilities to the general public for speech purposes could not deny a church group access to the school property. The school had designated its property as a limited forum, but had denied access to the religious group because of the content of its speech. As in *Widmar*, the Court rejected the argument that the school had a compelling interest in avoiding the establishment of religion that would result from allowing the religious group to use the facilities. Inclusion of religious speakers along with numerous others does not violate the Establishment Clause.

d. **Religious Student Publications. [§ 953]**

**A school may not deny funding to a religious student publication if it funds other student journals.**

*Rosenberger v. Rector and Visitors of the University of Virginia*, 515 U.S. 819 (1995). The Court ruled that the University of Virginia could not deny funding for the publication of a recognized student group's journal on the basis that the journal was religious in content. The university set up a program under which payments are made from a Student Activities Fund for the publication of student journals and magazines. When a religious student group, otherwise eligible for funding, applied for funding of its newspaper, Wide Awake: A Christian Perspective at the University of Virginia, the university turned them down, asserting that to fund a religious student publication would violate the Establishment Clause. The Court, relying on *Widmar* (See § 950) and *Lamb's Chapel*, said that a university does not establish religion by granting access to its facilities to a wide spectrum of student groups, even if some of them are religious. The Court saw no difference between a university granting access to its facilities (*Widmar*) and a university funding the publication of student journals; both cases involved the university creating a limited forum for the purpose of enhancing diversity of student expression.

e. **Display of Religious Symbols. [§ 954]**

**A state may not prohibit a private unattended display of a religious symbol in a public forum.**

*Capital Square Review and Advisory Board v. Pinette*, 515 U.S. 753 (1995). The Court ruled that a private, unattended display of a religious symbol in a public forum does not violate the Establishment Clause. In *Pinette*, the Ku Klux Klan applied to the Columbus, Ohio Capitol Square Review and Advisory Board for permission to place an unattended cross on the capitol square during the 1993 Christmas season. The Board denied the Klan permission to use the square which, under Ohio law, is a public forum. The Board asserted that it had a compelling interest in avoiding the establishment of religion which, it claimed, would occur if it permitted the Klan to erect a cross in the capitol square. The Court, relying on *Widmar* (See § 950), ruled that it would not establish religion to allow an unattended religious symbol to be placed in a public forum that is generally open to the public for speech purposes. There was not government sponsorship or endorsement of religion when there was simply private religious expressions and the Klan had to go through the same application process as any other potential user of the capitol square.

9. **Government Preference for One Religion Over Another. [§ 955]**

**When a government takes action which prefers one religious group over another, the court uses the strict scrutiny, compelling interest balancing test.**

# CHAPTER XVIII

*Larson v. Valente*, 456 U.S. 228 (1982). The Court invalidated a Minnesota law which imposed reporting and registration requirements only on those religious organizations that solicit more than fifty percent of their funds from nonmembers. The result of the law was to exempt mainstream religions with affiliated branches (like parishes) from the requirements, while burdening religions such as the Unification Church (which do not have organized affiliates). The Court applied strict scrutiny to this denominational preference, finding that the law was not narrowly tailored to any compelling government interest. **The Court noted that preference for some religions over others not only violates the Establishment Clause, but burdens the religious practices of other religions, creating a free exercise problem.**

10. **Religious Land Use and Institutionalized Persons Act. [§ 956]**

    **Congress may protect the religious rights of prisoners without violating the Establishment Clause.**

    *Cutter v. Wilkinson*, 544 U.S. 709 (2005). In a unanimous decision, the Court held that the Religious Land Use and Institutionalized Persons Act of 2000 (RLUIPA) does not violate the Establishment Clause. When prison inmates brought a claim against the Ohio Department of Rehabilitation and Correction asserting that Ohio prison officials failed to accommodate their religious exercise in violation of RLUIPA, the respondents mounted a facial challenge to RLUIPA, claiming that the Act improperly advances religion and violates the Establishment Clause. The Court held that RLUIPA—which prohibits government from substantially burdening the religious exercise of institutionalized persons unless the burden furthers a compelling governmental interest by the least restrictive means—does not exceed permissible limits of government accommodation of religion. While upholding the constitutionality of RLUIPA, the Court noted that the Act does not render religious accommodation more important than an institution's need to maintain order and safety.

## C. THE FREE EXERCISE CLAUSE. [§ 957]

**The First Amendment says that Congress shall make no law abridging the free exercise of religion. This is a fundamental right which applies against the states.** Government may never regulate religious beliefs, just actions. Government may not regulate actions because they are religious; the impact on religion must be incidental to some legitimate governmental goal. Government may never inquire into the truth of a religious belief, but it may examine the sincerity with which a person claims to hold a religious belief.

1. **Overview of Free Exercise Analysis. [§ 958]**

    The Court has given us specific methods of analysis to use in different kinds of Free Exercise cases. **To identify the appropriate analysis, you** must be very careful about two factors. First, is the law generally applicable? Laws that provide for individualized hearings or that have exceptions or exemptions built in (for example, apply only to certain religious groups) are not generally applicable. Second, is the challenge to the law based solely on the Free Exercise Clause, or on the Free Exercise Clause plus some other constitutional right such as freedom of speech, or the right to direct the education of your children? Here is how the Court will analyze Free Exercise cases under constitutional principles.

a. **Generally Applicable Laws. [§ 959]**

   Laws that apply equally to all persons (such as a criminal statute) are considered to be generally applicable.

   (1) **Challenges Based Solely on the Free Exercise Clause.**

   If a government has passed a generally applicable law, and the plaintiff's challenge to the law is based solely on the Free Exercise Clause, the law is good. There is no heightened scrutiny used.

   (2) **Challenges Based on the Free Exercise Clause Plus Some Other Constitutional Right.**

   If a government has passed a generally applicable law, and the plaintiff's challenge to the law is based on the Free Exercise Clause and some other constitutional right (free speech, rearing your children), strict scrutiny applies, and the government must show that the law is narrowly tailored to achieve a compelling government interest.

b. **Laws That Are Not Generally Applicable. [§ 960]**

   Laws that provide for individualized hearings or that have exceptions or exemptions built in are not generally applicable.

   **If a government has passed a law that is not generally applicable, strict scrutiny applies, and the government must show that the law is narrowly tailored to achieve a compelling government interest.** Look for two kinds of laws that are not generally applicable: unemployment compensation laws that provide individualized hearings on eligibility (*Sherbert, Hobbie* and *Thomas* cases, §§ 970, 971, 972); and laws which have built-in exceptions or exemptions (*Church of the Lukumi Babalu Aye* case, § 974).

c. **Types of Free Exercise Clause Analysis. [§ 961]**

   *Employment Division v. Smith*, 494 U.S. 872 (1990) is the leading Free Exercise case. Justice Scalia, for the Court, set forth the rules for the different kinds of cases.

# CHAPTER XVIII

In *Smith*, the Court upheld a state's power to criminalize the use of peyote, even when used by Native Americans as an essential part of their religion. Oregon had a generally applicable drug law (all uses of certain drugs were prohibited) which was challenged solely on the basis that it violated the Free Exercise rights of two drug counselors who had been fired for peyote use and then denied unemployment compensation because they were discharged for illegal conduct. The Court first said that a government may not regulate religious beliefs. It then set forth the rule that **a generally applicable law which has only an incidental effect of burdening religion does not offend the Free Exercise Clause. No heightened scrutiny is called for in such a case.**

In direct response to the *Smith* decision, Congress passed the Religious Freedom Restoration Act of 1993 Under the Act, a government could not substantially burden a person's free exercise of religion unless it had a compelling reason for the law and had chosen the least restrictive means of achieving that goal. The Religious Freedom Restoration Act was invalidated by the Court in *Boerne v. Flores*, 521 U.S. 507 (1997).

In *Boerne*, the Court by a 6–3 vote, held that the Religious Freedom Restoration Act (RFRA) exceeded Congress' enforcement power under § 5 of the Fourteenth Amendment. In *Boerne*, the Catholic Archbishop of San Antonio applied for a building permit to enlarge a church. The local zoning authorities denied the permit on the basis of a historic preservation ordinance which the zoning authorities said applied to the church. The Archbishop challenged the zoning ordinance, relying in part on RFRA, which would require the city to show a compelling reason for the permit denial and that it had chosen the least restrictive means to achieve the purposes of the historic preservation ordinance. RFRA applied to any branch of federal or state government, to all federal or state officials, and to all federal or state laws. § 5 of the Fourteenth Amendment gives Congress the power to enforce the equal protection and due process guarantee of the Fourteenth Amendment. The Court said that Congress does not have the power to define substantive rights under the Fourteenth Amendment; it only has the power to remedy violations of rights that have been defined by the Court under its power to interpret the Constitution. For Congress to define (not simply protect) substantive rights would violate separation-of-powers principles. The Court only struck down the application of RFRA to state and local governments. Since this was a Fourteenth Amendment case, the constitutionality of RFRA in relation to the federal government is still an open question.

*Gonzales v. O Centro Espirita Beneficente Uniao do Vegetal*, 546 U.S. 418 (2006). This case dealt with an application of the Religious Freedom Restoration Act (RFRA) to the federal government. Whereas Boerne (previous case) involved a statutory attempt by Congress to limit states under § 5 of the 14th Amendment, this case focused on whether Congress, through RFRA, could prohibit the federal government from substantially burdening a person's free exercise of religion, except when the government can show that its law furthers a compelling interest and is the least restrictive means of furthering that interest. Member of the respondent church (UDV) receive communion by drinking hoasca, a hallucinogenic tea brewed from plants unique to the Amazon rainforest. After U.S. Customs officials seized a hoasca shipment and threatened prosecution, UDV sought declaratory and injunctive relief alleging that applying the federal Controlled Substances Act (CSA) to UDV violated their rights under RFRA. The Court held that lower courts were correct in ruling that the government failed to show a compelling interest in barring UDV's sacramental use of hoasca. The Court rejected the Government's argument that it has a compelling interest in the uniform application of the CSA, asserting that RFRA's strict scrutiny test contemplates that the government must demonstrate that the compelling interest test be applied to a specific person—the specific claimant whose sincere exercise of religion is being substantially burdened.

**(1) Examples of Generally Applicable Laws Challenged Solely on Free Exercise Grounds. [§ 962]**

These laws receive no heightened scrutiny.

**(a) Anti–Polygamy Laws. [§ 963]**

A federal law prohibiting polygamy is constitutional.

*Reynolds v. U.S.*, 98 U.S. 145 (1878). The Court upheld a federal law prohibiting polygamy as applied to a Mormon whose religion required polygamy. The Court said that the Congress could not regulate religious beliefs, but could reach actions that were violative of social duties or subversive of good order. This law applied generally and was challenged solely on Free Exercise grounds.

**(b) Dress Codes. [§ 964]**

An Air Force regulation prohibiting wearing a yarmulke on duty is constitutional.

*Goldman v. Weinberger*, 475 U.S. 503 (1986). The Court upheld an Air Force regulation which prohibited an Orthodox

# CHAPTER XVIII

Jew from wearing his yarmulke while on duty. The Air Force regulations forbade all individualized headgear which was visible in public, a restriction which the Court thought sufficiently related to the military goals of unity and discipline.

**(2) Examples of Generally Applicable Laws Challenged on the Basis of the Free Exercise Clause and Another Constitutional Right. [§ 965]**

Strict scrutiny is used when a generally applicable law is challenged on the basis that it violates the Free Exercise Clause plus some other constitutional protection, such as freedom of speech or press, or the right of parents to direct the educational upbringing of their children.

**(a) Mandatory Education Laws. [§ 966]**

A state cannot apply a mandatory education law to the Old Order Amish.

*Wisconsin v. Yoder*, 406 U.S. 205 (1972). The Court upheld a state court's reversal of the convictions of members of the Old Order Amish community who refused to send their children to state-certified schools through the age of sixteen. The Amish children did go to school through the eighth grade. The Court applied strict scrutiny, asserting that the Wisconsin compulsory education law violated the Free Exercise rights of the Amish parents, as well as their unenumerated right to direct the educational upbringing of their children.

**(b) State Laws Requiring a Motto on a License Plate. [§ 967]**

A state may not force a person to use license plates which carry a message to which the person objects on religious grounds.

*Wooley v. Maynard*, 430 U.S. 705 (1977). The Court held that the state of New Hampshire could not require a Jehovah's Witness to display on his car a license plate with the state motto, "Live Free or Die." While the Court relied primarily on the plaintiff's "right to refrain from speaking," it also discussed his religious objections to being forced to disseminate such a message. The Court treated this challenge as one involving First Amendment rights of speech and religion.

# THE RELIGION CLAUSES OF THE FIRST AMENDMENT

(3) **Examples of Laws That Are Not Generally Applicable. [§ 968]**

In these cases, strict scrutiny applies, even though the law is challenged solely on Free Exercise grounds.

(a) **Unemployment Compensation Cases. [§ 969]**

Strict scrutiny is also used in unemployment compensation cases where benefits are denied to a person who has lost a job, but the government provides an individualized hearing to determine eligibility. The individualized hearing takes these cases out of the category of "generally applicable" laws.

(i) **Refusal to Work on the Sabbath. [§ 970]**

A state cannot deny benefits to a person who refuses to work on her Sabbath.

*Sherbert v. Verner*, 374 U.S. 398 (1963). The Court held that unemployment compensation benefits could not be denied to a Seventh Day Adventist who was fired because she would not work on Saturday, which was her Sabbath. The Court found that the State Employment Security Commission's refusal to grant Sherbert an exemption substantially burdened her exercise of religion, and that the state had no compelling reason to deny the exemption.

(ii) **Religious Objection to Making Weapons. [§ 971]**

A state cannot deny unemployment compensation benefits to a person who has religious reservations about making weapons.

*Thomas v. Review Board*, 450 U.S. 707 (1981). The Court reversed a state court's denial of unemployment compensation benefits to a Jehovah's Witness who quit his job because his religious beliefs would not allow him to participate in the production of armaments. He had been transferred to a department that made tank turrets. Relying on *Sherbert* (previous case), the Court found that the denial of benefits to Thomas substantially burdened the free exercise of his religion, and was not supported by any compelling government interest.

# CHAPTER XVIII

**(iii) Post–Hiring Development of Religious Beliefs. [§ 972]**

A state cannot deny benefits to a worker whose religious beliefs developed after she had been on the job.

*Hobbie v. Unemployment Appeals Commission*, 480 U.S. 136 (1987). The Court held violative of the Free Exercise Clause a state commission's refusal to grant unemployment benefits to a worker whose newly formed religious beliefs prohibited her from working from sundown Friday to sundown Saturday. Despite the fact that her religious beliefs had developed after she had been working awhile, the Court found that the denial of benefits substantially burdened her free exercise of religion, and was not justified by any compelling government interest.

**(b) Example of a Law That Is Not Generally Applicable Because It Has Exceptions Built Into It. [§ 973]**

If a law has exceptions or exemptions built into it, strict scrutiny will apply, even though the law is challenged solely on Free Exercise grounds.

**(i) Activities of Specific Religious Groups. [§ 974]**

A state cannot selectively prohibit activity engaged in by a specific religious group, while allowing other religious groups to engage in that activity.

*Church of the Lukumi Babalu Aye, Inc. v. Hialeah*, 508 U.S. 520 (1993). The Court invalidated ordinances of the city of Hialeah which, when read together, prohibited animal slaughter by members of the Santeria religion, but allowed it by other religious and commercial slaughterhouses. The Court found the purpose of the ordinance to be to keep the Santeria religion from operating in town. The Court said that a neutral, generally applicable law will not receive strict scrutiny, even if it incidentally burdens a religious practice. However, a law which is not neutral and generally applicable (because of exceptions or exemptions) must be narrowly tailored to achieve a compelling government interest. In addition to the free exercise argument of the Santeria religion, it is also arguable that the government is establishing religion by allowing other religious groups to maintain slaughterhouses.

## 2. What Counts as "Religion" for Free Exercise Clause Purposes? [§ 975]

Obviously someone who is a believer in or a member of an accepted mainstream religion will be able to make a Free Exercise challenge to a law. An issue arises when someone belongs to a new or non-mainstream religion, or has a religious belief system that is purely personal.

### a. Religious Belief as a Basis for Conscientious Objector Status. [§ 976]

**The Court looks to the importance of religion in the life of a recognized, mainstream adherent to evaluate the religion claims of conscientious objectors.**

#### (1) "Religion" for Purposes of Conscientious Objector Status.

**"Religion" for purposes of conscientious objector status depends on whether a person's religious belief system fills the same place in his life as a mainstream religion does in the life of one of its adherents.**

*U.S. v. Seeger*, 380 U.S. 163 (1965). The Court interpreted a federal law which exempted from combat a person who, by religious training and belief, is conscientiously opposed to participation in war in any form. The test of "belief in a relation to a Supreme Being" (statutory language) was whether a given belief that is sincere and meaningful occupies a place in the life of its possessor parallel to that filled by the orthodox belief in God of one who clearly qualifies for the exemption.

#### (2) Opposition to All War.

**Conscientious objectors must oppose all war, not just specific ones.**

*Gillette v. U.S.*, 401 U.S. 437 (1971). The Court upheld a provision of federal law which allows Congress to draft persons who oppose a particular war (not war in general) on religious grounds. The Court rejected the argument that the law abridged the Free Exercise rights of those who religiously opposed only unjust wars; the government interest in an efficient draft system overrode this argument.

# CHAPTER XVIII

b. **Sincerity of Religious Beliefs. [§ 977]**

**The government may not inquire into the truth or falsity of religious beliefs. It may, however, question the sincerity of a person's claimed religious belief. A government cannot declare some religious beliefs true and some false; that would be tantamount to establishment of religion.**

(1) **Jury Determination of Religious Beliefs. [§ 978]**

**A jury may not question the truth or falsity of religious beliefs.**

*U.S. v. Ballard*, 322 U.S. 78 (1944). The Court ruled that a jury may not be given the question of whether particular religious beliefs are true. The defendants in this case, who had been charged with mail fraud, claimed to be divine messengers who had talked with Jesus, and who had the power to cure incurable diseases. The Court held that the First Amendment guarantees the protection of a person's chosen form of religion regardless of how incomprehensible those views may be to others.

(2) **Exaggerated Claims of Religious Belief. [§ 979]**

**Some claims of religious belief just go too far.**

*U.S. v. Kuch*, 288 F.Supp. 439 (D.D.C. 1968). The district court refused to rule that the Free Exercise claim of the defendant in a drug case was based on a religion within the meaning of the First Amendment. Judith Kuch claimed to be a minister of the Neo–American Church, and asserted that her religious beliefs immunized her from criminal prosecution for federal drug offenses. The Neo–American Church was founded in California, and its leader was Chief Boo Hoo. Kuch was the primate of the Potomac, and supervised the Boo Hoos in her area. To join the church, one had to subscribe to the principle that marijuana and LSD are not drugs, but the true Host of the church, and that it was the religious duty of all members to partake of the sacraments on a regular basis. The church symbol was a three-eyed toad, its bulletin was the "Divine Toad Sweat," and its motto was "Victory over Horseshit!" The district court did not take Kuch's Free Exercise claims seriously.

3. **Religion and Political Office. [§ 980]**

**Religion may not be used to qualify or disqualify a person from holding political office. Article VI, clause 3 of the Constitution**

# THE RELIGION CLAUSES OF THE FIRST AMENDMENT

provides that "[N]o religious Test shall ever be required as a Qualification to any office or public Trust under the United States." The Court has applied this rule to protect the Free Exercise Clause rights of those seeking public office.

a. **Belief in God. [§ 981]**

**Office-seekers may not be required to declare a belief in God.**

*Torcaso v. Watkins*, 367 U.S. 488 (1961). The Court invalidated a Maryland law which required any person who wanted to hold public office to declare a belief in God. **A person's belief or non-belief in God cannot be the basis for granting or withholding access to government office or benefits.**

b. **Clergy Members as Legislators. [§ 982]**

**Members of the clergy may not be prohibited from being legislators.**

*McDaniel v. Paty*, 435 U.S. 618 (1978). The Court invalidated a Tennessee law which prohibited members of the clergy from serving as legislators. There was no majority opinion, but a majority of Justices thought there was a violation of the Free Exercise Clause. Justice Brennan, concurring, also thought the Establishment Clause was violated because the primary effect of the law was to inhibit religion (which is forbidden by *Lemon*).

4. **Taxes on Religious Institutions. [§ 983]**

Generally applicable taxes may be imposed on religious institutions, but churches may not be singled out for discriminatory taxation.

a. **Denial of Tax–Exempt Status. [§ 984]**

The federal government can deny tax-exempt status to schools that discriminate based on race.

*Bob Jones University v. U.S.*, 461 U.S. 574 (1983). The Court upheld an Internal Revenue Service denial of tax exempt status to all schools that engaged in racial discrimination, even if the discrimination was the result of sincerely held religious beliefs. The government interest in eliminating racial discrimination outweighed any incidental impact on the Free Exercise rights of the schools, their students, and the parents of those students.

**The federal government can deny tax deductions for expenses for mandatory church programs.**

# CHAPTER XVIII

*Hernandez v. Commissioner of Internal Revenue*, 490 U.S. 680 (1989). The Court found no violation of the Free Exercise Clause (or the Establishment Clause) as a result of the IRS denying a tax deduction to persons who make payments to the Church of Scientology for "auditing" and "training" sessions. The Church requires payment for these sessions, so the Court did not consider them "charitable contributions" that were deductible. The Court said that the government had an overriding interest in maintaining a sound tax system, free from numerous religious exceptions.

b. **Sales and Use Taxes. [§ 985]**

**Generally applicable sales and use taxes may be imposed on religious institutions.**

*Jimmy Swaggart Ministries v. Board of Equalization*, 493 U.S. 378 (1990). The Court upheld the imposition of generally applicable sales and use taxes on the sale of religious goods and literature by a religious organization. The taxes, which were applied to all sales and uses of tangible personal property in the state, were challenged under both the Establishment Clause and the Free Exercise Clause.

c. **Social Security Tax. [§ 986]**

**The federal government can apply the social security tax system to those whose religion forbids participation.**

*U.S. v. Lee*, 455 U.S. 252 (1982). The Court upheld the application of the Social Security tax system to members of the Old Order Amish religion, even though payment into the system and receipt of benefits were forbidden by the religion. The Court said that the government has an overriding interest in the fiscal integrity of the social security system, and mandatory participation is the only way to achieve it.

5. **Sunday Closing Laws. [§ 987]**

**A state law which requires businesses to close on Sundays does not violate the First Amendment.** Just because a law happens to coincide with the tenets of a religion does not mean that the law is unconstitutional.

a. **Sunday Closing Laws and the Establishment Clause. [§ 988]**

**Sunday closing laws do not violate the Establishment Clause.**

*McGowan v. Maryland*, 366 U.S. 420 (1961). The Court upheld Maryland's Sunday Closing Law against both Free Exercise and

# THE RELIGION CLAUSES OF THE FIRST AMENDMENT

Establishment Clause challenges. The purpose and effect of the law were secular (providing a uniform day of rest), so there was no establishment of religion. The law had no direct effect of burdening Free Exercise rights.

b. **Sunday Closing Laws and the Free Exercise Clause. [§ 989]**

**Sunday closing laws do not violate the Free Exercise Clause.**

*Braunfeld v. Brown*, 366 U.S. 599 (1961). The Court upheld a Sunday closing law against a challenge by orthodox Jewish merchants who claimed a special injury because their religious beliefs prohibited work on Saturday, so they lost two workdays out of the week. As in *McGowan* (previous case), there was no direct burden on Free Exercise rights, and the state could not be expected to recognize exceptions for all whose religions required a day of rest other than Sunday.

6. **Laws Affecting the Free Exercise Rights of Native Americans. [§ 990]**

The Court has not been sympathetic to the Free Exercise claims of Native Americans. **Be aware of how government action frequently makes it impossible for Native Americans to practice essential aspects of their religion.**

a. **Social Security Numbers. [§ 991]**

**Forcing Native Americans to submit and use an identification number does not violate the Free Exercise Clause.**

*Bowen v. Roy*, 476 U.S. 693 (1986). The Court held that it did not violate the Free Exercise rights of a Native American child and her parent for a state to require them to submit the child's Social Security number for the state to use to identify her. The child and her parent argued that the submission and use of such a number violated their sincerely held religious beliefs. The Court considered this only an incidental burden on Free Exercise rights, and one that was clearly outweighed by the interest in an efficient welfare system.

b. **Destruction of Sacred Sites. [§ 992]**

**Federal land may be used in a way that necessitates the destruction of sacred sites.**

*Lyng v. Northwest Indian Cemetery Protective Association*, 485 U.S. 439 (1988). The Court held that the federal government did not

# CHAPTER XVIII

violate the Free Exercise rights of Native Americans by building a road and allowing timber harvesting in a national forest which included sacred areas which were integral to the Native American religion. The Court said that the Free Exercise Clause cannot be read to require the federal government to conduct its own internal affairs in ways that comport with the religious beliefs of particular citizens.

    c.    **Sacramental Use of Peyote. [§ 993]**

**A state may criminalize the sacramental use of peyote by Native Americans.**

*Employment Division v. Smith*, 494 U.S. 872 (1990). The Court upheld a state's power to criminalize the use of peyote, even when used by Native Americans as an essential part of their religion. Oregon had a generally applicable drug law (all uses of certain drugs were prohibited) which was challenged solely on the basis that it violated the Free Exercise rights of two Native American drug counselors who had been fired for peyote use and then denied unemployment compensation because they were discharged for illegal conduct. The Court first said that a government may not regulate religious beliefs. It then set forth the rule that **a generally applicable law which has only an incidental effect of burdening religion does not offend the Free Exercise Clause. No heightened scrutiny is called for in such a case.**

7.    **State Refusal to Fund Scholarships for Theology Majors. [§ 994]**

**A state does not violate the Free Exercise rights of college theology majors by excluding them from a scholarship program open to students who meet academic and income criteria.**

In *Locke v. Davey*, 540 U.S. 712 (2004), the Court held that a state regulation making devotional theology majors ineligible for state-funded college scholarships awarded according to objective criteria furthers the state constitutional ban on using state funds for funding the ministry and does not reflect any animus toward religion. Even though including theology majors in the scholarship program would not violate the Establishment Clause (See §§ 930–931.1), excluding them from what is otherwise a generally available scholarship program does not violate the Free Exercise Clause. The Plaintiff challenged the operation of the state of Washington's Promise Scholarship Program. Plaintiff won a scholarship, but lost it when he refused to certify that he was not pursuing a degree in devotional theology. The plaintiff asserted that exclusion of theology majors from the program violated the Free Exercise Clause, but the Court held that the states disfavor of religion was relatively mild (compared to criminalizing religious activity) and that training for religious professions and training for secular professions are not fungible.

## D. ACCOMMODATION BETWEEN THE RELIGIOUS BELIEFS OF EMPLOYEES AND THE INTERESTS OF EMPLOYERS: TENSION BETWEEN THE FREE EXERCISE CLAUSE AND THE ESTABLISHMENT CLAUSE. [§ 995]

When a government accommodates the religious beliefs of employees (by forcing employers to recognize a chosen Sabbath), it runs the risk of establishing religion. The Court balances the religious beliefs of employees against the degree of hardship imposed on the employer by the accommodation.

1. **Refusal to Work on the Sabbath. [§ 996]**

   **Employees have no absolute right to a day off on their chosen Sabbath.**

   *Estate of Thornton v. Caldor, Inc.*, 472 U.S. 703 (1985). The Court invalidated a Connecticut law which required employers to give employees a day off work on the employee's chosen day of worship. This law violated the Establishment Clause because it had the primary effect of advancing the particular religious practice of any employee who demanded a certain day off. The state's attempt to accommodate religious beliefs crossed the line into establishment of religion.

2. **Exemption of Religious Organizations from Laws Banning Discrimination Based on Religion. [§ 997]**

   **Congress may exempt religious organizations from laws banning discrimination based on religion.**

   *Corporation of the Presiding Bishop of the Church of Jesus Christ of Latter–Day Saints v. Amos*, 483 U.S. 327 (1987). The Court upheld Title VII's exemption of religious organizations from the statute's prohibition against discrimination in employment based on religion. The Mormon Church fired a building engineer because he failed to qualify for a certificate that he was a member of the Church, and eligible to attend its temples. The Court applied the *Lemon* analysis, and found that the Title VII exemption for religious organizations met the purpose, effect, and entanglement prongs, thus avoiding any establishment of religion.

# CHAPTER XVIII

# REVIEW PROBLEMS—THE RELIGION CLAUSES OF THE FIRST AMENDMENT

**PROBLEM 1.** The State of Oz has a program of providing computerized "readers" for visually impaired students in its public schools. A student simply puts any printed material on the scanner of the reader, and a computerized voice reads what is on the page. Jamie Jaynes is a ninth-grader in the Id School District (in the State of Oz), and has been blind from birth. She applies for and is given the use of a computerized reader to help her with her schoolwork. Jamie attends St. Matthew's Catholic High School. A group called Keep Religion Out of Schools (KROOS) sues, arguing that providing Jamie with a reader violates the Establishment Clause. Will KROOS prevail?

**Answer:** No. Providing the computerized reader is a neutral, generally applicable benefit which the state gives to students in public, non-religious private, and parochial schools. Also, it is Jamie's decision, not the state's to use the reader in a parochial school. See § 914 for further review.

**PROBLEM 2.** The School District of the City of Id allows high school graduates to decide if they would want a prayer at their graduation ceremony. If they do, the students choose a classmate to deliver the prayer, and the class advisor makes sure that the prayer is non-sectarian. Is this practice constitutional?

**Answer:** Maybe. In *Lee v. Weisman*, 505 U.S. 577 (1992), see § 932, the Court invalidated the practice of a principal choosing a member of the clergy to deliver an invocation or benediction at a junior high school graduation. This case is different because the students decide whether or not to have a prayer, and they choose a student to deliver it. At least one lower federal court has approved this kind of arrangement. See *Jones v. Clear Creek Independent School District*, 930 F.2d 416 (5th Cir. 1991).

**PROBLEM 3.** Id High School, a public school in the State of Oz, opens its gymnasium to members of the general public for speech purposes. All groups are admitted unless they are engaged in illegal activity. The Church of the Sublime Essence (CSE) applies for permission to use the school facilities for its meetings. CSE admits that there will be praying, singing, and discussion of spiritual matters. The principal of Id High School, who is in charge of granting permission to speakers, denies CSE's request on the basis that allowing them to use the gym would establish religion, in violation of the First Amendment. Does CSE have a right to use the public school gym for its meetings?

**Answer:** Yes. Id High School has created a designated public forum. Any content-based exclusions from that forum receive strict scrutiny. The principal will argue that the government has a compelling interest in not

# THE RELIGION CLAUSES OF THE FIRST AMENDMENT

establishing religion. The problem with this argument is that allowing religious speakers to have access to this kind of forum does not establish religion, so there is no compelling reason for the school to exclude them. As long as a number of different kinds of speakers have access, religious speakers must also be allowed to use the government property. See § 952 for further review.

**PROBLEM 4.** The State of Oz has a law which requires that an autopsy be performed anytime a death occurs under certain, statutorily-defined circumstances. One of these circumstances is when a person's death is caused by or related to police activity. Gene Attroman belongs to a religion which prohibits autopsies as a desecration of the body of a deceased person. The religion also requires, as a matter of scriptural interpretation, that parents have control and dominion over the bodies of their deceased children. Gene's son, Jake, was killed in a high-speed chase with police. The state has Jake's body and wants to perform an autopsy as required by state law. Gene sues, claiming that the autopsy would violate his Free Exercise rights. Will Gene prevail?

**Answer:** Under *Employment Division v. Smith*, 494 U.S. 872 (1990), Gene will lose if he is challenging the mandatory autopsy law solely on free exercise grounds. A neutral, generally applicable law trumps free exercise claims. If Gene can inject another fundamental right into his argument, a court will use strict scrutiny, and may very well invalidate the application of the law to Gene. Remember that under the Religious Freedom Restoration Act of 1993, a court would use strict scrutiny to analyze Gene's case even if he is asserting only a free exercise argument. See § 961 for further review.

**PROBLEM 5.** Holy Harry's Divine Discount Emporium is a large retail store in the State of Oz that sells only religious items and literature. The State of Oz imposes its sales tax on all retail establishments in the state, including Holy Harry's. Harry challenges the imposition of this tax on his business, arguing that it violates his free exercise rights. Will Harry win?

**Answer:** No. A generally applicable sales tax, applied in a neutral fashion to all retail stores in the state, would not violate Harry's free exercise rights. If religious stores were singled out for special taxation, then there would be a problem. See § 983 for further review.

# Chapter XIX

## THE CONSTITUTION OF THE UNITED STATES

### PREAMBLE

We the People of the United States, in Order to form a more perfect Union, establish Justice, insure domestic Tranquility, provide for the common defence, promote the general Welfare, and secure the Blessings of Liberty to ourselves and our Posterity, do ordain and establish this Constitution for the United States of America.

### ARTICLE I

Section 1. All legislative Powers herein granted shall be vested in a Congress of the United States, which shall consist of a Senate and House of Representatives.

Section 2. [1] The House of Representatives shall be composed of Members chosen every second Year by the People of the several States, and the Electors in each State shall have the Qualifications requisite for Electors of the most numerous Branch of the State Legislature.

[2] No Person shall be a Representative who shall not have attained to the Age of twenty five Years, and been seven Years a Citizen of the United States, and who shall not, when elected, be an Inhabitant of that State in which he shall be chosen.

[3] Representatives and direct Taxes shall be apportioned among the several States which may be included within this Union, according to their respective Numbers, which shall be determined by adding to the whole Number of free Persons, including those bound to Service for a Term of Years, and excluding Indians not taxed, three fifths of all other Persons. The actual Enumeration shall be made within three Years after the first Meeting of the Congress of the United States, and within every subsequent Term of ten Years, in such Manner as they shall by Law direct. The Number of Representatives shall not exceed one for every thirty Thousand, but each State shall have at Least one Representative; and until such enumeration shall be made, the State of New Hampshire shall be entitled to chuse

# CHAPTER XIX

three, Massachusetts eight, Rhode Island and Providence Plantations one, Connecticut five, New York six, New Jersey four, Pennsylvania eight, Delaware one, Maryland six, Virginia ten, North Carolina five, South Carolina five, and Georgia three.

[4] When vacancies happen in the Representation from any State, the Executive Authority thereof shall issue Writs of Election to fill such Vacancies.

[5] The House of Representatives shall chuse their Speaker and other Officers; and shall have the sole Power of Impeachment.

Section 3. [1] The Senate of the United States shall be composed of two Senators from each State, chosen by the Legislature thereof, for six Years; and each Senator shall have one Vote.

[2] Immediately after they shall be assembled in Consequence of the first Election, they shall be divided as equally as may be into three Classes. The Seats of the Senators of the first Class shall be vacated at the Expiration of the Second Year, of the second Class at the Expiration of the fourth year, and of the third Class at the Expiration of the sixth Year, so that one third may be chosen every second Year; and if Vacancies happen by Resignation, or otherwise, during the Recess of the Legislature of any State, the Executive thereof may make temporary Appointments until the next Meeting of the Legislature, which shall then fill such Vacancies.

[3] No Person shall be a Senator who shall not have attained to the Age of thirty Years, and been nine years a Citizen of the United States, and who shall not, when elected, by an Inhabitant of that State for which he shall be chosen.

[4] The Vice President of the United States shall be President of the Senate, but shall have no Vote, unless they be equally divided.

[5] The Senate shall chuse their other Officers, and also a President pro tempore, in the Absence of the Vice President, or when he shall exercise the Office of President of the United States.

[6] The Senate shall have the sole Power to try all Impeachments. When sitting for that Purpose, they shall be on Oath or Affirmation. When the President of the United States is tried, the Chief Justice shall preside: And no Person shall be convicted without the Concurrence of two thirds of the Members present.

[7] Judgment in Cases of Impeachment shall not extend further than to removal from Office, and disqualification to hold and enjoy any Office of honor, Trust, or Profit under the United States: but the Party convicted shall nevertheless be liable and subject to Indictment, Trial, Judgment, and Punishment, according to Law.

# CONSTITUTION OF THE UNITED STATES

Section 4. [1] The Times, Places and Manner of holding Elections for Senators and Representatives, shall be prescribed in each State by the Legislature thereof; but the Congress may at any time by Law make or alter such Regulations, except as to the Places of chusing Senators.

[2] The Congress shall assemble at least once in every Year, and such Meeting shall be on the first Monday in December, unless they shall by Law appoint a different Day.

Section 5. [1] Each House shall be the Judge of the Elections, Returns, and Qualifications of its own Members, and a Majority of each shall constitute a Quorum to do Business; but a smaller Number may adjourn from day to day, and may be authorized to compel the Attendance of absent Members, in such Manner, and under such Penalties as each House may provide.

[2] Each House may determine the Rules of its Proceedings, punish its Members for disorderly Behavior, and, with the Concurrence of two thirds, expel a Member.

[3] Each House shall keep a Journal of its Proceedings, and from time to time publish the same, excepting such Parts as may in their Judgment require Secrecy; and the Yeas and Nays of the Members of either House on any question shall, at the Desire of one fifth of those Present, be entered on the Journal.

[4] Neither House, during the Session of Congress, shall without the Consent of the other, adjourn for more than three days, nor to any other Place than that in which the two Houses shall be sitting.

Section 6. [1] The Senators and Representatives shall receive a Compensation for their Services, to be ascertained by law, and paid out of the Treasury of the United States. They shall in all Cases, except Treason, Felony and Breach of the Peace, be privileged from Arrest during their Attendance at the Session of their respective Houses, and in going to and returning from the same; and for any Speech or Debate in either House, they shall not be questioned in any other Place.

[2] No Senator or Representative shall, during the Time for which he was elected, be appointed to any civil Office under the Authority of the United States, which shall have been created, or the Emoluments whereof shall have been increased during such time; and no Person holding any Office under the United States, shall be a Member of either House during his Continuance in Office.

Section 7. [1] All Bills for raising Revenue shall originate in the House of Representatives; but the Senate may propose or concur with Amendments as on other Bills.

# CHAPTER XIX

[2] Every Bill which shall have passed the House of Representatives and the Senate, shall, before it become a Law, be presented to the President of the United States; If he approve he shall sign it, but if not he shall return it, with his Objections to the House in which it shall have originated, who shall enter the Objections at large on their Journal, and proceed to reconsider it. If after such Reconsideration two thirds of that House shall agree to pass the Bill, it shall be sent together with the Objections, to the other House, by which it shall likewise be reconsidered, and if approved by two thirds of that House, it shall become a Law. But in all such Cases the Votes of both Houses shall be determined by yeas and Nays, and the Names of the Persons voting for and against the Bill shall be entered on the Journal of each house respectively. If any Bill shall not be returned by the President within ten Days (Sundays excepted) after it shall have been presented to him, the Same shall be a Law, in like Manner as if he had signed it, unless the Congress by their Adjournment prevent its Return in which Case it shall not be a Law.

[3] Every Order, Resolution, or Vote, to Which the Concurrence of the Senate and House of Representatives may be necessary (except on a question of Adjournment) shall be presented to the President of the United States; and before the Same shall take Effect, shall be approved by him, or being disapproved by him, shall be repassed by two thirds of the Senate and House of Representatives, according to the Rules and Limitations prescribed in the Case of a Bill.

Section 8. [1] The Congress shall have Power To lay and collect Taxes, Duties, Imposts, and Excises, to pay the Debts and provide for the common Defence and general Welfare of the United States; but all Duties, Imposts and Excises shall be uniform throughout the United States;

[2] To borrow money on the credit of the United States;

[3] To regulate Commerce with foreign Nations, and among the several States, and with the Indian Tribes;

[4] To establish an uniform Rule of Naturalization, and uniform Laws on the subject of Bankruptcies throughout the United States;

[5] To coin Money, regulate the Value thereof, and of foreign Coin, and fix the Standard of Weights and Measures;

[6] To provide for the Punishment of counterfeiting the Securities and current Coin of the United States;

[7] To Establish Post Offices and Post Roads;

[8] To promote the Progress of Science and useful Arts, by securing for limited Times to Authors and Inventors the exclusive Right to their respective Writings and Discoveries;

# CONSTITUTION OF THE UNITED STATES

[9] To constitute Tribunals inferior to the supreme Court;

[10] To define and punish Piracies and Felonies committed on the high Seas, and Offenses against the Law of Nations;

[11] To declare War, grant Letters of Marque and Reprisal, and make Rules concerning Captures on Land and Water;

[12] To raise and support Armies, but no Appropriation of Money to that Use shall be for a longer Term than two Years;

[13] To provide and maintain a Navy;

[14] To make Rules for the Government and Regulation of the land and naval Forces;

[15] To provide for calling forth the Militia to execute the Laws of the Union, suppress Insurrections and repel Invasions;

[16] To provide for organizing, arming, and disciplining, the Militia, and for governing such Part of them as may be employed in the Service of the United States, reserving to the States respectively, the Appointment of the Officers, and the Authority of training the Militia according to the discipline prescribed by Congress;

[17] To exercise exclusive Legislation in all Cases whatsoever, over such District (not exceeding ten Miles square) as may, by Cession of particular States, and the Acceptance of Congress, become the Seat of the Government of the United States, and to exercise like Authority over all Places purchased by the Consent of the Legislature of the State in which the Same shall be, for the Erection of Forts, Magazines, Arsenals, dock-Yards, and other needful Buildings;—And

[18] To make all laws which shall be necessary and proper for carrying into Execution the foregoing Powers, and all other Powers vested by this Constitution in the Government of the United States, or in any Department or Officer thereof.

Section 9. [1] The Migration of Importation of Such Persons as any of the States now existing shall think proper to admit, shall not be prohibited by the Congress prior to the Year one thousand eight hundred and eight, but a Tax or duty may be imposed on such Importation, not exceeding ten dollars for each Person.

[2] The privilege of the Writ of Habeas Corpus shall not be suspended, unless when in Cases of Rebellion or Invasion the public Safety may require it.

[3] No Bill of Attainder or ex post facto Law shall be passed.

# CHAPTER XIX

[4] No Capitation, or other direct, Tax shall be laid, unless in Proportion to the Census or Enumeration herein before directed to be taken.

[5] No Tax or Duty shall be laid on Articles exported from any State.

[6] No Preference shall be given by any Regulation of Commerce or Revenue to the Ports of one State over those of another: nor shall Vessels bound to, or from, one State be obliged to enter, clear, or pay Duties in another.

[7] No money shall be drawn from the Treasury, but in Consequence of Appropriations made by Law; and a regular Statement and Account of the Receipts and Expenditures of all public Money shall be published from time to time.

[8] No Title of Nobility shall be granted by the United States: And no Person holding any Office of Profit or Trust under them, shall, without the Consent of the Congress, accept of any present, Emolument, Office, or Title, of any kind whatever, from any King, Prince, or foreign State.

Section 10. [1] No State shall enter into any Treaty, Alliance, or Confederation; grant Letters of Marque and Reprisal; coin Money; emit Bills of Credit; make any Thing but gold and silver Coin a Tender in Payment of Debts; pass any Bill of Attainder, ex post facto Law, or Law impairing the Obligation of Contracts, or grant any Title of Nobility.

[2] No State shall, without the Consent of the Congress, lay any Imposts or Duties on Imports or Exports, except what may be absolutely necessary for executing it's inspection Laws: and the net Produce of all Duties and Imposts, laid by any State on Imports or Exports, shall be for the Use of the Treasury of the United States; and all such laws shall be subject to the Revision and Controul of the Congress.

[3] No State shall, without the Consent of Congress, lay any Duty of Tonnage, keep Troops, or Ships of War in time of Peace, enter into any Agreement or Compact with another State, or with a foreign Power, or engage in War, unless actually invaded, or in such imminent Danger as will not admit of delay.

## ARTICLE II

Section 1. [1] The executive Power shall be vested in a President of the United States of America. He shall hold his Office during the Term of four Years, and, together with the Vice President, chosen for the same Term, be elected, as follows:

[2] Each State shall appoint, in such Manner as the Legislature thereof may direct, a Number of Electors, equal to the whole Number of Senators and

# CONSTITUTION OF THE UNITED STATES

Representatives to which the State may be entitled in the Congress; but no Senator or Representative, or Person holding an Office of Trust or Profit under the United States, shall be appointed an Elector.

[3] The Electors shall meet in their respective States, and vote by Ballot for two Persons, of whom one at least shall not be an Inhabitant of the same State with themselves. And they shall make a List of all the Persons voted for, and of the Number of Votes for each; which List they shall sign and certify, and transmit sealed to the Seat of the Government of the United States, directed to the President of the Senate. The President of the Senate shall, in the Presence of the Senate and House of Representatives, open all the Certificates, and the Votes shall then be counted. The Person having the greatest Number of Votes shall be the President, if such Number be a Majority of the whole Number of Electors appointed; and if there be more than one who have such Majority, and have an equal Number of Votes, then the House of Representatives shall immediately chuse by Ballot one of them for President; and if no Person have a majority, then from the five highest on the List the said House shall in like Manner chuse the President. But in chusing the President, the Votes shall be taken by States the Representation from each State having one Vote; A quorum for this Purpose shall consist of a member or Members from two thirds of the States, and a Majority of all the States shall be necessary to a Choice. In every Case, after the Choice of the President, the Person having the greater Number of Votes of the Electors shall be the Vice President. But if there should remain two or more who have equal Votes, the Senate shall chuse from them by Ballot the Vice President.

[4] The Congress may determine the Time of chusing the Electors, and the Day on which they shall give their Votes; which Day shall be the same throughout the United States.

[5] No person except a natural born Citizen, or a Citizen of the United States, at the time of the Adoption of this Constitution, shall be eligible to the Office of President; neither shall any Person be eligible to that Office who shall not have attained to the Age of thirty five Years, and been fourteen Years a Resident within the United States.

[6] In case of the removal of the President from Office, or of his Death, Resignation or Inability to discharge the Powers and Duties of the said Office, the Same shall devolve on the Vice President, and the Congress may by Law provide for the Case of Removal, Death, Resignation or Inability, both of the President and Vice President, declaring what Officer shall then act as President, and such Officer shall act accordingly, until the Disability be removed, or a President shall be elected.

[7] The President shall, at stated Times, receive for his Services, a Compensation, which shall neither be increased nor diminished during the Period for which he

# CHAPTER XIX

shall have been elected, and he shall not receive within that Period any other Emolument from the United States, or any of them.

[8] Before he enter on the Execution of his Office, he shall take the following oath or Affirmation: "I do solemnly swear (or affirm) that I will faithfully execute the Office of President of the United States, and will to the best of my Ability, preserve, protect and defend the Constitution of the United States."

Section 2. [1] The President shall be Commander in Chief of the Army and Navy of the United States, and of the militia of the several States, when called into the actual Service of the United States; he may require the Opinion, in writing, of the principal Officer in each of the Executive Departments, upon any Subject relating to the Duties of their respective Offices, and he shall have Power to grant Reprieves and Pardons for Offenses against the United States, except in Cases of Impeachment.

[2] He shall have Power, by and with the Advice and Consent of the Senate to make Treaties, provided two thirds of the Senators present concur; and he shall nominate, and by and with the Advice and Consent of the Senate, shall appoint Ambassadors, other public Ministers and Consuls, Judges of the supreme Court, and all other Officers of the United States, whose Appointments are not herein otherwise provided for, and which shall be established by Law; but the Congress may by Law vest the Appointment of such inferior Officers, as they think proper, in the President alone, in the Courts of Law, or in the Heads of Departments.

[3] The President shall have Power to fill up all Vacancies that may happen during the Recess of the Senate, by granting Commissions which shall expire at the End of their next Session.

Section 3. He shall from time to time give to the Congress Information of the State of the Union, and recommend to their Consideration such Measures as he shall judge necessary and expedient; he may, on extraordinary Occasions, convene both Houses, or either of them, and in Case of Disagreement between them, with Respect to the Time of Adjournment, he may adjourn them to such Time as he shall think proper; he shall receive Ambassadors and other public Ministers; he shall take Care that the Laws be faithfully executed, and shall Commission all the Officers of the United States.

Section 4. The President, Vice President and all civil Officers of the United States, shall be removed from Office on Impeachment for, and Conviction of, Treason, Bribery, or other high Crimes and Misdemeanors.

## ARTICLE III

Section 1. The judicial Power of the United States, shall be vested in one supreme Court, and in such inferior Courts as the Congress may from time to time

# CONSTITUTION OF THE UNITED STATES

ordain and establish. The Judges, both of the supreme and inferior Courts, shall hold their Offices during good Behaviour, and shall, at stated Times, receive for their Services a Compensation, which shall not be diminished during their Continuance in Office.

Section 2. [1] The judicial Power shall extend to all Cases, in Law and Equity, arising under this Constitution, the Laws of the United States, and Treaties made, or which shall be made, under their Authority;—to all Cases affecting Ambassadors, other public Ministers and Consuls;—to all Cases of admiralty and maritime Jurisdiction;—to Controversies to which the United States shall be a Party;—to Controversies between two or more States;—between a State and Citizens of another State;—between Citizens of different States;—between Citizens of the same State claiming Lands under the Grants of different States, and between a State, or the Citizens thereof, and foreign States, Citizens or Subjects.

[2] In all Cases affecting Ambassadors, other public Ministers and Consuls, and those in which a State shall be a Party, the supreme Court shall have original Jurisdiction. In all the other Cases before mentioned, the supreme Court shall have appellate Jurisdiction, both as to Law and Fact, with such Exceptions, and under such Regulations as the Congress shall make.

[3] The trial of all Crimes, except in Cases of Impeachment, shall be by Jury; and such Trial shall be held in the State where the said Crimes shall have been committed; but when not committed within any State, the Trial shall be at such Place or Places as the Congress may by Law have directed.

Section 3. [1] Treason against the United States, shall consist only in levying War against them, or, in adhering to their Enemies, giving them Aid and Comfort. No Person shall be convicted of Treason unless on the Testimony of two Witnesses to the same overt Act, or on Confession in open Court.

[2] The Congress shall have Power to declare the Punishment of Treason, but no Attainder of Treason shall work Corruption of Blood, or Forfeiture except during the Life of the Person attainted.

## ARTICLE IV

Section 1. Full Faith and Credit shall be given in each State to the public Acts, Records, and judicial Proceedings of every other State. And the Congress may by general Laws prescribe the Manner in which such Acts, Records and Proceedings shall be proved, and the Effect thereof.

Section 2. [1] The Citizens of each State shall be entitled to all Privileges and Immunities of Citizens in the several States.

# CHAPTER XIX

[2] A Person charged in any State with Treason, Felony, or other Crime, who shall flee from Justice, and be found in another State, shall on demand of the executive Authority of the State from which he fled, be delivered up, to be removed to the State having Jurisdiction of the Crime.

[3] No Person held to Service or Labour in one State, under the Laws thereof, escaping into another, shall, in Consequence of any Law or Regulation therein, be discharged from such Service or Labour, but shall be delivered up on Claim of the Party to whom such Service or Labour may be due.

Section 3. [1] New States may be admitted by the Congress into this Union; but no new State shall be formed or erected within the Jurisdiction of any other State; nor any State be formed by the Junction of two or more States, or Parts of States, without the Consent of the Legislatures of the States concerned as well as of the Congress.

[2] The Congress shall have Power to dispose of and make all needful Rules and Regulations respecting the Territory or other Property belonging to the United States; and nothing in this Constitution shall be so construed as to Prejudice any Claims of the United States, or of any particular State.

Section 4. The United States shall guarantee to every State in this Union a Republican Form of Government, and shall protect each of them against Invasion; and on Application of the Legislature, or of the Executive (when the Legislature cannot be convened) against domestic Violence.

## ARTICLE V

The Congress, whenever two thirds of both Houses shall deem it necessary, shall propose Amendments to this Constitution, or, on the Application of the Legislatures of two thirds of the several States, shall call a Convention for proposing Amendments, which, in either Case, shall be valid to all Intents and Purposes, as part of this Constitution, when ratified by the Legislatures of three fourths of the several States, or by Conventions in three fourths thereof, as the one or the other Mode of Ratification may be proposed by the Congress; Provided that no Amendment which may be made prior to the Year One thousand eight hundred and eight shall in any Manner affect the first and fourth Clauses in the Ninth Section of the first Article; and that no State, without its Consent, shall be deprived of its equal Suffrage in the Senate.

## ARTICLE VI

[1] All Debts contracted and Engagements entered into, before the Adoption of this Constitution shall be as valid against the United States under this Constitution, as under the Confederation.

# CONSTITUTION OF THE UNITED STATES

[2] This Constitution, and the Laws of the United States which shall be made in Pursuance thereof; and all Treaties made, or which shall be made, under the Authority of the United States, shall be the supreme Law of the Land; and the Judges in every State shall be bound thereby, any Thing in the Constitution or Laws of any State to the Contrary notwithstanding.

[3] The Senators and Representatives before mentioned, and the Members of the several State Legislatures, and all executive and judicial Officers, both of the United States and of the several States, shall be bound by Oath or Affirmation, to support this Constitution; but no religious Test shall ever be required as a Qualification to any Office or public Trust under the United States.

## ARTICLE VII

The Ratification of the Conventions of nine States shall be sufficient for the Establishment of this Constitution between the States so ratifying the Same.

ARTICLES IN ADDITION TO, AND AMENDMENT OF, THE CONSTITUTION OF THE UNITED STATES OF AMERICA, PROPOSED BY CONGRESS, AND RATIFIED BY THE LEGISLATURES OF THE SEVERAL STATES PURSUANT TO THE FIFTH ARTICLE OF THE ORIGINAL CONSTITUTION.

## AMENDMENT I [1791]

Congress shall make no law respecting an establishment of religion, or prohibiting the free exercise thereof, or abridging the freedom of speech, or of the press; or the right of the people peaceably to assemble, and to petition the Government for a redress of grievances.

## AMENDMENT II [1791]

A well regulated Militia, being necessary to the security of a free State, the right of the people to keep and bear Arms, shall not be infringed.

## AMENDMENT III [1791]

No Soldier shall, in time of peace be quartered in any house, without the consent of the Owner, nor in time of war, but in a manner to be prescribed by law.

## AMENDMENT IV [1791]

The right of the people to be secure in their persons, houses, papers, and effects, against unreasonable searches and seizures, shall not be violated, and no

Warrants shall issue, but upon probable cause, supported by Oath or affirmation and particularly describing the place to be searched, and the persons or things to be seized.

### AMENDMENT V [1791]

No person shall be held to answer for a capital, or otherwise infamous crime, unless on a presentment or indictment of a Grand Jury, except in cases arising in the land or naval forces, or in the Militia, when in actual service in time of War or public danger; nor shall any person be subject for the same offence to be twice put in jeopardy of life or limb; nor shall be compelled in any criminal case to be a witness against himself, nor be deprived of life, liberty, or property, without due process of law; nor shall private property be taken for public use, without just compensation.

### AMENDMENT VI [1791]

In all criminal prosecutions, the accused shall enjoy the right to a speedy and public trial, by an impartial jury of the State and district wherein the crime shall have been committed, which district shall have been previously ascertained by law, and to be informed of the nature and cause of the accusation; to be confronted with the witnesses against him; to have compulsory process for obtaining witnesses in his favor, and to have the Assistance of Counsel for his defence.

### AMENDMENT VII [1791]

In Suits at common law, where the value in controversy shall exceed twenty dollars, the right of trial by jury shall be preserved, and no fact tried by jury, shall be otherwise re-examined in any Court of the United States, than according to the rules of the common law.

### AMENDMENT VIII [1791]

Excessive bail shall not be required, nor excessive fines imposed, nor cruel and unusual punishments inflicted.

### AMENDMENT IX [1791]

The enumeration in the Constitution, of certain rights, shall not be construed to deny or disparage others retained by the people.

### AMENDMENT X [1791]

The powers not delegated to the United States by the Constitution, nor prohibited by it to the States, are reserved to the States respectively, or to the people.

# CONSTITUTION OF THE UNITED STATES

## AMENDMENT XI [1798]

The Judicial power of the United States shall not be construed to extend to any suit in law or equity, commenced or prosecuted against one of the United States by Citizens of another State, or by Citizens or Subjects of any Foreign State.

## AMENDMENT XII [1804]

The Electors shall meet in their respective states and vote by ballot for President and Vice–President, one of whom, at least, shall not be an inhabitant of the same state with themselves; they shall name in their ballots the person voted for as President, and in distinct ballots the person voted for as Vice–President, and they shall make distinct lists of all persons voted for as President, and of all persons voted for as Vice–President, and of the number of votes for each, which lists they shall sign and certify, and transmit sealed to the seat of the government of the United States, directed to the President of the Senate;—The President of the Senate shall, in the presence of the Senate and House of Representatives, open all the certificates and the votes shall then be counted;—The person having the greatest number of votes for President, shall be the President, if such number be a majority of the whole number of Electors appointed; and if no person have such majority, then from the persons having the highest numbers not exceeding three on the list of those voted for as President, the House of Representatives shall choose immediately, by ballot, the President. But in choosing the President, the votes shall be taken by states, the representation from each state having one vote; a quorum for this purpose shall consist of a member or members from two-thirds of the states, and a majority of all the states shall be necessary to a choice. And if the House of Representatives shall not choose a President whenever the right of choice shall devolve upon them before the fourth day of March next following, then the Vice–President shall act as President, as in the case of the death or other constitutional disability of the President.—The person having the greatest number of votes as Vice–President, shall be the Vice–President, if such number be a majority of the whole number of Electors appointed, and if no person have a majority, then from the two highest numbers on the list, the Senate shall choose the Vice–President; a quorum for the purpose shall consist of two-thirds of the whole number of Senators, and a majority of the whole number shall be necessary to a choice. But no person constitutionally ineligible to the office of President shall be eligible to that of Vice–President of the United States.

## AMENDMENT XIII [1865]

Section 1.  Neither slavery nor involuntary servitude, except as a punishment for crime whereof the party shall have been duly convicted, shall exist within the United States, or any place subject to their jurisdiction.

Section 2.  Congress shall have power to enforce this article by appropriate legislation.

# CHAPTER XIX

## AMENDMENT XIV [1868]

Section 1.   All persons born or naturalized in the United States, and subject to the jurisdiction thereof, are citizens of the United States and of the State wherein they reside. No State shall make or enforce any law which shall abridge the privileges or immunities of citizens of the United States; nor shall any State deprive any person of life, liberty, or property, without due process of law; nor deny to any person within its jurisdiction the equal protection of the laws.

Section 2.   Representatives shall be apportioned among the several States according to their respective numbers, counting the whole number of persons in each State, excluding Indians not taxed. But when the right to vote at any election for the choice of electors for President and Vice President of the United States, Representatives in Congress, the Executive and Judicial officers of a State, or the members of the Legislature thereof, is denied to any of the male inhabitants of such State, being twenty-one years of age, and citizens of the United States, or in any way abridged, except for participation in rebellion, or other crime, the basis of representation therein shall be reduced in the proportion which the number of such male citizens shall bear to the whole number of male citizens twenty-one years of age in such State.

Section 3.   No person shall be a Senator or Representative in Congress, or elector of President and Vice President, or hold any office, civil or military, under the United States, or under any State, who having previously taken an oath, as a member of Congress, or as an officer of the United States, or as a member of any State legislature, or as an executive or judicial officer of any State, to support the Constitution of the United States, shall have engaged in insurrection or rebellion against the same, or given aid or comfort to the enemies thereof. But Congress may by a vote of two-thirds of each House, remove such disability.

Section 4.   The validity of the public debt of the United States, authorized by law, including debts incurred for payment of pensions and bounties for services in suppressing insurrection or rebellion, shall not be questioned. But neither the United States nor any State shall assume or pay any debt or obligation incurred in aid of insurrection or rebellion against the United States, or any claim for the loss or emancipation of any slave; but all such debts, obligations and claims shall be held illegal and void.

Section 5.   The Congress shall have power to enforce, by appropriate legislation, the provisions of this article.

## AMENDMENT XV [1870]

Section 1.   The right of citizens of the United States to vote shall not be denied or abridged by the United States or by any State on account of race, color, or previous condition of servitude.

# CONSTITUTION OF THE UNITED STATES

Section 2. The Congress shall have power to enforce this article by appropriate legislation.

## AMENDMENT XVI [1913]

The Congress shall have power to lay and collect taxes on incomes, from whatever source derived, without apportionment among the several States, and without regard to any census or enumeration.

## AMENDMENT XVII [1913]

[1] The Senate of the United States shall be composed of two Senators from each State, elected by the people thereof, for six years; and each Senator shall have one vote. The electors in each State shall have the qualifications requisite for electors of the most numerous branch of the State legislatures.

[2] When vacancies happen in the representation of any State in the Senate, the executive authority of such State shall issue writs of election to fill such vacancies: *Provided*, That the legislature of any State may empower the executive thereof to make temporary appointments until the people fill the vacancies by election as the legislature may direct.

[3] This amendment shall not be so construed as to affect the election or term of any Senator chosen before it becomes valid as part of the Constitution.

## AMENDMENT XVIII [1919]

Section 1. After one year from the ratification of this article the manufacture, sale, or transportation of intoxicating liquors within, the importation thereof into, or the exportation thereof from the United States and all territory subject to the jurisdiction thereof for beverage purposes is hereby prohibited.

Section 2. The Congress and the several States shall have concurrent power to enforce this article by appropriate legislation.

Section 3. This article shall be inoperative unless it shall have been ratified as an amendment to the Constitution by the legislatures of the several States, as provided in the Constitution, within seven years from the date of the submission hereof to the States by the Congress.

## AMENDMENT XIX [1920]

[1] The right of citizens of the United States to vote shall not be denied or abridged by the United States or by any State on account of sex.

# CHAPTER XIX

[2] Congress shall have power to enforce this article by appropriate legislation.

## AMENDMENT XX [1933]

Section 1.   The terms of the President and Vice President shall end at noon on the 20th day of January, and the terms of Senators and Representatives at noon on the 3d day of January, of the years in which such terms would have ended if this article had not been ratified; and the terms of their successors shall then begin.

Section 2.   The Congress shall assemble at least once in every year, and such meeting shall begin at noon on the 3d day of January, unless they shall by law appoint a different day.

Section 3.   If, at the time fixed for the beginning of the term of the President, the President elect shall have died, the Vice President elect shall become President. If the President shall not have been chosen before the time fixed for the beginning of his term, or if the President elect shall have failed to qualify, then the Vice President elect shall act as President until a President shall have qualified; and the Congress may by law provide for the case wherein neither a President elect nor a Vice President elect shall have qualified, declaring who shall then act as President, or the manner in which one who is to act shall be selected, and such person shall act accordingly until a President or Vice President shall have qualified.

Section 4.   The Congress may by law provide for the case of the death of any of the persons from whom the House of Representatives may choose a President whenever the right of choice shall have devolved upon them, and for the case of the death of any of the persons from whom the Senate may choose a Vice President whenever the right of choice shall have devolved upon them.

Section 5.   Sections 1 and 2 shall take effect on the 15th day of October following the ratification of this article.

Section 6.   This article shall be inoperative unless it shall have been ratified as an amendment to the Constitution by the legislatures of three-fourths of the several States within seven years from the date of its submission.

## AMENDMENT XXI [1933]

Section 1.   The eighteenth article of amendment to the Constitution of the United States is hereby repealed.

Section 2.   The transportation or importation into any State, Territory, or possession of the United States for delivery or use therein of intoxicating liquors, in violation of the laws thereof, is hereby prohibited.

Section 3. This article shall be inoperative unless it shall have been ratified as an amendment to the Constitution by conventions in the several States, as provided in the Constitution, within seven years from the date of the submission hereof to the States by the Congress.

## AMENDMENT XXII [1951]

Section 1. No person shall be elected to the office of the President more than twice, and no person who has held the office of President, or acted as President, for more than two years of a term to which some other person was elected President shall be elected to the office of President more than once. But this Article shall not apply to any person holding the office of President when this Article was proposed by the Congress, and shall not prevent any person who may be holding the office of President, or acting as President, during the term within which this Article becomes operative from holding the office of President or acting as President during the remainder of such term.

Section 2. This article shall be inoperative unless it shall have been ratified as an amendment to the Constitution by the legislatures of three-fourths of the several States within seven years from the date of its submission to the States by the Congress.

## AMENDMENT XXIII [1961]

Section 1. The District constituting the seat of Government of the United States shall appoint in such manner as the Congress may direct:

A number of electors of President and Vice President equal to the whole number of Senators and Representatives in Congress to which the District would be entitled if it were a State, but in no event more than the least populous state; they shall be in addition to those appointed by the states, but they shall be considered, for the purposes of the election of President and Vice President, to be electors appointed by a state; and they shall meet in the District and perform such duties as provided by the twelfth article of amendment.

Section 2. The Congress shall have power to enforce this article by appropriate legislation.

## AMENDMENT XXIV [1964]

Section 1. The right of citizens of the United States to vote in any primary or other election for President or Vice President, for electors for President or Vice President, or for Senator or Representative in Congress, shall not be denied or abridged by the United States or any State by reason of failure to pay any poll tax or other tax.

# CHAPTER XIX

Section 2. The Congress shall have power to enforce this article by appropriate legislation.

## AMENDMENT XXV [1967]

Section 1. In case of the removal of the President from office or of his death or resignation, the Vice President shall become President.

Section 2. Whenever there is a vacancy in the office of the Vice President, the President shall nominate a Vice President who shall take office upon confirmation by a majority vote of both Houses of Congress.

Section 3. Whenever the President transmits to the President pro tempore of the Senate and the Speaker of the House of Representatives his written declaration that he is unable to discharge the powers and duties of his office, and until he transmits to them a written declaration to the contrary, such powers and duties shall be discharged by the Vice President as Acting President.

Section 4. Whenever the Vice President and a majority of either the principal officers of the executive departments or of such other body as Congress may by law provide, transmit to the President pro tempore of the Senate and the Speaker of the House of Representatives their written declaration that the President is unable to discharge the powers and duties of his office, the Vice President shall immediately assume the powers and duties of the office as Acting President.

Thereafter, when the President transmits to the President pro tempore of the Senate and the Speaker of the House of Representatives his written declaration that no inability exists, he shall resume the powers and duties of his office unless the Vice President and a majority of either the principal officers of the executive department or of such other body as Congress may by law provide, transmit within four days to the President pro tempore of the Senate and the Speaker of the House of Representatives their written declaration that the President is unable to discharge the powers and duties of his office. Thereupon Congress shall decide the issue, assembling within forty-eight hours for that purpose if not in session. If the Congress, within twenty-one days after receipt of the latter written declaration, or, if Congress is not in session, within twenty-one days after Congress is required to assemble, determines by two-thirds vote of both Houses that the President is unable to discharge the powers and duties of his office, the Vice President shall continue to discharge the same as Acting President; otherwise, the President shall resume the powers and duties of his office.

## AMENDMENT XXVI [1971]

Section 1. The right of citizens of the United States, who are eighteen years of age or older, to vote shall not be denied or abridged by the United States or by any State on account of age.

# CONSTITUTION OF THE UNITED STATES

Section 2. The Congress shall have power to enforce this article by appropriate legislation.

## AMENDMENT XXVII [1992]

No law, varying compensation for the services of Senators and Representatives, shall take effect, until an election of Representatives shall have intervened.

# TABLE OF CASES

Abrams v. U.S.—§ 720
Adarand Construction Inc. v. Pena—§ 585
Adderley v. Florida—§ 804
Addington v. Texas—§ 444
Afroyim v. Rusk—§ 204
Agins v. City of Tiburon—§ 424
Agostini v. Felton—§§ 904, 922
Aguilar v. Felton—§ 921
Alden v. Maine—§ 110
Allee v. Medrano—§ 130
Allegeyer v. Louisiana—§ 473
Allegheny, County of v. ACLU—§ 942
Allen v. Wright—§§ 60, 64
Allied Structural Steel Co. v. Spannaus—§ 406
Aloha Airlines, Inc. v. Director of Taxation—§ 340
Altria Group v. Good—§ 340
Ambach v. Norwick—§ 599
American Booksellers Association v. Hudnut—§ 762
American Library Association, Inc., U.S. v.—§ 737
American Trucking Association v. Michigan Public Service Commission—§ 290
Anderson v. Celebrezze—§ 818
Apprendi v. New Jersey—§ 744
Arkansas Educational Television Commission v. Forbes—§ 854
Arkansas Writers' Project, Inc. v. Ragland—§ 856
Arlington Heights v. Metropolitan Housing Development Corp.—§ 543
Asarco v. Kadish—§ 72

Ashcroft v. American Civil Liberties Union—§ 737
Ashcroft v. Free Speech Coalition—§ 757
Associated Industries of Missouri v. Lohman—§ 332
Association of Data Processing v. Camp—§ 86
Austin v. Michigan State Chamber of Commerce—§ 826
Ayotte v. Planned Parenthood of Northern New England—§ 501

Bailey v. Drexel Furniture Co.—§ 174
Baker v. Carr—§ 32
Baldwin v. Fish and Game Commission of Montana—§ 308
Baldwin v. Seelig—§ 264
Ballard, U.S. v.—§ 978
Bantam Books v. Sullivan—§ 687
Barclay's Bank PLC v. Franchise Tax Board of California—§ 320
Barnard v. Thorstenn—§ 306
Barnes v. Glen Theatre, Inc.—§ 788
Barrows v. Jackson—§§ 77, 367
Bartnicki v. Vopper—§ 681
Batson v. Kentucky—§ 547
Belle Terre v. Boraas—§ 512
Bellotti v. Baird—§ 501
Berman v. Parker—§ 412
Bernal v. Fainter—§ 601
Bethel School District v. Fraser—§ 793

Bibb v. Navajo Freight Lines—§ 286
BMW of North America v. Gore—§ 464
Board of Airport Commissioners v. Jews for Jesus, Inc.—§ 662
Board of County Commissioners v. Umbehr—§ 833
Board of Curators v. Horowitz—§ 462
Board of Education v. Allen—§ 909
Board of Education v. Mergens—§§ 814, 951
Board of Education v. Pico—§ 794
Board of Education of Kiryas Joel Village School District v. Grumet—§ 912
Board of Regents v. Roth—§ 456
Board of Regents of the University of Wisconsin v. Southworth—§ 866
Board of Trustees of the University of Alabama v. Garrett—§ 113
Bob Jones University v. U.S.—§ 984
Boddie v. Connecticut—§ 531
Boerne v. Flores—§§ 386, 961
Bolling v. Sharpe—§§ 533, 558
Boos v. Barry—§§ 706, 808
Boston Stock Exchange v. State Tax Commission—§ 322
Bowen v. Kendrick—§ 948
Bowen v. Roy—§ 991
Bowers v. Hardwick—§ 508
Bowsher v. Synar—§ 232
Boumediene v. Bush—§ 251

# TABLE OF CASES

Boy Scouts of America v. Dale—§ 871
Bradwell v. Illinois—§ 607
Brandenburg v. Ohio—§ 726
Braniff Airways, Inc. v. Nebraska State Board of Equalization and Assessment—§ 328
Branti v. Finkel—§ 839
Branzburg v. Hayes—§ 887
Braunfeld v. Brown—§ 989
Breard v. Alexandria—§ 271
Brentwood Academy v. Tennessee Secondary School Athletic Association—§ 354
Brewster, U.S. v.—§ 242
Broadrick v. Oklahoma—§ 673
Brockett v. Spokane Arcades, Inc.—§ 674
Brown v. Board of Education I—§ 556
Brown v. Board of Education II—§ 557
Brown v. Louisiana—§ 800
Brown, U.S. v.—§ 399
Buckley v. Valeo—§§ 223, 820
Burbank v. Lockheed Air Terminal, Inc.—§ 341
Burson v. Freeman—§ 707
Burton v. Wilmington Parking Authority—§ 346
Bush v. Gore—§ 516
Bush v. Vera—§ 551
Butler v. Michigan—§ 759
Butler, U.S. v.—§ 181

C & A Carbone v. Town of Charlestown, New York—§ 276
Caban v. Mohamed—§ 633
Cabell v. Chavez–Salido—§ 600
Califano v. Goldfarb—§ 183
Califano v. Webster—§ 617
California Democratic Party v. Jones—§ 525
Campbell v. Louisiana—§ 547
Camps Newfound/Owatonna, Inc. v. Harrison—§ 277

Cantwell v. Connecticut—§ 730
Caperton v. A.T. Massey Coal Co., Inc.—§ 438
Capitol Square Review and Advisory Board v. Pinette—§ 954
Carey v. Population Services International—§§ 498, 641
Carmell v. Texas—§ 396
Carolene Products Co., U.S. v.—§ 478
Carroll v. President and Commissioners of Princess Anne—§ 713
Carter v. Carter Coal Co.—§ 154
Castaneda v. Partida—§ 546
Castle Rock v. Gonzales—§ 465
Causby, U.S. v.—§ 418
CBS v. Democratic National Committee—§ 894
Central Hudson Gas & Electric Corporation v. Public Service Commission—§ 766
Central Virginia Community College v. Katz—§ 117
Chaplinsky v. New Hampshire—§ 731
Chemical Waste Management v. Hunt—§ 274
Cheney v. U.S. District Court—§ 236
Chicago v. Morales—§ 671
Christian Legal Society v. Martinez—§ 874.1
Church of the Lukumi Babalu Aye, Inc. v. Hialeah—§ 974
Cincinnati, City of v. Discovery Network, Inc.—§ 768
Citizens United v. Federal Election Commission—§ 826.1
Civil Rights Cases—§ 381
Clark v. Community for Creative Non–Violence (CCNV)—§§ 703, 790
Clark v. Jeter—§§ 624, 637
Cleburne, City of v. Cleburne Living Center, Inc.—§ 643

Cleveland Board of Education v. LaFleur—§ 655
Cleveland Board of Education v. Loudermill—§ 458
Clingman v. Beaver—§ 526
Clinton v. City of New York—§ 221
Clinton v. Jones—§ 239
Coates v. Cincinnati—§ 675
Cohen v. California—§ 734
Cohen v. Cowles Media, Co.—§ 890
Cohens v. Virginia—§ 22
Coleman v. Miller—§ 58
Cole v. Richardson—§ 830
Colgate v. Harvey—§ 468
College Savings Bank v. Florida Prepaid Postsecondary Education Expense Board—§ 114
Colorado Republican Federal Campaign Committee v. Federal Election Commission—§ 827
Columbus Board of Education v. Penick—§ 565
Committee for Public Education and Religious Liberty v. Nyquist—§ 911
Commonwealth Edison v. Montana—§ 323
Complete Auto Transit, Inc. v. Brady—§ 313
Comstock, U.S. v.—§ 146
Conn v. Gabbert—§ 483
Connecticut Dept. of Public Safety v. Doe—§ 453
Connick v. Meyers—§ 833
Container Corporation v. Franchise Tax Board—§ 319
Cook v. Gralike—§ 36
Cooley v. Board of Wardens—§ 283
Cooper v. Aaron—§ 561
Cornelius v. NAACP Legal Defense and Educational Fund, Inc.—§ 710
Corporation of the Presiding Bishop of the Church of Jesus Christ of Latter–Day Saints v. Amos—§ 997
Craig v. Boren—§§ 79, 610
Crawford v. Marion County Election Board—§ 518

# TABLE OF CASES

Cruzan v. Director, Missouri Department of Health—§ 509
Curtiss–Wright Export Corp., U.S. v.—§ 186
Cutter v. Wilkinson—§ 956

Dallas v. Stanglin—§ 873
DaimlerChrysler Corp. v. Cuno—§ 74
Dames & Moore v. Regan—§ 213
Daniels v. Williams—§ 441
Davis v. Bandemer—§ 31
Dawson v. Delaware—§ 742
Day–Brite Lighting v. Missouri—§ 479
Dean Milk v. Madison—§ 269
DeFunis v. Odegaard—§ 91
Dennis v. U.S.—§ 723
Denver Area Educational Telecommunications Consortium Inc. v. FCC—§ 738
Department of Revenue of Kentucky v. Davis—§ 292
DeShaney v. Winnebago Dept. of Social Services—§ 368
District of Columbia v. Heller—§ 467
Doe v. Bolton—§ 301
Doe v. Reed—§ 709
Dolan v. Tigard—§ 431
Dombrowski v. Pfister—§ 131
Dothard v. Rawlinson—§ 620
Douglas v. California—§ 530
Duke Power Co. v. Carolina Environmental Study Group, Inc.—§ 482
Dunn v. Blumstein—§§ 300, 519

Easley v. Cromartie—§ 552
Eastern Enterprises v. Apfel—§ 434
E.C. Knight Co., U.S. v.—§ 152
Edelman v. Jordan—§ 106
Edenfield v. Fane—§ 776
Edge Broadcasting Co., U.S. v.—§ 769

Edmonson v. Leesville Concrete Co.—§§ 361, 547
Edwards v. Aguillard—§ 926
Eichman, U.S. v.—§ 787
Eisenstadt v. Baird—§ 497
Elfbrandt v. Russell—§ 830
Elk Grove Unified School District v. Newdow—§§ 81, 935
Elrod v. Burns—§ 838
Employment Division v. Smith—§§ 788, 961, 993
Energy Reserves Group v. Kansas Power & Light Co.—§§ 402, 407
Engel v. Vitale—§ 930
England v. Louisiana State Board of Medical Examiners—§ 126
Engquist v. Oregon Department of Agriculture—§ 534
Epperson v. Arkansas—§ 925
Erie, City of v. Pap's A.M.—§ 788
Eu v. San Francisco County Democratic Central Committee—§ 818
Evans v. Newton—§ 347
Everson v. Board of Education—§ 908
Exxon Corp. v. Maryland—§ 288

FCC v. League of Women Voters—§ 851
FCC v. Pacifica Foundation—§§ 701, 735
Federal Election Commission v. Akins—§ 55
Federal Election Commission v. Colorado Republican Federal Campaign Committee—§ 828
Federal Election Commission v. Massachusetts Citizens for Life—§ 826
Federal Election Commission v. National Conservative Political Action Committee—§ 825
Federal Election Commission v. National Right to Work Committee—§ 824
Ferguson v. Skrupa—§ 481

First English Evangelical Lutheran Church v. County of Los Angeles—§ 432
First National Bank v. Bellotti—§ 823
Fitzpatrick v. Bitzer—§ 112
Flagg Bros., Inc. v. Brooks—§ 364
Flast v. Cohen—§§ 68, 72
Florida Bar v. Went For It, Inc.—§ 779
Florida Dept. of State v. Treasure Salvors, Inc.—§ 108
Florida Prepaid Postsendary Education Expense Board v. College Savings Bank—§ 114
Foley v. Connelie—§ 598
Fordice, U.S. v.—§ 572
Forsyth County v. The Nationalist Movement—§ 810
Fort Gratiot Sanitary Landfill, Inc. v. Michigan Dept. of Natural Resources—§ 269
Forty–Four (44) Liquormart, Inc. v. Rhode Island—§§ 768, 771
Foster v. Love—§ 338
Free Enterprise Fund and Beckstead and Watts, LLP v. Public Company Accounting Oversight Board—§ 232.1
Freedman v. Maryland—§ 685
Freeman v. Pitts—§ 570
Friends of the Earth, Inc. v. Laidlaw Environmental Services—§ 89
Frisby v. Schultz—§§ 704, 809
Frontiero v. Richardson—§ 609
Frothingham v. Mellon—§§ 67, 73
Fullilove v. Klutznick—§ 583

Gagnon v. Scarpelli—§ 445
Gannett Co., Inc. v. De Pasquale—§ 882
Garcetti v. Ceballos—§ 833
Garcia v. San Antonio Metropolitan Transit Authority—§ 169

# TABLE OF CASES

Garner v. Jones—§ 395
Geduldig v. Aiello—§§ 614
General Motors v. Washington—§ 325
Georgia, U.S. v.—§ 113
Gilbert v. Homar—§ 459
Gillette v. U.S.—§ 976
Ginsberg v. New York—§ 761
Gitlow v. New York—§ 721
Glickman v. Wileman Brothers & Elliot, Inc.—§ 867
Globe Newspapers Co. v. Superior Court—§ 884
Glona v. American Guarantee & Liability Insurance Co.—§ 626
Goldberg v. Kelly—§ 461
Goldman v. Weinberger—§ 964
Goldwater v. Carter—§ 30
Gomillion v. Lightfoot—§ 549
Gonzales v. Carhart—§ 507
Gonzales v. Centro Espirita Beneficente Uniao do Vegetal—§ 961
Gonzales v. Raich—§ 163
Good News Club v. Milford Central School—§ 815
Goss v. Lopez—§ 462
Grace, U.S. v.—§ 702
Graham v. Richardson—§ 604
Grand Rapids School District v. Ball—§ 920
Granholm v. Heald—§ 278
Gratz v. Bollinger—§ 576
Gravel v. U.S.—§ 243
Grayned v. Rockford—§§ 700, 806
Great A. & P. Tea Co. v. Cottrell—§ 266
Greater New Orleans Broadcasting Association, Inc. v. U.S.—§ 769
Green v. County School Board—§ 563
Greer v. Spock—§ 799
Gregory v. Ashcroft—§§ 340, 640
Griffin v. County School Board—§ 562
Griffin v. Breckenridge—§ 378
Griffin v. Illinois—§ 528
Griffiths, In re—§ 597

Griswold v. Connecticut—§§ 78, 496
Grutter v. Bollinger—§ 577
Gryger v. Burke—§ 395
Guest, U.S. v.—§ 383

Hague v. C.I.O.—§ 802
Hamdan v. Rumsfeld—§ 252
Hamdi v. Rumsfeld—§ 250
Hammer v. Dagenhart—§ 153
Hampton v. Wong—§ 594
Harisiades v. Shaughnessy—§ 395
Harlow v. Fitzgerald—§ 240
Harper v. Virginia State Board of Elections—§ 517
Harris v. McRae—§ 502
Hatter, U.S. v.—§ 178
Hawaii Housing Authority v. Midkiff—§ 413
Hays, U.S. v.—§ 61
Haywood v. Drown—§ 342.1
Hazelwood School District v. Kuhlmeier—§ 793
Healy v. Beer Institute—§ 287
Hein v. Freedom From Religion Foundation, Inc.—§ 71
Heller v. Doe—§ 644
Henneford v. Silas Mason—§ 331
Herbert v. Lando—§ 889
Herndon v. Lowry—§ 668
Hernandez v. Commissioner of Internal Revenue—§ 984
Hess v. Indiana—§ 727
Hess v. Port Authority Trans-Hudson Corp.—§ 122
Hewitt v. Helms—§ 446
Hicklin v. Orbeck—§ 304
Hicks v. Miranda—§ 132
Hill v. Colorado—§ 714
Hillside Dairy, Inc. v. Lyons—§ 298
Hines v. Davidowitz—§ 339
Hobbie v. Unemployment Appeals Commission—§ 972
Hodel v. Virginia Surface Mining and Reclamation Association—§ 160
Hodgson v. Minnesota—§ 504

Holder v. Humanitarian Law Project—§ 725.1
Home Building & Loan Association v. Blaisdell—§ 404
Honda Motor Co. v. Oberg—§ 463
Hooven & Allison Co. v. Evatt—§ 198
Houchins v. KQED—§ 881
Hudgens v. NLRB—§ 360
Huffman v. Pursue Ltd.—§ 134
Hughes v. Alexandria Scrap—§ 293
Hughes v. Oklahoma—§ 261
Humphrey's Executor v. U.S.—§ 229
Hunt v. McNair—§ 938
Hurley v. Irish–American Gay, Lesbian and Bisexual Group of Boston—§ 848
Hutchinson v. Proxmire—§ 244

Ibanez v. Florida Department of Business and Professional Regulation, Board of Accountancy—§ 777
Ingraham v. Wright—§ 447
INS v. Chadha—§ 218
International Society for Krishna Consciousness v. Lee—§ 811

Jackson v. Metropolitan Edison Co.—§ 363
J.E.B. v. Alabama ex rel T.B.—§§ 547, 611
Jefferson County v. Acker—§ 177
Jimmy Swaggart Ministries v. Board of Equalization—§ 985
Johanns v. Livestock Marketing Association—§ 867
Johnson v. California—§ 553
Johnson v. Maryland—§ 177
Jones v. Alfred H. Mayer Co.—§ 375

# TABLE OF CASES

Jones v. Flowers—§ 466
Jones v. U.S.—§ 164
Jones v. Wolf—§ 947
Juidice v. Vail—§ 136

Kadrmas v. Dickinson Public Schools—§ 491
Kahn v. Shevin—§ 616
Kanapaux v. Ellisor—§ 302
Kansas v. Colorado—§ 100
Kansas v. Crane—§ 395
Kansas v. Hendricks—§ 395
Kassel v. Consolidated Freightways Corp.—§ 285
Katzenbach v. McClung—§ 162
Katzenbach v. Morgan—§ 384
Keller v. State Bar of California—§ 865
Kelley v. Johnson—§ 483
Kelo v. New London, Connecticut—§ 414
Keyes v. School District—§ 564
Keystone Bituminous Coal Association v. DeBenedictis—§ 422
Kimel v. Florida Board of Regents—§ 386
Kleindienst v. Mandel—§ 201
Kleppe v. New Mexico—§ 197
Kolender v. Lawson—§ 670
Kovacs v. Cooper—§ 698
Kramer v. Union Free School District—§ 518
Kras, U.S. v.—§ 532
Kuch, U.S. v.—§ 979

Labine v. Vincent—§ 627
Ladue v. Gilleo—§ 708
Lalli v. Lalli—§ 632
Lamb's Chapel v. Center Moriches Union Free School District—§§ 815, 952
Lapides v. Board of Regents of the University System of Georgia—§ 119
Larkin v. Grendel's Den—§ 946

Larson v. Valente—§§ 905, 955
Lassiter v. Dept. of Social Services—§ 449
Lawrence v. Texas—§ 508
League of United Latin American Citizens v. Perry—§ 31
Leathers v. Medlock—§ 899
Lebron v. National Railroad Passenger Corp.—§ 369
Lee, U.S. v.—§ 986
Lee v. Weisman—§ 932
Legal Services Corporation v. Velazquez—§ 855
Lemon v. Kurtzman—§§ 904, 910
Levy v. Louisiana—§ 625
Lincoln County v. Luning—§ 111
Linda R. S. v. Richard D.—§ 65
Lingle v. Chevron U.S.A., Inc.—§ 426
Littleton, Colo. v. Z.J. Gifts D-4 LLC—§ 685
Lochner v. New York—§ 474
Locke v. Davey—§ 994
Locke v. Karass—§ 864
Lopez v. Monterey County—§ 391
Lopez, U.S. v.—§ 164
Loretto v. Teleprompter Manhattan CATV Corp.—§ 417
Lorillard Tobacco v. Reilly—§ 772
Los Angeles v. Alameda Books Inc—§ 693
Los Angeles v. Preferred Communications, Inc.—§ 896
Los Angeles City Council v. Taxpayers for Vincent—§ 789
Lovett, U.S. v.—§ 399
Loving v. Virginia—§ 589
Lubin v. Parish—§ 523
Lucas v. South Carolina Coastal Council—§ 427
Lugar v. Edmonson Oil Co.—§ 351
Lujan v. Defenders of Wildlife—§ 57

Lujan v. G & G Fire Sprinklers, Inc.—§ 460
Lunding v. New York Tax Appeals Tribunal—§ 307
Lynce v. Mathis—§ 396
Lynch v. Donnelly—§§ 904, 922, 941
Lyng v. UAW—§ 872
Lyng v. Northwest Indian Cemetery Protective Association—§ 992

Madsen v. Women's Health Center, Inc.—§ 714
Maher v. Roe—§ 502
Maine v. Taylor—§ 262
Marbury v. Madison—§ 21
Marchetti v. U.S.—§ 176
Marsh v. Alabama—§ 359
Marsh v. Chambers—§ 933
Martin v. Hunter's Lessee—§ 22
Massachusetts v. U.S.—§ 176
Massachusetts Board of Retirement v. Murgia—§ 640
Mathews v. Diaz—§ 593
Mathews v. Eldridge—§§ 439, 461
Mathews v. Lucas—§ 630
McCardle, Ex parte—§ 247
McCollum v. Board of Education—§ 917
McConnell v. Federal Election Commission—§ 820
McCreary County v. ACLU—§ 928
McCulloch v. Maryland—§ 146
McDaniel v. Paty—§ 982
McDonald v. Chicago—§ 467
McDonald v. Santa Fe Trail Transportation Co.—§ 377
McGowan v. Maryland—§ 988
McIntyre v. Ohio Elections Commission—§ 709
McLaughlin v. Florida—§ 588
Medellin v. Texas—§ 188
Memoirs v. Massachusetts—§ 748
Memorial Hospital v. Maricopa County—§ 513

# TABLE OF CASES

Metro Broadcasting v. FCC—§ 584
Metropolitan Life Insurance Co. v. Ward—§§ 311, 329
Metropolitan Washington Airports Authority v. Citizens for the Abatement of Aircraft Noise, Inc.—§ 219
Meyer v. Nebraska—§ 489
Miami Herald Publishing Co. v. Tornillo—§ 893
Michael H. v. Gerald D.—§ 658
Michael M. v. Superior Court—§ 621
Michelin Tire Corp. v. Wages—§ 329
Michigan v. Long—§ 37
Middlesex County Ethics Committee v. Garden State Bar Association—§ 138
Miller v. California—§ 749
Miller v. Florida—§ 396
Miller v. Johnson—§ 551
Miller v. Schoene—§ 428
Milliken v. Bradley—§§ 107, 568
Mills v. Habluetzel—§ 635
Minneapolis Star & Tribune Co. v. Minnesota Commissioner of Revenue—§ 898
Minnesota v. Clover Leaf Creamery—§ 289
Mississippi University for Women v. Hogan—§ 612
Missouri v. Holland—§ 194
Missouri v. Jenkins—§ 571
Mistretta v. U.S.—§ 248
Mitchell v. Helms—§ 923
M.L.B. v. S.L.J.—§ 451, 529
Monell v. Dept. of Social Services—§ 111
Moore v. East Cleveland—§ 512
Moore v. Ogilvie—§ 95
Moore v. Sims—§ 137
Moorman Manufacturing Co. v. Bair—§ 318
Moose Lodge v. Irvis—§ 349
Morrison v. Olson—§ 231
Morrison, U.S. v.—§ 164
Morrissey v. Brewer—§ 445

Morse v. Frederick—§ 793
Mt. Healthy City School District v. Doyle—§ 109, 111
Mueller v. Allen—§ 945
Mullane v. Central Hanover Bank & Trust Co.—§ 466
Muskrat v. U.S.—§ 24
Myers v. U.S.—§ 228

NAACP v. Alabama—§§ 85, 863
NAACP v. Clairborne Hardware Co.—§ 869
National Endowment for the Arts v. Finley—§ 853
National League of Cities v. Usery—§ 168
National Treasury Employees Union, U.S. v.—§ 835
NCAA v. Tarkanian—§ 353
Near v. Minnesota—§ 679
Nebbia v. New York—§ 476
Nebraska Press Association v. Stuart—§ 878
Nevada v. Hall—§ 109
New Hampshire v. Piper—§ 306
New Jersey Welfare Rights Organization v. Cahill—§ 629
New Orleans v. Dukes—§ 648
New York v. Ferber—§ 755
New York v. U.S.—§ 170
New York City Transit Authority v. Beazer—§ 649
New York State Board of Elections v. Lopez Torres—§ 522
New York Times Co. v. U.S.—§ 680
Nguyen v. Immigration and Naturalization Services—§§ 623, 638
Nixon v. Administrator of General Services—§§ 235, 400
Nixon v. Fitzgerald—§ 238
Nixon v. Missouri Municipal League—§ 340
Nixon v. Shrink Missouri Government PAC—§ 821

Nixon v. U.S.—§ 29
Nixon, U.S. v.—§ 234
NLRB v. Jones & Laughlin Steel Corp.—§ 157
Nollan v. California Coastal Commission—§ 430
Northwest Austin Municipal Utility District Number One v. Holder—§ 391.1

O'Brien, U.S. v.—§ 786
O'Connor v. Donaldson—§ 444
O'Hare Truck Service, Inc. v. Northlake—§ 840
Ohio Civil Rights Commission v. Dayton Christian Schools—§ 139
Ohralik v. Ohio State Bar Association—§ 775
Oklahoma City Board of Education v. Dowell—§ 569
Oklahoma Tax Commission v. Jefferson Lines, Inc.—§ 326
Olim v. Wakinekona—§ 446
Oregon v. Mitchell—§ 385
Oregon Waste Systems, Inc. v. Dept. of Environmental Quality of Oregon—§§ 263, 275
Orr v. Orr—§ 618
Osborne v. Ohio—§ 756

Pace v. Alabama—§ 587
Pacific Gas & Electric Co. v. Public Utilities Commission—§ 846
Pacific States Telephone & Telegraph Co. v. Oregon—§ 27
Pacific Gas & Electric Co., v. State Energy Resources Conservation & Development Commission—§ 340
Palmore v. Sidoti—§ 590
Parents Involved in Community Schools v. Seattle School District No. 1—§ 578
Parham v. Hughes—§ 634

# TABLE OF CASES

Parham v. J.R.—§ **444**
Paris Adult Theatre I v. Slaton—§ **753**
Paul v. Davis—§ **452**
Pell v. Procunier—§ **880**
Penn Central Transportation Co. v. New York City—§ **423**
Pennhurst State School and Hospital v. Halderman—§ **102**
Pennsylvania v. Nelson—§ **342**
Pennsylvania v. Union Gas Co.—§ **116**
Pennsylvania Coal Co. v. Mahon—§ **421**
Pennzoil Co. v. Texaco, Inc.—§ **140**
Perez v. U.S.—§ **159**
Perry v. Sindermann—§ **457**
Perry Educational Association v. Perry Local Educators' Association—§ **807**
Personnel Administrator v. Feeney—§ **544**
Philadelphia v. New Jersey—§ **273**
Phillips v. Washington Legal Foundation—§ **436**
Pickering v. Board of Education—§ **833**
Pickett v. Brown—§ **636**
Pierce v. Society of Sisters—§ **489**
Pierce County v. Guillen—§ **164**
Pike v. Bruce Church—§§ **268, 279**
Pinkus v. U.S.—§ **760**
Pittsburgh Press Co. v. Pittsburgh Commission on Human Relations—§ **895**
Planned Parenthood v. Danforth—§ **500**
Planned Parenthood of Southeastern Pennsylvania v. Casey—§ **506**
Playboy Enterprises Group, U.S. v.—§ **738**
Pleasant Grove City v. Sammum—§ **928**
Plessy v. Ferguson—§ **555**
Plyler v. Doe—§ **491**
Poe v. Ullman—§ **42**

Police Department of Chicago v. Mosley—§§ **699, 805**
Polk County v. Dodson—§ **362**
Pope v. Illinois—§ **750**
Port Authority Trans–Hudson Corp. v. Feeney—§ **118**
Posadas de Puerto Rico Associates v. Tourism Company of Puerto Rico—§ **767**
Powell v. McCormack—§ **34**
Powers v. Ohio—§§ **80, 547**
Press Enterprise Co. v. Superior Court—§ **885**
Price, U.S. v.—§ **382**
Primus, In re—§ **778**
Printz v. U.S.—§ **171**
Prudential Insurance Co. v. Benjamin—§ **310**
Pruneyard Shopping Center v. Robins—§§ **360, 868**

Quill Corp. v. North Dakota—§ **328**

R.A.V. v. St. Paul—§ **740**
Railroad Commission v. Pullman Co.—§ **124**
Railway Express Agency v. New York—§ **647**
Raines v. Byrd—§ **58**
Randall v. Sorrell—§ **822**
Rankin v. McPherson—§ **833**
Rasul v. Bush—§ **251**
Red Lion Broadcasting Co. v. FCC—§ **892**
Reed v. Reed—§ **608**
Reeves v. Stake—§ **294**
Regan v. Taxation With Representation of Washington—§ **850**
Regents of the University of California v. Bakke—§ **575**
Reid v. Covert—§ **195**
Reitman v. Mulkey—§ **348**
Rendell–Baker v. Kohn—§ **350**
Reno v. American Civil Liberties Union—§ **737**
Reno v. Condon—§ **172**

Renton v. Playtime Theaters, Inc.—§ **693**
Republican Party of Minnesota v. White—§ **676**
Reynolds v. Sims—§ **515**
Reynolds v. U.S.—§ **963**
Rice v. Cayetano—§ **520**
Richmond v. J.A. Croson Co.—§ **580**
Richmond Newspapers, Inc. v. Virginia—§ **883**
Riley v. National Federation of the Blind of North Carolina, Inc.—§ **686**
Roberts v. U.S. Jaycees—§ **870**
Roe v. Wade—§§ **94, 499**
Roemer v. Board of Public Works—§ **939**
Rogers v. Bellei—§ **205**
Rogers v. Tennessee—§ **393**
Rome v. U.S.—§ **390**
Romer v. Evans—§ **645**
Rooney v. North Dakota—§ **395**
Rosenberger v. Rector and Visitors of the University of Virginia—§§ **816, 953**
Rostker v. Goldberg—§ **622**
Roth v. U.S.—§ **747**
Rubin v. Coors Brewing Co.—§ **770**
Rumsfeld v. Forum for Academic and Institutional Rights—§ **874**
Runyon v. McCrary—§ **376**
Rust v. Sullivan—§§ **505, 852**
Rutan v. Republican Party of Illinois—§ **841**

Sable Communications v. Federal Communications Commission—§ **736**
Sabri v. U.S.—§ **179**
Saenz v. Roe—§§ **468, 513**
San Antonio Independent School District v. Rodriguez—§ **491**
San Francisco Arts & Athletics, Inc. v. U.S. Olympic Committee—§ **352**
Santa Fe Independent School District v. Doe—§ **934**

# TABLE OF CASES

Santosky v. Kramer—§ 450
Scales v. U.S.—§ 725
Schenck v. Pro–Choice Network of Western New York—§ 714
Schenck v. U.S.—§ 719
Scheuer v. Rhodes—§ 121
Schlesinger v. Reservists Committee to Stop the War—§ 57
Schneider v. Irvington—§ 803
School District of Abington v. Schempp—§ 54
SCRAP, U.S. v.—§ 88
Seeger, U.S. v.—§ 976
Selective Service System v. Minnesota Public Interest Research Group—§§ 398, 400
Seling v. Young—§ 395
Seminole Tribe of Florida v. Florida—§ 116
Shapero v. Kentucky Bar Association—§ 781
Shapiro v. Thompson—§ 513
Shaw v. Hunt—§ 550
Shaw v. Reno—§ 550
Shelley v. Kraemer—§ 366
Sheppard v. Maxwell—§ 877
Sherbert v. Verner—§ 970
Shuttlesworth v. Birmingham—§ 682
Sibron v. New York—§ 98
Sierra Club v. Morton—§§ 53, 59
Simon v. Eastern Kentucky Welfare Rights Organization—§ 63
Simon & Schuster, Inc. v. New York State Crime Victims Board—§ 900
Singleton v. Wulff—§ 51
Skinner v. Oklahoma—§ 494
Slaughterhouse Cases—§§ 468, 513
Smith v. Allwright—§ 356
Smith v. Doe—§ 395
Smith v. Goguen—§ 669
Snepp v. U.S.—§ 688
South Carolina v. Baker—§ 176
South Carolina v. Katzenbach—§ 388

South Central Bell Telephone Co. v. Alabama—§ 324
South–Central Timber Development Co. v. Wunnicke—§ 296
South Dakota v. Dole—§ 182
Southern Pacific v. Arizona—§ 284
Southland Corp. v. Keating—§ 337
Sporhase v. Nebraska—§ 267
Stanley v. Georgia—§ 752
Stanley v. Illinois—§ 652
Starns v. Malkerson—§ 513
State Farm v. Campbell—§ 464
Stenberg v. Carhart—§ 507
Stevens, U.S. v.—§ 676.1
Stogner v. California—§ 396
Stone v. Graham—§ 927
Stop the Beach Renourishment v. Florida Department of Environmental Protection—§ 410
Stromberg v. California—§ 667
Sugarman v. Dougall—§ 596
Summers v. Earth Island Institute—§ 59
Supreme Court of Virginia v. Friedman—§ 306
Swann v. Charlotte–Mecklenburg Board of Education—§ 567

Tahoe–Sierra Preservation Council Inc. v. Tahoe Regional Planning Agency—§ 433
Talley v. California—§ 709
Tashjian v. Republican Party of Connecticut—§ 818
Tennessee v. Lane—§ 113
Terminiello v. Chicago—§ 732
Terry v. Adams—§ 356
Texas v. Johnson—§ 787
Texas, U.S. v.—§ 120
Texas Monthly, Inc. v. Bullock—§ 856
Thomas v. Chicago Park District—§ 705
Thomas v. Review Board—§ 971

Thompson v. Western States Medical Center—§ 773
Thornton, Estate of v. Caldor, Inc.—§ 996
Tilton v. Richardson—§ 937
Times Film Corp. v. Chicago—§ 684
Timmons v. Twin Cities Area New Party—§ 524
Tinker v. Des Moines School District—§ 792
Toll v. Moreno—§ 603
Toomer v. Witsell—§ 303
Torcaso v. Watkins—§ 981
Trafficante v. Metropolitan Life Insurance Co.—§ 87
Trainor v. Hernandez—§ 135
Trimble v. Gordon—§ 631
Troxel v. Granville—§ 490
Turner Broadcasting System v. Federal Communications Commission I—§ 847
Turner Broadcasting System v. Federal Communications Commission II—§ 847

United Brotherhood of Carpenters v. Scott—§ 379
United Building and Construction Trades Council v. Camden—§§ 295, 305
United Food, Inc., U.S. v.—§ 867
United Jewish Organizations v. Carey—§ 389
United Public Workers v. Mitchell—§ 43
**United States v. (see opposing party)**
United States Civil Service Commission v. National Association of Letter Carriers—§ 834
United States Department of Agriculture v. Murry—§ 654
United States Railroad Retirement Board v. Fritz—§ 650
United States Term Limits, Inc. v. Thornton—§ 35
United States Trust v. New Jersey—§ 405

# TABLE OF CASES

Usery v. Turner Elkhorn Mining Co.—§ 657

Vacco v. Quill—§ 511
Valley Forge Christian College v. American United for Separation of Church and State—§ 70,
Vance v. Bradley—§ 641
Vance v. Terrazas—§ 203
Van Orden v. Perry—§ 928
Vieth v. Jubelirer—§ 31
Virginia v. Black—§ 741
Virginia, U.S. v.—§ 613
Virginia State Board of Pharmacy v. Virginia Citizens Consumer Council—§ 765
Vitek v. Jones—§ 444
Vlandis v. Kline—§ 653

Walker v. Birmingham—§ 682
Wallace v. Jaffree—§ 931
Walz v. Tax Commission—§ 944
Ward v. Rock Against Racism—§ 692
Warth v. Seldin—§ 83
Washington v. Davis—§§ 539, 542
Washington v. Glucksberg—§ 510
Washington State Grange v. Washington State Republican Party—§ 525

Watchtower Bible & Tract Society v. Stratton, Ohio—§ 711
Waters v. Churchill—§ 833
Watts v. United States—§ 741
Weaver v. Graham—§ 396
Weber v. Aetna Casualty & Surety Co.—§ 628
Webster v. Reproductive Health Services—§ 503
Weinberger v. Salfi—§ 656
Weiss v. U.S.—§ 224
West Lynn Creamery v. Healy—§ 270
West Coast Hotel Co. v. Parrish—§ 477
West Virginia State Board of Education v. Barnette—§ 844
Western Live Stock v. Bureau of Revenue—§ 316
Whalen v. Roe—§ 483
White v. Massachusetts Council—§ 295
Whitney v. California—§ 722
Wickard v. Filburn—§ 158
Widmar v. Vincent—§§ 813, 950
Wilkinson v. Austin—§ 444
Williams v. Rhodes—§ 522
Williams, U.S. v.—§ 757
Williamson v. Lee Optical—§ 480
Willowbrook v. Olech—§ 534
Wisconsin v. J. C. Penney Co.—§ 315
Wisconsin v. Mitchell—§ 743
Wisconsin v. Yoder—§ 966

Witters v. Washington Department of Services for the Blind—§ 913
Woods v. Cloyd W. Miller Co.—§ 184
Wooley v. Maynard—§§ 846, 967
W. T. Grant Co., U.S. v.—§ 96
Wygant v. Jackson Board of Education—§ 579

Yakus v. U.S.—§ 216
Yates v. U.S.—§ 724
Yee v. City of Escondido—§ 425
Yick Wo v. Hopkins—§ 541
Young v. American Mini Theatres, Inc.—§ 693
Young, Ex parte—§ 102
Younger v. Harris—§ 127
Youngstown Sheet & Tube v. Sawyer—§ 212
Ysursa v. Pocatello Education Association—§ 864

Zablocki v. Redhail—§ 495
Zauderer v. Office of Disciplinary Counsel—§ 780
Zelman v. Simmons–Harris—§ 915
Zobrest v. Catalina Foothills School District—§ 914
Zorach v. Clauson—§ 918
Zurcher v. Stanford Daily—§ 888

# INDEX

References are to section numbers

**ABORTION**
   Generally 499–507
Government funding of abortions, 502
Judicial bypass for minors, 501
*Roe v. Wade*, 499
Spousal consent laws, 500
Two-parent notification, 504
"Undue burden" analysis, 506
Waiting periods, 504; 506

**ABSTENTION**
   Generally, 123–133
*Pullman* abstention, 124–126
*Younger* abstention, 127–133

**ACCESS TO COURTS**
Generally 527–532

**ADEQUATE AND INDEPENDENT STATE GROUNDS**
   Generally, 37–39
State Constitution confers greater protection, 39

**ADVISORY OPINIONS**, 24

**AFFIRMATIVE ACTION**
   Generally, 573–585
Federal, 581–585
State, 574–580

**AGE CLASSIFICATIONS, 639–641**

**ALIENAGE CLASSIFICATIONS**
   Generally, 591–604
Federal laws, 592–594

Political function exception 594
State laws 595–604

**ASSOCIATION, FREEDOM OF**
   Generally, 857–874
Business association, 858
First Amendment association, 860–867
Personal association, 859

**BILL OF ATTAINDER**
   Generally, 397–400
Factors to consider, 398

**CLEAR AND PRESENT DANGER ANALYSIS**
Generally, 716–727

**COMMERCE POWER**
   Generally, 147–172
Federalism and commerce power, 165–172
Scope of commerce power, 147–164

**COMMERCIAL SPEECH**
   Generally, 763–781
Lawyer advertising, 774–777
Power to prohibit includes power to channel advertising, 767
Prevailing test, 766

**CONGRESSIONAL ENFORCEMENT OF CIVIL RIGHTS**
   Generally, 370–391.1
Fifteenth Amendment, 370; 387–391.1
Fourteenth Amendment, 370; 380–386

465

# INDEX

Thirteenth Amendment, 370; 374–379

**CONGRESSIONAL POWERS**
Generally, 141–205; 223–232
Action affecting the judiciary, 245–248
Legislative immunity, 241–244
Legislative vetoes, 214–220
Restrictions on President's removal power, 225–232

**CONTRACEPTIVES** 496–498

**CONTRACTS CLAUSE**
Generally, 401–407
Current test, 402

**DESEGREGATION**
Generally, 557–573
Remedies, 569–572
Separate but equal, 554–556
Termination of federal court supervision, 569–572

**DORMANT COMMERCE CLAUSE**
Generally, 253–296
Discrimination against out-of-staters, 254–278
Market participant exception, 291–296
State laws that burden interstate commerce, 279–290

**DUE PROCESS**
*See* Procedural Due Process; Substantive Due Process

**ELEVENTH AMENDMENT**
Generally, 99–122
Congressional abrogation, 110; 112–116
Only applies in federal court, 109
Relief available, 103–107
State waiver, 118
Suing a state official as a way around the Eleventh Amendment Bar, 102

**ELECTORAL PROCESS AND THE FIRST AMENDMENT**
Generally, 817–828
Campaign contributions and expenditures, 819–828
Restricting on voting and becoming a candidate. 818

**ESTABLISHMENT CLAUSE**
Generally, 901–956
Aid to colleges, 936–939
Evolution, teaching of, 924–926
Holiday displays, 940–942
*Lemon* test, 904
Preferring one religion over another, 905; 955
Public Forum, 949–954
Religion in public schools, 906–939
School prayer, 929–935
Tax exemptions and deductions, 943–945

**EQUAL PROTECTION**
Generally, 533–658
Affirmative action, 573–585
Age classifications, 639–641
Alienage classifications, 591–604
Burden of proof, 535–538
Gender classifications, 605–623
Illegitimacy classifications, 624–638
Intent requirement, 539–552
Irrebuttable presumptions, 651–658
Levels of scrutiny, 535–538
Mental status classifications, 642–644
Pregnancy classifications, 614
Racial classifications, 553–590
School desegregation, 559–572
Sexual Orientation Classifications, 645
Socio-economic classifications, 646–650

**EX POST FACTO LAWS**, 394–396

**EXECUTIVE AGREEMENTS**, 189–193

**EXECUTIVE IMMUNITY**, 237–240

**EXECUTIVE POWERS**
*See* Presidential Powers

# INDEX

**FEDERALISM**
Commerce power, 165–172
Foreign affairs, 185–195
Preemption of state laws, 333–340

**FIFTEENTH AMENDMENT**, 387–391.1

**FIGHTING WORDS**, 728–732

**FOREIGN AFFAIRS POWERS**
Generally, 185–195
Congressional delegation to President, 186
Federalism and foreign affairs, 190
Treaties and executive agreements, 187–195

**FREE EXERCISE CLAUSE**
Generally, 957–994
Definition of religion, 975–979
*Employment Division v. Smith*, 961
Religion as qualification for public office, 980–982
Sincerity of religious belief, 977–979
Sunday closing laws, 987–989
Taxation of religious institutions, 983–986
Truth of religious belief, 977

**FUNDAMENTAL RIGHTS**
*See* Substantive Due Process

**GENDER CLASSIFICATIONS**
Generally, 605–623
Pregnancy discrimination, 614
Remedial discrimination, 615–618

**GOVERNMENT EMPLOYEE SPEECH**
Generally, 829–841
Loyalty oaths, 830
Political activity and political patronage, 831–841

**GRANDPARENT VISITATION RIGHTS**, 490

**HATE SPEECH**, 739–744

**HOMOSEXUAL ACTIVITY**, 508

**ILLEGITIMACY CLASSIFICATIONS**
Generally, 624–638
Inheritance, 627; 630–632
Welfare benefits, 629

**IMMIGRATION AND NATURALIZATION**
Generally, 199–205
Loss of citizenship, 202–205
Rationality review, 200

**INTERSTATE TRAVEL, RIGHT TO**, 513

**IRREBUTTABLE PRESUMPTIONS**
Generally, 651–658
Child born to a married woman is child of husband, 658
Pregnant teachers unable to teach, 655
Unmarried fathers as unfit parents, 652

**JUDICIAL REVIEW**
Generally, 20–133
Abstention, 123–133
Adequate and independent state grounds, 37–39
Advisory opinions, 24
Appeal, 11–13
Certiorari, 13
Detention of detainees in war on terrorism, 251–252
Eleventh Amendment, 99–122
*Marbury v. Madison*, 21
Mootness, 90–97
Political questions, 25–32
Ripeness, 41–43
Standing, 44–89

**LIBERTY INTERESTS**
Generally, 443–453

# INDEX

Commitment to mental institutions, 444–446
Parental rights, 448–451
Prisoners, 446
Reputation, 452–453

**MARRY, RIGHT TO**, 494–495

**MENTAL STATUS CLASSIFICATIONS**, 642–644

**MOOTNESS**
Generally, 90–97
"Capable of repetition" exception, 93–95
"Collateral consequences" exception, 97
"Voluntary cessation of illegal activity", exception 96

**NATIONAL LEGISLATIVE POWER**
Generally, 141–205
Commerce power, 147–172
Enumerated powers of Congress, 145
Foreign affairs powers, 185–195
Immigration and naturalization power, 199–205
Necessary and Proper Clause, 146
Property power, 196–198
Taxing power, 178
Spending power, 179–182
War power, 184

**OBSCENITY**
Generally, 745–762
Child pornography, 754–757
*Miller v. California* test, 749–750
Pornography as sex discrimination, 762
Right to possess, 751–754

**POLITICAL ASSOCIATION**
Generally, 521–526
Access to the ballot, 522
Filing fee for candidates, 523

**POLITICAL QUESTIONS**
Generally, 25–32

Constitutional commitment to another branch, 26–30
Prudential political questions, 32

**PORNOGRAPHY**
Child, 754–757
Sex discrimination, 762

**PREEMPTION**
Generally, 333–342
Congressional statement of intent to preempt, 340
Conflicting laws, 336–339
Pervasive congressional regulation, 341–342

**PRESIDENTIAL POWERS**
Generally, 209–213; 222–233
Appointment power, 222–224
Executive immunity, 237–240
Executive privilege, 233–236
List of powers, 210
Removal of executive officials, 225–232
Seizure of property, 211–212

**PRESS, FREEDOM OF**
Generally, 875–900
Courtroom access, 879; 882–885
Fair trial, right to, 876–878
Media privilege exempting compliance with generally applicable laws, 886–890
Required access to mass media, 891–896
Taxation of the press, 897–900

**PRIOR RESTRAINTS**
Generally, 677–688
Injunctive orders, 678–681
Movie licensing systems, 683–685

**PRIVACY, RIGHT TO**
Generally, 492–512
Abortion and reproductive freedom, 499–507
Family living arrangements, 512

**468**

# INDEX

Homosexual activity, 508
Refusal of medical treatment, 511

**PRIVILEGES AND IMMUNITIES CLAUSE OF ARTICLE IV**
Generally, 297–308
Standard of review, 298

**PRIVILEGES OR IMMUNITIES CLAUSE OF THE FOURTEENTH AMENDMENT**
*Slaughterhouse* cases, 468

**PROCEDURAL DUE PROCESS**
Generally, 437–466
Government action requirement, 440
Intentional deprivation, 441
Liberty interests, 442–453
*Mathews v. Eldridge* test, 439
Property interests, 454–466

**PROCREATE, RIGHT TO**, 494

**PROPERTY INTERESTS**
Generally, 454–466
Employment, 455–460
Government benefits, 461
School attendance, 462

**PROPERTY POWER**
Generally, 196–198
Wild animals, 197

**PUBLIC FORUM ANALYSIS**
Generally, 795–816
Commandeered public forum, 800
Designated public forum, 797–799
Religious speakers in, 812–816
Traditional public forum, 796

**PUBLIC SCHOOL SPEECH**
Generally, 791–794
Non-school-sponsored speech, 792
Removal of books from school library, 794
School-sponsored speech, 793

**QUALIFICATIONS CLAUSES**, 32–33

**RACIAL CLASSIFICATIONS**
Generally, 553–590
Affirmative action, federal, 581–585
Affirmative action, state, 573–580
School desegregation, 559–572
"Separate but equal", 554–558

**RELIGION CLAUSES**
Generally, 901–997
Establishment Clause, 901–956;
Free Exercise Clause, 957–997

**REPRODUCTIVE FREEDOM, RIGHT TO**
Generally, 492–507
Abortion, 499–507
Contraceptives, 496–498
Marry, right to, 494–495
Procreate, right to, 494

**RIGHT TO DIE**, 509–510

**RIPENESS**, 41–43

**SCHOOLS**
Desegregation, 556–572
Religion, 906–939
Speech, 791–794

**SEPARATION OF POWERS**
Generally, 206–252
Appointment power, 222–232
Congressional action affecting the President, 214–221
Congressional action affecting the judiciary, 245–248
Executive immunity, 237–240
Executive privilege, 233–236
Legislative immunity, 241–244
Legislative veto, 215–219
Powers of the President, 210
Presidential action affecting Congress, 211–213

# INDEX

**SPEECH, FREEDOM OF**
Generally, 659–874
Association, right of, 857–874
Child pornography, 754–757
Clear and present danger analysis, 716–727
Commercial speech, 763–781
Compelled speech, freedom from, 843–848
Electoral process and the First Amendment, 817–828
Fighting words, 728–732
Government employees, speech of, 829–841
Hate speech, 739–744
Obscenity, 745–762
Offensive speech, 733–738
Overbreadth, 662; 672–676
Pornography as sex discrimination, 762
Prior restraints, 677–688
Public forum analysis, 795–816
Public schools, speech in, 791–794
Religious speakers in public forums, 812–816
Symbolic speech, 782–790
Time, place, or manner restrictions, 689–714
Vagueness, 661; 666–671

**SOCIO–ECONOMIC CLASSIFICATIONS**, 646–650

**SPENDING POWER**
Generally, 179–183
Regulation through spending, 180–183

**STANDING**
Generally, 44–89
Associational standing, 82–85
Congressional creation of standing, 86–89
Constitutional requirements, 45–47
Federal taxpayer standing, 66–71
Prudential requirements, 48
Third-party standing, 75–81

**STATE ACTION REQUIREMENT**
Generally, 343–369
Governmental assistance, 345–354
Private actors, 368
*Sum & Substance* QUICK REVIEW of Constitutional Law, 409
Restrictive covenant cases, 360–362
Traditional government function, 350–359

**STATE POWER TO REGULATE COMMERCE**
Generally, 253–332
Congressional authorization of discrimination, 309–311
Dormant Commerce Clause, 254–296
Market participant exception to Dormant Commerce Clause, 291–296
Privileges and Immunities Clause of Article IV, 297–308

**STATE TAXATION OF INTERSTATE COMMERCE**
Generally, 312–332
*Complete Auto Transit* test, 313–325
Due process considerations, 327–328
Equal protection considerations, 329
Foreign commerce, 325
Use taxes, 330–332

**SUBSTANTIVE DUE PROCESS**
Generally, 467–532
Abortion, 499–507
Access to courts, right to, 527–532
Direct educational upbringing of children, right to, 488–491
Economic legislation, 471–482
Family living arrangements, 512
Fundamental rights, 484–532
Homosexual activity, 508
Interstate travel, right to, 513
Levels of scrutiny, 470
Marry, right to, 494–495
Political association, right to, 521–526
Refusal of medical treatment, 509–511

# INDEX

Reproductive freedom, right to, 493–507
Right to privacy, 492–512
Vote, right to, 514–520

**SUSPECT CLASSES**
See Equal protection

**SUPREMACY CLAUSE**
See Preemption

**SYMBOLIC SPEECH**
Generally, 782–790
Prohibition of, 783
Time, place, or manner restrictions on, 784

**TAKINGS CLAUSE**
Generally, 408–436
Conditions on granting building permits, 429–431
"Just compensation", 435
"Public use" requirement, 411–414
Regulatory takings, 415–422
Temporary takings, 432

**TAXING POWER**, 173
Generally, 173–178
Constitutional limitations on the taxing power, 175–178
Two ways a tax can be valid, 174

**THIRTEENTH AMENDMENT**
**TIME, PLACE, OR MANNER RESTRICTIONS**
Generally, 689–714
Content-neutrality, 690–692
Injunction imposing, 711–713
Public forum, 696–710

**TREATIES**, 187–195

**VOTING RIGHTS**
Generally, 514–518
Durational residency requirements, 519
One-person, one-vote, 515
Poll taxes, 517

**WAR POWER**, 184
410 *Sum & Substance* QUICK REVIEW of Constitutional Law